Parameters
and
Universals

OXFORD STUDIES IN COMPARATIVE SYNTAX
Richard Kayne, *General Editor*

Parameters and Universals

RICHARD S. KAYNE

OXFORD

UNIVERSITY PRESS

2000

OXFORD

UNIVERSITY PRESS

Oxford   New York

Athens   Auckland   Bangkok   Bogotá   Bombay   Buenos Aires   Calcutta
Cape Town   Chennai   Dar es Salaam   Delhi   Florence   Hong Kong   Istanbul
Karachi   Kuala Lumpur   Madrid   Melbourne   Mexico City   Mumbai
Nairobi   Paris   São Paulo   Singapore   Taipei   Tokyo   Toronto   Warsaw

and associated companies in
Berlin   Ibadan

Published by Oxford University Press, Inc.
198 Madison Avenue, New York, New York 10016

Oxford is a registered trademark of Oxford University Press

Library of Congress Cataloging-in-Publication Data
Kayne, Richard S.
Parameters and universals / Richard S. Kayne.
p.   cm.—(Oxford studies in comparative syntax)
Includes bibliographical references and index.
ISBN 0-19-510235-5; ISBN 0-19-510236-3 (pbk.)
1. Grammar, Comparative and general—Syntax.   2. Principles and parameters
(Linguistics)   3. Universals (Linguistics)   I. Title.   II. Series.
P291.K36   2000
415—dc21   98–38013

P
291
.K36
2000

9 8 7 6 5 4 3 2 1

Printed in the United States of America
on acid-free paper

To Nicolas Ruwet

PREFACE

The study of syntactic parameters and the study of syntactic universals go hand in hand. The various essays in this collection may emphasize one of these facets of syntactic theory more than the other; none can fail to take both into account.

The essays in Part I take Romance languages as their window into UG. Chapter 1 can be read as an introduction to small-scale comparative syntax. Chapters 2 (here translated from French) and 3 treat past participle agreement of the sort found in French and Italian and related dialects. While sensitive to the differences among these languages, the analysis developed adopts a highly unified approach to such agreement, one that takes past participle agreement to be strongly similar to finite verb agreement (both necessarily involve a Spec-head configuration of the sort that Chomsky (1999) has recently moved away from; whether his Agree operation can account for the intricate patterns of Romance past participle agreement is an important open question).

Chapters 4, 5 and 6 address the phenomenon of clitic climbing and other questions having to do with pronominal clitics. Chapter 4 is particularly concerned with the relation between clitic climbing and null subjects, taking the position that for clitic climbing to be possible in a given language that language must allow (some) null subjects. Since its writing, it has become more and more evident how important the North Italian dialects are for a proper understanding of null subjects. The same is true for clitic climbing, since, as discussed briefly in chapter 6, the North Italian dialects lie, informally speaking, somewhere between French and Italian there, too. (In addition, they often allow clitic climbing much more readily when the higher verb is itself non-finite, for reasons that have yet to be elucidated.)

Chapter 5 is, in turn, concerned with the relation between clitics and control, more specifically with the surprising correlation between infinitive-clitic order and the possibility of control in cases like *John doesn't know if to go home*; these are found only in those Romance languages that allow clitics to follow infinitives, with potentially important implications for Binding Theory. Chapter 6 pursues the question of clitic-infinitive vs. infinitive-clitic order, arguing that their distribution across

Romance supports the conclusion that certain Italian imperatives contain a null aux-iliary (to which clitics can climb).

Auxiliaries are the focus of chapter 7, too, but there it is a matter of the distribu-tion of the two overt auxiliaries *have* and *be*. It is argued that UG allows no 'auxil-iary selection rule'; rather, the appearance of one or the other depends on the inter-action of a host of factors. The syntax is highly decompositional in a sense like that of Chomsky's (1970) analysis of passive. The building blocks of syntax are smaller than they appear to be.

Chapter 8 argues for another, more familiar, kind of decomposition in the case of (many) pronouns. Non-clitic pronouns in French and Italian (and perhaps univer-sally) are not monomorphemic. Nor are non-clitic reflexives (which are a subtype of pronoun), even those that might seem to be.

Chapter 9 takes up the little-studied question of clitic doubling in French and attempts to characterize the environments in which it is obligatory. There are impli-cations for the syntax of *pro* (and its sensitivity to person), for the null subject phe-nomenon, and for past participle agreement.

The chapters that constitute Part II turn to English, especially to certain non-standard varieties of English. Chapters 10 and 11 use, in particular, the variety of English brought to theoretical light by Kimball and Aissen (1971) in which it is pos-sible to have *Which kids do John think should be invited?*, with *do* instead of *does*. The analysis bears on a number of issues, including successive cyclicity and the sta-tus of number agreement.

Chapter 12 demonstrates, I think, that it is entirely plausible that some varieties of English would have a complementizer *of* in cases like *John should of left*. The key, in part, is to refrain from thinking about the question solely in terms of English, and to bring to bear on this ultimately UG question elements of the syntax of (at least) French, Italian, and Scandinavian.

Chapter 13, beginning Part III, addresses the obviously UG question of the sta-tus of covert (LF) movement. It attempts to show that an extensive class of move-ments usually analyzed as covert are better understood in terms only of overt move-ment. The overt movements in question are partly of the relatively familiar 'negative phrase movement' type, partly of the less familiar VP/AspP/TP movement type (in particular in languages in which the verb normally precedes its complement).

Chapter 14, too, uses movement of the VP/AspP/TP type. It is argued that prepo-sitional complementizers are not merged with their associated IP. Those comple-mentizers are, instead, merged with VP (subsequent to V merging with IP) and 'get together with' IP as the result of IP moving up to them. Subsequent VP/Asp/TP movement plays a central role in establishing the correct word order.

Word order universals of the Greenbergian type are explicitly discussed in chapter 15, and some are claimed to follow from the approach to prepositional complementizers (generalized to all complementizers and adpositions) set out in chapter 14. (Chapter 15, which has implications for the status of what has been called extraposition, also suggests a new approach to the notion of 'heaviness'.)

New York   R. S. K.
January, 2000

ACKNOWLEDGMENTS

Chapter 1, "Microparametric Syntax. Some Introductory Remarks," originally appeared in J. R. Black and V. Motapanyane, eds. (1996), *Microparametric Syntax and Dialect Variation*, John Benjamins, Amsterdam and Philadelphia, ix–xvii, and is reprinted with permission.

Chapter 2, "Past Participle Agreement in French and Italian," originally appeared in French in *Modèles Linguistiques*, VII (1985), 73–89, and is reprinted with permission (English translation by the author).

Chapter 3, "Facets of Romance Past Participle Agreement," originally appeared in P. Benincà, ed. (1989), *Dialect Variation and the Theory of Grammar*, Foris, Dordrecht, 85–103, and is reprinted with permission.

Chapter 4, "Null Subjects and Clitic Climbing," originally appeared in O. Jaeggli and K. Safir, eds. (1989), *The Null Subject Parameter*, Reidel, Dordrecht, 239–261, and is reprinted with kind permission from Kluwer Academic Publishers.

Chapter 5, "Romance Clitics, Verb Movement, and PRO," originally appeared in *Linguisitc Inquiry*, 22 (1991), 647–686, and is reprinted with permission from The MIT Press.

Chapter 6, "Italian Negative Infinitival Imperatives and Clitic Climbing," originally appeared in L. Tasmowski and A. Zribi-Hertz, eds. (1992), *De la musique à la linguistique. Hommages à Nicolas Ruwet*, Communication & Cognition, Ghent, 300–312, and is reprinted with permission.

Chapter 7, "Toward a Modular Theory of Auxiliary Selection," originally appeared in *Studia Linguistica*, 47 (1993), 3–31, and is reprinted with permission from Blackwell Publishers.

Chapter 8, "Person Morphemes and Reflexives in Italian, French, and Related Languages," dedicated to Paola Benincà, and Chapter 9, "A Note on Clitic Doubling in French," dedicated to Lorenzo Renzi, are due to appear separately.

Chapter 10, "Notes on English Agreement," originally appeared in *C(entral) I(nstitute of) E(nglish and) F(oreign) L(anguages) Bulletin* (Hyderabad, India), 1 (1989), 41–67, and is reprinted with permission.

Chapter 11, "Agreement and Verb Morphology in Three Varieties of English," originally appeared in H. Haider, S. Olsen, and S. Vikner, eds. (1995), *Studies in Comparative Germanic Syntax*, Kluwer, Dordrecht, 159–165, and is reprinted with kind permission from Kluwer Academic Publishers.

Chapter 12, "The English Complementizer *of*," originally appeared in *Journal of Comparative Germanic Linguistics*, 1 (1997), 43–54, and is reprinted with kind permission from Kluwer Academic Publishers.

Chapter 13, "Overt versus Covert Movement," originally appeared in *Syntax*, 1 (1998), 128–191, and is reprinted with permission from Blackwell Publishers.

Chapter 14, "Prepositional Complementizers as Attractors," originally appeared in *Probus*, 11 (1999), 39–73, and is reprinted with permission from Mouton de Gruyter.

Chapter 15, "A Note on Prepositions, Complementizers, and Word Order Universals" is a slightly revised version of a paper contributed to the Chomsky Virtual Celebration (http://mitpress.mit.edu/celebration).

Some of the material in Chapters 1, 7, 8, and 9 is based upon work supported by the National Science Foundation under Grant No. SBR-9120615, for which I am grateful.

CONTENTS

I

ROMANCE

1

Microparametric Syntax

Some Introductory Remarks

Comparative syntax can be thought of as that facet of syntactic theory directly concerned with the question of how best to characterize the properties of human languages that are not universal. Put another way, comparative syntax directly addresses the question of how best to understand the notion of parameter taken to underlie syntactic variation.

The study of differences among languages must obviously proceed in tandem with the study of what they have in common, that is, with the study of the principles of Universal Grammar (UG) that interact with language-specific parameters to yield observed variation. Similarly, there is every reason to believe that the search for universal syntactic principles cannot proceed without close attention being paid to syntactic variation.

At its most successful, comparative syntax simultaneously achieves two primary kinds of results: It accounts for observed clusterings of syntactic properties by showing that the several properties in question can all be traced back to a single relatively more abstract parameter setting. And it shows that that optimal parametric account depends on particular assumptions about the proper formulation or understanding of the principles of universal grammar. In the latter way, comparative syntax provides evidence bearing on questions that are not themselves comparative in nature.

My own work in comparative syntax was at first limited to problems that arose from a comparison of French and English. I argued, for example, that the absence in French of the so-called Exceptional Case Marking (ECM) construction (*John considers Bill to have been mistaken*) need not, as Chomsky had thought, be seen as an irreducible difference between the two languages.[1] Rather, that French-English difference should be related to others involving prepositions and prepositional complementizers[2] and ultimately be derived from an abstract difference in the governing properties of prepositions in the two languages.

If correct or largely correct, this clustering of properties (involving ECM constructions, *for* + lexical subject, preposition stranding, and double object constructions) provides evidence in favor of a certain approach to ECM constructions (with an essential role played by an abstract prepositional head) and against various others (e.g. the S-bar deletion approach) and thereby tells us something about how UG is put together that we might not have discovered without doing this kind of comparative work.

In the early to mid-1980s, it became apparent to me that a direct comparison of French and English raised difficult problems to a greater extent than direct comparison of French and Italian. In essence, in searching for clusters of properties, one must make decisions about what syntactic differences can plausibly be linked to what other syntactic differences. To a certain extent one is guided by one's knowledge of syntax in general and by the theory within the framework of which one is working. Such general considerations do place limits on the set of hypotheses one takes seriously, but typically the set of plausible linkings remains larger than one would like. The size of that set will of course be affected by the number of syntactic differences there are between the two languages in question. The more there are to begin with, the harder it will be, all other things being equal, to figure out the correct linkings.

A related point can be made by considering the question of how one goes about testing one's comparative syntax hypotheses. Any proposal of the form 'These two (or three . . .) differences between the languages in question are related to one another' can in principle be tested indirectly by examining the theoretical consequences of the hypotheses about parameters and about universal principles that flow from the original claim concerning the related differences. But there is in addition a more direct way of testing such a claim, and that is to examine other languages to see if the particular properties in question actually do systematically cluster together. In pursuing this kind of examination, one finds that hypotheses concerning French versus English lead very directly to questions concerning both other Romance languages and other Germanic languages. (Languages further afield can sometimes be relevant, but they can also be too different—for example, a hypothesis concerning past participles cannot be tested in any direct manner in a language that has no past participles.) Hypotheses concerning French versus Italian often do not immediately lead beyond the Romance languages: in this sense, the hypothesis testing task generated by French-Italian comparison may be more manageable than the one generated by French-English comparison.

This advantage of French-Italian over French-English comparative work led me to concentrate on the former pair. I attempted, for example, to relate certain differences between French and Italian past participle agreement to other aspects of their syntax, in particular to a difference between them concerning passives of causatives, and to another concerning inversion and null subjects (see chapter 2).

Although French and Italian are relatively similar syntactically, they still show a rather large number of syntactic differences, so the task of deciding which pairs or sets of differences are significantly related to one another and therefore to be thought of as being traceable back to a single parametric difference between the two languages is, even if somewhat easier than in the case of French-English, still a difficult one.

It is consequently natural to take into comparative account languages that are syntactically closer to French or Italian (or to each other) than French is to Italian.

And comparative syntax hypotheses, including those that originate with work on French and Italian, do turn out to be testable with great profit on the less well-known dialects of France and Italy,[3] the study of which permits the discovery of clusterings of syntactic properties that otherwise would in all likelihood go unnoticed.

There is, for example, a strong correlation across these languages between the possibility of having (some) null subjects and the possibility of having clitic climbing out of an infinitival clause into the matrix (noncausative) clause; related to this is movement of a clitic across a preinfinitival adverbial (see chapter 4). If correct to a significant degree, this correlation supports decomposing clitic climbing into several steps, in the spirit of successive cyclicity. A decompositional approach receives additional support from the existence of 'clitic splitting', where two clitics originating as complements of the same infinitive can surface in two different positions. Clitic splitting in noncausatives had been thought not to exist in Romance, but it turns out that there are a number of little-known Romance languages that do have it. It appears, however, to be limited to those Romance languages with clitic-infinitive order.[4]

There is another correlation in Romance that involves the order between clitic and infinitive: a Romance language/dialect will allow the counterpart of English *John doesn't know if to go to the movies tonight* (with controlled PRO in the presence of *if*), if and only if it has the order infinitive-clitic (see chapter 5). This correlation, particularly striking if one looks at little-studied (from a syntactic point of view) null subject languages that have clitic-infinitive order (Sardinian, Occitan, Gardenese), appears to favor over other approaches an approach to PRO based on a modified version of Chomsky's (1986b) analysis and to support (a certain revision of) principles A and B of his binding theory.

Italian, although it almost invariably shows infinitive-clitic order, has an apparently anomalous preinfinitival clitic in infinitival imperatives. This anomaly can be made sense of by taking advantage of a correlation that holds quite strongly across the dialects of Italy between preinfinitival clitics in these imperatives and clitic climbing of the familiar sort. The analysis called for involves an abstract auxiliary to which the clitics can raise in the manner of clitic climbing (see chapter 6).

The study of Italian dialects also radically changes one's perception of Romance auxiliary selection. The picture and theory of auxiliary selection that one arrives at by studying the most widely spoken Romance languages must be considerably modified and enriched if one is to account for the remarkable diversity found in the dialects (see chapter 7).

Comparative work on the syntax of a large number of closely related languages can be thought of as a new research tool, one that is capable of providing results of an unusually fine-grained and particularly solid character.[5] If it were possible to experiment on languages, a syntactician would construct an experiment of the following type: take a language, alter a single one of its observable syntactic properties, examine the result to see what, if any, other property has changed as a consequence. If some property has changed, conclude that it and the property that was altered are linked to one another by some abstract parameter.

Although such experiments cannot be performed, I think that by examining pairs (and larger sets) of ever more closely related languages, one can begin to approximate the results of such an experiment. To the extent that one can find languages that are syntactically extremely similar to one another, yet clearly distinguishable and readily examinable, one can hope to reach a point such that the number of observable differences is so small that one can virtually see one property covarying with another.[6]

In addition to facilitating the accurate individuation of parameters and of the principles of Universal Grammar required to interact with them, the technique of examining a large number of very closely related languages promises to provide a broad understanding of parameters at their finest-grained (microparameters), that is, to provide a handle on the question, What are the minimal units of syntactic variation?

Consider, for example, the phenomenon of past participle agreement. Study of the better-known Romance languages shows past participle agreement with the subject in SPEC·IP in passives to be general, perhaps exceptionless. In active sentences, on the other hand, past participle agreement is found in French and Italian, and to some extent in Catalan, but not in Spanish or Portuguese. On the basis of these, one might postulate a parameter one setting of which allows past-participle agreement in actives.

Yet consideration of lesser-known Romance languages indicates that there must be parameters with finer-grained effects to account for facts such as the following: Some of these languages allow past participle agreement in both WH- and clitic constructions, some only in the latter. No Romance language/dialect, as far as I can see, has past participle agreement with WH-phrases but not with object clitics (see chapter 3).

Some allow past participle agreement with all direct-object clitics, but some, while having it with third-person clitics, prohibit it with first- and second-person clitics. Some allow past participle agreement with the partitive clitic; others do not. Of those that allow clitics to follow past participles in the auxiliary-past participle construction, some allow past participle agreement only when the clitic has moved up to the auxiliary, while others are freer. As far as I know, all Romance languages with past participle agreement in actives allow such agreement in at least some reflexive clitic constructions when the auxiliary is the equivalent of *be*. When there is a reflexive clitic in addition to an accusative clitic, some require agreement with the accusative; others do not. When the auxiliary is *have*, some prohibit agreement with the reflexive clitic (or its antecedent) completely, while others do not.

Our understanding of all of these points will benefit from a closer look at even more of these languages/dialects. In many of these cases, it is not clear yet what the exact form of the relevant parameters will be, or whether they will concern agreement per se, or whether they will more centrally involve properties of the pronouns/clitics, or of the auxiliaries, or of the participles, or some combination of these.

It seems reasonable to expect work in microparametric syntax to play a privileged role in the future in answering the more general question concerning the form that syntactic parameters may take.[7] Chomsky's recent work, for example, suggests the possibility that all syntactic variation might be expressible in terms of strong/weak features on various functional heads;[8] microparametric work will enable us to test this kind of hypothesis in a particularly interesting way.

In the preceding discussion, I have assumed that the enormous amount of syntactic variation that can be observed even within the set of Romance languages/dialects lends itself to insightful characterization in terms of the notion 'parameter' as it has developed over the past fifteen or twenty years. Alternatively put, we can take the study of microparametric variation to provide an ideal testing ground for the very hypothesis that syntactic variation can be reduced to a finite set of parameters (inter- acting with a set of universal principles).

Related to this is the question of how many irreducible syntactic parameters there really are. Again, work in microparametric syntax should be invaluable and should begin to give us some sense of a lower bound for the number of parameters (which in turn will bear on questions of learnability/acquisition). It is also clear that the study of minimal syntactic variation is bound to provide crucial evidence bearing on ques- tions of diachronic syntax (which involves the study of the minimally different stages in the evolution of the syntax of a language).

The question of the number of syntactic parameters leads in turn to the question of the number of syntactically distinct languages/dialects. To begin with, I take it for granted that there is no syntactically significant distinction to be drawn between 'lan- guage' and 'dialect' and no justification for neglecting the latter. Now it is often estimated that the number of languages presently in existence is 4000–5000.[9] Such estimates must evaluate the contribution of Italy as one.

Yet Renzi and Vanelli (1983) showed that in Northern Italy alone one can indi- viduate at least 25 syntactically distinct languages/dialects solely by studying the syntax of subject clitics. More recently, I have had the privilege of participating in a Padua-based syntactic atlas/ (micro)comparative syntax project with Paola Benincà,[10] Cecilia Poletto, and Laura Vanelli, on the basis of which it is evident that one can easily individuate at least 100 syntactically distinct languages/dialects in Northern Italy.[11] A very conservative estimate would be that present-day Italy has at least 500 syntactically distinct languages/dialects. 500,000 would in consequence, I think, then be a very conservative extrapolation to the number of syntactically distinct languages/ dialects in the world at present.

It is possible to arrive at a much more radical reevaluation based on the follow- ing question: Can anyone think of another person with whom they agree 100 percent of the time on syntactic judgments (even counting only sharp disagreements)? Or, more precisely, are there any two people who have exactly the same syntactic judg- ments without exception?

By the nature of the question, it is not possible to give a positive answer, since one could never be sure that two people who seemed to agree with each other con- sistently would not disagree (sharply) on some judgment at some subsequent time. On the other hand, it is easy to think of many pairs of English speakers, for example, who do differ sharply on some set of judgments. For such pairs, the seemingly in- nocuous conclusion is that they do not speak exactly the same variety of English.

Now we know that there are distinct varieties of English—many syntactic dif- ferences have been discussed that distinguish American from British English.[12] And various regional syntactic differences within the United States or within the United Kingdom are well known.[13] But what if it turned out that for every single pair of English speakers (and similarly for other languages) one could find at least one clear syntactic difference?

My own experience in observing the syntax of English speakers, both linguists and nonlinguists, makes me think that it is entirely likely that no two speakers of

English have exactly the same syntactic judgments. In which case there must be many more varieties of English than is usually assumed. In fact, if it is true that no two English speakers have the same (syntactic) grammar,[14] then the number of varieties of English/ distinct grammars of English must be at least as great as the number of native speakers of English. Extrapolating to the world at large, one would reach the conclusion that the number of syntactically distinct languages/dialects is at least as great as the number of individuals presently alive (i.e. more than 5 billion).

Adding in those languages/dialects that have existed but no longer exist and those that will exist but do not yet exist, it becomes clear that the number of syntactically distinct (potential) human languages is substantially greater than 5 billion.

One might object at this point that many of these languages will be distinct from one another only to an insignificant degree. For example, two English speakers might have identical judgments everywhere except in particle constructions, and even there, the differences might readily lend themselves to being called 'tiny', especially if they had no effect on mutual comprehension. Yet such tiny differences may (or may not) be of substantial theoretical importance.[15]

What if it is really true that the commonly cited number of 4000–5000 should, for the purposes of our attempt to understand the human language faculty, be replaced by some number substantially greater than 5 billion?

It would of course be true that an exhaustive study of the syntax of the world's languages would be rather more arduous than is sometimes thought. (Nor will those linguists be comforted who admit that linguistic theorizing is important but who think that it should wait until all languages have been studied.) But if we set aside the unjustified and now entirely unrealistic idea that such an exhaustive study (which would of course be arbitrarily limited to those languages that happen to be spoken now and to a tiny number of extinct languages) is a necessary component of the linguistic enterprise, we can focus instead on a more important question: What is the significance of the number of possible human languages for the acquisition of syntax?

Under the assumption that acqustion proceeds by parameter setting, the child does not pick its language whole out of a set consisting of all possible languages. Rather, it sets individual (syntactic) parameters, the end result of which is (the syntactic component of) a grammar. If the number of possible languages were so large that the number of parameters the child had to set was unmanageable (i.e. not learnable in the amount of time available), there would indeed be a problem.

However, the number of independent binary-valued syntactic parameters needed to allow for 5 billion syntactically distinct grammars is only 33 (2 raised to the 33rd power is about 8.5 billion). Although we do not yet have a clear idea of the number of irreducible syntactic parameters, it seems likely that the number will turn out to be greater than 33. At the same time, although again there is a lot yet to be understood, it seems plausible that the child is capable of setting at least that many syntactic parameters.

If the number of independent parameters is somewhat larger, say 50, then the corresponding number of syntactically distinct grammars is somewhat more than one thousand trillion. If the parameters are 100 in manageable number, then the corresponding number of grammars is, innocuously, over one million trillion trillion (i.e. greater than 10 raised to the 30th power).

Alongside these numbers, the increase in numerical coverage due to work in microparametric syntax in recent years is quantitatively modest. Yet it may not be premature to speak of the beginnings of a qualitative improvement in our understanding of syntactic variation. Microparametric syntax is a powerful tool, whose growth is perhaps to be compared with the development of the earliest microscopes, that allows us to probe questions concerning the most primitive units of syntactic variation. And since the invariant principles of UG can hardly be understood in isolation from syntactic variation, this tool promises to provide invaluable evidence that will shape our understanding of those principles themselves.

NOTES

1. See Chomsky (1980; 1981a) and Kayne (1981e).

2. A related proposal concerning double object constructions is given in Kayne (1983c). The absence of double object constructions in French and Italian is not expected from the perspective of Collins & Thráinsson (1993), whose analysis lacks the crucial abstract preposition.

3. Also, Belgium, Quebec and Switzerland.

4. At least one variety of Milanese seems to allow split clitics despite being an infinitive-clitic language. This (yet to be understood) exception is probably correlated to the property of allowing a copy of the 'climbed' clitic to follow the embedded infinitive.

5. As illustrated in particular by the various articles in this volume, most of which treat Romance or Germanic languages. Johns's article on Inuttut and Cheng, Huang, and Tang's article on Chinese demonstrate the importance of microparametric syntax for other language families. I make no attempt in these introductory remarks at a systematic survey of microparametric work.

6. In the extreme case, one may find an isolated property distinguishing two very close dialects—see Henry (1995; 1996).

7. The term 'micro-comparative' was used by Hellan and Christensen (1986). For discussion of (microparameters vs.) macroparameters, see Baker (1996).

8. See Chomsky (1995). In a general way, this seems compatible with the implications of the approach of Kayne (1994) to word order variation.

9. For some discussion, see Comrie (1987, 2–5) and Crystal (1987, 284–285).

10. See Benincà (1994).

11. See Poletto (1995).

12. See, for example, Zandwoort (1965, 343), Merat (1974), Johansson (1979), and Trudgill and Hannah (1994, 56–82).

13. See, for example, Klima (1964b), Trudgill and Chambers (1991); also Henry (1995).

14. Here and elsewhere, I gloss over the distinction between language/dialect and grammar. For relevant discussion, see Chomsky (1995) on E-language versus I-language.

15. For an example of theoretically important variation within English particle constructions, see Emonds (1976, 83–86); for recent discussion, see den Dikken (1995b).

2

Past Participle Agreement in French and Italian

2.1 Problems

Past participle agreement is illustrated in the following sentences:

(1) Ils l'ont repeinte. ('they it$_{fem.}$ have repainted$_{fem.}$.')

(2) Je sais combien de tables ils ont repeintes. ('I know how-many of tables they have repainted$_{fem.pl.}$.')

For many speakers, this agreement is not made in spoken French; for others it still is. In a certain number of cases even those who don't use this agreement are capable of making differential judgments between cases in which agreement might be possible and cases in which it is clearly excluded. For example, it is generally agreed that there is a sharp difference in contemporary French between (1) and (2) on the one hand and (3) on the other:

(3) *Ils ont repeinte la table. (they have repainted$_{fem.}$ the table')

In Italian, past participle agreement as in (1) is obligatory with a third-person direct-object clitic but is not found in sentences comparable to (3) in the nonformal spoken language (cf. Burzio (1981, 92); Calabrese (1988, 554); Salvi (1991, 239)):

(4) Li ho visti. ('them$_{masc.pl.}$ I-have seen$_{masc.pl.}$.')

(5) *Ho visti i ragazzi. ('I-have seen$_{m.pl.}$ the boys')

Past participle agreement has several properties that have never been explained. For example, it is well known that (6) behaves like (3) in French:

(6)   *Il a été repeintes quelques tables. ('it(expletive) has been repainted some tables')

(The only possibility is to have no agreement, i.e., to have *repeint*.) Nonetheless, (7) does not behave like (2):

(7)   *Combien de tables a-t-il été repeintes? ('how-many of tables has it been repainted')

Why is past participle agreement not possible here?

The absence of agreement in (8) poses a second problem:

(8)   a. Quelle chaleur atroce il a fait ces jours-ci! ('what heat átrocious it has made these days' = 'How atrociously hot it has been recently!')

   b. *Quelle chaleur atroce il a faite ces jours-ci! ('. . . heat$_{fem.}$ . . . made$_{fem.}$ . . . ')

A third problem, pointed out by Ruwet (1982, 150), has to do with the following contrast:

(9)   une femme qu'on a dite belle ('a woman that one has said$_{fem.}$ beautiful')

(10)   *?une femme qu'on a dite ne pas être belle ('a woman that one has said$_{fem.}$ neg. not be(infin.) beautiful')

(vs. *une femme qu'on a dit ne pas être belle*, without past participle agreement).

A fourth problem, which arises from a comparison between French and Italian, is posed by causative constructions, as illustrated by the contrast in the next pair, with past participle agreement possible in (12) (Italian) but not in (11) (French):

(11)   *Il les a faites réparer par un ami. ('he them$_{fem.pl.}$ has made$_{fem.pl.}$ repair(infin.) by a friend' = 'he has had them repaired . . .')

(12)   Le ha fatte riparare da un amico. ('them$_{fem.pl.}$ he-has made$_{fem.pl.}$ . . .')

French and Italian also differ with respect to the clitic *en/ne*. In French, past participle agreement with *en* is usually (though not always) rejected (cf. Grevisse (1993, sect. 910), Martinon (1927, 482)), whereas in Italian the corresponding agreement with *ne* is straightforwardly acceptable:

(13)   *Il en a reprises deux. ('he of-them has taken-back$_{fem.pl.}$ two')

(14)   Ne ha riprese due. ('of-them he-has taken-back$_{fem.pl.}$ two')

A sixth problem appears very clearly within Italian:

(15)   a. Maria lo è stata. ('M it is been$_{fem.}$' = 'M has been that')

   b. *Maria lo è stato. ('M it is been$_{masc.}$')

This contrast indicates that the past participle cannot agree with *lo* when that clitic is a pro-predicate.

I will attempt to show that all these problems can be solved, given a theory that incorporates the notions 'empty category' and 'small clause'.

2.2.   Locality

Let us begin with (2). What exactly is the past participle agreeing with? In light of the lack of agreement in (3), it would be implausible to think that the element triggering agreement is the trace in postverbal object position of *combien de tables* ('how-many of tables').[1] The most common answer is that the past participle in (2) agrees directly with *combien de tables*. Let us, however, compare past participle agreement with finite verb agreement:

(16)   Les garçons iront au cinéma. ('the boys will-go to-the movies')

Finite verb agreement is always local, in the sense that the nominal phrase with which the verb agrees is the subject of that verb:

(17)   *Les garçons pensent que tu iront au cinéma. ('the boys think that you will-go$_{3pl.}$ to-the movies')

If the structure of the sentence is [NP [INFL VP]], such that INFL contains the AGR element that appears as *-ont/-ent* in (16) and (17), and if INFL is the head of the sentence, then one can account for (17) by requiring the antecedent of AGR to be contained in a category that is a projection of that very AGR/INFL.[2]

It would be entirely reasonable to think that the kind of locality restriction found with finite verb agreement should also be found with past participle agreement. It is, on the other hand, not very likely that *combien de tables* in (2) is contained in a projection of the AGR found on the past participle. It follows that *repeintes* in (2) is not agreeing directly with *combien de tables*.

This paradox dissolves if one considers sentences like (18):

(18)   Je croyais ces tables repeintes. ('I thought those tables (were) repainted')

Example (18) presumably corresponds to: '. . . [ces tables$_i$ [repeintes [e]$_i$]]', where [e] is the trace of *ces tables*. The past participle agreement seen in (18) is surely local: The word *repeintes* agrees with *ces tables*, which is almost certainly contained in a projection of *repeintes* (or of the AGR associated with *repeintes*, if the more highly articulated representation of note 1 is correct):

(19)   . . . [ces tables [AGR [repeintes [e]]]]

The constituent '[ces tables repeintes]' of (18) is to be considered a 'small clause' (i.e., a verbless sentence).[3]

My hypothesis is that (2) contains a small clause and that, by virtue of containing such a small clause, (2) is in fact an instance of local past participle agreement. As a first approximation, the structure of (2) is:

(20)   . . . combien de tables$_i$ ils ont [[e]$_i$ repeintes [e]$_i$] ('. . . how-many of tables they have repainted')

The constituent '[[e]$_i$ repeintes [e]$_i$]' of (20) is a small clause comparable to that of (18), as well as to that of:

(21)   Je sais combien de tables$_i$ elle croyait [[e]$_i$ repeintes [e]$_i$] ('I know how-many of tables she thought (were) repainted')

The small clause of (20) is a complement of the auxiliary *avoir* ('have'), whereas in (18) and (21) the small clause is a complement of *croire* ('think').

The analysis of (2)/(20) just proposed might appear surprising to the extent that (22) is impossible with an interpretation equal to that of (23):

(22)   *Ils ont beaucoup de tables repeintes. ('they have many of tables repainted')

(23)   Ils ont repeint beaucoup de tables.

There are, however, other well-known cases in French of well-formed Wh-movement for which the corresponding nonmovement structure is ill formed:

(24)   la personne que je croyais avoir disparu ('the person that I believed to-have disappeared')

(25)   *Je croyais cette personne avoir disparu. ('I believed that person to-have disappeared')

In other work, I have proposed an analysis of (24) vs. (25) that assigns them parallel constituent structure, while making the desired distinction in terms of case and government.[4] The contrast between (20) and (22) will now be analyzed in the same way. At the same time, the problem of (22) and that of (25) must be kept apart to some degree, given the difference with respect to clitics:

(26)   Ils l'ont repeinte. (=(1))

(27)   *?Je la croyais avoir disparu. ('I her believed to-have disappeared')

In the references cited in note 4, the deviance of (27) is basically attributed to the fact that the subject position of an infinitive can in general not be governed in French by a verb like *croire* ('believe/think'). The subject position of a small clause can be governed from above more easily, as shown by:

(28)   a. Je la croyais disparue. ('I her believed disappeared')

      b. Je les croyais repeintes. ('I them believed repainted')

Let us assume that auxiliary *avoir* can govern the subject position of its small clause complement and that the representation of (26) is (29), which has *repeinte* agreeing, locally, with the empty category to its left (which is the derived subject of the small clause):

(29)   Ils $l_i$ont [[e]$_i$ repeinte [e]$_i$]

Let us assume further that auxiliary *avoir* (and perhaps more generally all temporal auxiliaries) cannot assign case. This implies that the case of the clitic *l'* in (29) must be assigned by *repeinte* rather than by *avoir*. That the past participle *repeinte* can assign (objective) case to its object (i.e., to the empty category to its right) in French is supported by the existence of:[5]

(30)   comme il me l'a été dit ('as it$_{expletive}$ to-me it$_{expletive}$ has been said')

Consequently, the chain in (29) that contains the clitic *l'/la* and the two empty categories respects the case filter.[6]

    The following principle will exclude (22):

(31)   If a chain headed by an A-position has case, then that case must be assigned to the head of the chain.

This suffices to exclude (22), given that the head of the chain there, namely *beaucoup de tables*, is in an A-position (subject of the small clause), yet that A-position is not assigned any case. Example (26)/(29) is compatible with (31), on the other hand, since the head of the chain there is the clitic *la*, which is not in an A-position.

    A thematic chain cannot contain an operator, so *combien de tables* is not contained in any chain in (20). The first empty category is consequently the head of the chain there; thus, (20) violates (31) in the same way that (22) does. The grammatical (2) must therefore have the representation:

(32)   ... combien de tables$_i$ ils ont [[e]$_i$ [[e]$_i$ repeintes [e]$_i$]]

Example (32) has an empty category in the COMP of the small clause.[7] This empty category counts as head of the chain (cf. Kayne (1983b, sect. 1), which allows (32) to avoid violating (31), since COMP is not an A-position. (The chain in (32) will get its case from *repeintes*.)

    If (29) is correct, one might wonder why it is not possible to add an agent phrase:

(33)   *Ils l'ont repeinte par Marie. ('they it have repainted by M')

The answer, I think, comes from theta theory and raises the question how *ils* in (29) gets its theta-role. The auxiliary *avoir* is plausibly not the source of the theta-role of *ils*, which must rather get the theta-role normally assigned by *repeindre* ('repaint') to its underlying subject. Let us assume that passive past participles 'absorb' the theta-role that the corresponding verb would normally assign to its subject position.[8] We know that this theta-role can subsequently be assigned to the object of the preposition *par* ('by'):

(34)   Cette table a été repeinte par Marie. ('this table has been repainted by M')

Were that to take place in (33), however, *ils* would be without any theta-role ((34) has no NP corresponding to the *ils* of (33)), and (33) would violate the theta criterion (which requires that every argument bear some theta-role).

What about (29), then? Let me adopt the basic idea of Hoekstra (1984, 282), which is that *avoir* has the property of transmitting to its subject the theta-role absorbed by the past participle.[9] This amounts to saying that in (29) the theta-role absorbed by *repeinte* is transmitted to *ils* by *avoir*, which makes (29) compatible with the theta criterion.

2.3.   Solutions

We are now in a position to address the six problems brought up in section 2.1. Let us begin by asking why (7), repeated as (35), is ungrammatical:

(35)   *Je ne sais pas combien de tables il a été repeintes. ('I neg know not how-many of tables it$_{expletive}$ has been repainted$_{fem.pl.}$')

We know that *repeintes* cannot agree directly with *combien de tables*, which is too far away from it. The question is then why (35) could not have a representation like that in (32), which would give:

(36)   ... [combien de tables]$_j$ il a été [e]$_j$ [e]$_j$ repeintes [e]$_j$

It is tempting to relate the contrast between (2)/(32) and (35)/(36) to the following:

(37)   les tables qu'on a dit qui seraient repeintes (les premières) ('the tables that they have said that would-be repainted (first)')

(38)   *les tables qu'il a été dit qui seraient repeintes (les premières) ('the tables that it$_{expletive}$ has been said that would-be ...')

Extraction of the subject of the embedded sentence, which is possible in (37) (with complementizer *qui*) is not possible in (38), whose matrix subject is the expletive *il*. Example (36) likewise contains an expletive subject *il* and is also an instance of embedded subject extraction (of the subject of a small clause).

The reason for the deviance of (35) and (38) may be as follows. Assume that expletive *il* must be coindexed with the sentential/small-clause complement, that the head of that complement is *qui* in (38) and the first empty category in (35)/(36), and that head and projection bear the same index.[10] Then, by transitivity of coindexing, the empty category in embedded subject position will, in both (35)/(36) and (38), have the same index as *il*. However, that empty category is supposed in each case to be a variable (bound by the relative operator in (38) and by the interrogative wh-phrase in (35)). As a variable, it may not legitimately have expletive *il* as its local antecedent[11] and is consequently ruled out.

The second problem mentioned in section 2.1. concerned the impossibility of past participle agreement in (8) (again with an expletive *il*), repeated here:

(39)   *Quelle chaleur atroce il a faite ces jours-ci! ('what heat atrocious it has made these days' = 'How atrociously hot it has been recently!')

Given the analysis proposed so far, the representation must be:

(40)   quelle chaleur atroce$_i$ il a [e]$_j$ [e]$_j$ faite [e]$_j$

We know, however, that such impersonals cannot be passivized:

(41)   Il a fait une chaleur atroce. ('it has made a heat atrocious')

(42)   *Une chaleur atroce a été faite ces jours-ci. ('a heat atrocious has been made these days')

The ungrammaticality of (39) can therefore be related, given my analysis, to that of (42).[12]

A third problem was posed by the contrast between (9) and (10), repeated here:

(43)   une femme qu'on a dite belle ('a woman that one has said$_{fem}$/called beautiful')

(44)   *?une femme qu'on a dite ne pas être belle ('a woman that one has said$_{fem.}$ neg. not be(infin.) beautiful')

(43) has the representation:

(45)   . . . a [e]$_j$ [e]$_j$ dite [e]$_j$ belle

No principle is violated. Example (44) must then be:

(46)   . . . a [e]$_j$ [e]$_j$ dite [e]$_j$ ne pas être belle

The embedded participial structure of (43)/(45) is independently attested as well formed (see (47)), but that of (44)/(46) is not, as shown by (48):

(47)   Cette femme a été dite belle. ('this woman has been said beautiful')

(48)   *?Cette femme a été dite ne pas être belle. ('this woman has been said neg not to-be beautiful')

This analysis of past participle agreement allows us to reduce the contrast between (43) and (44) to that between (47) and (48).[13]
   The fourth problem under consideration concerns causatives:

(49)   *Il les a faites réparer par un ami. (= (11) 'he them has made$_{fem.pl.}$ repair(infin.) by a friend' = 'he has had them repaired . . .')

For (49) to be possible, there must be a participial small clause embedded under *avoir* (see (29)), given the proposal I have been developing:

(50)   . . . les$_i$ a [e]$_i$ faites réparer [e]$_I$ . . .

The impossibility of past participle agreement in (49) therefore reduces to the impossibility of (51), with a parallel participial small clause in a passive:

(51)   *Elles ont été faites réparer par un ami. ('they have been made repair by a friend')

   Although causatives do not passivize in French, they do in Italian:[14]

(52)   Sono state fatte riparare da un amico. ('they-are been made repair (infin.) by a friend')

This observation provides, from the present perspective, an immediate answer to the question why the Italian counterpart of (49) is grammatical:

(53)   Le ha fatte riparare da un amico. ('them he-has made$_{fem.pl.}$ . . .')

   The correlation between past participle agreement and passive might seem weakened, in Italian, by:

(54)   Gianni le ha volute riparare. ('G them$_{fem.pl.}$ has wanted$_{fem.pl.}$ to-repair')

(55)   *Sono state volute riparare da Gianni. ('they-are been wanted to-repair by G')

However, I will follow Burzio (1981, 576) in taking (55) to be excluded as a result of the fact that the PRO subject of the infinitive there lacks a controller/antecedent that c-commands it. In (55) *Gianni* does not c-command PRO, although PRO is c-commanded by *Gianni* (which receives the subject theta-role of *volere* ('want') by transmission)[15] in (54), as shown in (56):

(56)   Gianni$_i$ le$_j$ ha [[e]$_j$ volute PRO$_i$ riparare [e]$_j$]

The fifth problem mentioned earlier is the following. Why do French and Italian contrast with respect to *en*, as illustrated by (13) versus (14), repeated here:

(57)   *Paul en a reprises deux. ('P of-them has taken-back$_{fem.pl.}$ two')

(58)   Paolo ne ha riprese due. ('P of-them he-has taken-back$_{fem.pl.}$ two')

Let us begin with French, by asking why the past participle does not agree with *en* in the way it does with accusative clitics. The analysis I have proposed implies that the past participle can agree directly neither with *en* nor with an accusative clitic. The past participle agrees, rather, with its own subject NP, which can have an accusative clitic as antecedent, as in (29), repeated here:

(59)   Paul les$_i$ a [e]$_i$ reprises [e]$_i$ ('P them has taken-back')

The question, then, is why (60) is not as well formed as (59):

(60)   Paul en a [e] reprises [deux [e]]

The essential difference lies, I think, in the fact that *en* corresponds to only part of a NP, as opposed to *les*. This difference affects the distribution of the pronominal features of *les* and *en*. In (59), we can take the empty category subject of the small clause to be pronominal (i.e., to share the pronominal features of its antecedent *les*), while taking the empty category in object position to be a nonpronominal anaphor.

In (60), on the other hand, it is not very plausible, given the special status of *en*, to take the empty category subject, which is a full NP, to have the pronominal features of *en*. Assume that those features are instead shared by the empty category contained in the object. Now, if this pronominal empty category were bound by the one in subject position, there would be a violation of Condition B of the Binding Theory (taking the governing category of the [e] within the object to be the small clause). Binding depends on coindexation. The subject empty category is what determines the past participle agreement in (60). It must therefore be coindexed with the object of *reprises*:

(61)   Paul en a [e]$_i$ reprises [deux [e]]$_i$

Pollock (1986) has shown that there is in general coindexation between *en*, the trace of *en*, and the NP of which the trace of *en* is head.[16] The complete coindexing of (57)/(60) is therefore:

(62)   Paul en$_i$ a [e]$_i$ reprises [deux [e]$_i$]$_i$

In (62) the pronominal empty category (the second one) is indeed bound by the other, so Condition B excludes (57). (There is no comparable violation in (59), since the pronominal empty category in (59) is the first one.)

The French/Italian contrast in (57)/(58) can now be seen to follow from the 'free inversion' character of Italian. Example (57)/(58) resembles:

(63)   *?le jour où en ont été repris(es) deux (Fr. 'the day when of-them have been taken-back two')

(64)   il giorno in cui ne sono stati/e ripresi/e due (Ital. 'the day in which of-them are been taken-back two')

Example (63) is excluded, according to Pollock (1986), by Binding Theory, since *en* (or its trace; see note 16) is bound by the empty category subject (of the finite auxiliary). Pollock suggests distinguishing (64) from (63) by having the corresponding subject position not count as an A-position in Italian. (That would be a property intimately linked to the 'free inversion' property.) If, as suggested in Kayne (1983b, sect. 9), Condition B looks only at antecedents in A-positions, (64) will not constitute a violation of it.

Taken together, these hypotheses allow an explanation of the well-formedness of (65), the representation of (58):

(65)   Paolo ne$_i$ ha [[e]$_i$ riprese [due [e]$_i$]$_i$]

The second empty category, which is pronominal, is bound by the first, but, since the first is not in an A-position, there is no violation in Italian (as opposed to the French counterpart (62)).[17]

There is a contrast in Italian between (58) and (66) (although the latter is possible in a formal register):

(66)   (*)Paolo ha riprese due cose. ('P has taken-back two things')

This contrast strongly suggests that the empty category subject in (65) is licensed by *ne*, which is its antecedent. There is no corresponding antecedent in (66).[18]

Belletti (1981) has noted a contrast between (67) (which has the status of (5) or (66)) and (68):

(67)   *Gianni ha conosciuta Maria. ('G has known/met M')

(68)   Conosciuta Maria, Gianni è cambiato del tutto. ('(having) known/met M, G is changed completely')

She develops an analysis of (68) with a PRO controlled by Gianni: 'PRO conosciuta Maria, . . .'. That amounts to having the past participle agree directly with the following object, a possibility that I have excluded. I am therefore led to sketch an analysis of (68) that has *Maria* as the subject of a small clause. (If *Maria* were in object position, (68) would be parallel to (66).)

This leads in turn to the proposal that (68) involves moving the participle *conosciuta* to the left, much as one observes in Italian in the case of gerunds (cf. Rizzi (1982a)):

(69)   Avendo Maria comprato il libro, Gianni . . . ('having M bought the book, G . . .')

The absence of (68) in French now reduces to the absence of (69):

(70)   *Connue Marie, Jean a changé complètement. (=(68))

(71)   *Ayant Marie acheté le livre, Jean . . . (=(69))

The representation of (68) is thus:

(72)   conosciuta$_j$ Maria$_i$ [e]$_j$ [e]$_i$ . . .

Maria receives objective case from *conosciuta* (shown by *Conosciuta me*, . . . vs. **Conosciuta io* . . . , as pointed out by Belletti). The agreement in (68)/(72) takes place prior to the movement of the participle (as in *Where have you been?*). The control interpretation in (68) recalls theta-role transmission by *avoir* (cf. the discussion of (33)). (In any event, postulating a PRO does not suffice to account for *?Une fois la main mise à la pâte, tout devient facile* ('one time the hand put to the paste, everything becomes easy' = 'once one lends a hand, . . .'); example from Ruwet (1983, note 136).) Although the apparently obligatory character of this control in Italian remains to be explained,[19] once granted, it suffices to account for (73), in a way parallel to the discussion of (33):

(73)   *Conosciuta Maria da Gianni, . . . ('known/met M by G, . . .')

The sixth problem mentioned in section 2.1 had to do with the absence of past participle agreement in (15b) versus (15a), repeated as (75) versus (74):

(74)   Maria lo è stata. ('M it is been$_{fem.sg.}$')

(75)   *Maria lo è stato. ('. . . been$_{masc.sg.}$')

The question is, What is the status of the following past participle agreement structure?:

(76)   Maria$_j$ lo$_i$ è [e]$_i$ stato ([e]$_j$) [e]$_i$

(*Maria* probably binds a trace; see Couquaux (1979).) Example (76) contains a small clause that resembles the passive of a predicate complement of *essere* ('be'). Put another way, (76) has the status of (77):

(77)   *Intelligent été, Jean est devenu bête. ('intelligent been, J is become stupid')

Thus, (75) itself must have the status of (77), as desired, since both are ungrammatical.

2.4. Subjects

Every well-formed example of past participle agreement has turned out to be analyzable in terms of a structure in which the past participle directly agrees with its own subject.

If Burzio (1981, 644ff.) is correct to analyze passives as generally containing a small clause '[NP $V_{past\ part.}$ NP]', then (78), too, is an instance of a past participle agreeing with its own subject:

(78)   La ville sera détruite par l'ennemi. ('the city will-be destroyed by the enemy')

(79)   la ville$_i$ sera [[e]$_i$ détruite [e]$_i$ par l'ennemi]

I proposed earlier that auxiliary *avoir* ('have') can be followed by a small clause. If we generalize this analysis to the auxiliary *être* ('be') of (80), then (80) will have a representation illustrated in (81):

(80)   Les victimes sont mortes il y des années. ('the victims are died years ago')

(81)   les victimes$_i$ sont [[e]$_i$ mortes [e]$_i$] . . .

The second empty category is motivated by work of Perlmutter (1978; 1989), Burzio (1981; 1986), Hoekstra (1984) and Pollock (1983a; 1985). Example (80) again shows a participle agreeing with its own subject.

Assume, as I have implicitly been doing, that participle agreement always has this strongly local character.[20] We can now attempt an explanation of the impossibility of past participle agreement with the subject of a transitive:

(82)   *Marie a reprise tout cela. (Fr. 'M has taken-back$_{fem.sg.}$ all that')

(83)   *Maria ha ripresa tutto questo. (Ital., same)

Marie is not the configurational subject of *reprise*, strictly speaking, but is rather the subject of auxiliary *avoir*. Example (82)/(83) would therefore be possible only if there were a small clause: 'Marie a [[e] reprise tout cela]'. The empty category could not be PRO, because PRO cannot be governed. The position to which the subject theta-role is assigned (by *avoir*) is that of *Marie*. Assume that the features of the argument of a chain never appear in a position lower than the position in which the theta-role is assigned. Even if a chain could be formed in (82)/(83), past participle agreement would be excluded.[21]

2.5. Conclusion

I have looked at the question of French and Italian past participle agreement in a new perspective, within the framework of a theory that makes use of both small clauses and empty categories. The results obtained provide substantial support for that type of theory.

NOTES

1. For a possible answer to the question why the participle cannot agree with a following object, see Fauconnier (1974), who proposes relating the ungrammaticality of (3) to the impossibility of having *il* and *Jean* coreferential in a sentence like (i):

(i)   Il a photographié le fils de Jean. ('he has photographed the son of J')

Another proposal (that would be relatively close to Fauconnier's) would postulate the structure:

(ii)   ... [AGR [V$_{\text{past part.}}$ NP]]

(with movement of AGR onto the participle) and would require that AGR (abstracting away from that movement) be c-commanded by the NP with which it is coindexed, which is not the case in (ii). (A c-commands B if the first branching node that dominates A also dominates B.)

2. A second possibility would be to treat AGR as an anaphor and to bring in Binding Theory, but that would risk complicating my approach to (2), given the agreement phenomenon described by Kimball and Aissen (1971), a counterpart of which perhaps exists in Portuguese (cf. Moreira da Silva (1983)). For more details concerning AGR in (16), see Chomsky (1981a), Pollock (1983b), and Rouveret (1980).

3. The lack of verb is not necessarily the result of a deletion rule. See Stowell (1983); also Belletti (1981).

4. See Kayne (1980b; 1981e). For important refinements, see Pollock (1983a; 1985).

5. For other arguments supporting case assignment by a past participle, see Pollock (1981; 1983a; 1985).

6. Which requires that every thematic chain (apart from those headed by PRO) have a case. On the notion of chain, see Chomsky (1981a, chap. 6), Kayne (1983b), and Pollock (1983b).

7. That a small clause can have a Comp position is clear from Mouchaweh (1984; 1985); see also Pesetsky (1984). The extra complexity attributed to (32) as compared with (29) is justified by the fact that in Italian (2) is marginal (as opposed to (4)) and for some speakers even has the status of (5); see Burzio (1981, 92). Example (32) bears a structural resemblance to (24), according to the references of note 4.

Example (3) shows that applying rightward movement to (22) would not neutralize the violation of (31), presumably because the adjoined position could not be part of a thematic chain.

8. See Burzio (1981; 1986) and Chomsky (1981a).

9. As Hoekstra suggests, this may allow one to do away with the distinction between active and passive past participle (if there is no morphological difference). Absorption could take place consistently and transmission occur even in simple cases lacking a small clause, as in *Ils ont repeint la table* ('they have repainted the table'). Such transmission might be close to the theta-percolation proposed by Kayne (1985). See, however, chapter 7.

10. This would hold, too, if the head were INFL, given the coindexation between INFL and *qui*/[e]$_j$ in these cases. The idea that head and projection bear the same index goes back to Williams (1982) (for French, see Pollock (1986)).

11. For additional examples of this type of violation, see Pollock (1983a; 1983b) and Kayne (1983b).

12. If the hypothesis based on Hoekstra (1984) alluded to in note 9 is correct, (39) and (42) cannot, given (41), be treated as in Burzio (1981), which disallows the formation of a passive past participle starting from a verb with a nonthematic subject. An alternative promising approach might involve relating (39) and (35).

13. On the ungrammaticality of (48), see Kayne (1981e) and Pollock (1983a; 1985).

14. For discussion of this contrast, see Zubizarreta (1986).

15. This reasoning, which is independent of the question whether Burzio is right to postulate movement of '*riparare* [e]ⱼ' to the left of PRO, extends to *potere* ('be able'):

(i)   Gianniᵢ leⱼ ha [e]ⱼ potute [e]ᵢ riparare [e]ⱼ

This structure suggests that the small clause, which is not an argument in the strict sense, does not count as an opaque domain. The '?' that Burzio (1981, 606) assigns to a similar sentence with *andare* ('go') might, from my perspective, not be the result of a case conflict.

Example (49), which involves neither control of PRO nor raising, is unaffected by this argument. (There are examples of (49) in Harmer (1979, 75); the text analysis predicts that a French speaker who accepts (49) should also accept (51).).

16. See also the earlier discussion of (35)-(38). That the trace of a clitic is subject to Condition B is clear from:

(i)   ?Jean me le lui a fait présenter. ('J me him him has made introduce' = 'J had me introduce him to him')

Those who accept (i) allow *lui*, but not *le*, to have *Jean* as antecedent (cf. Morin (1979a)), which suggests that Condition B takes clitic traces into account (this does not affect the essentials of Pollock (1986)).

Example (ii) is excluded parallel to (57):

(ii)   *Paul en a reprises. ('P of-them has taken-back (some)')

The structure is: '. . . reprises [0 [e]]', with a 0 determiner; see Kayne (1975, sect. 2.9). Example (iii) is excluded in the relevant interpretation by (31), parallel to (22), since (*en*, [*deux* [e]], [e]) is an ill-formed chain (by virtue of containing two arguments, even though the two are coindexed).

(iii)   *Paul en a deux reprises. ('P of-them has two taken-back')

17. The past participle agreement in (65) holds between *riprese* and the first empty category. There may be a link here with agreement between a finite verb and a 'topic'; see note 2. A chain ([e], [*due* [e]]) in (65) would not violate (31), since the head would not be in an A-position.

18. The empty category subject in (64) does not need an antecedent because it is adequately 'identified' by AGR. In (65) and (66) AGR does not suffice to identify nonnominative [e], since AGR there is not marked for person (but only for number and gender); see Borer (1984; 1986).

As far as the register of Italian is concerned in which (66) is acceptable (e.g., Lepschy and Lepschy (1981, 169–171)), it might be that *avere* can assign a case, as seems to be true for middle French; see Martin and Wilmet (1980, 221).

19. For Belletti's analysis, the problem arises as to how to exclude (72). The impossibility of embedding (72) under *avere* (at least in ordinary Italian—such embedding would allow (66)) might be linked to that of embedding a structure with a preposed finite verb; see Kayne (1982).

Having a PRO in (68) is incompatible (in the case of a verb with a thematic subject, which would allow 'PRO *elogiatosi* [e]' if Burzio (1981) is correct) with Hoekstra's proposal, mentioned in note 9. That proposal accounts straightforwardly for *Telefonato a Gianni*, . . . (example from Belletti; comparable examples are accepted, in other contexts, by Burzio (1981, 536) and Manzini (1983, 128)).

Belletti's example *Elogiato solo se stesso*, . . . ('praised only himself, . . .) could be related to (i) (and similarly for Italian; cf. Fresina (1980, 241)):

(i)   Une chose comme ça ne devrait pas être dite de soi-même. ('a thing like that neg.
      should not be said of reflex.(oneself)')

The impossibility of *Detto che-S*, . . . could be related to that of *That she was departing announced*, . . . , where what is at issue is probably not agreement but rather differences between S-bar and NP; see Koster (1978).

How best to express the obligatoriness of the agreement in (4) (with the clitics *lo, la, li, le*) remains an open question.

20. See the discussion of (16)ff. Example (i), with a transitive verb and dative reflexive clitic, is comparable to (81) (and to (59)):

(i)   Jean se les$_i$ est [e]$_i$ offertes [e]$_i$ ('J refl. them is offered')

21. Without it being necessary to state a complex rule specific to past participle agreement of the sort proposed in Burzio (1981). Left open is the question of (i) vs. (ii) (cf. Burzio (1981, 446)):

(i)   Si è comprata due libri. (Ital. 'refl. she-is bought$_{fem.sg.}$ two books')

(ii) *Elle s'est offerte deux livres. (Fr. 'she refl. is offered$_{fem.sg.}$ two books')

3

Facets of Romance
Past Participle Agreement

This article will address itself primarily to the agreement found in past participle constructions containing an auxiliary comparable to English 'have'. As seen in (1)–(3), the past participle in French does not agree with a following NP but may agree in the corresponding accusative clitic construction or Wh-construction:

(1) a. Paul a repeint les chaises. ('P has repainted the chairs')

   b. *Paul a repeintes les chaises. (same, with agreement added)

(2) Paul les a repeintes. ('P them-has repainted')

(3) les chaises que Paul a repeintes ('the chairs that . . .')

It is usual to say that in (2) and (3), the past participle agrees with the clitic or Wh-phrase, much as the auxiliary 'a' in (l)–(3) is said to agree with the subject NP 'Paul'. We shall argue, however, that this parallelism is only partially valid and that there is a significant distinction to be drawn between the two types of agreement, namely that although the finite auxiliary does agree directly with its subject, the past participle in (2) and (3) does not agree directly in the same sense with either clitic or Wh-phrase. Rather, the past participle agreement in (2) and (3) must be mediated by an empty category that intervenes between the clitic or Wh-phrase and the past participle.

What this means for (2), for example, is that the S-structure representation 'Paul les$_i$ a repeintes [e]$_{I}$', with one empty category corresponding to the D-structure position of the clitic, is not adequate and that we should adopt instead a representation like (4):

(4) Paul les$_i$ a [e]$_i$ repeintes [e]$_i$

25

In (4), a direct agreement relation will hold between the participle and the empty category preceding it, rather than between participle and clitic. (Given the ungrammaticality of (1b), we do not want to say that there is a direct agreement relation between the participle and the empty category in object position).

The reasons for adopting (4) are of two kinds: On the one hand, it will give us a more restrictive characterization of agreement than would be available if (4) were not adopted. On the other, there are certain empirical properties of past participle agreement that (4), but not an analysis lacking the first empty category, will allow us to elucidate. To mention one before closing this introductory section, the agreement in (3) is impossible if the subject of the auxiliary is an expletive; we will show how (the Wh counterpart of) (4) leads to an account.

3.1. A unified theory

We start from the position that, all other things being equal, it is desirable to have a maximally unified theory of past participle agreement and finite verb agreement. The latter is generally analyzed as involving a node AGR: 'NP AGR $[_{VP}$ V . . .]', and we will do the same for the former:

(5)   Paul les$_i$ a [e]$_i$ AGR$_i$ repeintes [e]$_i$

(At some point in the derivation AGR will lower to V or V raise to AGR—the choice does not affect what follows.) The presence of AGR in (5) will allow us to distinguish French and Italian straightforwardly from Spanish, which does not have (2) (or (3)), by saying that Spanish active past participles are incompatible with AGR (a possible reason is mentioned below), and occur only in a structure like 'NP CL$_i$ V$_{aux}$ V$_{pp}$ [e]$_I$'.

The agreement relation will now be expressed by coindexing (or linking, in Higginbotham's (1983) sense) AGR with some NP. We know from the case of finite verb agreement that this relation is subject to locality conditions. Thus, the finite verb will agree with its own subject, but not with the subject of the next highest verb up. Having an empty category preceding AGR in (5) yields a more strongly local agreement relation than would be the case if AGR were linked directly to the clitic. This consideration has particular force in the Wh counterpart of (5), for example, in (7), corresponding to the sentence (6):

(6)   Je me demande combien de tables Paul a repeintes. ('I wonder how-many of tables P has repainted')

(7)   . . . combien de tables$_i$ Paul a [e]$_i$ AGR$_i$ repeintes [e]$_i$

Were the first empty category absent, AGR$_i$ would have to be linked directly to the Wh-phrase, across the IP headed by that AGR$_i$, the VP headed by the auxiliary, and the IP headed by the (unlike indexed) agreement associated with the auxiliary. If, on the other hand, we adopt (7), we can maintain the characterization of AGR as link-

ing only with a NP that it governs (or, perhaps, that governs it), given that a government relation does hold between the first empty category and AGR, although not
between the Wh-phrase and AGR.

Thinking of the agreement relation in terms of government, as in Chomsky
(1981a, 211), gives us a straightforward account of the ungrammaticality of (1b) in
French, since in '. . . AGR [$_{VP}$ repeint(*es) les chaises]', no government relation can
hold between AGR and the NP governed by V (although AGR m-commands that
NP, the intervening V creates a minimality barrier, in Chomsky's (1986a, 42) sense).

The postulation of an extra empty category in (5) and (7) leads to the question
of why that position could not be filled by a lexical NP:

(8)   *Paul a ces tables repeint(es). ('P has these tables repainted')

(8) is sharply ungrammatical with 'a' taken as tense auxiliary 'have', with or without past participle agreement. The contrast between (8) and (6)/(7) is not, however,
unfamiliar, in that a rather similar one occurs elsewhere in French, in the case of
infinitival complements embedded under verbs like 'croire' ('believe'):

(9)   la personne que je croyais avoir disparu ('the person that I believed to-have disap-
      peared')

(10)   *Je croyais cette personne avoir disparu.

In Kayne (1980b, sect. 1.3; 1981e, sect. 3), it is argued that this can be accounted for
if 'cette personne' in (10) is not in a case-marked position (unlike its English counterpart) and if Wh-movement in (9) has the effect of allowing case to be assigned to
the relevant chain via another position (comp). The reason that 'cette personne' in
(10) is not in a case-marked position is not that 'croire' is not a case-assigner (it is)
but rather that the infinitival subject position is too far away from 'croire' (in present
terms, it is separated from it by both CP and IP).

Now the ungrammaticality of (10) and that of (8), although similar, must not be
fully identified, since their clitic counterparts diverge sharply, that of (8) being fully
grammatical, as in (2)/(5), while that of (10) is quite deviant:

(11)   *?Je la croyais avoir disparu. ('I her-believed to-have disappeared')

Our proposal is that (8) and (10) both violate case theory requirements, that in both
the offending lexical NP is in a noncase marked position (whence the similarity) but
that the reason for case not reaching that position is different in the two constructions: Whereas in (10), it is that a case-assigning verb is too far away, in (8) the higher
verb (the auxiliary), though near enough, is incapable of assigning case at all.[1]

That tense auxiliary 'avoir' is not a case-assigner is further supported by the
observation that 'avoir' is incompatible with the accusative clitic 'le' that can stand
for various predicate elements, and in particular for (passive) past participles:

(12)   Paul sera photographié par Marie. ('P will-be ph. by M')

(13)   Paul le sera par Marie.[2]

If we take (the trace of) 'le' in (13) to receive case from copula 'être' ('be'), and if tense auxiliary 'avoir' cannot assign case, then (14) vs. (15) falls into place:

(14)   Paul a téléphoné (à Marie). ('P has tel. to M')

(15)   *Paul l'a (à Marie).

Against the background of the ungrammaticality of (8), which crucially involves the inability of auxiliary 'avoir' to assign case, consider again (2), repeated here as (16):

(16)   Paul les a repeintes.

If the accusative case of the clitic cannot be due to 'avoir', as now must be true, then that case must come from the participle 'repeintes'. That is, in (17) 'repeintes' assigns case to the NP position that it governs:[3]

(17)   Paul les a [e] AGR repeintes [e]$_{Case}$

That an active past participle can assign case is clearly supported by an Italian construction studied by Belletti (1981), in which one finds an active past participle unaccompanied by any auxiliary, yet taking an object and assigning accusative case to it:

(18)   Conosciuto me, Maria . . . ('known/met me, M . . .')

Although (18) is absent from French, that is arguably due to independent considerations (cf. section 3.6.), so we can plausibly take (18) as support for French (17), as well as for the equivalent of (17) in Italian.[4]

  If past participles in French (and Italian) can assign case, then more must be said about the ungrammaticality of (8), that is, about the ill-formedness of (19):

(19)   *Paul a ces tables AGR repeintes [e]$_{Case}$

Consider a principle such as (20):[5]

(20)   If a case-marked chain is headed by an A-position, then that A-position must be assigned case.

Since nothing about (19) would allow one to say that 'ces tables' is in an A-bar-position, (19) is ruled out by (20). Example (17), on the other hand, contains a chain headed by the position of the clitic, which is not an A-position.

  We are now in a position to return to the Wh case of past participle agreement illustrated in (7), repeated here as (21), with case added:

(21)   . . . combien de tables$_i$ Paul a [e]$_i$ AGR$_i$ repeintes [e]$_{i, \ Case}$

Since the Wh-phrase 'combien de tables' is, being an operator, not part of the relevant chain, it follows from (20) that the first empty category must not be in an A-position. Let us take it, then, to be adjoined to the IP (strictly speaking AGRP) headed by AGR_i as in (22):

(22)   ... combien de tables$_i$ Paul a [$_{IP}$ [e]$_i$ [$_{IP}$ AGR_i repeintes [e]$_{i,\ Case}$]]

(If there is in addition an [e]$_i$ in the spec position of AGR_i, then the adjoined [e]$_i$, which is not in an A-position, must be taken to be the head of the chain, so that (20) does not come into play; if there is no such [e]$_i$ in spec position, then [e]$_i$ in object position can be taken as head.) In the framework of Chomsky (1986a), the intervening lower IP segment in (22) will not block the government relation between the first [e]$_i$ and AGR_i, as desired.

Summing up this section, we see that a restrictive theory of agreement imposes the presence of an extra [e]$_i$ in (22) (and (17)), and that, given the inability of auxiliary 'avoir' to assign case, this [e]$_i$ must, for case-theoretic reasons, be taken in (22) to be in an A-bar-position. In the next section, we attempt to show that the presence of this [e]$_i$ in A-bar-position in (22) has distinctly favorable empirical consequences.

3.2.   Expletives

The conclusion we have just reached is, in effect, that two Wh-movement sentences, one with and one without past participle agreement, will, even if otherwise identical, have category-wise different representations. Compare (22) with (23), which corresponds to the same sentence less agreement:

(23)   ... combien de tables$_i$ Paul a [$_{VP}$ repeint [e]$_{i,\ Case}$]

'Repeint' is the participle of a verb that is associated with a subject theta-role. Consider the effect on (22) and (23) of replacing 'repeint' by the participle of a verb not associated with a subject theta-role. Schematically, this will result in (24) and (25), where 'il' is the French expletive pronoun:

(24)   ... Wh-phrase$_i$ il V_{aux} [$_{IP}$ [e]$_i$ [$_{IP}$ AGR_i V_{pp} [e]$_i$]]

(25)   ... Wh-phrase$_i$ il V_{aux} V_{pp} [e]$_i$

Let us further adopt Chomsky's (1986b, 179) proposal concerning expletives, namely that they are replaced in LF. In (25), 'il' will be replaced by [e]$_i$, much as in a corresponding simple sentence with no Wh-movement.

In (24), we would expect 'il' to have to be replaced by the first [e]$_i$. But that yields a case of improper movement (from an A-bar-position to an A-position), in Chomsky's (1986b, 114; 1986a, 22) sense.[6] Therefore, (24) can correspond to no well-formed sentence. In other words, the analysis developed here leads us to expect that past participle agreement of the Wh- type should be impossible when the subject of the auxiliary is an expletive.

That expectation is met. Since an analysis of past participle agreement that does not force the postulation in (22) and (24) of an extra [e]$_i$ generates no comparable expectation, the relevant facts, to which we now turn, strongly support the approach to agreement taken here.

That it is not possible for a past participle to display agreement with a Wh-phrase in the context of expletive 'il' is seen in several different subconstructions. First there is the weather expression of (26):

(26)   Il a fait une chaleur atroce. ('it has made a heat atrocious')

Wh-movement is possible, but not past participle agreement:[7]

(27)   Quelle chaleur atroce il a fait(*e)! ('what . . .')

(28)   les chaleurs qu'il a fait(*es)

Second, there are unaccusative verbs that in French take auxiliary 'have'. Of these, a few have past participles whose masculine and feminine forms are phonetically distinct. Although the expletive construction often gives marginal results that are exacerbated by Wh-movement, the difference between the nonagreeing sentence and its agreeing counterpart is clear:[8]

(29)   ?Je me demande combien de couleurs il a déteint(*es) (sur ce vêtement) ('I wonder how many of colors it/there has run on that clothing')

Third is the case of expletive 'il' in constructions where the auxiliary is être' ('be') rather than 'avoir'. There is no instance of past participle agreement triggered by a Wh-phrase object. The primary candidate would be impersonal passives:

(30)   Il sera repeint beaucoup de chaises cette année. ('it/there will-be repainted many of chairs this year')

Wh-movement is possible, but there is no agreement with the Wh-phrase:[9]

(31)   Je me demande combien de chaises il sera repeint(*es) cette année.

Fourth and last, there is the case of 'falloir' ('to be necessary'), which is notable in being able to assign accusative case (and to thereby nullify the constraint against definites usually found in expletive 'Il V NP' contexts) to an argument NP despite taking an expletive subject:

(32)   Il me les faut. ('it me$_{dative}$ them$_{accus}$. is-necessary')

(33)   Il me faut ces chaises.

What evidence there is suggests that the accusative case does not waive the expletive replacement requirement, in that past participle agreement with Wh-movement
is generally felt to be impossible (cf. Grevisse (1964, section 787), Martinon (1927,
479)), although the judgment has a delicate status because of the absence of any
phonetic distinction between masculine and feminine for this participle:[10]

(34) Il m'aurait fallu ces chaises—là. ('it/there me-would-have been-necessary those
       chairs there')

(35)   les chaises qu'il m'aurait fallu(*es)

For all of the four subconstructions described, we continue to assume case to be assigned to the rightmost [e]$_i$, by the past participle and not to be assignable at all by
the auxiliary. For the three with auxiliary 'avoir', this simply corresponds to the
position taken earlier. In (30)/(31), however, the auxiliary is copula 'be', which appears to be a case assigner in (13). Example (13) contrasts, though, with (36) (cf.
Pollock (1983a, 146)):

(36)   *Il sera beaucoup de chaises repeint(es) cette année.

It will suffice for our purposes if this 'be' can in French assign case to a predicative
element (as in (13)) but not to an argument. If so, then it is again clear that in (30)/
(31) case must be assigned by the participle.

   To close our account of the impossibility of past participle agreement with a Wh-
phrase in an expletive construction, one further assumption should be made explicit,
and that is that in none of the sentences given earlier can there be S-structure case transmission from expletive 'il' to the first [e]$_i$ of (24), since if there were, then (20) would
no longer prevent that [e]$_i$ from being reinterpreted as being in an A-position. Put another way, it must not be possible to take 'il' to be the head of the relevant S-structure
chain.[11]

3.3. ECM

Ruwet (1982, 150) has observed an interesting contrast between the following two
constructions:

(37)   une femme qu'on a dit belle ('a woman that one has said beautiful')

(38)   une femme qu'on a dit ne pas être belle ('. . . neg. not to-be . . .')

Example (37) is an instance of Wh-movement applied to the subject of a small clause
embedded under 'dire', and (38) an example of the same except that the small clause
is replaced by an infinitive. Ruwet's observation is that past participle agreement,
although possible in (37), yields a deviant result in (38):

(39)   une femme qu'on a dite belle

(40)   *?une femme qu'on a dite ne pas être belle

The relevant substructure of (39) is 'Wh$_i$ NP a [$_{IP}$ [e]$_i$ [$_{IP}$ AGR$_i$ dite [[e]$_i$ belle]]] in which the second [e]$_i$ is governed by the participle across the small-clause boundary. The corresponding representation for (40) must involve more than simply replacing the small clause by an infinitival IP, however, since as discussed earlier for (9) and (10), French does not permit the subject of an embedded infinitive to be governed across a boundary by a verb like 'dire'. Our proposal for (9), and similarly (38)/(40), has attributed an essential role to the trace in Comp left by Wh-movement. Thus, (38) will have a representation such as '. . . Wh$_i$ NP a dit [$_{CP}$ [e]$_i$ [$_{IP}$[e]$_i$ ne pas être belle]]'.[12] That of (40) will be the same, except that the theory of agreement adopted here forces the postulation of an extra empty category adjoined to the IP headed by the participial AGR:

(41)   . . . Wh$_i$ NP a [$_{IP}$ [e]$_i$ [$_{IP}$ AGR$_i$ dite [$_{CP}$ [e]$_i$ [$_{IP}$[e]$_i$ . . .]]]]

In discussing (22), we noted that it might be the case that we should also have an [e]$_i$ in the Spec of AGR$_i$. If so, then we will have a clear violation of the 'improper movement' constraint seen to play a role in the preceding section, in that in (41) the [e]$_i$ in Spec of CP, an A-bar-position, will be bound by this [e]$_i$ in Spec of AGR$_i$, an A-position. If, on the other hand, there were no such [e]$_i$ that must be added to (41), then we would apparently have to interpret 'improper movement' broadly enough that the binding of [e]$_i$ in Spec of CP by AGR$_i$ itself triggers the violation.[13] This might not be necessary, however, if we took (41) to violate a stronger form of improper movement than is currently assumed, namely one that would go back to Chomsky (1973, section 3) and prohibit a category in Spec of CP from being bound (within the scope of the maximal operator) by any phrase not itself in the Spec of some CP. In this way the [e]$_i$ adjoined to IP in (41) would become the illicit binder.[14]

     Thus (40) is accounted for, and correctly distinguished from (39). (39) differs from (40) precisely in that the subject position of the small clause is accessible to government by the matrix verb.[15] Hence the presence of an [e]$_i$ Spec of CP is not required, so that the [e]$_i$ adjoined to IP in (39) yields no illicit binding relation.

3.4.   Wh- vs. clitics

We have postulated the existence of an IP-adjoined empty category in the Wh past participle agreement construction. For the comparable construction in which the participle agrees with a clitic, we have not been led to suppose that there is such an IP-adjoined category; see (17), with the empty category in Spec of AGR. We take this difference in representation to be supported by the fact that, contrary to the impression perhaps given by French, these two subcases of past participle agreement are not always found together. This is seen most readily in nonformal spoken Italian, which has the past participle agreeing with a clitic but not with a Wh-phrase:[16]

(42) Paolo ha visto le ragazze. ('P has seen the girls')

(43) Paolo le ha viste.

(44) le ragazze che Paolo ha visto/*viste

As it turns out, neither French nor Italian constitutes an isolated case. In fact, French itself is not homogeneous, in that there are many speakers who have past participle agreement neither with object clitics nor with object Wh-phrases (i.e., these speakers share the Spanish paradigm).[17] Those who do have it always, as far as we know, have it both with clitics and with Wh-phrases. The French situation is further complicated by the fact that past participle agreement is one of the areas most discussed by normative grammarians. So it is in a sense welcome to find that the combination of agreement with clitic and agreement with Wh-phrases is attested in various nearby languages/dialects, for example those varieties of Occitan described by Camproux (1958, 323), Kelly (1973, 196, 200), as well as that referred to by Seguy (1950, 53); also the Vaudois of Reymond and Bossard (1979, 93, 147), the Normandy dialect of Lepelley (1974, 107, 113) and apparently the Brittany dialect of Hervé (1973, 84).

On the other hand, the Italian paradigm of (43)–(44), with clitic agreement but without Wh-agreement, is also robust, shared as it is[18] by Catalan according to Fabra (1981, para. 73), by the varieties of Occitan described in Rohlfs (1977, 223), Bonnaud (1974, 39, 57), Lamouche (1902, 106), Marshall (1984, 66), and Miremont (1976, 54, 55), by the Beuil dialect described by Blinkenberg (1948, 118), and by the Corsican, Milanese, Cremonese, and Bolognese dialects of Italian, to judge by Yvia Croce (1979, 137), Beretta (1984, 124, 145), Rossini (1975, 126), and Mainoldi (1950, 63), respectively.

What is to the best of our knowledge notably lacking, though, is a language having the Wh-case of object agreement but not the clitic case. This means that adjunction of NP to the IP complement of the auxiliary is not automatically available,[19] even to a language that otherwise uses the '$[_{IP} [e]_i \, AGR_i \, V_{pp} \, [e]_i, \, _{Case}]$' structure that underlies clitic agreement. Conversely, it means that if a language allows '$[_{IP} [e]_i [_{IP} \, AGR_i \, V_{pp} \, [e]_i, \, _{Case}]]$', then the corresponding structure with $[e]_i$ in Spec of AGR but with no IP adjunction is straightforward.

We could interpret this asymmetry as simply reflecting the extra complexity of the IP-adjunction structure, or perhaps of the agreement relation in that structure. A stronger result, however, would consist in showing that the subset of languages allowing Wh-agreement, within the set of clitic-agreement languages, is not a random one but that the property of Wh-agreement correlated with some other.

Given the heterogeneity found among the varieties of Occitan mentioned, it is not clear that such a property must exist. On the other hand, the contrast between the Italian dialects and the northern French ones mentioned makes one wonder if there might not be some correlation with so-called 'free inversion', and more precisely, if there might not be an inverse correlation between having (a verb form agree productively with) a NP adjoined somewhere to the right (as in the 'free inversion' construction of Italian) and allowing left-adjunction of NP to IP. This would be especially plausible (though not necessarily true) if a recent suggestion by Raposo (1987b) is correct, namely that free inversion in Romance is right-adjunction to IP, which would allow saying that in the normal case a language must choose (as an option for a subject NP not in A-position) between right- and left-adjunction to a given category, much as it chooses direction of government, etc. This would require that Italian topicalization and left-dislocation (cf. Cinque (1990a)) not involve adjunction to IP, and would lead us to hope that the various varieties of Occitan differ in the extent, at least, to which they countenance 'free inversion'. Unable to pursue this further at present, we end this section by noting only that the impossibility of short Wh-movement in Italian brought to light by Rizzi (1982a, 151ff.) and plausibly related to free inversion (it doesn't hold for French, as he notes) also does not hold for at least one of the varieties of Occitan that allows Wh-agreement, to judge by an example in Camproux (1958, 315).

3.5. Postverbal NPs

In a more literary Italian (cf. Lepschy and Lepschy (1977, 200)), as well as in an Italian that Parisi (1976,78) calls substandard, agreement is possible in (42):

(45)   Paolo ha viste le ragazze.

This possibility seems thoroughly absent from French. It is stated explicitly not to exist in Milanese and Corsican by Beretta (1984, 145) and Yvia Croce (1979, 137), and the same is said by Rohlfs (1977, 223) for (almost all of) Gascon and Blinkenberg (1948, 118). On the other hand, the equivalent of (45) is possible in the Salentino dialect of southern Italy (Andrea Calabrese, p.c.) and in the Corese dialect of Chiominto (1984, 179) and is attested in several varieties of Occitan (see Camproux (1958, 323), Dansereau (1985, 81), Granier (1978, 46), Lafont (1967, 180), and Miremont (1976, 55)).[20]

The possibility of (45) does not correlate with that of agreement with a Wh-phrase, which is lacking both in Salentino, according to Calabrese, and in the Occitan of Miremont, as noted earlier. For Calabrese, (45) in Salentino feels like right dislocation, and Miremont makes a rather similar remark ("celui qui s'exprime s'attache ... à l'objet"). That (45) is not neutral is likewise suggested by Fornaciari's (1974 (1881), 310) observation that the construction is not possible if the object NP is an idiom chunk.

Conceivably, (45) could be right dislocation with a phonetically unrealized object clitic, which would reduce (45) to the standard clitic case, as far as agreement is concerned. Alternatively, the object NP in (45) has been moved and adjoined to VP or IP, from where it can be governed by AGR. Either approach would cover the idiom chunk restriction[21] as well as account for the following contrast (observed by Granier (1978, 46) for Occitan) in literary Italian:

(46)   Paolo ha potute vedere le ragazze. ('P has been-able to-see the girls')

(47)   *Paolo ha potute vederle.

In (46), the modal participle agrees with the object of the infinitive. Since agreement with an overt clitic is possible: 'Paolo le ha potute vedere', (with a pre-auxiliary clitic), the invisible clitic approach could account straightforwardly for these by postulating an invisible pre-auxiliary one in (46).[22] Under the adjunction approach, (46) must involve adjoining 'le ragazze' to the VP headed by 'potute' or to the IP just above it, with such 'raising' presumably possible only under 'restructuring'[23] and with (47) excluded because the raised empty object would not be c-commanded by its clitic antecedent.

The question remains as to whether there is some pattern to the set of languages permitting (45). Although the answer is not yet clear, it may be that all such languages freely allow null subject positions or that they all allow some rightward subject inversion or that some related third property holds.

In any event, it seems highly likely that (45) does not involve agreement with a governed NP located in its postverbal D-structure position, so the earlier[24] characterization of agreement as involving a government relation between AGR and some NP stands unaffected.

3.6. Aux-to-comp

Belletti (1981) has studied a construction in Italian that appears at first glance to involve agreement between a past participle and a following NP in D-structure object position:

(48)   Conosciuta me, Gianni è cambiato molto. ('known/met me, G is changed much')

Here the object 'me' bears accusative case, which is assigned by the past participle, which agrees with that object. Note that the Italian described by Belletti does not have (45) (cf., similarly, Parisi (1976, 97)) and that (48) is possible with idiom chunks (cf. Belletti (1981, 10)), so it is unlikely that (48) should be analyzed via the same mechanism as (45).

Our proposal is that (48) involves Rizzi's (1982a, 83ff.) Aux-to-Comp rule, with the participle here moving left in the way the Aux does in the cases he discusses, and that the object NP itself moves into subject position:

(49)   conosciuta [$_{IP}$ me$_i$ AGR$_i$ [$_{VP}$ [$_V$ e] [e]$_i$]]

The participle must assign case from its derived position to the NP in subject position (in order to respect (20) above). There is no potential case conflict since this (nonperson) AGR is not a case assigner.[25] The fact that French lacks (48) can now be related to the fact that French lacks the whole range of Aux-to-Comp constructions discussed by Rizzi.[26]

If (49) is on the right track, then (48) will be compatible with our general characterization of agreement.[27]

3.7. Conclusion

Various Romance languages, to varying degrees, have constructions in which it appears that a past participle is agreeing with its object NP. We have argued that all such cases should be interpreted otherwise: The past participle never agrees directly with an NP in object position. Rather, when there is agreement, that agreement is due to the NP's having moved to (or through) a position governed by an abstract element AGR generated as sister to the VP headed by the participle.[28]

The question arises as to whether this characterization of agreement between a verbal form and an NP as always being mediated by such an AGR and by a government relation with that AGR should be taken to be valid within Romance or more widely. The widest possible interpretation, the study of the consequence of which is well beyond the scope of this article, would require that many apparent cases of agreement between a verbal form and an NP object (more generally: NP governed by V) be analyzed as involving clitics (i.e., clitic doubling of some sort), rather than AGR.

NOTES

1. We assume that the participial AGR is not itself capable of assigning case. This might in turn follow from Raposo's (1987b) proposal that for AGR to assign case, it must itself receive case and, assuming no case-assigning tense to be associated with the participial phrase, from the text claim that auxiliary 'avoir' is not a case-assigner. If + person AGR always requires case, then the absence of participial agreement marked for person would follow here, too (although not in the case of passive past participles (or adjectives), given (13) in the text).

2. This construction is not straightforwardly compatible with Jaeggli's (1986) proposal that the external theta-role in passives is necessarily associated with the participle suffix.

3. We take 'avoir' in (17) to L-mark its IP complement, thereby permitting antecedent-government of the first empty category by the clitic. In (11), there is an extra CP node, which prevents 'croire' from L-marking IP, so that antecedent-government there of the [e] in subject position by the clitic is not available. On the sometime partial acceptability of (11), cf. Rizzi (1981, Appendix), and Pollock (1985). Case-marking by the past participle alone in (17) and (18) goes against Rouveret and Vergnaud (1980, note 69).

4. The absence of (18) from Spanish and Portuguese is more surprising. If active past participles in those two languages differed minimally from those of French and Italian in not being case-assigners, then the clitic chain in (the equivalent of) (17) would, assuming the presence of AGR there to interfere with any possibility of case transmission in Rouveret and Vergnaud's (1980, Appendix A) sense, or of case composition, have no way of getting case at all, which might provide an account for the absence in Spanish and Portuguese of (16) (and (6)) (alternatively, cf. the rather different approach of Taraldsen (1991), parts of which are not compatible with the present one).

5. See Sportiche (1983, 53).

6. If the A'-to-A constraint were a constraint on movement per se (rather than a constraint (having the effect of) barring representations of the form '... A_i ... A'_i ...') then we would have to ensure that movement of the second $[e]_i$ to the position of 'il' in (24) not be an available option, for example, by having an antecedent-government requirement on movement links. It must also be the case that expletive replacement cannot be effected in (24) by IP, and similarly for the infinitival CP in '*la personne qu'il a été dit avoir disparu' ('the person that it has been said to-have disappeared'), which contrasts minimally with (9). The slightly less sharp status of the tensed CP counterpart '*?la personne qu'il a été dit qui a disparu'

may be a result of the marginal possibility of allowing overt 'qui' to license the deletion of the trace in its spec.

7. As noted by Martinon (1927, 479) and Grevisse (1964, sect. 787). Example (26) is notable in that 'il' cannot be replaced in the syntax: '*Une chaleur atroce a fait', this perhaps related to Ruwet's (1989, sect. 3.4) suggestion that the NP is a predicate (although if (26) were an unaccusative structure, we might expect auxiliary 'be' in Italian). See the restriction on '*That S seems', discussed recently in partially similar terms by Rothstein (1985, 168).

8. Pollock (1981, 232ff.; 1983a) has studied certain complex expressions that in some ways mimic unaccusatives. There, too, agreement is impossible: '?Combien d'idées croyez-vous qu'il a pris(*es) forme . . .'.

9. It may be that the participle in (31) is agreeing with the expletive, but that does not tell us why the alternative agreement with the Wh-phrase is so strongly unavailable—note in particular that Burzio (1986, 369) gives a case with 'be' in Italian where both subject and clitic object agreement are (marginally) possible.

For some speakers, '??Combien de chaises sera-t-il repeintes?' is less sharp than (31), presumably because the syntactic cliticization of 'il' here (to the inverted auxiliary; see Kayne (1983b)) allows marginally taking the subject [e] to be a (nonexpletive) variable locally bound by the Wh-phrase.

10. Judgments are less negative on the clitic counterpart to (35): 'Il me les aurait fallu(?es)' (an example (without a dative) seems to be considered unacceptable by Grevisse (op. cit.)), and an example from Gascon with audible agreement (and clitic climbing) is actually given by Rohlfs (1977, 223). If the clitic case is grammatical, then 'il' there must be replaced at LF by the accusative clitic, that is, an X^0 element (of category N and lacking oblique case) can occupy a subject position at LF (cf. the possibility that French subject clitics might be X^0 subjects in the syntax, as well as the existence of an X^0 operator for French and Italian 'easy to please' postulated in chapter 4, note 50. No improper movement problem will arise if improper movement reduces to Condition C of the Binding Theory (cf. Chomsky (1986a, note 20)) and if empty categories bound by clitics do not count as variables.

It is essential that expletive replacement not be satisfiable by the dative clitic in (35) (if it were, nothing would force the A'-to-A violation), this presumably related to the fact that subject position may not be filled by a dative in French. On expletive replacement with respect to impersonal passives lacking an appropriate overt NP, cf. Reuland (1983b) and Christensen and Taraldsen (1989, sect. 5).

11. That there is no case transmission with 'il' was first proposed by Pollock (1981). See also Belletti (1988) and the fact that there is no agreement between 'il' and the relevant NP.

12. We omit C, which is not central to what follows, although it may be important in mediating the relation between the two $[e]_i$. See Rizzi (1990).

13. This does not seem right, given Kimball and Aissen's (1971) dialect examples of agreement with what should now advantageously be reinterpreted as successive cyclic movement (e.g., 'Where are the boys who Tom think Dick believe to be late?').

14. If successive cyclic Wh-movement proceeds by adjunction to VP, as in Chomsky (1986a), then [e] adjoined to VP would have to be deleted, whereas the IP-adjoined $[e]_i$ in (41) would have not to be, presumably because it is needed for AGR_i (on such deletion, cf. Lasnik and Saito (1984, 258)).

15. The '?' of (40) is a result of the marginal possibility for certain such verbs to act as if they do govern the embedded infinitival subject position. See Rizzi (1981, Appendix) and Pollock (1985). If Pollock is correct in claiming that in (38) or (9) case can be assigned to the Wh-trace governed by 'être' or 'disparu', then (20) implies either that the infinitive has no subject position or that the [e] in Spec of CP heads the chain; see the discussion of (22).

The possibility that AGR$_i$ in (22) has no Spec but does have another position (the adjoined one) with which to be coindexed recalls Borer (1986).

16. See Parisi (1976, 99), Cinque (1975, 143), and Burzio (1986, 430).

17. Or, more to the point, the paradigm of those dialects that show no agreement with either clitic or Wh-phrase. See Alex (1965, 117), Flutre (1955, 59), and Remacle (1956, 148).

18. Some of the following are explicit about ruling out Wh-agreement with relatives but give no examples of interrogatives or exclamatives. However, to judge by Martinon (1927, 478), relatives are precisely the Wh-construction potentially most favorable to agreement (which might explain a felt lack of need to be more explicit). The favored status of relatives is perhaps significant, if the following is correct: In (22), the question arises as to the location of the variable. The first [e] may not be eligible since it is not in an A-position, nor the second, which is not locally bound by the Wh-phrase. Consequently, there can be no true variable in (22) but only an A-bar-bound pro in the sense of Cinque (1990a) and Obenauer (1984), which element might, like overt resumptive pronouns, favor relatives.

19. If Chomsky (1986a, 6) is correct, then the IP complement of the tense auxiliary must not be an argument.

20. Spanish has 'Juan tiene escrita la carta', but that seems clearly related to its also having 'Juan tiene la carta escrita', which calls for case assignment from 'tener' to the small-clause subject (cf. Lois (1990)); 'tener' is quite different from the tense auxiliary 'avoir'/ 'avere', etc., we have been concentrating on. Case assignment from 'avere' could conceivably be available in the literary Italian that allows (45).

21. The Occitan described by Miremont requires that Wh-movement be unable to apply to (the structure corresponding to) (45), presumably because 'le ragazze' there is not in an A-position. See Kayne (1985, 120).

22. Unless the (counterintuitive) prediction it makes about dialects having 'Paolo le può vederle' (cf. chapter 4, note 37), namely that they, if they have past participle agreement with clitics, should allow (47), turns out to be false.

23. From the perspective of chapter 4, only in conjunction with I-to-(C to-)I movement.

24. See the discussion of (7).

25. See note 1. The fact that at least some idioms compatible with (48)/(49) are impossible in passives (cf. Belletti (1981, 10)) may mean that those passives are excluded for some reason having to do with the external theta-role being absorbed (in a way that it is not in (48)/(49) (cf. Kayne (1975, sect. 3.5), and/or it may have to do with a difference in Case assignment.

26. Thus: '*Ayant Jean gagné, . . .', '*Jean croit avoir Paul disparu', '*Arrivée Marie, . . .'. French does have 'Une fois arrivée Marie, . . .' ('once arrived M, . . .'), but that arguably involves only rightward movement of the subject, as in so-called 'stylistic inversion'. See Kayne and Pollock (1978), Kayne (1986a). Not all Italian dialects have (48), to judge by Yvia Croce (1979, 138) and Rossini (1975, 125–126).

27. Belletti argues that (48) involves control. Contrary to chapter 2, an earlier stage of this work, we suspect that that is not incompatible with (49), if there is a position for PRO within the participial VP, a question beyond the scope of this article, as is the related question of why unaccusative verbs tend to show no past participle agreement when the auxiliary is 'have' (cf. Benincà (1984)). Christensen and Taraldsen (1989) adopt a proposal of ours (1986b) based on obligatory case assignment that we have not followed here, one consideration being that there are dialects for which this lack of agreement with subject of 'have' seems not to hold. See Tintou (1959, 69), Dansereau (1985, 82), Salentino (A. Calabrese, p.c.), Rohlfs (1977, 224n) (with a reflexive), Miremont (1976, 67), and Camproux (1958, 46, 49) (the last

two with examples containing two auxiliaries, the second being 'have' and the participle following it showing agreement with the subject).

Given the reflexive in the (not perfect) '?Elogiata se stessa, Maria . . .' ('praised herself, M . . .'), there must be some form of reconstruction at work, perhaps sensitive to the case-marking.

28. This approach requires no specific rule such as that in Burzio (1986, 55).

4

Null Subjects and
Clitic Climbing

4.1. Clitic climbing

4.1.1. No restructuring rule

In earlier work,[1] we proposed that the contrast between French and Italian seen in the clitic climbing construction in (1) should be related to the contrast between them seen in (2) concerning null subjects:

(1) a. *Jean les veut voir.

    b. Gianni li vuole vedere.
       John them-wants to-see

(2) a. *Pleut

    b. Piove.
       Rains

This proposal was taken up by Rizzi (1982a, 172), who suggested that the restructuring rule underlying (1b) might be excluded from applying in French if it were sensitive to some notion of adjacency and if, following Chomsky (1981a), there were a syntactic rule lowering INFL to the verb in null subject languages like Italian, but not in French. We have expressed doubts elsewhere[2] as to the syntactic relevance of adjacency, Chomsky (1986a, 74) has moved away from his INFL-lowering analysis, and we now also doubt the correctness of a restructuring approach to (1b). The present article will consequently explore the possibility of expressing a relation between clitic climbing and null subjects within an approach to the former that makes no use of a restructuring rule (though our analysis of that relation will agree with Rizzi's in attributing a crucial role to INFL).

4.1.2.   Intervening adverbs

There have been a number of approaches to clitic climbing besides Rizzi's (1976; 1982a)—for example, Aissen and Perlmutter's (1983) fairly similar clause reduction analysis within a relational grammar framework, Goodall's (1985) restructuring as union of phrase markers, Fresina's (1982) use of VP-complementation, Burzio's (1986) VP-movement analysis, Quicoli's (1976) Equi-NP Deletion approach, Lujan's (1978) Equi-NP plus adjacency analysis, Zubizarreta's (1980) thematic restructuring, Di Sciullo and Williams's (1987) coanalysis, and others. As far as we can see, none of these successfully expresses a relation between clitic climbing and null subjects.

Moreover, none of these has taken into account what we, in agreement with Vey (1978 (1911), 192), interpret as a construction essentially analogous to (1b):

(3)   (*)Jean a promis de les bien faire.
       John has promised for/to them well do.

Although ungrammatical in contemporary French (like (1a)), this construction, in which the clitic *les* is separated from the following infinitive by an adverb or quantifier, is rather widespread in Romance: It existed in earlier stages of French (cf. Galet (1971, 463ff) and Engver (1972, II)) and is attested in numerous dialects,[3] all of which have clitic climbing of the standard sort (1b) as did earlier French.[4] It thus seems perfectly appropriate to consider (3) to be an instance of clitic climbing, that is, to consider that any adequate analysis of (1b) must also cover (3). As far as we can see, none of the analyses mentioned achieves this.

Example (3) shows clearly that attachment to V is not a fundamental property of Romance clitics.[5] Since (3) is analogous to (1b), since (1b) is in some relation to the null subject construction (2b), and since null subjects are in some significant relation to INFL (henceforth I), it is natural to suggest that the clitic in (3) is attached to the head I of the infinitival IP: . . . Cl + I Adv VP . . . , which in addition makes sense of the order of constituents.

As mentioned, (3) is not possible in contemporary French, where one would have instead (4):

(4)   Jean a promis de bien les faire.

Let us propose that in (4) the clitic has attached itself to V. From this perspective, Romance clitics have two options: attachment to V or attachment to I. With tensed V, which in French (and Italian) arguably adjoins to I, as in Emonds (1978), the two options converge.[6] But when I and V remain separate, the two options yield visibly different results. The question is now to understand why attachment to such a separate I, as in (3), is no longer available to contemporary French.

For a clitic to attach to I, it must move out of its VP. Assume, then, with Chomsky (1986a) (cf. also Koster (1987)) that VP is potentially a barrier to antecedent government but that it can lose its barrierhood if it is L-marked (in the sense of Chomsky (1986a)) by I. This will always hold if a lexical V moves to I. Assume that in French (cf. Emonds (1978) and Pollock (1989)), the infinitival V does not move up to I and, furthermore, that the infinitival I is not by itself strong enough to L-mark VP. Then, in French the clitic will not be able to move out of the infinitival VP (since if it did, its trace would not be properly governed,[7] VP remaining a barrier) and will have only the option of adjoining to V. Hence, (4) will be possible, but not (3).

The two options that we are allowing clitics, namely adjunction to V and adjunction to I, have in common the property of both being adjunction to a head, in the sense of X-bar theory. This should be correlated with the categorial status of the clitics themselves, which are arguably heads. In other words, following Baltin (1982, 4) and Chomsky (1986a, 73), we may claim that clitics, being heads, may adjoin to another head, but never to a maximal projection. This will ensure that clitics cannot escape from VP in the way that Wh-phrases can, that is, by adjunction to VP.[8]

To allow (3), we propose that, in a Romance language that licenses null subjects, I is strong enough to L-mark VP even if the V does not raise up to it. Consequently, the clitic will be able to move to I, crossing a VP-adjoined adverb, if there is one.

The type of licensing that we have in mind is what Rizzi (1986a, 518) calls 'formal licensing'. A language that formally licenses null subjects need not look as generous as Italian, since the actual interpretation of the null subject will depend on how the particular language can assign it content (cf. also Rizzi (1982a, chap. 4)). The Walloon described by Remacle (1952, 224–227), for example, has a much narrower range of null subjects than Italian (though more than French[9]), yet still allows (3).

4.1.3.   Adjunction is to the left

If, in Italian and other null subject Romance languages, I is strong enough to L-mark VP on its own, then we might expect the head V to be able to move out of VP without passing through I. It is tempting to take exactly this to play a role in the French versus Italian contrast in (5):

(5)   a.   Lui parler serait une erreur.
           him_{dat} +(to)speak would be an error.

      b.   Parlargli sarebbe un errore.
           (to)speak + him_{dat.} . . .

Postinfinitival clitics are possible in Romance only in null subject languages.

To exclude French (6), we suggest first that the French weak I prevents the infinitive from leaving VP and second that clitics in Romance must always be adjoined to the left of a head, perhaps because the derived clitic-head relation is formally parallel to a specifier-head relation:

(6)   *Parler-lui serait une erreur.

Example (5b) will now have the clitic adjoined to (the left of) I, rather than directly to the right of V, with I distinct from and following the moved inifnitive.

Alternatively, one might be tempted to relate (5b) directly to the ease with which subjects can be postverbal in Italian. That does not seem sufficient, however, given the order of clitic and finite verb in Italian:

(7) a. Gianni gli parlava.

　　 b. *Gianni parlavagli.
　　　　 John him$_{dat.}$ spoke.

We tentatively conclude that (5b) does have at some level of representation the structure: '$V_{infin.}$ [CL + I [$_{VP}$ [$_V$e] . . .]] *sarebbe* . . .' (and that leftward V-movement past I is not available to finite V in Italian[10]).

4.2. Constraints on Clitic Climbing

4.2.1. Infinitival I

To express the strong correlation that exists between (3) (. . . CL Adv $V_{infin.}$ . . .) and the better known clitic climbing construction in (1b), and simultaneously to link the latter, too, to the formal licensing of null subjects, is now straightforward: For a clitic to move up from an infinitival complement to the matrix V (or matrix I) as in (1b), it must minimally be able to escape from the infinitival VP. That will be possible in a language like Italian (or Walloon) with a sufficiently strong infinitival I, but impossible in French. Thus (1a) is excluded in French for essentially the same reason that (3) is.

4.2.2. Causatives

French does allow a clitic to move up in certain causative constructions:

(8) Jean la fait manger par/à Paul.
　　 John it-makes eat by/to Paul.

This means that causative verbs must have the ability to take a VP complement, as Burzio (1986, 4.2) had already suggested for the *par* version of (8). We must extend his proposal to at least certain instances of *à*.

　　Clitic climbing in (8) is, however, blocked by an intervening *ne*. Some speakers marginally accept (9):[11]

(9) ??Jean/Cela a fait ne pas manger sa soupe à l'enfant.
　　 John/that has made NEG not eat his soup to the child.

Cliticization of the object of the infinitive yields (10):

(10) *Jean/Cela l'a fait ne pas manger à l'enfant.

Cliticization of the underlying subject of the infinitive does not, on the other hand, result in a drop in acceptability:

(11)   ??Jean/Cela lui a fait ne pas manger sa soupe.

We can distinguish (10) from (11) by supposing that *ne* is hierarchically below *à l'enfant* but above *sa soupe*: . . . [*ne pas* [*manger sa soupe*]] *à l'enfant*. . . . The question is, Why should an intervening *ne* ever block clitic climbing?

In (8), the clitic antecedent-governs its trace in the VP, which has been L-marked by the causative V.[12] Our proposal for (10) is that *ne* is a head in the sense of X-bar theory, that in (10) *ne* m-commands the infinitival VP, and that the presence of such a head intervening between the V/I bearing the adjoined clitic and the base position of that clitic blocks antecedent government. This will follow if *ne*, which we take to be of the same general class of heads as C and I, has the property, like French infinitival I, of being unable to L-mark its complement, here VP. Thus, the infinitival VP will be a barrier for the clitic-trace relation in (10) just as it is in French in (3) and (1a).

Taking *ne* to be a head whose lack of L-marking ability prevents clitics from moving past it accounts directly for the facts of (12), without the need for any special statement concerning ordering among clitics:[13]

(12)   a. Jean ne les voit pas.

   b. *Jean les ne voit pas.
      John ne them-sees not.

4.2.3.   Negation as head

The blocking effect on clitic climbing in causatives of French *ne* is mirrored by the (more widely visible) blocking effect on clitic climbing of Italian *non*:[14]

(13)   Gianni non li vuole vedere.
        John NEG them-wants to-see.

(14)   a. Gianni vuole non vederli.

   b. *Gianni li vuole non vedere.

Our proposal for (10) and (12b) carries over straightforwardly to (14b), if *non* is unable to L-mark its sister constituent. (Thus, although Italian infinitival I has the null subject related property of being capable of L-marking, which French I does not, the negative elements *ne* and *non* are alike in the two languages.)

4.2.4.   Stepwise climbing

We have taken the position that the citic in (13) can move out of the infinitival VP by virtue of I L-marking that VP, without the clitic having to (and without it being able to) use a VP-adjunction escape hatch. The question arises as to whether the clitic moves directly to its S-structure position, or whether it does so stepwise. One consideration is that of the impossibility of (15), with a tensed complement in place of the infinitive:

(15)   *Gianni (non) li vuole che (Maria) veda.
      John (NEG) them-wants that M/she see$_{subjunctive}$

The status of (15) is especially notable given the (marginal) acceptability of clitic climbing out of (infinitival) Wh-islands noted by Rizzi (1982a, 36):

(16)   Non ti saprei che dire.
      (I) NEG you$_{DAT}$-would-know what to-say.

Clitic climbing thus appears to display behavior that is in a sense opposite to that of Wh-movement, which is always readily acceptable out of subjunctive complements of verbs like 'want' and delicate out of Wh-islands, even infinitival ones.

    In earlier work,[15] we excluded (15) by invoking the Specified Subject Condition. Such an approach leads either to deleting the embedded subject in (13) and (16) or to moving the VP out past that subject position. The latter solution runs into the problem concerning the position of *pas* mentioned in note 11 and does not extend naturally to (16). The former is not quite in the spirit of the present framework, in particular with respect to the Projection Principle. Furthermore, it is not clear that the now Principle A of Binding Theory should be relevant to the clitic-trace relation in the first place.[16]

    It is highly desirable, of course, that (15) continue to be excluded by a principle or principles of some generality.[17] Our proposal now is that (15) fails to maintain antecedent government and hence violates ECP, just as (14b), (12b), (10), (3), and (1a).

    If (13) and especially (16) involved the clitic moving directly to its S-structure position, it would be hard to see why (15) would be so sharply excluded. We conclude that the clitic can climb stepwise.[18] We can solve the problem of the contrast between (15) and (17) by invoking the ability of a Wh-phrase to move through (the specifier position of) comp, granting that a clitic cannot move through that position:

(17)   la persona che Gianni vuole che Maria veda
      the person that . . . .

This leaves the problem of distinguishing (15) from the French (18), with leftward quantifier movement:[19]

(18)   ?Jean veut tout qu'elle refasse.
      John wants everything that she redo (≠ relative)

While contrasting with clitic climbing, this type of movement remains far less free than Wh-movement, which might suggest that it, too, is unable to use the comp escape hatch. More specific arguments that *tout* (and other non-Wh quantifiers like *beaucoup*) cannot move through comp are given in Kayne (1981d, 1981b).[20]

Let us suggest the following trifurcation: Wh-phrases can move through the specifier of C position, but neither non-Wh-quantifiers nor clitics can. Non-Wh-quantifiers can adjoin to IP (just as they can to VP), but clitics cannot (just as they cannot adjoin to VP, as discussed earlier).[21]

Returning to (15), we see that the clitic in Italian can reach the embedded I, but from there it cannot move to the matrix V or I, since from that S-structure position it would not antecedent-govern its trace, the reason being that that trace would be included within (non-L-marked) IP, so that CP would count as a barrier for it, by inheritance. (The same holds if the clitic moves directly from its base position to its S-structure position in (15).) We are assuming here that the nonoperator status of the clitic makes it impossible to evade the ECP violation by deleting the intermediate trace.[22]

Before taking up again the instances of well-formed long clitic climbing in Italian, we note that the contrast in French between (19) and (20) is straightforwardly accounted for:

(19)   *Les vouloir refaire serait absurde.
        them-to-want to-redo would-be . . . .

(20)   Tout vouloir refaire serait absurde.
        everything . . . .

In (19), the infinitival VP constitutes a barrier to antecedent government, which can be evaded by *tout* in (20), by virtue of *tout* being able to adjoin to VP (and then to IP). Thus, recourse to binding theory (in terms of variable vs. nonvariable), as in Kayne (1981b), is no longer necessary.

4.2.5.   Blocking by C

Consider again (13) and (16), repeated here as (21) and (22):

(21)   Gianni non li vuole vedere.

(22)   Non ti saprei che dire.

The clitic in Italian can reach the infinitival I position. In (22), there is clearly a CP. Movement directly from the lower I position to the S-structure position of *ti* is not possible, since CP would constitute a barrier to antecedent government just as in the discussion of (15). Consequently, we shall take over an idea proposed in a different context (that of the LF movement of long-distance reflexives) by Pica (1987), namely that a pronominal element can move from I to C on its way out of CP.

For the S-structure phenomena that we are concerned with,[23] passage of a clitic through C would seem intuitively to imply that C is otherwise empty. Let us henceforth assume, then, that a clitic in Italian has the option of moving through an empty C, and in so doing of neutralizing a potential ECP violation. (The trace in C will properly govern the trace in I since IP can not be an inherent barrier,[24] and the clitic, from its position in the matrix I, will properly govern the trace in C, since CP in all the relevant cases is L-marked by V.)

The claim that the clitic in (22) has moved through C is supported by the following observation: Rizzi (1982a, 36) gives a variety of examples like (22), with differing degrees of acceptability, (22) being the most acceptable. The choice of Wh-phrase seems to be relevant. Now of all such examples, we have found that the most severe violations seem clearly to be those with *se* ('if'):

(23)   Non so se farli.
      (I) NEG know if to-do-them.

(24)   *Non li so se fare.

This is at first glance surprising, since extraction from Wh-islands is usually easiest with Wh-islands headed by 'if' (e.g., in English, with Wh-movement out of tensed Wh-islands). The facts follow, however, if Italian *se*, probably like English 'if', is not a true Wh-phrase, but rather an instance of C,[25] like English 'that'. In other words, the contrast between (22) and (24) is due to the former's empty C position versus the latter's filled one and to the fact that clitic movement, unlike Wh-movement, is forced to move through C in order to leave CP.

The ungrammaticality of (15) now reflects the fact that the complementizer *che* blocks movement through C just as *se* does. One might wonder about tensed complements with an empty C. It is not clear that Romance null subject languages ever have them (at least some apparent cases may involve V moving to C; cf. Torrego (1983), Rizzi (1982a, 85)), so the question is difficult to pursue. On the other hand, although an empty C seems necessary for long clitic climbing,[26] it is clear that it is not sufficient, since there are many verbs from whose C-less infinitival complements clitics may not be extracted. We return to this question later.

Although (22) visibly involves a CP, (21) could conceivably be analyzed as IP. That would, however, create problems having to do with the distribution of PRO, as well as with that of NP-trace, which we want to exclude with verbs like 'want'. Furthermore, taking (21) to instantiate IP complementation would yield what would arguably be an undesirable kind of derivational ambiguity. Namely, (21) could be derived either by stepwise clitic movement, as we saw was necessary for (22), or by one long movement of the clitic, since in the absence of CP, no barrier would intervene. We tentatively conclude that (21), too, is an instance of CP complementation.[27]

4.2.6.   Clitic splitting

If (21) contains CP, there is a slightly different form of suspect derivational ambiguity that arises, which in any case exists in (22), namely that nothing appears to prevent the clitic from moving directly from its base position to C. This possibility seems to be available in addition to the one we have proposed (adapting Pica's idea), according to which the clitic moves first to I and then to C.

Consider the relevant substructure of (22):

$$\ldots \text{CL}_j + \text{I} \ldots [_{\text{CP}}[\text{Wh-phrase}]\ \text{C}_{(j)}\ [_{\text{IP}} \ldots \text{I}_{(j)}\ [_{\text{VP}} \ldots [\text{e}]_j \ldots]] \ldots$$

We noted that movement from base position directly to the matrix I is impossible, since antecedent government would not hold. Direct movement to C, which seems suspect, can be excluded in exactly parallel fashion, if IP is a potential barrier (other than just by inheritance)[28] and if C does not L-mark IP. This requires adopting Frampton's (1990) proposal that adjunction of a Wh-phrase to IP is possible.[29]

At first glance, taking IP in (22) to be a potential barrier seems not to help, in that it seems to exclude not only direct movement to C but also the I-to-C step of the derivation we propose. At second glance, we note that we have so far left unclear exactly what we mean by saying that the clitic moves to I and then to C. Assume that after the clitic adjoins to I yielding $[_I\ \text{CL I}]$, what moves on to C is not just the clitic but the whole newly formed I constituent that includes the clitic.[30] Let us further assume that, in moving to C, Italian I retains its ability to L-mark its sister constituent, that is, that, once in the C position, $[_I\ \text{CL I}]$ can L-mark IP, voiding barrierhood. The crucial point is that it is I, not the clitic, that has this L-marking ability, so if the clitic adjoined directly to C skipping I, there would be nothing in C capable of L-marking IP, and the resulting representation would violate ECP.

Let us return to (21), repeated essentially as (25):

(25)   Gianni li vuole vedere.

We have argued against allowing direct clitic movement to the matrix I, against direct movement to C, and for movement to the embedded I, followed by movement out of IP. There are two sets of further empirical considerations that seem to us to favor the last, more densely stepped, approach.

The first concerns the equivalent of (25) with two clitics:

(26)   Gianni ve li vuole mostrare.
         John you$_{\text{DAT}}$-them-wants to-show.

It is possible for both clitics to remain together on the embedded I, but impossible for one to move up to the matrix I without the other (cf. Rizzi (1982a, 44)):

(27)   Gianni vuole mostrarveli.

(28)   a. *Gianni vi vuole mostrarli.

         b. *Gianni li vuole mostrarvi.

If the clitic in (25) were capable of moving directly to the matrix 1, then it would be difficult to see what would prevent one of the clitics in (the base structure corresponding to) (26)/(27) from so doing while the other moved only as far as the embedded I, yielding the ungrammatical (28). Taking this to show that direct movement to the matrix I is prohibited, we conclude somewhat less tentatively than in the previous section that (25) (and (26)) do not involve IP complementation.[31] (The same type of argument will also hold against direct movement to C, except if it were to turn out that in (27), the infinitive is itself in C (cf. note 10), in which case no conclusion could be drawn.)

From our perspective, (28) follows immediately from the claim that Italian clitics must move first to the embedded I plus the claim that once attached to I a clitic cannot move any further without the entire I moving along at the same time.[32]

The ill-formedness of (28) in Italian (and Spanish) is well known.[33] It turns out, though, that (28) is not fully representative, as there are dialects that allow such 'clitic splitting'.[34] These dialects differ from Italian and Spanish in having pre-infinitival rather than postinfinitival clitics, so one has the equivalent of (29):

(29)   a. (*)Jean vous veut les montrer. (same as (26))

     b. (*)Jean les veut vous montrer.

(The morphemes in (29) are given in French, in which such sentences are impossible.) The existence of (29) in some dialects is unexpected under previous approaches, which in addition do not seem capable of expressing the generalization (true to the best of our current knowledge) that (29) is found only in dialects having their clitics pre- rather than postinfinitival.

Our tentative proposal is as follows: One clitic in (29) adjoins to the infinitival V itself, while the other adjoins to the embedded I,[35] subsequently moving (to C and then) into the matrix. This double possibility is unavailable in French since in French VP, not being L-marked by I,[36] is a barrier, so no clitic can move to the infinitival I at all.

As for Italian, the crucial fact is that the Italian infinitive has itself moved out of VP, past I (cf. the earlier discussion of (5). Consequently, adjunction to the (empty) V position within VP is not possible, for the reason mentioned in note 32. In the discussion of (5), we further suggested that clitics invariably adjoin to the left of V or I. Hence, in (28) the second clitic cannot be adjoined directly to the infinitive itself in its derived position, but only to I. In which case (the text to) note 32 again is sufficient to exclude (28).[37]

4.2.7.   Impersonals

A second area in which it is arguably advantageous to have the clitic forced to move through the embedded infinitival I is that of the interaction of clitic climbing and control. Virtually all the standard cases of clitic climbing are cases of subject control or raising. What is conspicuously absent is object control. Some cases seem to exist in Spanish (cf. Lujan (1978, 123)), but we conjecture that they are hidden instances of the causative construction (see note 38). If so, an explanation is required for the incompatibility of clitic climbing with true object control.

In subject control examples like (26) (and similarly for raising), I to (C to) I movement has the effect of coindexing the matrix and embedded I, and in particular the matrix and embedded AGR. This is consistent with the fact that in subject control and raising structures, the matrix and embedded subjects are themselves coindexed. Comparable I to (C to) I movement in object control structures, however, would coindex two AGR whose respective subjects are themselves not essentially coindexed. This is arguably the source of incompatibility. This account goes through, though, only if movement through the embedded I position necessarily takes place in all sentences in which a clitic climbs to a higher verb.[38]

There is another restriction that we think is related to this, namely that clitic climbing in Italian and Spanish is prohibited if the matrix verb is impersonal.[39] Now Longobardi (1980) has shown that Italian impersonal verbs followed by an infinitive fall into two classes. In one the infinitival complement seems to pattern with inverted subjects with respect to Wh-movement and other phenomena. In the other, Wh-movement out of the complement is straightforward, and Longobardi suggests for this and other reasons that these infinitives are in true complement position. It is for this latter class that the ill-formedness of clitic climbing is surprising. All the more so as clitic climbing out of the infinitival complement of an impersonal verb is possible in earlier French, in present literary French (cf. note 9), and in assorted varieties of Occitan. Thus, we have the following contrasts:

(30)   a. *Lo bisogna fare. (Italian)

       b. *Lo hay que hacer. (Spanish)

(31)   a. Il le faut faire. (earlier French)[40]

       b. Lo cal far. (Occitan)[41]
          (*It*) it$_{accus.}$ *is-necessary to-do.*

Note that Occitan is like Spanish and Italian in having no overt expletive.

Our proposal follows Longobardi (1980, note 18 bis) in taking (Spanish and) Italian to be languages that must assign nominative case to a postverbal NP in the absence of a distinct thematic subject. Generalizing to postverbal infinitival complements and associating nominative with AGR, we arrive at the hypothesis that in Spanish and Italian the infinitival complement of an impersonal verb will be coindexed with the matrix AGR. So that I to (C to) I movement will yield a pair of like indexed I, the lower coindexed with its PRO subject and the upper coindexed with the infinitival complement itself—an impossible situation.[42]

In French, as seen clearly in (32), the postverbal NP of an impersonal construction need not trigger verb agreement:

(32)   Il me faut ces livres.
       it me$_{DAT}$ *is*$_{sing}$-*necessary these books.*

This correlates with the possibility of accusative case on the postverbal NP, seen with clitics:

(33)   a. Il me les faut.

       b. Il le faut.
          It is-necessary it/so.

Both (33a) and (33b) appear to exist in Occitan,[43] but not in Spanish or Italian:

(34)   *Lo bisogna. (= (33b))

If so, then we are justified in claiming that the property mentioned earlier concerning nominative case holds for neither French nor Occitan, so (30) vs. (31) is accounted for[44]—but only under the assumption that clitic climbing must use the embedded I position (otherwise no agreement conflict would be forced in (30)).

4.2.8. Tense

Among the class of subject control verbs, some allow clitic climbing and some do not. Luján (1978) has made the interesting hypothesis that (approximately) verbs that take infinitival complements associated with an independent tense do not allow clitic climbing.[45] Luján's idea can be adapted into our framework by combining it with Raposo's (1987b) proposal that an abstract tense element can be located in the C position. If so, then we can take such a T to block I to (C to) I movement in a way parallel to the case of the overt C's *se* and *che*.

Recourse to tense is probably not sufficient to account for all cases of subject control recalcitrant to clitic climbing. For example, Italian 'want' allows it, but Italian 'hate', 'desire' do not or only marginally do.[46] No one has succeeded in providing a precise account of this kind of contrast. Nor will we. But it is worth saying what formal property might be involved, from our perspective. Matrix verbs that allow clitic climbing allow I to (C to) I movement,[47] the result of which is to leave these verbs with a complement having an empty head position bound from without. This property might then be compatible only with certain types of matrix verbs.

4.3. French vs. Italian

4.3.1. Easy-to-please

Rizzi (1982a, 26) notes that his notion of restructuring appears to be relevant to the Italian 'easy-to-please' construction, in the sense that, when the gap is two infinitives distant, the higher infinitive must be of the class that allows clitic climbing. For example, *cominciare* ('begin') is of this class but *promettere* ('promise') is not, and there is the contrast:

(35)   a. Questa canzone è facile da cominciare a cantare . . .
            This song is easy to begin to sing . . . .

        b. *Questo lavoro è facile da promettere di finire per domani.
            This work is easy to promise to finish by tomorrow.

Similarly, this construction is in Italian incompatible with object control infinitives (which in general disallow clitic climbing):

(36)   *Questo libro è difficile da convincere Mario a finire prima di lunedì.
        This book is difficult to convince Mario to finish before Monday.

Neither of the above restrictions holds for English, which allows the equivalents of
(35b) and (36) fairly easily.

Now the contrast in (35) seems valid in French:

(37)   a. ?(Pour moi), ce livre serait impossible à commencer à lire aujourd'hui.[48]
            For me this book would-be impossible to begin to read today.

        b. *Ce genre de livre est facile à promettre de lire.
            This kind of book is easy to promise to read.

The restriction concerning object control holds, too:

(38)   *Ce genre de livre serait difficile à convaincre Jean de lire.
        This kind of book would-be hard to convince John to read.

Remarkably, the following is more acceptable than (37b), despite involving a
Wh-island:

(39)   ?Ce genre d'article est difficile à savoir où classer.
        This kind of article is hard to know where to-file.

In other words, Rizzi's generalization has some validity for French, with (39) now
seen to match up with the Italian clitic-cimbing-out-of-Wh-island example (22).

This may seem paradoxical, since French itself allows clitic-climbing neither
with (37a) nor with (39). We offer the following interpretation: In both Italian and
French, the 'easy-to-please' construction is possible with two levels of embedding
only if the highest infinitive is of the class of verbs compatible with a CP complement having an empty head bound from without. More specifically, let us propose
that in (37a) and in (39) the lowest infinitival I has moved out of its S into the upper
infinitival domain, that is, that I to (C to) I/V has applied (perhaps in LF), with C
definitely involved in (39) and possibly in (37a). In other words, the I to (C to) I
movement that plays a central role in Italian clitic climbing does also in both the Italian and French 'easy-to-please' constructions.

The paradox disappears when we recall that Italian clitic climbing depends on
more than just I to (C to) I movement, and in particular on the clitic being able to
escape from the domain of the lower infinitive. That escape possibility depends in
turn on I L-marking VP, which Italian allows and French not. Put another way, there
are two necessary conditions for clitic climbing up to a higher V: First, the infinitival
I must be able to L-mark VP, and, second, the matrix V must be compatible with I to
(C to) I movement. Crucially, neither of these two conditions is by itself sufficient.[49]

Italian meets the first and so can display clitic climbing with those verbs that
meet the second. French does not meet the first, so such verbs have no opportunity
to display their special character with clitic climbing, although they do elsewhere, as
in (37)–(39).[50]

4.3.2. Infinitival *if*

In attributing to Italian infinitival I the ability to L-mark VP and in claiming that that ability is linked to the empty subject licensing property of Italian, we are in effect taking the position that this licensing property generalizes from tensed I to infinitival I. And in fact Rizzi (1982a, 83ff.) has shown that in what he calls the Aux-to-Comp construction null subjects can be licensed by infinitival I (their interpretation will have a narrower range than with a tensed I).

There is a second context in which it seems advantageous to allow an infinitival I to license a null subject, and that is one given by Rigau (1984, 251) for Catalan:

(40)　En Pere no sap si fer-ho.
　　　Pere NEG knows if to-do-it.

A corresponding Italian sentence would be grammatical, too (similarly for Spanish):

(41)　Gianni non sa se andare al cinema.
　　　Gianni NEG knows if to-go to-the cinema.

The French equivalent is sharply ungrammatical, however:

(42)　*Je ne sais pas si aller au cinéma.

This is so despite the fact that controlled infinitival interrogatives are otherwise well formed:

(43)　Je ne sais pas où aller.
　　　I NEG know not where to-go.

We can interpret (42) versus (43) à la Borer (1989) by taking control in French to necessarily be mediated by the C position, on the assumption, already seen to be justified indirectly by (24), that Romance *si/se*, like English 'if', is a C, and not a phrase capable of occupying a specifier position (unlike 'whether'):

(44)　I don't know whether/*if to go to the movies.

This implies that Catalan and Italian control are not necessarily mediated by the C position. Following essentially Borer (1989), we take this to reflect the fact that control involves identifying the empty infinitival subject. In French and English, it is necessary that this identification be mediated by C, presumably by having I move to C at LF (cf. the last paragraph of note 50),[51] where it will be able to pick up the requisite features from the NP controller, the idea then being that in Catalan and Italian infinitival I has sufficient features inherently and so does not need an empty C position to move to.

4.3.3. Auxiliaries

Rizzi's analysis of clitic climbing touched on a very wide range of issues, several more of which we will briefly mention in this section. Clitic climbing is blocked when a locative phrase intervenes between the matrix V and the infinitive, but certain other intervening adverbials are permitted (cf. Rizzi (1982a, 12, 38). Let us assume that base structures can be of the form . . . (AdvP$_1$) V CP (AdvP$_2$) . . . and that V can move to the left across the preceding AdvP, yielding . . . V AdvP$_1$ [$_V$ e] CP (AdvP$_2$) . . . , with an 'intervening' AdvP. Assume further that locatives are invariably in the AdvP$_2$ position, and that to get them to 'intervene' requires moving CP to the right: . . . (AdvP$_1$) V [$_{CP}$ e] AdvP$_2$ CP. . . . It suffices now to grant that in such a structure V cannot L-mark CP (and that the property of being L-marked cannot be inherited from a trace) for it to follow that clitic climbing will be prohibited across such as AdvP$_2$, as desired.[52] (That it is not prohibited across AdvP$_1$ above means that the trace of V remains an L-marker.)

Rizzi (1982a, 9) notes that clitic climbing is incompatible with clefting the infinitival complement. His account depends on a claim about constituent structure that is not naturally integrable into our analysis. An alternative account is that the infinitival phrase (whether IP or CP) cannot be L-marked in its S-structure clefted position (nor can L-marking be inherited), so that the trace of [$_I$ CL I] contained in the infinitival phrase is not properly antecedent-governed.[53]

Beyond the scope of this article (although it will clearly have an analysis a subpart of which will be an I-(C-)I type relation) is the auxiliary phenomenon that Rizzi shows to be significantly correlated with clitic climbing.[54] We note only that rather than being coextensive with clitic climbing, the range of this phenomenon, whereby auxiliary 'be' is licensed in some sense by the embedded infinitive, is definitely more restricted than that of clitic climbing, as indicated by Burzio's (1986, 381) remark on di-infinitivals and Boysen's (1977) on sapere ('know'), by Canepari (1986, 83, 98), and by the fact that the sharp incompatibility of clitic climbing and non in (14b) is not matched by the (weaker) deviance of (45):

(45)   ??Sarebbe voluto non andare al mare.
         (He) would-be wanted NEG to-go . . . .

In addition, although an archaicizing French would allow clitic climbing (even more than in note 9)), it would still not allow the use of 'be' in the Italian fashion:

(46)   *Jean serait voulu aller à la mer.

4.3.4. Conclusion

We have analyzed Romance clitic climbing (and its relation to null subjects) from the perspective of the highly articulated theory of conditions on antecedent government proposed in Chomsky (1986a), and found that clitic climbing is less exotic than it might appear. Clitics differ from Wh-phrases and quantifier phrases precisely in being heads, rather than phrases (maximal projections). Modulo that distinction, once recognized, the principles determining how far a clitic can move are seen to be of essentially the same cloth as the principles determining how far a Wh- or quantified phrase can move.

Part of the syntax of clitic climbing turns on I to (C to) I movement, which we found to play a role even in French. Not all matrix verbs, even of subject control, are compatible with the effect of this movement.[55]

NOTES

This essay corresponds in its essentials to a talk given at the 1987 GLOW Workshop on Dialectology. For helpful comments on an earlier version of this paper, we are grateful to Osvaldo Jaeggli, Jean-Yves Pollock, and Kenneth Safir.

1. Kayne (1980a, 40).
2. See Kayne (1984, Introd.; 1987).
3. See Remacle (1952, 268) (at least with a negative adverb), Camproux (1958, 111, 297, 339, 354, 370, 377, 477, 479), Reymond and Bossard (1979, 217), Miremont (1976, 100, 136, 162, 188), Blinkenberg (1948, 92), Vey (1978 (1911), 192). Note that the intervening adverb can be visibly phrasal—see de Kok (1985, 339, 346) and literary French . . . *n'en presque rien dire,* . . . *en fort bien parler* ('NEG it$_{gen.}$ almost nothing to-say', it$_{gen.}$ very well to-speak').
4. For the dialects, see Remacle (1952, 261ff.), Camproux (1958, 352), Reymond and Bossard (1979, 94), Miremont (1976, 27, 52, 93, 94), Blinkenberg (1948, 91), Vey (1978 (1911), 192). For earlier French, see Galet (1971) and de Kok (1985). The absence of (3) in Italian is related to the absence of pre-infinitival clitics there (apart from familiar negative imperatives).
5. We differ here from Benacchio and Renzi (1987, 32), which did not take (3) into account.
6. Rumanian allows the order CL-Adv-V even with tensed V—see Sandfeld and Olsen (1936, 98).
7. We assume here that proper government can only be met by antecedent government, i.e. that theta-government by V is not sufficient—v. Chomsky (1986a, 77ff.).
8. Leftward-moved quantifier phrases pattern here with Wh-phrases. The difference in X-bar status between clitics, which are heads and never phrases, and these quantifier phrases, can be seen in Kayne (1975, sect. 2.3). Pollock (1989) has argued that in French a verb can be adjoined to VP—if so, then the more restricted behavior of clitics must be attributed either to their specific clitic character or perhaps to the fact that an adjoined V could be interpreted as a derived head (cf. Kayne (1983b, sect. 2)) of the newly created VP. The precise way in which NP movement would breach a non-L-marked VP is left open.
9. Literary French actually still allows (3) with the clitics *en* and *y* (cf. Kayne (1975, chap. 2, note 7) and Taraldsen (1983, 308)), and also still allows null expletive subjects in a very limited set of contexts, in particular with impersonal passives (cf. Kayne and Pollock (1978, sect. 3). We take the licensing of the empty subject in inversion examples such as *ce que voit Jean* ('that that sees John') in a style less literary than the above to be effected not by I but by the NP (in combination with the Wh-phrase—cf. Kayne (1986a)).

We take the northern Italian dialects to have a strong I, in particular those that show V_{infin} + CL as in (5b). Some of these appear not to have clitic climbing, in which case we would be led to look for some subsidiary factor, taking a strong I to be a necessary, but not sufficient condition for clitic climbing. (The dialect atlas died by Beninca (1986) has clitic climbing uniformly absent from those dialects, but that must be overstated, given Rossini (1975, 142), who notes in particular that in his Cremona dialect the presence of two clitics (as opposed to just one) facilitates preposing them to the matrix verb.)

10. As opposed, arguably to European Portuguese, which allows (7b) in certain root contexts. ((7) holds of French, too.) Both French and Italian allow the order of (7b) with positive imperatives, again a root context (cf. Kayne (1972, note 20)). This suggests a link with the impossibility of embedded V to C in Germanic in the general case, and in French inversion with subject clitics; see Kayne (1983b, sect. 10). The exact landing site in (5b) (for which leftward V-movement was proposed by Sauzet (1986)) is left open, as is the problem of the positioning of the subject in Rizzi's (1982a, chap. 3) Aux-to-Comp construction. The absence in Romance (with the (so far) limited dialect exception mentioned by Chauveau (1984, 198) concerning reflexive imperatives with the adverb 'donc') of the mirror image of (3), that is, of '. . . $V_{(infin.)}$Adv CL . . .' might be explicable in terms of Adv not being able to attach within IP to the left of I (cf. Holmberg (1987)).

11. Viviane Déprez has noted that '*Jean/Cela a fait ne manger pas sa soupe à l'enfant' is impossible and that that constitutes evidence against the leftward verb (–phrase) movement proposed by Kayne (1975, sect. 4.9). The ill-formedness of certain examples of dative clitic climbing in causative constructions is beyond the scope of this article. (For an interesting recent suggestion, see Koster (1987, 311).) The embedding of an I-less verbal constituent, as in (8), is also found in auxiliary + past participle constructions.

12. Contrary to (5b), here the embedded V cannot move past the head above it (cf. perhaps the immobility of C or P heads embedded under V in Romance). On the necessary nonrelevance of minimality in (8), see note 35.

13. To what extent other clitic ordering statements of the kind proposed by Perlmutter (1971, chap. 2) can be derived from more general principles is an open question. Some interesting discussion can be found in Seuren (1976). The text proposal extends to '?Jean a promis de ne pas ne pas en parler', '??Jean a promis de ne pas n'en pas parler' versus '*Jean a promis de n'en pas ne pas parler'. Whether the Portuguese example resembling (12b) given by Bourciez (1967, sect. 382) indicates a difference in the status of the negative morpheme or an extra movement possibility for what look like clitics is an open question.

14. Which has been mentioned by: Remacle (1952, 265), Strozer (1976, 344ff.), de Kok (1985, 427), Pizzini (1981, 417), Roldán (1974, 133), Fresina (1982, 288), and Rizzi (1976, 13), among others, for various Romance languages. The idea that a negative morpheme can be a head has been proposed for Japanese by Kitagawa (1986, sect. 2.4.3).

15. Kayne (1975, sect. 4.3) (for infinitival constructions) and (1981b). We note that (16) is (marginally) accepted by the few Spanish speakers we have asked and that comparable sentences are attested in Remacle (1952, 263) for sixteenth- and seventeenth-century Liegeois, Martin and Wilmet (1980, 159), Foulet (1968, 146), Gougenheim (1971, 181), and Flutre (1970, 518).

16. See Chomsky's (1986a, sect. 11) analysis of NP-movement, which eschews a binding approach in favor of an ECP approach, much as we are proposing here for clitic movement.

17. Aissen and Perlmutter (1983, 364) make use of a condition specific to clitics. The text use of antecedent government is, modulo 'barriers', similar to the approach to clitics in terms of government of Borer (1984).

18. Stepwise clitic climbing is proposed by Luján (1978) and by Burzio (1986).

19. See Kayne (1975, chap. 1).

20. Quantifier movement out of a Wh-island is marginally acceptable: *?Elle a tout su où mettre* ('she has everything known where to put').

21. See (text to) note 8. Adjunction to IP is of course what quantifier phrases are standardly taken to be able to do at LF.

22. Whether or not such is possible with traces of operator phrases.

23. Though not in any simple way for those studied by Pica.

24. A revision proposed below will bear on the status of IP here.

25. See Kayne (1972, note 17) for evidence that French *si* is more like 'if' than like 'whether'. That *si* is a complementizer has been proposed by Huot (1974, 47).

26. The *que* of Spanish *Lo tengo que hacer* ('I) it have *que* to-do') can be analyzed as a specifier of an empty C (as *que* clearly is in some contexts), as can the *di* of *Lo finisco di fare* ('(I) it-finish *di* to-do'), the latter without losing the account given in Kayne (1981e) of the incompatibility of *di* with raising. (Another likely instance of a prepositional specifier is French and Italian partitive *de/di*.) This seems more plausible than taking *di* to be a head capable of L-marking IP. (If there can exist no L-marking by a prepositional C, then English 'For John to win would . . .' must be assimilated to an adjunction structure (possible, since 'for' and 'to' are of like category), much as Chomsky (1986a, 76) on auxiliary plus participle.)

27. See also the discussion following (25). If verbs like *sembrare* ('seem') are compatible with infinitival IP complementation, the text ambiguity reappears (such verbs allow clitic climbing for some speakers; v. Burzio (1986, 392)) in a limited fashion. Christensen (1985) has suggested that raising might involve movement through the specifier of C, a peculiarity that might then be related to 'seem' not taking a true argument (cf. Rothstein (1985)).

28. As had been suggested to us in other contexts by Manuela Ambar and Tarald Taraldsen.

29. With implications for extraction from Wh-islands. We find semi-acceptable in the appropriate reading: '???How exactly were you wondering whether to fix it?', '?For that sort of reason, I'm not sure who would have resigned.' See Aoun (1986, 125).

30. This would follow from Baker's (1985, 89; 1988, 73) prohibition against traces dominated by a zero-level category, which also makes clear why a clitic cannot move through a filled C, as in (24). See also note 12.

I's retention of L-marking discussed below might suggest that I-to-C is substitution rather than adjunction. See Chomsky (1986a, note 50).

31. Strictly speaking, (28) by itself would not be incompatible with an IP analysis as long as (a) some principle(s) could force the clitic to move first to the embedded I (on minimality, cf. note 35 below) and (b) the distribution of PRO and NP-trace in subject position could be managed.

32. See note 30. Baker's prohibition would also exclude attaching a second clitic to a trace of I whose antecedent was the first clitic plus I (cf. the problem discussed in Aissen and Perlmutter (1983, note 5)).

33. See for Spanish, Luján (1978, 106) and Aissen and Perlmutter (1983, 366).

34. See Boillot (1929, 260, 262), Olszyna-Marzys (1964, 48), Reymond and Bossard (1979, 94). The last explicitly has both variants of (29). Remacle (1952, 262) has a more complex well-formed example, of the form (*)*Jean vous viendra les aider* (*à*) *abattre* ('J you-will-come them-help slaughter'), where *vous* is a complement of 'help' and *les* of 'slaughter'. This type of example is explicitly discussed by Aissen and Perlmutter (1983, 367), but only on the basis of its ungrammaticality in Spanish. We leave open the question of Rumanian *o* (cf. Sandfeld and Olsen (1936, 97–98)) cf. perhaps Italian *loro* (Rizzi (1982a, 23–25)), which we would take not to be syntactically adjoined to a head.

35. Note that (our analysis of) (29) suggests strongly that the clitic-trace relation must not be taken to be sensitive to minimality barriers in the sense of Chomsky (1986a).

36. L-marking by I of VP must take place in the dialects that have (29). These dialects do have null subjects to a degree greater than that of French. See Boillot (1929, 45, 71, 115), Olszyna-Marzys (1964, 35), Reymond and Bossard (1979, 78), and Remacle (1952, 224–227).

37. As to why Italian couldn't have the exact equivalent of (29), there are really two, subquestions: Why must the Italian infinitive apparently move out of VP? Why can't a clitic adjoin to the left of the infinitive in the latter's derived position? We leave both open, along with that of the (apparent) absence of (29) in the history of standard French.

Although (28) seems not to exist, there are dialects with postinfinitival clitics that show the same clitic both in the matrix and in the embedded sentence (cf. Rohlfs (1977, 185), Beninca (1986, 474), Bec (1968, 234–235), Morin (1979b, note 5), Kany (1976, 160), and (with pre-infinitival clitic) Camproux (1958, 489)), that is, the equivalent of (*)*Gianni li vuole vederli*. These may turn out to be analyzable as involving movement to the infinitival I, with further movement leaving a copy of that I.

38. Except for certain causatives which lack an embedded I. See the discussion of (8). Causatives with a pre-infinitival subject probably have an I, in which case the text account will extend to them, even if they are not cases of object control. Something further will need to be said about passives of object control structures.

39. See Lujan (1978, 119) and Burzio (1986, 392).

40. See Galet (1971) and de Kok (1985).

41. See Camproux (1958, 352), Miremont (1976, *52*, 94), Kelly (1973, 203), Sauzet (1986, 166), and Dansereau (1985, 65, 84, 86, 107, 108, 109).

42. We must assume here that in the general case, perhaps contrary to Williams (1982), I does not transmit its index to CP when moving through C.

43. On (33b), Miremont (1976, 97) and, for earlier French, Rickard (1970, 68). Interestingly, both (31b) and at least (33a) appear to be ungrammatical in Catalan.

44. As long as nondistinctness (rather than identity) of the two AGR is all that is required. Spanish agreementless *Las hay* (v. Torrego (1984b)) could be licensed by an abstract locative clitic compatible with NP but not CP.

45. Cf. perhaps Rizzi's (1982a, 39) discussion of Aux-V-Aux-V sequences. The blocking effect of T will also exclude the tensed equivalent of (22).

46. Cf. Rizzi (1982a, 31), van Tiel-di Maio (1978, 128), Lo Cascio (1970, 156–238), and Napoli (1981b, 858–884).

47. Recall that passage through C is necessary in (22). Direct I to I would exist if the option of note 31 turned out to be viable.

48. Example from Kayne (1976, 288). On (38), see also Kayne (1975, chap. 4, note 76).

49. This conclusion is in the spirit of Bordelois (1986), which in addition contains the idea that 'restructuring' should involve the coindexing of two I nodes (cf. also Choe (1988)).

50. A further question is why French and Italian are not more like English here. In the terms of Chomsky (1977), it could be that unlike English they do not have available the requisite null operator. This could then be related to their lacking English-style topicalisation (cf. Cinque (1990a) and Kayne (1975, 2.9, 2.11)).

The link between (37)–(39) and Italian clitic climbing leads one to ask, given (14b), about negation, and there does seem to be a clear contrast between 'Mary is hard not to like' and *Marie est difficile à ne pas aimer*, which suggests that in French the object of the infinitive is necessarily a nonovert (pronominal) element which must move up cliticwise (in LF) at least as far as the infinitival C position (which an intervening *ne* will prevent it from doing), in which position it will be licensed by the matrix subject—in effect, French and Italian use the X^0 counterpart of the null X^{max} operator of English.

In a special context such as 'This book is easy to read; that one is easy not to read', this French restriction is weakened (a similar weakening occurs with Italian clitic climbing; see Rizzi (1976, note 9) and Napoli (1981b, 853)), raising the possibility that in such contexts *ne* is not present at the relevant level of representation as a head m-commanding the entire VP.

The suggestion of the paragraph before last implies either that French infinitival I can L-mark VP at LF or that the class of potential barriers is smaller at LF than at S-structure.

51. I_{tense} to C is suggested by Stowell (1982) and by Pesetsky (1982, 4.3.3).

52. Similarly for **Lo è andato Gianni a prendere* if Belletti (1988) is right in taking *a . . . VP* to necessarily have been moved rightward, versus Burzio (1986, 333). In *Lo è andato a prendere Gianni*, we must take the *a*-phrase to be in its base-position, and to be L-marked there. In Spanish, $AdvP_2$ also covers adverbs like *mucho*; see Lujan (1978). In *?Il en est arrivé exprès un très grand nombre*, it is possible that rightward movement of *un . . .* strands the trace of *en*.

53. See note 22. Our proposal is close to that of Zubizarreta (1980, 148); see also Rizzi (1982b) on clefts and raising. It may be possible to distinguish the clefting violation from the well-formed example of VP-preposing given by Longobardi (1985, 186, ix) on the basis that his example involves an auxiliary plus participle structure, which arguably requires no intermediate attachment to I (cf. note 11).

54. Similarly for the reflexive clitic construction with NP preposing.

55. In taking I to (C to) I to apply freely, with the resulting structure subject to further well-formedness conditions, we hold, modulo restructuring, a view close to that of Napoli (1981b).

5

Romance Clitics, Verb Movement, and PRO

Pronominal clitics in Romance may either precede or follow the verb they are associated with, depending on a number of factors, some of which I shall try to elucidate
in this article. My analysis will take Romance clitics to invariably left-adjoin to a
functional head. In cases where that functional head dominates the verb, this will
straightforwardly yield the order clitic-verb. The order verb-clitic will, on the other
hand, be claimed to result from the verb's having moved leftward past the functional
head to which the clitic has adjoined (rather than having the clitic right-adjoin to the
verb). I shall focus on the question of clitic/verb order as it applies to embedded sentences, leaving for future work certain extra possibilities that appear in root sentences
such as imperatives, and in certain other types of root sentences in languages such as
Portuguese and Galician.

The order verb-clitic is found in embedded infinitives in Italian, but not in French.
I shall take the Italian infinitive to move leftward past the clitic and to adjoin to the
single-bar projection whose head the clitic has adjoined to. In the case of control
infinitives this will produce a structure in which the controlled subject PRO is governed by the infinitive. I shall claim that government of PRO by the infinitive always
holds in Italian (not only in the presence of a clitic). Such government is not compatible with Chomsky's *Lectures on Government and Binding* (*LGB*) theory of PRO,
but I shall argue that it is compatible with, and in fact supports, a particular interpretation of the modification of the *LGB* binding theory that Chomsky has suggested in
Knowledge of Language.

More specifically, I shall argue that controlled PRO is always governed and,
paradoxically, that the PRO theorem nonetheless continues to hold to a significant
degree of generality and continues to play a major role in determining the distribution of PRO.

I shall claim further that this approach makes better sense of the little-studied
contrast with respect to control between *whether* and *if*, and in particular of the corresponding complex array of data in Romance, than alternative approaches to con-

trol. If this is correct, then we will have found evidence in this area to support the general approach to PRO that takes its distribution to follow from Binding Theory (and hence for the specific analysis of PRO as being simultaneously anaphoric and pronominal), as well as having found evidence for the presence of an element PRO in syntactic representations.

5.1.   Romance clitics

5.1.1.   Infinitives

French and Italian differ in that French clitics precede embedded infinitives, whereas Italian clitics follow them:

(1)   Lui   parler serait   une erreur.
      him$_{DAT}$ to-speak   would-be   an   error

(2)   *Parler-lui   serait   une erreur.

(3)   Parlargli   sarebbe un errore.
      to-speak him$_{DAT}$ would-be an   error

(4)   *Gli parlare sarebbe un errore.

A possible approach to this contrast would be to distinguish the two languages in terms of type of adjunction: French would left-adjoin its clitics to the infinitive, whereas Italian would right-adjoin its. In chapter 4, sect. 4.1.3. I rejected this approach, in part because it would allow no interesting account of the fact that Italian does not permit its clitics to follow a finite verb:

(5)   Sarebbe   assurdo che tu   gli   parlassi.
      it-would-be absurd that you him$_{DAT}$ spoke

(6)   *Sarebbe assurdo che tu parlassigli.

The contrast between (3) and (6) will turn out to be indirectly related to the fact that the embedded verb in (6) is specified for both agreement and tense, whereas the infinitive of (3) is not. We can note immediately, however, that no simple statement of the sort "A clitic may not follow an agreeing verb form" would suffice (even descriptively), since the order verb-clitic is possible with Portuguese infinitives, even with those that show agreement and since clitics may follow agreeing finite verbs in Portuguese root clauses, as well as in both French and italian imperatives. Similarly, there is no simple prohibition against a clitic following a tensed verb, as seen again in Portuguese root clauses, as well as in a Friulian construction to be discussed later.

   On the basis of these considerations and others that will follow, I continue to consider that an approach to (1) versus (3) in terms of left- versus right-adjunction of the clitic is not to be pursued. This leaves us, in turn, with the question of why right-adjunction is not available to object clitics. One possible answer would be that right-adjunction is not available at all but that seems too strong a position to take, especially thinking of Chung and McCloskey's (1987, 195) discussion of pronoun postposing in Irish, as well as Rizzi's (1982a, chap. 4) and my (1980b, sect. 2.2) analysis of subject inversion/postposition in French and Italian.[1] A potentially more promising answer would be to generalize Williams's (1981) proposal about right-headedness in morphology to instances of X^0 constituents created by adjunction. If such constituents must be right-headed (at least in languages of the sort under discussion), then adjunction to X^0 must always be left-adjunction, given the standard interpretation of adjunction as creating a category of the same type as the element adjoined to.[2]

I am assuming that Romance clitics have the (perhaps defining) property that they must adjoin to some X^0 element.[3] Let us assume further, at least for the purposes of exposition, that they must adjoin to a nonlexical X^0, that is, to a functional head.[4] Thus, in (5) the clitic *gli* has adjoined to the functional head position in which the verb is found as a result of V-to-I movement of the familiar type (for discussion, see Chomsky (1986a) and Pollock (1989)). The same will be true of *lui* in (1), assuming the verb to move out of VP in French infinitival structures, as Pollock (1989, sect. 2.4.1) argues.

Turning to (3), we see that if *gli* there is not right-adjoined to the infinitive itself, then it must be left-adjoined to some empty head position. It seems unlikely that that position could be that of the V-trace within VP, since that would amount to allowing a trace to be a proper subpart of an X^0 constituent (see Baker (1985, 89) and Emonds (1985, 198)). Furthermore, that would prevent us from making the required distinction between infinitives and finite verbs (that is, if the clitic were adjoined to the V-trace in (3), why would this not be possible in (6)?)[5] We conclude, instead, that *gli* in (3) must be left-adjoined to an empty I-type position. Moreover, the preceding considerations that count against the idea of having a clitic adjoined to a V-trace carry over to the idea that a clitic might be adjoined to an I-trace. In other words, the empty I position to which the clitic is adjoined in (3) must not have been moved through by the infinitive.

This leads to the following representation,

(7) ... V ... Cl + I ... [$_{VP}$[$_V$ e] ...] ...

in which the clitic has adjoined to I and V has moved leftward, skipping over I. I would like to propose that, in so doing, V adjoins to I' (I-bar). (I return to the implications for PRO in section 2.) Adjunction of the infinitive to I' is compatible with Chomsky's (1986a, 73) discussion of restrictions on head movement.[6] As far as Chomsky's (1986a, 42) Minimality Condition is concerned, I' will not count as a minimality barrier for V by virtue of V's having adjoined to it.[7]

We are now in a position to return to the contrast between (3) and (6), that is, to the question of why V in (7) can be an infinitive but not an embedded finite verb. I adopt a suggestion made to me by Esther Torrego in response to an earlier presentation of this work, namely that finite verbs cannot mimic infinitives here because the former, unlike the latter, must pick up a suffix corresponding to each functional head. In effect, my earlier claim that I in (7) cannot be a trace (also see chapter 4 sect. 4.2.6.)) means that the I in (7) corresponds to a functional head position that V need not move through. Put another way, my proposal concerning the structure of sentences with verb-clitic order requires that there exist such an abstract I for the clitic to adjoin to. Torrego's idea amounts to saying that in finite sentences there can be no such abstract I.

In the context of Pollock's (1989) proposals concerning multiple I positions, more must be said, however. If in certain cases there can be two I positions, ... I_1 ... I_2 ... V ... (for example, AGR and T(ense)), such that V must move through both, then it is true that the clitic has no (nontrace) empty I position to attach itself to and so must adjoin to the I position in which the verb finds itself at S-structure. What needs to be said further is that Universal Grammar (UG) does not permit the use of a "wild card" I-type node (call it I_W) that could appear in a representation like ... I_W ... I_1 ... I_2 ... V ... in such a way that the clitic could adjoin to I_W, while V moves through the two usual nodes (AGR and T) and subsequently adjoins to I_W', yielding the order ... V ... Cl + I_W ... with V an embedded finite verb. Let us assume, then, that UG permits empty I nodes of only two types: (a) traces (to which a clitic may never adjoin) and (b) nontrace abstract I nodes that are the nonovert counterpart of an otherwise legitimate I-type category. More specifically, (b) will allow an abstract T or an abstract AGR, but if T and AGR are the only two functional categories that appear in embedded Ss,[8] then (b) allows for nothing else. Given this restriction on available I nodes, the absence of embedded V-Cl order in the case of finite verbs will follow from the unavailability of any free I node for Cl to adjoin to, as a func-tion of the fact that a finite verb must merge with both T and AGR.

In (7), on the other hand—that is. in the case of infinitives—we can take Cl to adjoin to the free I node that is available by virtue of the infinitive's not being obliged to merge with both T and AGR.[9] The precise identity of the free abstract I node in (7) is not immediately clear, however, since the infinitive verb shows neither an overt AGR suffix nor an overt T suffix in Italian. For much of what follows, the exact label of the free I to which Cl attaches in (7) will not be relevant. For concreteness, let us tentatively take it to be T, rather than AGR.[10] Let us in addition follow Raposo (1987a) in taking the infinitival -*r*(*e*) suffix of Italian and French to correspond to a functional head having nominal properties, somewhat like English -*ing*. Calling this element Infn and adding it to (7), we arrive at the more highly specified representa-tion in (8),

(8) *Italian*
     ... V + Infn ... Cl + T ... [$_{Infn}$ e] ... [$_{VP}$[$_V$ e] ...

in which V has adjoined to Infn and V + Infn has then adjoined to T'.

From this perspective, French infinitives will involve raising V to Infn, but will not involve any additional movement of the V. Furthermore, instead of adjoining to T, as shown in (8) for Italian infinitives, Cl in French will adjoin to Infn:

(9) *French*
     T ... Cl + [$_{Infn}$ V + Infn] ... [$_{VP}$[$_V$ e] ...

On the assumption that certain adverbs can be generated between Infn and VP (for instance, left-adjoined to VP), the raising of V to Infn will have the effect of moving V across those adverbs, much as in Pollock (1989. sect. 2.4). while leaving open the question of why there is no comparable raising of V to Infn in mainland Scandinavian.[11]

Consider now the case of adverbs or similar elements generated (or subsequently placed) between T and Infn (for example, left-adjoined to Infn-P). V-to-Infn raising will not change the relative order of such adverbs and the verb, so in French they will appear at S-structure to the left of the infinitive. In Italian, on the other hand, the infinitive moves again, left-adjoining to T'. This additional movement will carry the infinitive to the left of any adverb occurring between T and Infn. Put another way, Italian will differ from French with respect to these adverbs in having them necessarily to the right of the infinitive at S-structure. This is essentially equivalent to the point made by Pollock (1989, 412).[12]

If some adverbs can be left-adjoined to VP and others to Infn-P, the question arises whether any can be left-adjoined to TP. If there are adverbs with that property, then we might expect to be able to see that property reflected in Italian, since such adverbs would, by virtue of being left-adjoined to TP, hence higher than the infinitive left-adjoined to T', appear at S-structure to the left of the infinitive, unlike those adjoined to Infn-P (or VP). (In French it would be harder to distinguish them from those adjoined to Infn-P, given the reduced scope of infinitive movement.) Some examples of adverbs appearing to the left of Italian infinitives are in fact given in Rizzi (1982a, 103).

For the case of an infinitive accompanied by a clitic and by an adverb left-adjoined to TP, the order in Italian will be . . . Adv Inf Cl . . . , with the three elements left-adjoined to TP, T', and T, respectively. If the adverb is of the type that cannot be adjoined to Infn-P or VP, then the order . . . Inf Cl Adv . . . will be excluded. A relevant pair of examples, provided by Guglielmo Cinque, is the following:

(10)   senza   forse   invitarlo
        without perhaps to-invite-him

(11)   *senza invitarlo forse

On the other hand, with no adverb is it possible to have the order *. . . Inf Adv Cl . . . . This will follow if adverbs can never left-adjoin to T', as opposed to TP.[13]

Partially similar is the case of the Piedmontese negative morpheme *nen*, which obligatorily appears to the left of the infinitive (despite appearing obligatorily to the right of the finite verb).[14] In its positioning with respect to the infinitive and finite verb, Piedmontese *nen* strongly resembles French *pas*, discussed by Pollock (1989), who takes *pas* to be generated between T and AGR (between T and Infn, from the perspective of (8) and (9)). The finite verb in French raises to T, across *pas*, whereas the infinitive raises only as far as AGR, leaving *pas* to its left. This analysis of *pas* does not transpose to Piedmontese in a way compatible with our analysis of verb-clitic order. The problem (which does not arise in French) is that Piedmontese is exactly like Italian (and unlike French) in having the order infinitive-clitic. Thus, one must account for the fact that Piedmontese infinitives cannot move past *nen* even though they can move past the clitic. More specifically, the problem is that if the order *nen*-infinitive is attributed to a (French-like) necessarily short movement of the infinitive (up to Infn, from the present perspective), then there is no way to account for the position of the clitic, and in particular for the Piedmontese-French contrast with respect to clitic order.

I am led to propose, then, that *nen* is higher up (farther to the left) than Pollock suggested for *pas*:

(12)   *Piedmontese*
　　　... *nen* ... V + Infn ... Cl + T ... [$_{Infn}$ e] ... [VP[$_V$ e] ...

Here, V has moved through Infn and then adjoined to T' as before, but *nen* is to the left of T rather than between T and Infn. Taking *nen* to be adjoined to the left of TP, we have a consistent structure.[15] Since the infinitive adjoins to T', it must follow *nen*, as in the discussion of (10).

The similarity between *nen* and *pas* is emphasized by the fact that in auxiliary–past participle sentences the preferred position for *nen*, like that of *pas*, is to the left of the infinitival auxiliary (Luigi Burzio (personal communication)). One is led to wonder, then, whether *pas* should not also be considered to be adjoined to the left of TP, rather than below T, as Pollock has it. This would raise the question of how exactly to allow for the order infinitive-*pas* where the infinitive is an auxiliary (a question that arises in any event for Piedmontese), and it would presumably require postulating the presence of another functional head node above T into which (only) the auxiliary could move. Somewhat similarly, if it is the case that *pas/nen* are left-adjoined to TP in finite clauses, too, there would have to be a higher X[0] for the finite verb to move into, presumably the AGR of Chomsky (1991) and Belletti (1990).

Summing up, I have claimed that infinitives in Italian left-adjoin to T', that clitics in Italian infinitival clauses left-adjoin to T, that infinitives in French move up only to Infn, and that clitics in French infinitival clauses left-adjoin to Infn. In addition, I have taken Piedmontese infinitives and associated clitics to behave as in Italian, despite certain differences with respect to negation.[16]

In the languages discussed so far, infinitive adjunction to T' is paired with clitic adjunction to T, and infinitive movement to Infn is paired with clitic adjunction to Infn. Given the constraint assumed earlier against clitic adjunction to trace, it is not possible to combine clitic adjunction to Infn with infinitive adjunction to T', since the latter presupposes infinitive movement through Infn (to pick up the infinitival suffix). However, there is no reason why in some language clitic adjunction to T could not be paired with infinitive movement to Infn.[17] This, I would argue, is precisely the case in Occitan, in earlier French, and to some extent still in literary French. For example, in literary French (but not in colloquial French) it is possible for the clitics *y* and *en* to be separated from the following infinitive by certain adverbs:

(13)   ... en   bien parler ...
　　　　of-it well to-speak

We can take this possibility to correspond to (14),[18]

(14)   ... Cl + T ... Adv ... V + Infn ... $[_{VP}[_V e]$ ...

in which V has raised to Infn and Cl has moved across Adv to T.[19]

Another configuration that comes to mind would be one in which V moved up through Infn but, instead of adjoining to T', moved into T itself. As before, this would preclude the Cl from adjoining to Infn, since Infn would be a trace but would be compatible with Cl adjoining to T:

(15)   *Sardinian*
       ... Cl + $[[V + Infn] T]$ ... $[_{Infn} e]$ ... $[_{VP}[_V e]$ ...

This arguably corresponds to the situation in Sardinian, which has the order clitic-infinitive, apparently like French and Occitan, but in fact differs from them in prohibiting in most contexts the order adverb-infinitive where the adverb is of the type that can precede the infinitive in French and Occitan, but not in Italian.[20] Having the infinitive move into T accounts directly for the position of the clitic, since, under my analysis, a verb can be followed by its clitic only if the verb is adjoined to some X'. The adverb contrast between Sardinian and French/Occitan will follow if the adverbs in question (those corresponding to French *bien* 'well', *mieux* 'better', *mal* 'badly', as well as the leftward-moved quantifiers like French *tous* 'all', *tout* 'everything', *rien* 'nothing'; see Kayne (1975, chap. 1)) can adjoin to Infn-P, but not to TP.[21]

Sardinian does allow these moved quantifiers to precede the infinitive in modal constructions of the sort that show clitic climbing. I suggest that in such sentences the moved quantifier has moved out of the embedded sentence entirely; That is, it is not found anywhere in the representation shown in (15). Instead, we have (16),

(16)   ... Modal ... QP ... $[_{Modal} e]$ ... $[[V + Infn] T]$ ...

in which the QP has moved out of the embedded clause past the base position of the modal verb and adjoined probably to the higher VP. Since the modal verb itself will have raised to its T or AGR, the QP will end up between the modal and the embedded infinitive. In this way, we can maintain the account suggested in the preceding paragraph for the fact that in contexts with no higher modal the QP must remain postinfinitival. Such raising of QP past the base position of a higher modal is supported by French examples such as (17),

(17)   ... tout   pouvoir   faire ...
        everything to-be-able to-do

in which the object of the lower infinitive appears visibly to the left of the higher modal. Of course, the Sardinian example looks more like (18):

(18)   Jean peut   tout   faire,
        Jean is-able everything to-do

That Sardinian does not have the word-for-word equivalent of (17) is akin to the fact that French does not have (19):

(19)   *Jean tout peut faire.

When the modal itself must move up to T or beyond. as is true of French finite modals and all Sardinian modals, the raised QP will appear to the right of the modal in S-Structure even though the QP is contained in the matrix clause.[22]

This approach to Sardinian . . . Modal . . . QP . . . Inf . . . will probably turn out to be supported by the very fact that there is no counterpart to these structures in Sardinian with QP replaced by one of the above-mentioned adverbs (taken to modify the infinitive). This asymmetry between QP and Adv can be related, given my proposal, to the fact that there is a corresponding asymmetry in French between QP and these adverbs as far as raising into a higher sentence is concerned, namely, that whereas (17) and similar examples are perfectly common in French, parallel examples with a moved adverb are very difficult to find (although not completely nonexistent).[23]

Further support may come from a contrast between English and mainland Scandinavian concerning negation. In English, double negation of the following sort is possible:

(20)   He says that he has not not done it.

In mainland Scandinavian, this seems to be impossible, as the following Swedish example shows (example from Christer Platzack (personal communication)):

(21)   *Han säger att   han inte har inte gjort det.
         he   says that he   not has not done it

Without the second *inte*, the sentence would be fine (embedded *inte* precedes the finite verb in mainland Scandinavian). If the second *not* in the English example were contained in the participial clause, we would have to say that for some unclear reason Scandinavian participial clauses differ. My proposal is that neither English nor Scandinavian past participial clauses can contain the negative morpheme and that the contrast between (20) and (21) should be related to the independently needed contrast between English and mainland Scandinavian concerning auxiliary raising, which takes place in the former, but not in the latter.[24] More precisely, let us take English (20) to have a D-structure representation of the form . . . *not . . . not . . . have . . .* , with *have* raising to T or AGR not merely across one *not*, as is generally supposed to be possible, but here across two.[25] If this is the only way of deriving (20), then (21) will be unavailable in mainland Scandinavian simply as a consequence of the fact that those languages lack auxiliary raising. If this is correct, then (20) is like (16) in having an element in a higher clause (the second *not* of (20), the QP of (16)) that at first glance seemed to be in the lower clause (participial in (20), infinitival in (16)).

In conclusion, then, the Sardinian . . . Modal . . . QP . . . Inf . . . construction seems ultimately to be compatible with the analysis of Sardinian infinitives as moving to T, that is, to a higher functional head than the one French infinitives move to. The extra distance moved by the Sardinian infinitive as compared with the French one is what is responsible for the much more limited availability in the former of infinitives preceded by QP or Adv. Italian is more like Sardinian than like French in this respect, due, I claim, to the fact that Italian infinitives also move up to the T level.[26] At the same time, the difference between Italian infinitive adjunction to T' and Sardinian infinitive movement to T accounts for Italian's having infinitive-clitic order and Sardinian's having the order clitic-infinitive.

Before leaving infinitives for past participles, let us ask whether these differences in verb movement could possibly be correlated with other properties of these languages. One point to consider is that Occitan, Sardinian, and Italian are all null subject languages, in the core sense of the term; that is, all three are languages that normally fail to express a pronominal subject. If I am correct in taking Occitan to have V-to-Infn movement with the possibility of no additional V-movement, then it follows that having null subjects cannot be a sufficient condition for having systematic V-raising to a position above Infn. On the other hand, it might be the case, in the spirit of chapter 4 and Belletti (1990), that having null subjects is a necessary condition for such long V-raising—in other words, that French infinitives raise no farther than Infn for principled reasons.[27]

The Italian-Sardinian contrast between adjunction to T' and movement to T does not lend itself to any simple null subject approach. However, there may possibly be a link with the so-called free (subject) inversion construction, insofar as Sardinian, according to Jones (1993), tends to avoid that construction with indefinite NPs that are in an agreement relation with the verb.[28] In addition, Jones (1990) has noted that subject inversion in Sardinian is "inhibited by certain postverbal complements" in the manner of French Stylistic Inversion.[29]

5.1.2.   Past participles

Clitics occur with past participles in Romance rather little. The order clitic–past participle is attested in Belgium[30] but is absent from standard French. There are two kinds of environments in which one might have expected to find it, one with and one without a preceding auxiliary. In French, when there is an auxiliary, the clitic adjoins to the left of that auxiliary:

(22)   Marie nous a   parlé.
       Marie us$_{DAT}$ has spoken

(23)   *Marie a nous parlé.

This might be related in part to the sometimes obligatory raising of clitics to the causative verb in complex causative constructions (see Kayne (1975, chaps. 4 and 6; 1981a, fn. 31), Rouveret and Vergnaud (1980), Burzio (1986)).

(24)   Jean nous fait   photographier par Paul.
       Jean us   makes to-photograph by Paul
       'Jean has us photographed by Paul.'

(25) *Jean fait nous photographier par Paul.

But that would not cover (26), in which there is no auxiliary:

(26) *tout individu nous présenté
     any person us$_{DAT}$ introduced

Here the participial relative clause provides no well-formed means of using a dative clitic in standard French. Examples comparable to (26) are given by Grevisse (1964, sec. 477) for Belgian French. The order participle-clitic is found in no type of French, as far as I know:

(27) *tout individu présenté-nous

I have no interesting proposal to make concerning (26).

The absence of (27) from all types of French is plausibly to be derived from the absence of infinitive-clitic order.[31] It also appears to be the case that if a language allows clitic-past participle order, then it allows clitic-infinitive. Of the languages that have infinitive-clitic order, some allow neither participle-clitic nor clitic-participle. Some have participle-clitic order. One is Italian, which allows the equivalent of (27),[32] although with an auxiliary, the clitic must raise:

(28) ogni persona presentataci . . .
     every person introduced-us$_{DAT}$

(29) *Maria ha parlatoci.
     Maria has spoken-us$_{DAT}$

(30) Maria ci ha parlato. (= (22))

Italian also allows past participle–clitic order in the so-called absolute construction studied by Belletti (1981: 1989); see chapter 3, sect. 3.6.):

(31) Una volta conosciutami, Gianni . . .
     once   known-me   Gianni

The analysis of verb-clitic order developed so far has the clitic necessarily left-adjoined to an empty (nontrace) functional head position. In (28) and (31) the underlined *a* in *presentataci* and *conosciutami* represents feminine singular agreement (with the head of the relative in (28) and with the accusative object clitic in (31)), so that the clitic following *a* can clearly not be taken to be left-adjoined to this participial AGR. Let us therefore take it to be adjoined to an abstract T, as in (32),

(32) . . . V$_{pp}$ + Agr . . . Cl + T . . . [$_{Agr}$ e] . . . [$_{VP}$[$_V$ e] . . .

in which the past participial V merges with AGR and then left-adjoins to T'.[33]

Although Italian does not allow (29), comparable sentences are possible in the Franco-Provençal dialect described by Chenal (1986, 545):[34]

(33)   Dz'i batia-la tot solet.
     I have built-it all alone

In this example, as in (28) and (31), the underlined a of the past participle *bati̱a* corresponds to the past participial AGR, in this case agreeing with the clitic *la*. Let us propose that here too we have the structure given in (32), this time embedded under the auxiliary.[35]

Taking the past participle here to left-adjoin to T' amounts to establishing a strong parallelism between it and the Italian infinitive, which also left-adjoins to T', as argued above. As noted in the discussion following (15), this longer movement of the Italian infinitive, as compared with the French one, correlates with contrasts like the following one:

(34)   *Tutto rifare sarebbe difficile.
     everything to-redo would-be difficult

(35)   Tout refaire serait difficile.

The quantifier *tout* can move leftward from its base position following the infinitive in French, left-adjoining to Infn-P (the infinitive in French left-adjoins to $Infn^0$), but it cannot move up to the T level (in either language), so that the Italian counterpart is not possible.[36] Given the proposed parallelism between Italian infinitives and past participles, then, we would expect the participial equivalent of (34) not to be possible in Italian, although it could well be in French, if the infinitive-participle parallel extends to French. The facts are as expected:

(36)   *Gianni ha tutto rifatto.
     Gianni has everything redone

(37)   Jean a tout refait.

There is, however, an apparent complication. I have taken (33) to indicate that in that Franco-Provençal dialect, the past participle moves as far leftward as it does in Italian, at the very least in such examples with the order participle-clitic. It might therefore seem that leftward quantifier movement across the participle should be impossible in that dialect, too, in particular in participle-clitic sentences. But Chenal (1986, 340) contains the following example:

(38)   L'an tot portà-lèi vià.
     they have everything carried-him$_{DAT}$ away
     'They have taken everything away from him.'

The solution that I would like to propose is to take (38) to be the exact counterpart of the Sardinian examples with leftward quantifier movement across an infinitive, referred to in the discussion of (16), and, more precisely, to claim that in (38) *tot* has moved out of the participial clause entirely, past the base position of the auxiliary, probably adjoining to the VP headed by the auxiliary. The surface order will then follow from the fact that the auxiliary itself raises leftward out of its base position up to the finite AGR.[37]

5.1.3. Split clitics

Let us return now more specifically to the question of verb-clitic order. I have claimed that participle-clitic order is derived in a way strongly similar to the way in which infinitive-clitic order is derived. In both cases the clitic left-adjoins to a functional head (T), to the single-bar projection of which (T') the participle/infinitive left-adjoins. This parallelism might at first glance seem to be weakened by an asymmetry that holds between past participles and infinitives with respect to the phenomenon of *split clitics*. I shall argue that although this asymmetry does show that past participle constructions differ in an important respect from infinitival constructions, it does so in a way that leaves intact the analysis of the preceding section.

By split clitics, I have in mind the case of a verb associated with more than one clitic (two, in all the examples to be considered), such that the two clitics find themselves in distinct S-structure positions. A known example is that of French infinitival causative constructions involving a reflexive clitic associated with the embedded infinitive. Martinon (1927, 302) gives the following instance:

(39)   Voilà ce qui l'en a fait se souvenir.
       here-is that which him of-it has made REFL to-remember
       'Here's what made him remember it.'

The reflexive clitic remains adjoined to the infinitive, while the clitic *en*, which corresponds to a complement of the infinitive, raises up to the causative verb (for discussion, see Kayne (1975, chap. 6)). Since causative constructions have a number of very particular properties, it may not seem surprising that Italian noncausative infinitive constructions never display split clitics:

(40)   Gianni vuole darceli.
       Gianni wants to-give-us$_{DAT}$-them

(41)   Gianni ce li vuole dare.

(42)   *Gianni ci vuole darli.

(43)   *Gianni li vuole darci.

In (40) both clitics have adjoined to the lower T; in (41) both have raised up to the matrix verb (which has itself moved into the matrix finite AGR). Neither clitic can raise to the matrix verb alone, while the other remains below (see, for example, Rizzi (1982a, 44)).

Against the background of (40)–(43), it is notable, however, that Chenal (1986, 398, 399) gives two examples of split clitics in the Franco-Provençal auxiliary-participle construction:

(44)   T'an- të prèdzà- nen?
        you$_{DAT}$-have they spoken of-it

(45)   T'an- të deut- lo?
        you$_{DAT}$-have they said it

In both of these, the dative clitic is raised to the auxiliary, while the other object clitic adjoins to the embedded T (past which the participle moves). Similar examples have been attested for the nearby dialects studied by R. Harris (1969).

We can distinguish (44)–(45) from (42)–(43) as follows: Assume that once a clitic is adjoined to some X^0, it cannot be detached from it. $Cl + X^0$ can subsequently move as a constituent; but Cl cannot move, leaving X^0 behind.[38] If two clitics are adjoined to the same X^0, neither can be detached from it, nor, therefore, can they be detached from one another. It must then be the case that in (44)–(45) the dative clitic t' has raised up to the auxiliary without passing through the embedded T position to which the lower clitic is adjoined. This allows us to account for the impossibility of (42)–(43) by saying that although a clitic can move from an A-position out of a participial clause directly up to a higher auxiliary, a complement clitic is unable to move from an A-position out of an infinitival clause directly up to a higher verb (*volere* 'want', in (42) and (43)).

The reason for this asymmetry is plausibly that an infinitival complement of a higher verb is necessarily a full CP,[39] whereas the participial complement of a verbal auxiliary is not. Thus, long clitic movement would cross a CP barrier (by inheritance from IP, in the sense of Chomsky (1986a)) in the infinitival case, but in the auxiliary–participle construction there would be no equivalent CP, so that IP (TP) could be L-marked by the auxiliary, yielding no crossed barriers.[40]

The clitic climbing seen in (41) must now clearly not involve long movement of the clitics, since that would cross a CP barrier. Rather, the two clitics must be adjoined to the abstract infinitival T, and that T itself must subsequently move through the C position, evading the CP barrier[41] and carrying the two clitics together with it.

The ungrammaticality of split clitic constructions in Italian with matrix verb and infinitival complement as in (42) and (43) appears to hold for every Romance infinitive-clitic language.[42] It does not, however, hold for every Romance language, since at least some of those clitic-infinitive languages that allow clitic climbing allow split clitics, that is, sentences of the following form:

(46)   (*)Jean nous veut les donner.
        Jean us$_{DAT}$ wants them to-give

        'Jean wants to give them to us.'

(47)   (*)Jean les veut nous donner.

Examples from seventeenth-century French have been collected by de Kok (1985, 594), and there are also modern dialect examples.[43] Standard modern French does not allow such cases because it does not allow clitic climbing.

The contrast between clitic-infinitive constructions, which can display split clitics, and infinitive-clitic constructions, which cannot, is unexpected under an approach to clitic climbing such as that developed in Rizzi (1982a, chap. 1) or Aissen and Perlmutter (1983). Under the present approach, the contrast follows from the different position of the infinitive in the two types of language, combined with the stepwise analysis of clitic climbing proposed in chapter 4. The absence of split clitics in infinitive-clitic constructions was accounted for. Its existence in clitic-infinitive constructions is licensed as follows: The infinitive moves to $Infn^0$. One clitic adjoins to $Infn^0$ and stays there. The other clitic adjoins to T^0 and subsequently moves farther up with T^0.[44] The essential difference is that in these clitic-infinitive constructions, there are two adjunction sites (T^0 and $Infn^0$) available to the clitics within the infinitival complement, whereas in infinitive-clitic constructions, there is only one (T^0), by virtue of the infinitive's having moved through $Infn^0$.

5.1.4.   Finite verbs

The fact that embedded finite verbs do not show the verb-clitic possibility in Romance was discussed earlier, in the text surrounding (6) and (7). Here I briefly mention two exceptions. The first is found in written archaic Italian and seems to be limited to the impersonal clitic *si* (see Fornaciari (1974 (1881), 456)). I have not seen any attestation for a spoken dialect. Conceivably, *si* in this written Italian can be taken to be a true suffix (that is, an X^0 element to which the inflected verb adjoins), reversing the usual relation between clitic and inflected verb/empty functional head.[45]

The second case does come from a spoken dialect, more exactly from certain varieties of Friulian, in which what looks like an embedded finite verb can be followed by a clitic when it is preceded by the impersonal clitic *si*.[46] In Italian this clitic precedes the finite verb, along with other clitics:

(48)   a. Si parla.
           SI speaks

       b. Se ne   parla.
           SI of-it speaks

       c. Lo si vede.
           him SI sees

In these varieties of Friulian, the clitic instead follows the verb: . . . *si* V Cl . . . . I do not know why this possibility is found in these dialects and not in others, or not in Italian, but I will attempt to account for the fact that within the relevant dialects the order finite verb-clitic seems to depend on the presence of impersonal *si*.

Burzio (1986, 59) (also see Cinque (1988, 537)) discusses the fact that with Italian impersonal *si* the tensed verb never shows agreement, even in cases where a participle does:

(49)   Si è   arrivati.
        SI is(3SG.) arrived(PL.)

More exactly, he takes the 3sg. form to be the neutral (default) form of the tensed verb, so that there is truly no agreement between *è* and *si* in sentences like (49) (for reasons not directly relevant here). An important question is whether the absence of finite verb agreement in (48) and (49) corresponds to the absence of any agreement morpheme or simply to the presence of an agreement morpheme in default form. For past participles, it is clear that there is a morpheme in default form in Italian. On the other hand, in J. W. Harris's (1969) analysis of Spanish, the person-number morpheme for 3sg. is taken to be zero for several tenses. Let us conjecture that a phonological analysis of the relevant varieties of Friulian will be compatible with taking the 3sg. person-number morpheme to be zero in all cases of . . . *si* V Cl. . . . If so, that would allow us to claim that in those cases there is in fact no person-number morpheme at all suffixed to the verb, so that the representation (50) would be available,

(50) . . . *si* . . . V + T . . . Cl + AGR . . . [$_T$ e] . . . [$_{VP}$[$_V$ e] . . .

in which V raises to T followed by the tensed V left-adjoining to the AGR' headed by the abstract AGR that was not obliged to merge with V by virtue of there being no syntactic agreement.[47]

In conclusion, then, the Friulian . . . *si* V Cl . . . construction may provide additional support for the general approach to (embedded) verb-clitic order that I have adopted, one in which the clitic left-adjoins to an abstract functional head and the verb to the single-bar projection of that functional head. In section 2 I explore the way in which such verb adjunction impinges, in the case of infinitives, on patterns of control.

5.2.   PRO

5.2.1.   English

There is in English a contrast between *whether* and *if* with respect to control:

(51)   He doesn't know whether to go to the movies.

(52)   *He doesn't know if to go to the movies.

Both *whether* and *if* are of course possible in the finite counterparts to these:

(53)   He doesn't know whether he should go to the movies.

(54)   He doesn't know if he should go to the movies.

The grammaticality of (51) can be straightforwardly assimilated to that of other *wh*-infinitive constructions such as (55) if, following Katz and Postal (1964, 96) and Larson (1985, 238), we take *whether* to be a *wh*-phrase:

(55)   He doesn't know when to go to the movies.

From this perspective, the *whether* construction of (56) is akin to (57):

(56)   Whether they give him a seat or not, he'll be happy.

(57)   Wherever they put him, he'll be happy.

The ungrammaticality of (52) leads naturally to the claim that *if* is not a *wh*-phrase, which is supported by the absence of (58):

(58)   *If they give him a seat or not, he'll be happy.

Both Katz and Postal and Larson take *whether* to be the *wh*-counterpart of *either* (*neither* being the negative counterpart). This presumably contributes to licensing the combination *whether or not*, as in (59):

(59)   He doesn't know whether or not he should go to the movies.

If *if* has no direct relation to *either* and in particular is not a *wh*-phrase counterpart of it, the ungrammaticality of (60) is not surprising:

(60)   *He doesn't know if or not he should go to the movies.[48]

Conversely, the *if* of (54) almost certainly bears some relation to that of conditionals:

(61)   If you had not left, he would have been a lot happier.

Since this *if* does not alternate with *wh*-phrases, it is not surprising that *whether*, a *wh*-phrase, is not found:

(62)   *Whether you had not left, he would have been happier.

The conclusion I would like to draw from all this is that the primary difference between *whether* and *if* is that the former is a *wh*-phrase and the latter is not, and furthermore, that this difference in syntactic status is responsible for the contrast in behavior with respect to control seen in (51) versus (52).

As for the exact status of *if*, I will, in agreement with Emonds (1985, 287), take it to be a complementizer, and more precisely, to be an X^0 element. Emonds takes *if*, like other complementizers, to be of category P^0, as opposed to Chomsky's (1986a) C^0. I will call it C^0, while keeping in mind that P^0 might perhaps be compatible with what follows, in particular a non-case-assigning P^0.

The basic proposal will be that control is incompatible with the presence of a lexical complementizer, and hence incompatible with *if*. Control is, on the other hand, compatible with *whether* since *whether* is not a lexical complementizer, but a *wh*-phrase (that is, it is not a C^0 but a phrase in the Specifier position of CP); nor is there any element in (51) that is a C^0. As for the exact reason why a lexical complementizer inhibits control in (52), let us adopt as a first approximation the theory of control developed in Chomsky (1981a) (*LGB*), which takes the controlled subject NP to be the element PRO, having the features [+ anaphoric] and [+ pronominal]. Principles A and B of the binding theory combine to yield the so-called PRO theorem, which states that PRO must be ungoverned. Assume now that a lexically filled C^0 counts as a governor for the PRO in subject position, but that a nonlexical C^0 position does not. (This is straightforward if IP is an inherent barrier, if government of Spec, IP by C^0 depends on L-marking in Chomsky's (1986a) sense, and if a lexically filled C^0 is an L-marker.[49] If IP is not an inherent barrier, then the irrelevance of a nonlexical C^0 should be taken to follow directly from the requirement that for the purposes of binding theory, a governing category can be induced only by a lexical governor (see Chomsky (1986b, 169)).) Then the contrast between (51) and (52) follows from the *LGB* theory of control, via the PRO theorem.

5.2.2.   French

French is substantially like English with respect to the phenomena of the previous section, once we abstract away from a major difference, namely that French lacks any counterpart to English *whether*. Corresponding to (53) and (54) French has only (63):

(63)   Marie ne sait pas si elle devrait aller au cinéma.

This alone is not sufficient to tell us whether French *si* corresponds more to English *if* or to English *whether*. However, if we run through the various distinguishing properties noted earlier, we see that *si* corresponds strongly to *if* and not at all to *whether*. First, the control counterpart of (63) is ungrammatical, like *if* in (52):

(64)   *Marie ne sait pas si aller au cinéma (ou non).

Second, the French counterpart to (56) cannot have *si*, just as English does not use *if* (see (58)):

(65)   *Si on lui donne une place ou non, il sera heureux.

(Possible is *Qu'on lui donne* . . . , with the basic complementizer *que*.) Third, the contrast between *whether or not* and **if or not* in (59) versus (60) places *si* with *if*:

(66)   *Marie ne sait pas si ou non elle devrait aller au cinéma.

Finally, conditionals in French do use *si* as English uses *if* (see (61)):

(67)   Si vous n'étiez pas parti, il aurait été plus heureux.

The very fact that *si* corresponds to *if* and not to *whether* (plus the fact that no other French word corresponds to *whether* either) can be understood in terms of Katz and Postal's and Larson's idea discussed earlier that *whether* is a *wh*-phrase based on *either*. This is so because French lacks any single word for *either*, too (and similarly for *neither*) (see Kayne (1972, n. 17)).

That *si* is a complementizer (see Huot (1974, 47)) and more specifically a C^0 makes it possible to account for (64) in exactly the same way as proposed earlier for English (52), that is, in terms of the PRO theorem and government of PRO by *si*.[50]

Both *si* and *if* must of course be taken not to be Case assigners (contrary to English *for*) to exclude (68) and (69):

(68)   *Marie ne sait pas si Jean aller au cinéma.

(69)   *Mary doesn't know if John to go to the movies.

In being non-case-assigning governors (across IP), *si* and *if* have something in common with adjectives such as English *likely*. With respect to Empty Category Principle (ECP) effects, these C^0s pattern like the usual complementizers *que* and *that*; that is, they do not permit extraction from the subject position just below them. This indicates that government by X^0 is not a sufficient condition for a *wh*-trace to meet the ECP (see Kayne (1983a), Chomsky (1986a, 47, 79), and Rizzi (1990)).

The *de* that precedes many French infinitives must now not be an instance of C^0 in, for example, (70). If it were, it would induce a PRO theorem violation parallel to that of (64) and (52):

(70)   Jean essaie de comprendre.
       Jean tries DE to-understand

At the same time I would like to maintain my earlier account of the fact that *de* is incompatible with core cases of raising to subject position, with the nearest French counterpart to exceptional case marking (ECM) constructions, and with a *wh*-phrase in Spec of CP, as well as of the fact that *de* must precede negation (see Kayne (1981e)). The arguments given there show clearly that *de* is not configurationally parallel to English *to* and that it is at the CP level. I would like to propose, then, that it is in Spec of CP. This leaves intact the account given of the four properties just listed, while allowing *de* to cooccur with PRO.

De can now cooccur with PRO because from the Spec position it does not govern PRO. If IP can be an intrinsic barrier,[51] this follows from the fact that there is no lexical C^0 in (70) combined with the fact that it is in general not possible for a Specifier to be an L-marker. (If IP cannot be an intrinsic barrier, then we would have to allow C^1 to inherit barrierhood from IP (and *wh*-phrases to adjoin to IP; see Frampton (1990)).)

Taking *de* to be in Spec of CP (and generalizing that hypothesis to the very similar Italian *di*)[52] has the additional advantage of permitting a straightforward account of the fact that Italian *di* can to some extent be crossed by clitics moving out of the infinitive up into the matrix, whereas Italian *se* (the counterpart to French *si* and a C^0 also, as we shall see) cannot be (see chapter 4, sect. 4.2.5). A further advantage lies in the fact that, although many French and Italian dialects have doubly filled Comps with finite complementizer *que*, I know of none that allow *de* or *di* to cooccur with an immediately preceding (or following) *wh*-phrase. This asymmetry will follow from *que* = C^0 versus *de* = Spec, CP under the standard assumption that *wh*-phrases must occupy Spec of CP themselves (plus the equally standard assumption that a Spec position can host only one phrase).

Finally, note that there is a sharp asymmetry in Italian between *che* 'that' and *di* with respect to the possibility of being preceded by a preposition. Cinque (1990a, sect. 1.7.1) discusses the fact that *che* can in a more formal style be preceded by the preposition *a*:[53]

(71)   Sono contrario a   che tu   parta subito.
       I-am against   to that you leave right-away

If *di* were a C^0 like *che*, we might expect it to behave the same, but in fact (72) and similar sentences are impossible:

(72)   *Sono contrario a di partire subito.
       I-am against to DI to-leave right-away

What is possible is (73), without the *di*:

(73)   Sono contrario a partire subito.

Cinque argues that although the *a* of (73) looks like a true preposition, it is better analyzed as a complementizer, the simplest reason being that infinitives in Italian can never be preceded by a subcategorized preposition; the only exceptions are with *a* and *di*, precisely those prepositions that independently occur as complementizers. Cinque's argument against taking the *a* of (73) to be a true preposition (that is, a P^0 taking CP as complement) is convincing, but since he takes that *a* to be a C^0, he is unable to bring (71) into the same paradigm (given the presence there of *che* = C^0).

The perspective developed above allows me to make a partially different proposal: The *a* of (73) is not a true preposition, but neither is it a C^0. Rather, it, like French *de* (and Italian *di*) in (70), is a P^0 occupying the Spec of CP position. This immediately accounts for the ungrammaticality of (72) (which would have had two Specs of CP)[54] in a way parallel to my account of (74) (see the discussion two paragraphs back):

(74)   *Jean ne sait pas où de dormir.
       Jean NEG knows not where DE to-sleep

Furthermore, it allows us to extend Cinque's analysis of these instances of *a* to the *a* of (71) by saying that there, too, the *a* is in Spec of CP. The special stylistic status of (71) then presumably correlates with the fact that it, unlike (73), has a particular sort of doubly filled Comp, that is, a P-filled Spec of CP at the same time as a filled C^0.[55]

In conclusion, the syntax of French infinitival *de* appears to be compatible with my proposal to exclude French *si* and English *if* from control structures by using the PRO theorem and the C^0 status of *si* and *if*.[56]

5.2.3. Italian

There is no single word for *either* (or *neither*) in Italian, and, as we would then expect, no word corresponding to *whether*. There is, on the other hand, a word *se*, which resembles French *si*, and which, like French *si*, has much in common with English *if*. Like *si* and *if*, Italian *se* occurs both in embedded interrogative contexts and in conditionals:

(75)   Gianni non sa se dovrebbe andare al cinema.
       Gianni NEG knows if he-should to-go to-the movies

(76)   Se Gianni avesse fatto questo, Paolo . . .
       if Gianni had done this Paolo

Furthermore, it is not used in the construction represented by English (56), just as French *si* is not, as noted in (65). Nor can it occur in a constituent like *whether or not*, and in that respect it again resembles French *si* in (66), as well as English *if*. There thus appears to be every reason to take Italian *se* to be an instance of C^0.

Support for this position comes from dialects like those described by Ganzoni (1983, 160) and Poletto (1990a) in which subordinating conjunctions, as well as embedded *wh*-phrases, are invariably followed by the complementizer *cha/che* 'that', with one exception: *scha/se* 'if'. I interpret this to reflect the C^0 status of *scha/se* versus the non-C^0 status of subordinating conjunctions and *wh*-phrases.[57]

Additional support for this hypothesis comes from clitic-climbing considerations. As noted in chapter 4, sect. 4.2.5., *se* blocks clitic climbing into a matrix sentence more strongly than *wh*-phrases do in general. This asymmetry, which is the opposite of what is often found with respect to extractions of other phrases, can be accounted for by taking *se* to be a C^0 (and *wh*-phrases not to be), and by forcing clitic climbing to use C^0 as an escape hatch. A somewhat similar and at least as surprising asymmetry is found in the Italian counterpart to the *easy to please* construction, which is in general much more constrained than it is in English. In particular, the Italian equivalents of sentences like (77) are usually ungrammatical:

(77)   This book is hard to convince people to read.

For the empty category bound by the matrix subject to be able to appear in an embedded sentence, the verb below the adjective must be of the type that allows clitic climbing. My proposal (sect. 4.3.1.) was that Italian (and French) *easy to please* involved an abstract equivalent of clitic movement. Relevant to the present discussion is the fact that an intervening *se* seems to block this construction more strongly than an intervening *wh*-phrase:

(78)   ??Questi libri sono difficili da sapere dove mettere.
      these books are hard DA to-know where to-put

(79)   *Questi libri sono difficili da sapere se rileggere.
      these books are hard DA to-know if to-reread

Again, we can take the asymmetry to follow from the blocking of (abstract) clitic movement by *se* = C^0.

Despite these many ways in which Italian *se* seems definitely to be a C^0 like French *si* and English *if*, there is one major unexpected disparity in behavior. Unlike *si* and *if*, Italian *se* is compatible with control:

(80)   Gianni non sa se andare al cinema.
      Gianni NEG knows if to-go to-the movies

In light of the first three paragraphs of this section, it would be totally implausible to try to interpret *se* as an Italian equivalent of *whether*. But if so, the contrast between (80) and its French counterpart (64), repeated here as (81), seems mysterious:

(81)   *Marie ne sait pas si aller au cinéma.

The analysis developed here so far would lead us to expect (80) to be ungrammatical, too—*se*, being a C^0, should govern PRO across IP and thereby induce a PRO theorem violation.

5.2.4. Romance

In the spirit of the comparative syntax work of the past ten or more years, we must ask whether this Italian-French difference is related to any other, in the hope that if a correlation is discovered, it will point the way toward a solution to the problem. In chapter 4, sect. 4.3.2. I suggested a correlation with the null subject parameter, but consideration of additional Romance languages seems to indicate that that was incorrect.[58]

Though it is true that the null subject languages Catalan[59] and Spanish appear to pattern with Italian as far as (80) versus (81) is concerned, the null subject languages Occitan and Sardinian pattern instead with French; that is, they do not allow control with their counterpart to *if* (*se* in Occitan (82), *si* in Sardinian (83)):[60]

(82)   *Sabi pas se anar al cinema.
      I-know not if to-go to-the movies

(83)   *No'isco si andare.
      NEG I-know if to-go

I conclude that being a null subject language is not a sufficient condition for permitting control with *if* and therefore that there must be some other factor at issue in the Italian/French contrast between (80) and (81).

The question, then, is to figure out what Italian, Catalan, and Spanish have in common that sets them off from French, Occitan, and Sardinian. I propose that the key property is that of infinitive-clitic order, which holds for the first three but not for the last three, which show clitic-infinitive order.[61] Before going on to ask why control with *if* correlates with infinitive-clitic order, I will briefly mention some further Romance languages.

The languages/dialects of northern Italy are what might informally be called partial null subject languages, in that they typically allow a pronominal subject to fail to appear at all in some cases, but not in the systematic way found in Italian (see Renzi and Vanelli (1983)). In most of these languages, a pronominal subject, when required to appear overtly, appears as a pronominal clitic.[62] Within this set of languages, I have information concerning control with *if* in four. In Piedmontese, Milanese, and Paduan such control is possible,[63] as in Italian. In Gardenese it appears not to be.[64] Piedmontese, Milanese, and Paduan are infinitive-clitic languages, like Italian. Gardenese is a clitic-infinitive language.

In the remainder of this article I shall attempt to explain why control with the equivalent of *if* is possible in Romance only in infinitive-clitic languages.[65]

5.2.5.   Infinitive adjunction interferes with C^0–government

In section 1 I took infinitive-clitic languages to differ from clitic-infinitive languages in having their infinitive left-adjoin to the I' just below the C projection, the clitic itself being left-adjoined to the corresponding I (which I took to be T):

(84)   ... V_{inf} + [$_{I'}$ ... Cl + I ...

The order clitic-infinitive in the other class of languages involved no such adjunction to I', but rather movement of the infinitive into some I position and adjunction of the clitic either to that I position or to some higher one.

Recall now that I have suggested interpreting the ungrammaticality of control with *if/si/se* in French, Sardinian, Occitan, Gardenese (and English) as due to the government of PRO by the lexical C^0 and to the consequent violation of the PRO theorem:

(85)   ... *if* ... [$_{IP}$ PRO ...

In clitic-infinitive languages, the infinitive ends up in an I position below PRO. In the absence of *if*, control is perfectly possible and the standard conclusion is that the infinitive there does not govern PRO. In the presence of *if*, the infinitive moves to the same I and the same conclusion holds. In other words, in (86) PRO is governed by *si/se* and is not governed by the infinitive (independently of whether any clitic is present):

(86)   ... *si* ... [$_{IP}$ PRO ... V_{inf} + I ...

By virtue of being governed by C^0, PRO in (86) violates the PRO theorem, that is, the conjunction of Principles A and B of the *LGB* binding theory.

Fleshing out (84) to show PRO and to show where the lexical C^0 is (when it is present), we have (87):

(87)   ... *se* ... [$_{IP}$ PRO ... [$_{I'}$ V_{inf} + [$_{I'}$ ... (Cl +)I ...

I have taken the infinitive to left-adjoin to I' in these languages, whether or not a clitic is present. Put another way, in the infinitive-clitic languages like Italian, the infinitive will in the general case move into a position that is hierarchically closer to PRO than the position it moves into in the clitic-infinitive languages. I would like to propose, now, that in so doing the infinitive in (87) blocks off government of PRO by C^0 and thereby eliminates the potential PRO theorem violation induced by that C^0.

The precise mechanism involved will probably be minimality, in the sense of Chomsky (1986a, 10). I take c-command to be sensitive to the distinction between nodes and segments of nodes (see May (1985, 63)), so being dominated by one segment of I' in (87) does not prevent the adjoined infinitive from c-commanding and hence governing PRO (whereas the infinitive in (86) does not govern PRO, as noted earlier).[66]

The question now is whether in (87) *se* governs PRO. Since V_{inf} is a closer governor,[67] it would seem that *se* should not govern PRO. However, the definition of minimality barrier given in Chomsky (1986a, 42) requires that the minimality barrier be a projection of the relevant closer governor, which is not the case in (87), given standard assumptions about adjoined structures. Thus, we must revise the characterization of minimality barrier to allow for the case in which the minimality barrier (here, IP) is not a projection of that governor, but only contains it.[68]

Summing up, the idea that I am pursuing is that a lexical C^0 will be expected to induce a PRO theorem violation when PRO is the subject of the IP sister of that C^0. However, the government relation between C^0 and PRO that would be the cause of such a violation can be blocked by the presence of a closer governor. In languages that have the order infinitive-clitic, and only in those, the infinitive itself can be the required closer governor, having moved into an appropriate position by adjoining to I'.

It should be noted that this account of the correlation between control with a lexical C^0 and infinitive-clitic order, insofar as it depends crucially on the sensitivity of PRO to government by that C^0, supports the very postulation of a category PRO, that is, of a type of empty NP with a particular position in the syntactic structure and with the features [+ anaphoric] and [+ pronominal] given it by the *LGB* binding theory.

In effect, we can think of the process of looking at a set of Romance languages, moving from one with clitic-infinitive order to the opposite type and back, as a kind of experiment in which we hold the basic structure of a language—Romance—(relatively) constant,[69] while varying the position of the infinitive. What we learn is that as we so vary its position, the grammaticality of control sentences with *si/se* varies in step. If my theoretical proposal is correct, then we can interpret this covariance as reflecting the sensitivity of PRO to the position of the infinitive, that is, to the presence versus absence of a government relation with *si/se*.

5.2.6. Binding theory and PRO

The question arises why the infinitive adjoined to I' in the Italian-type languages does not itself induce a PRO theorem violation. There are two kinds of possible answer. One might take the position that the blocking effect of the adjoined infinitive does not actually depend on its governing PRO at all. For example, it might be feasible to allow some category X to create a minimality block with respect to Y without X governing Y itself, as in Reuland (1983a, 117, 122). I shall, however, pursue a different approach (still compatible with the basic idea that infinitive movement in the Italian-type languages blocks the potentially offending government from lexical C^0), in part because I do not see precisely how to formulate the preceding approach satisfactorily (for example, Reuland's specific proposal would not carry over to this case), and in part because of a consideration that will become clearer below, having to do with the determination of the antecedent of PRO, which is left open by the *LGB* Binding Theory.

Let us adopt the paradoxical position that infinitive adjunction in Italian does create a configuration in which the infinitive comes to govern PRO, that the PRO theorem continues to play an important role in UG, and yet that there is no PRO theorem violation here.

Consider the revision of Binding Theory suggested by Chomsky in *Knowledge of Language (KL)* (pp. 170ff.)[70] in which a slight discrepancy is introduced (in terms of BT-compatibility) between the governing category for an anaphor and the governing category for a pronoun. This discrepancy concerns in particular anaphors and pronouns in subject position. It is relevant when the subject position in question is governed by a lexical category that is found inside (rather than outside, as is more usual) the X^{max} of which the anaphor or pronoun is the subject. In that case the governing category of the pronoun would be X^{max}, the smallest category containing both the governor and a subject position.

However, in the case of an anaphor in such an internally governed subject position, the governing category is not X^{max} but rather the next category up containing a subject position, the reason being that, although X^{max} contains the governor of the anaphor, its subject position is not a potential binder for the anaphor (informally put, it would be unreasonable to require an anaphor to be bound within a category containing no position that could contain a potential binder—comparable unreasonableness is not an issue in the case of pronouns).

It follows from the simplest interpretation of this revision that the PRO theorem should no longer hold in full generality, although it will continue to hold over a restricted (but still wide) range.[71] This is so since the PRO theorem follows from the strict parallelism between Principles A and B of the Binding Theory. To the extent that strict parallelism fails to hold over some range of environments, the PRO theorem will fail to hold for that range. More specifically, it will fail to hold for any subject PRO governed by a lexical category found within the category of which PRO is the subject, since in such a case the governing category for PRO qua anaphor will not be identical to the governing category for PRO qua pronoun.

On the other hand, the PRO theorem will continue to hold, as in *LGB*, for all object PROs[72] as well as for all subject PROs governed by an element outside the category of which PRO is the subject.

In particular, when a lexical complementizer governs PRO, a PRO theorem violation continues to hold, since the complementizer is outside the IP of which PRO is in subject/Spec position. This is what excludes .. *if PRO to go to the movies* and the comparable examples discussed above for French, Occitan, Sardinian, and Gardenese (see (81)–(83)).

The difference between the *KL* Binding Theory and the *LGB* Binding Theory becomes important when we turn to the languages like Italian in which the infinitive left-adjoins to I':

(88)   ... *se* ... $[_{IP}$ PRO ... $[_{I'}$ V_{inf} + $[_{I'}$ ...

By hypothesis, *se* no longer governs PRO in this configuration, but V_{inf} does. In the *LGB* theory, this would have led to a PRO theorem violation. In the *KL* theory, on the other hand. that is not the case, as follows: The governing category for PRO qua pronoun is IP, since that is the smallest category that contains a subject position and contains the governor of the pronoun.[73]

This is not yet different from the *LGB* state of affairs. The crucial difference lies in how the two theories determine the governing category of PRO qua anaphor in (88). For the *LGB* theory, it is again IP, the same as for PRO qua pronoun, leading to a typical PRO theorem violation. For the *KL* theory, that is not the case. IP in (88) does contain the governor, but it does not contain a suitably accessible potential binder and so does not qualify as governing category for PRO qua anaphor. Rather, the governing category for PRO qua anaphor will be the next category up containing a subject position, in effect, the next IP up (not shown in (88)). Since this governing category is distinct from that assigned to PRO qua pronoun, there is no violation of the PRO theorem sort, as desired.

Thus, the *KL* Binding Theory[74] is capable of distinguishing the Italian construction represented by (88) from the corresponding French and English one.[75]

In assigning to PRO qua anaphor the next IP up as governing category, the binding theory adopted here excludes the possibility that the antecedent of PRO in (88) could be taken to be a subject NP two IPs up. This accounts correctly for the fact that in (89) the antecedent of PRO must be *Gianni* and cannot be *Maria*:

(89)   Maria pensa che Gianni non sappia se andare al cinema.
       Maria thinks that Gianni NEG knows if to-go to-the movies

This pattern is of course widespread for control infinitivals that are verb complements, as, for example, in (90), in which again the antecedent of PRO must be the subject of 'decide' and cannot be that of 'thinks'.

(90)   Maria pensa che Gianni abbia deciso di andare.
       Maria thinks that Gianni has decided DI to-go

This resolves a paradox noted by Lasnik (1989), namely that the *LGB* Binding Theory accounts for the distribution of PRO (by excluding it from governed positions) but at the same time fails to assign it a governing category and so makes no claim at all about the location of its antecedent. My extension of the *KL* Binding Theory to PRO retains the distributional account (by excluding PRO from all governed positions except those subject positions governed by an element inside the XP of which PRO is the subject) and at the same time does assign PRO a governing category[76] and so does make some claim about the location of the antecedent.

This approach to PRO, in having Binding Theory determine a governing category for PRO and hence delimit the possible positions for the antecedent of PRO, is significantly similar to that of Manzini (1983b) but has the advantage that there is no need to add to Binding Theory any notion of domain-governing category. From our perspective, the same effect is achieved in the Italian infinitive cases by the basic characterization of Principle A as picking out as governing category the smallest category containing a governor and an accessible subject. Since where PRO is the subject of an infinitive, that subject position does not count as accessible, Principle A will look for the next largest category containing one, which, in the case of the infinitive as complement of V, will straightforwardly be the next IP up (and there will be no PRO theorem violation, as discussed).

The approach developed here has the further advantage of allowing an account of the Italian-French contrast with respect to control in the presence of *se/si*, which depends on the *KL* binding theory and in particular on the analysis of PRO as simultaneously anaphoric and pronominal, whereas Manzini took PRO here to be a pure anaphor.[77]

5.2.7. Levels

My account of the Italian-French contrast with respect to control in the presence of *se/si* 'if' depended in part on postulating a rule of leftward infinitive adjunction to I' that applies in Italian but not in French. The left-adjoined infinitive governs PRO in Italian, with the consequences noted in the previous two sections. The absence of comparable infinitive movement in French means that in French the infinitive does not govern PRO—this is precisely what allows a lexical C^0 in French to induce a PRO theorem violation. In the absence of a lexical C^0, as in (91), French PRO is therefore ungoverned:[78]

(91) Jean veut aller au cinéma.
      Jean wants to-go to-the movies

This is of course expected within the *LGB* perspective and is perfectly compatible with what I have said so far. This is so, in the sense that I have argued that PRO can be governed under certain very specific conditions, but have in effect left open the possibility that it can also be ungoverned.

A problem arises, however, with respect to the paradox adduced by Lasnik that was mentioned earlier. I argued that his paradox is resolved for Italian by the fact that PRO there is governed by the preposed infinitive, hence gets a governing category, so that binding theory actually does provide an indication of where the antecedent of PRO must be. But if PRO remains ungoverned in French, Lasnik's paradox reappears there. I would like to propose, then, that French is to Italian with respect to leftward infinitive adjunction to I' as Chinese is to Italian with respect to wh-movement,[79] in other words, that French actually does have such infinitive movement, but only at the level of LF.[80]

This leads to the following proposal:

(92)   All controlled PROs are governed at some level of representation.

Proposal (92) holds even though the PRO theorem is largely true. This is so in the sense that the PRO theorem continues to hold for all PROs other than those that are in subject position and governed by an internal governor. On the other hand, if I am correct in putting forth (92), then any controlled PRO that is ungoverned at all levels of representation is equally excluded.

I take the reason for the existence of (92) to be that it is via government that PRO qua anaphor receives a governing category. Assuming further that an antecedent for PRO must be within PRO's governing category (that is, that an ungoverned PRO would not be able to be associated with any antecedent at all), (92) follows. In effect, I have reached the conclusion that PRO is less exotic than it was in the *LGB* framework, since PRO is now like other empty categories in being licensed in part via government; at the same time, the present theory maintains the specificity of PRO, and in particular its exclusion from most governed positions (see footnote 77).

Proposal (92) is stated in such a way as to allow for the possibility that there exist instances of ungoverned noncontrolled PRO, that is, instances of ungoverned PRO_{arb}. However, PRO_{arb} seems to exist in Italian with infinitives, as, for example, in (93) (also see Manzini (1979)):

(93)   Tu conosci il modo migliore per comportarsi a tavola.
        you know the way best for to-behave-self$_{arb}$ at table

But, by my analysis, the infinitive in (93) has moved into a position from which it governs PRO (notice the clitic in (93) following the infinitive and serving as a visible indication of that general movement). Therefore, the PRO_{arb} of (93) cannot be ungoverned, which suggests in turn that (92) should be taken to extend to all instances of PRO—in other words, that PRO_{arb} is really a subcase of controlled PRO, as proposed by Epstein (1984), who argues that many instances of PRO_{arb} should be taken to be controlled by a hidden dative (also see Higginbotham (1989, 324)). The most recalcitrant cases are those of (94) and (95):

(94)   ?John knows how to get oneself elected.

(95)   a. John knows the best way to get oneself elected.

        b. John knows the best way of getting oneself elected.

The fact that these seem best when embedded within a larger NP (as suggested by Petrovitz (1990)) might indicate that these instances of PRO_{arb} must, in the spirit of

Lebeaux (1984) and Authier (1989), be bound by some null operator sitting in a position provided by the NP.

Returning to the idea that controlled PRO is governed even in French (at LF), let us reconsider two kinds of examples:

(96)   *Jean ne sait pas si aller au cinéma.
       Jean NEG knows not if to-go to-the movies

(97)   Jean veut aller au cinéma.
       Jean wants to-go to-the movies

My idea has been that (96) is excluded because the lexical C^0 *si* governs PRO and induces a PRO theorem violation. Yet I am now proposing that in (97) PRO is governed by the infinitive at LF. There is no contradiction, since in (97) government will be of the internal type (that is, the governor is internal to the IP of which PRO is the subject), whereas in (96) it is of the external type (*si* is external to that IP), and in my analysis the (revised) PRO theorem holds for subject PRO only over the domain of external government configurations,

It is important, however, to ensure that LF movement of the infinitive does not have the undesirable consequence of making (96) legitimate, the point being that subsequent to such LF movement PRO in (96) will be governed by the infinitive and will no longer be governed by *si*. I conclude that a PRO theorem-type violation at S-structure, as in (96), cannot be neutralized at LF. Considering more closely the exact nature of the violation in (96), note that by virtue of being governed by *si*, PRO qua anaphor receives as governing category the matrix IP, which is perfectly reasonable—if (96) were grammatical, that is where we would expect the antecedent to be. The problem with (96) is really that PRO qua pronoun also receives the matrix IP as governing category,[81] yielding the familiar contradiction. If LF movement of the infinitive were able to neutralize such a violation, it would have to be by virtue of changing what counts as the governing category of PRO qua pronoun. Since the violation remains, I conclude that a governing category assigned by Principle B to a given pronominal element must be taken to stick to it.

Put more perspicuously, a given indexing must respect Principle B at all levels.[82] Thus, if PRO in (96) is coindexed with *Jean*, a violation will ensue since Principle B will not have been respected at S-structure. On the other hand, if I am correct in thinking that PRO cannot be assigned an antecedent without having a governing, category, then in (97) PRO has an antecedent only at LF. In other words, Principle A must be met at some level of representation, but does not need to be met at all levels. This asymmetry between Principle A and Principle B recalls the conclusion reached in Belletti and Rizzi (1988, 318).[83]

If we now ask why there should exist such an asymmetry, the following answer suggests itself: Binding principles are properly thought of as applying to a set of levels of representation associated with a given sentence. Principle A has intrinsically existential character (for a given anaphor, there must exist an antecedent within the appropriate syntactic domain). Interpreting this existential character consistently yields: For a given anaphor, there must exist some antecedent at some level (that is, somewhere in the set) within the appropriate syntactic domain. Principle B, on the other hand, has intrinsically universal character (a given pronoun must be free from all antecedents within the appropriate syntactic domain). Interpreting this consistently yields: A given pronoun must be free from all antecedents at all levels (that is, everywhere in the set) within the appropriate syntactic domain.

NOTES

This article is a revised and expanded version of Kayne (1990), which was first presented in the guise of comments at the MIT Workshop on Control held in April 1989. The phrase "Verb Movement" added to the title corresponds to a topic of central importance that has undergone a significant change in analysis from the earlier version to this one. For helpful comments on the 1990 version, I am indebted to Guglielmo Cinque. Carmen Dobrovie-Sorin, and Carlos Otero.

1. Also see Haegeman and Van Riemsdijk's (1986) discussion of Germanic (rightward) verb projection (perhaps always VP; see Kayne (1985, note 43)) raising.

2. An account in terms of headedness would not be compatible with my (1983b, sect. 5) claim that French subject clitics cliticize to the right of a preceding finite verb in the syntax. (A similar question arises with respect to Germanic subject pronouns that appear to cliticize to a complementizer; see, for example, Bayer (1983).)

My proposal that Romance object clitics never right-adjoin is very likely not compatible with Uriagereka's (1988) analysis of Galician articles as undergoing syntactic cliticization, nor with the particular way in which he pursues his important attempt to account for the relative order of accusative and dative clitics.

3. See Baltin (1982, 4). I shall hold strongly to this assumption as far as the languages of France and Italy are concerned. The extra finite verb-clitic possibilities in Portuguese and Galician might perhaps reflect adjunction to X^1, as suggested in Kayne (1988). Similarly, perhaps, for Romanian; see Dobrovie-Sorin (1990).

4. The existence in Old Italian and in certain North Italian dialects of preposition-clitic, as noted by Renzi (1989, 369), would then imply that at least some PPs could be embedded under a functional X^0, to which a clitic could adjoin, and past which P could move.

5. As in the previous paragraph, I suspect that a clitic may not be adjoined to a filled V position, either (as opposed to a filled, or empty (in the sense given later), functional head position).

6. My earlier (1990) proposal that V adjoins to IP fit in less straightforwardly.

7. Again, this is more straightforward than under my (1990) proposal of adjunction to IP.

8. Recall that Portuguese and Galician do allow in root contexts the order finite verb-clitic, suggesting either the existence of another I-type node limited to root contexts (a possibility explored in Uriagereka (1988)) or the adjunction of clitics to a root C (*root* here must be taken in a somewhat extended sense; see Uriagereka (1988)): also see footnote 3. Equally beyond the scope of this article is the potential category M as discussed by Rivero (1988).

9. The idea of an I node not obliged to merge with V is supported by an English construction discussed in chapter 10.

10. On the possibility of an abstract T in (English) infinitives, see Stowell (1982) and McCawley (1988, 216).

It is also possible that at least some infinitives have both abstract T and abstract AGR. If I in (7) were AGR, it would probably have not to be coindexed with PRO, thinking of the fact that inflected infinitives in Portuguese give the impression of not corresponding to true cases of control.

11. Pollock's approach was to take French AGR to be transparent to θ-marking even in infinitives.

12. And to my 1986 suggestion that he mentions, with the difference (among others) that that earlier idea, like both his formulation and Belletti's (1990), did not contain the proposal about infinitive adjunction to X'.

13. This prohibition could not be formulated under my (1990) approach in which the infinitive itself adjoined to TP. The prohibition in question might derive from the XP status of adverbs, combined with a restriction against adjoining XP to Y'; alternatively, the adjunction of XP to Y' might be possible, but it might yield a node nondistinct from YP, to which a Z^0 like an infinitive could not adjoin. For relevant discussion, see Rizzi and Roberts (1989).

14. Unlike Italian *non*, which obligatorily precedes both infinitives and finite verbs and which I take to be itself an X^0 element, as in chapter 4, sect. 4.2.3., rather than an adjoined adverb-like element. (On Piedmontese negation, see Zanuttini (1987; 1990; 1997).

15. Alternatively, *nen* could be in Spec of NegP, as Pollock (1989, 414) suggests for *pas*, but only if NegP is higher than TP, contrary to what he assumes.

16. Beyond the scope of this article is the question of how best to express the fact that clitic climbing (into a matrix sentence) is, in the case of finite matrix verbs (see Parry (1989)), marginal in Piedmontese as compared with Italian, though available to a greater degree than in French.

17. In using the word *movement* rather than the more explicit *adjunction*. I am leaving open the possibility that V-to-Infn might be substitution in the sense of Rizzi and Roberts (1989).

18. Where Adv is adjoined to Infn-P. Note that these intervening adverbs/quantifiers can be phrasal, as for example in the literary French (i) and (ii) (see de Kok (1985, 339, 346)), supporting the idea of adjunction to a maximal projection.

(i) n'en   presque rien   dire
     NEG of-it almost nothing to-say

(ii) en   fort   bien parler
     of-it strong well to-speak

The Romanian Cl Adv V construction differs in this respect, in that it does not allow Adv to be visibly phrasal, for reasons that are unclear: partially differing approaches to the Romanian construction can be found in Dobrovie-Sorin (1990). Motapanyane (1989), and Rivero (1988).

19. The contrast here between Occitan, etc. and colloquial French may be related to null subject considerations: see chapter 4. The possibility of (i)

(i) n'en   pas parler
    NEG of-it not to-speak

in literary French might indicate that Cl can move to an X^0 higher than T: see the previous text discussion concerning the order of auxiliary and *pas*. Such an X^0 might also be available to those varieties of Occitan that allow, like Catalan, the order infinitive-*pas*: compare also the dialect of Bergamo, whose *mìa* thus appears (Bernini (1987, 115)) to differ minimally from Piedmontese *nen*. Alternatively, it might be that languages can differ with respect to where they attach their (nonhead) negative morpheme.

20. All the Sardinian data discussed are from Michael Jones (personal communication): see, in general, Jones (1988; 1993).

21. Note also that these adverbs and quantifiers must follow negative *pas*.

22. From this perspective, French (18) is probably ambiguous between the finite counterpart of (17) and the finite counterpart of . . . *pouvoir tout faire* . . .

23. For example:

(i) J'ai   mal dû   raccrocher.
    I have badly must to-hang-up
    'I must have hung (the phone) up badly/wrong.'

24. Why auxiliary raising is limited to English, of the two, is unclear. Perhaps there is a link to the extra agreement morphology in English; see chapter 10.

25. At least some Scandinavian speakers actually accept . . . *att han inte inte har gjort det*. The acceptability of *You could have not done it* implies raising of nonfinite *have*; see Pollock (1989, 376) and Johnson (1988).

26. The fact that Italian generally lacks the . . . Modal . . . QP . . . Inf . . . construction (where QP is associated with a (nonheavy) infinitive) that Sardinian has is not yet accounted for.

On the other hand, Belletti (1990) has argued that Italian does have some (short) leftward quantifier movement (to a position to the right of the S-structure position of the verb); see the argument mentioned in Pollock (1989, footnote 7).

Judging from Ganzoni (1983) and Signorell et al. (1987), there are at least two varieties of Rhaeto-Romance that likewise (appear to) lack this construction. If so, that is notable, since they are like Sardinian in having clitic-infinitive order. It may be that they move the infinitive to T as Sardinian does, yet fail to have any long leftward quantifier movement at all, for reasons that remain to be elucidated.

Ganzoni (1983, 180) contains an example with a modal infinitive followed by clitic plus embedded infinitive, suggesting that the variety in question lacks Longobardi's (1980) double infinitive filter. If so, it suggests that his filter might come into play only in languages whose infinitives adjoin to T'.

27. If the text decision to have Cl adjoin in infinitival clauses to T rather than AGR is correct, then the null subject parameter would have to involve T in a way not envisaged in chapter 4. This is not implausible if Rizzi (1986a, 518) (see Rizzi (1982a, 130)) is correct in distinguishing a "formal licensing" aspect of the null subject phenomenon, and if formal licensing depends on some property of T.

The implications of my analysis of infinitive-clitic order for Rizzi's (1982a, 83ff.) Aux-to-Comp construction are as follows: It is possible to have . . . Aux_{inf} . . . Cl . . . NP . . . V_{PP} . . . , where the NP is the nominative lexical subject of the Aux. Thus, this NP cannot systematically be in standard subject position unless Cl is adjoined to C and Aux to C'. Alternatively, Aux could be adjoined to T' (or conceivably AGR') and Cl to T (or AGR) as in the text, with the NP lower in the structure.

The impossibility of having the lexical NP separate Aux from Cl in the above structure (that is. *. . . Aux . . . NP . . . Cl . . .) seems completely general in Romance when Cl follows V (and contrasts with the possibility of . . . Cl . . . NP . . . V_{fin} . . . in Galician; see Alvarez, Monteagudo, and Regueira (1986. 205), Uriagereka (1988)). It follows from Aux adjoining at the X^1-level, much as in the discussion of footnote 13.

28. Perhaps agreement with a postverbal indefinite NP somehow involves adjunction of V to X'. Occitan, which is like Sardinian in having clitics precede the infinitive, also seems to have less subject inversion than Italian (and less than Sardinian), despite being a null subject language in the core sense (see, for example, Doniol (1877, 40, 52)).

The fact that Sardinian (but not Occitan) gerunds precede their associated clitics, however, suggests that Sardinian does not systematically refuse V-adjunction to X'. Occitan appears to have some form of leftward verb movement in interrogatives and imperatives, as Sauzet (1989, note 11) suggests.

Consideration of Gascon is beyond the scope of this article.

29. Despite Sardinian's not requiring a trigger in the French manner. For the relevant French details, see Kayne (1972; 1980b, sect. 2).

30. See Grevisse (1964, sect. 477) and Remacle (1952, 228n, 265; 1956, 131). Also see Mattoso Camara (1972, 226) on Brazilian Portuguese and Signorell et al. (1987, 90) for a Rhaeto-Romance dialect.

31. However, the Val d'Aosta dialect of northwestern Italy described by Chenal (1986) has a robust use of past participle-clitic order (at least with a preceding auxiliary), yet is predominantly clitic-infinitive (although infinitive-clitic is not absent; see p. 358).

32. See Burzio (1986) on small clause relatives.

33. Whether or not there can be further movement to the C level (see Cinque (1990b, note 25)) will be left an open question (that recalls the second paragraph of footnote 27).

34. For some speakers of Italian, whether or not the auxiliary itself is tensed seems to play a role, in that they accept to some degree some sentences like (29) in which the auxiliary is untensed (infinitival or gerundial).

35. Chenal (1986, 222, 226) also contains examples similar to (33) but without past participle agreement. Furthermore, Piedmontese, which has . . . Aux V_{pp} Cl . . . (see Burzio (1986, 123)), never shows past participle agreement there (although it does in those environments in which the clitic can raise to the auxiliary). In such cases it might be, as I have suggested (Kayne (1990)), that Cl is adjoined to the participial AGR.

Alternatively, the absence of agreement might ultimately have a different interpretation (yet to be discovered). That would permit the claim that abstract participial AGR can never host a clitic. Extended to the similar adjectival AGR (both involve gender but not person) and combined with the idea that abstract T can be associated with past participles, but never with adjectives, this claim would yield the (correct, as far as I know) result that there could never be any . . . Adj-Cl . . . in Romance, since the clitic would have no functional head to adjoin to.

36. Except with a heavy infinitival VP. See footnote 26 and Belletti's (1990) suggestion that in comparable examples with *spesso* 'often' plus past participle only "heavy VP shift" is involved.

37. The ungrammaticality of (36) must then reflect the lack of long quantifier movement in Italian; recall footnote 26. Whether French (37) involves long movement as in (38) or short movement within the participial clause is now surprisingly difficult to ascertain. (36) improves with a heavy VP, as before.

38. Recall my earlier assumption that a trace cannot be a proper subpart of an X^0 constituent, following Baker (1985, 89; 1988, 73).

Note that the severe limitations holding of clitic splitting are, from Roberts's (1991, 212) perspective, unexpected.

39. Except perhaps in those languages, like Sardinian (see Jones (1988, 337; 1993), that have obligatory clitic climbing out of infinitival complements such as those under discussion. In that kind of language, the absence of split clitics could be seen as a subcase of the obligatoriness of clitic climbing in general.

40. The participial AGRP under T must either be defective (see Pollock (1989, 397)) or else be L-marked by T; recall the first paragraph of footnote 27.

41. In the manner of successive cyclicity; see chapter 4, sect. 4.2.5., going back to a proposal in a different context by Pica (1987).

The Sardinian counterpart of (41) cannot involve movement of Cl + Cl + T to C, since the Sardinian infinitive moves into T itself. Rather, Sardinian (41) must contain an infinitival complement that is a TP (and not a CP) that is L-marked by the matrix V, thereby permitting long movement of both clitics directly into the matrix (recall footnote 39). Alternatively, that infinitival complement could actually be a CP, if the TP just below it were not a barrier in the way it is in Italian (see chapter 4, sect. 4.2.6.)), so that in Sardinian (but not in Italian) both clitics could move directly into C on their way into the matrix, without landing in any lower I-type node.

42. The Romanian analytic future and conditional constructions look in part more like the auxiliary-participle construction discussed earlier than like the infinitival one (although there is neither a participial nor an-$r(e)$-like infinitival suffix on the embedded verb). Either there is no CP or Dobrovie-Sorin (1989; 1990) is correct in postulating movement of that (bare) V to C, with such movement licensed (from our perspective) either by the absence of suffix or by the special character of the Romanian auxiliary that she brings out.

43. See the references cited in chapter 4, note 34. It needs to be ascertained whether any of the Occitan languages fall into this class.

44. A language that allows . . . Cl Adv Inf . . . (see (13)) might then allow . . . Cl Adv Cl Inf . . . if Cl+T could fail to move. And in fact I have found two French speakers who accept a sentence of the form shown in (i), with clitics *y* and *en* separated by *plus*:

(i)   ?N'y plus en trouver serait surprenant.

    NEG there no-longer of-it to-find would-be surprising

Luigi Rizzi has pointed out to me an interesting prediction made by the text analysis, namely, that in a three-tiered structure, with both clitics complements of the most embedded verb, and the other two verbs of the type of the matrix verb in (46) (taking CP complements), it should not be possible to have . . . Cl_i V Cl_j V V t_i t_j . . . (order of the two traces irrelevant). This prediction has not yet been tested.

45. Compare perhaps Russian -*sja* and Scandinavian -*s*.

46. See Benincà (1989a). On Italian impersonal *si*, see Cinque (1988).

47. As opposed to the case of 3sg. verbs without *si*. The absence of verb-clitic order there might have to be attributed to V's having to pass through AGR despite AGR's not corresponding to an overt morpheme. In essence, a nonovert coindexed AGR would appear to pattern here with overt coindexed AGR (versus the nonovert noncoindexed AGR of (50)) with respect to V-AGR merger; this would conflict with chapter 10.

Alternatively, the solution might be that adjunction of V + T to AGR' is possible only when AGR is not coindexed with the NP in its spec position.

As for the position of *si* in (50), Belletti's (1990) proposal that (finite) AGR can be iterated might be relevant.

48. See Kayne (1972, note 17) and Emonds (1985, 286n). The construction *if he should . . . or not* is presumably to be thought of as a reduction, in some sense to be made precise, of *if he should . . . or if he should not*.

49. If L-marking is defined as in Chomsky (1986a, 70), then such a C^0 must be taken to θ-mark IP.

Concerning the status of IP as an inherent barrier, see chapter 4, sect. 4.2.6. and references cited there.

50. Over the years I have found one speaker who accepts (some sentences like) (64). Conceivably, he can allow *si* to occur in Spec of CP (contrary to the general case).

51. See (the text to) footnote 49. Another candidate for prepositional specifier is the *de* found in French partitives such as (i).

(i) Jean a   de la viande.

Jean has of the meat

Jean has some meat.'

and similarly for Italian *di*.

My present proposal that *de* is not a C^0 has something in common with Manzini's (1982) proposal that Italian *di* is adjoined to IP, which would have some of the same advantages as mine but not all.

Taking *de/di* to be in Spec of CP does not imply that their effect on extraction is identical to that of *wh*-phrases; see Frampton (1990). Cinque (1990a), and Rizzi (1990).

52. Note, however, that such a generalization is not forced by control considerations, since even if Italian *di* were a C^0, there would be no PRO theorem violation, just as there is none with the Italian counterpart to *if*; see below.

53. Left open are the questions of why *di* is not compatible with *che* in Italian and why (71) is ungrammatical in French.

54. If Italian *se* 'if' is a C^0, as I will argue below, then my proposal correctly accounts for the sharp contrast between (72) and (i), with the latter to be analyzed like (71). (This point was brought to my attention by Raffaella Zanuttini and Maria-Teresa Guasti.)

(i) ?Sto pensando a se partire.

I-am thinking to if to-leave

Why the example with *se* is marginal compared with (71) remains to be explained.

The contrast between (71) and (72) is repeated with certain prepositions that introduce adjuncts (for example, French *pour que tu partes* 'for that you leave' versus *pour (*de) partir*; similarly for *sans* 'without', *après* 'after'), suggesting that these are also in spec of CP. (The more nominal *afin* in order', *avant* 'before', and others will not be.) Similarly for certain Italian adjunct-introducing prepositions such as *per* 'for' and *senza* 'without'. These differ from *di* in that they, but not *di*, are compatible with the Aux-to-Comp construction mentioned in footnote 27. Perhaps that construction is licensed by case assignment to AGR, in the spirit of Raposo (1987b), with AGR in C^0 (see Rizzi (1990)) and *di* not an appropriate case assigner.

Dutch *om* appears to have the same status as French *de*, to judge by Bennis and Hoekstra's (1984, 51) data and partially similar analysis, and Dutch *zonder* 'without' and *na* 'after' appear to have the same status as *sans* and *après*. Why English does not allow the infinitive with these two is unclear (but consider the difference between English and Dutch/German with respect to ECM).

55. With a potential effect on the extraction facts Cinque discusses.

56. English does allow *John got up as if to leave*. This might involve a reduction of some sort from . . . as *if he were to leave*. There is in addition evidence, shown by the contrast between (i) and (ii), that *as if* is a constituent,

(i) . . . as if, in my opinion, to leave.

(ii) *. . . as, in my opinion, if to leave.

so that *if* here is arguably not a C^0 (essential, if this is really a control structure).

Similarly, in the French construction *bien que sachant* . . . 'although knowing . . .', *bien que* must be a constituent not equal to C^0 (see Kayne (1976, (text to) n. 42)). This is supported by (iii),

(iii)   *bien qu' ayant . . . et que sachant . . .
      although having and that knowing

in which the second *que*, being bare, must be a C^0 and hence induce a PRO theorem violation (if the verbs are finite, this kind of construction is fine).

Rigau (1984) notes that the Catalan equivalent of *si/if* creates a series of island effects not created by (the Catalan equivalent of) *que/that*. and she suggests that it be considered a modality operator. We can adopt her proposal in the following form: *si/if*, and so on, are necessarily accompanied by an abstract operator in Spec of CP. This will fit with the fact that no overt element occurs there, neither a *wh*-phrase nor (modulo the perhaps related marginality of the first paragraph of footnote 54) a preposition.

57. Together with the noniterability of CP. Note in this regard the occasional Germanic construction apparently containing three elements at the C-level: see Reinholtz (1989), Koster (1987, 207), and perhaps Klima (1964, note 5) on earlier English.

58. Skepticism about the null subject correlation had been expressed by Borer (1989, note 5) for a different reason.

59. See the example in Rigau (1984, 251) cited in chapter 4, sect. 4.3.2.

60. I am grateful for the Occitan data to Patrick Sauzet, and for the Sardinian data to Michael Jones.

61. This holds of the dialects of Sardinia other than those in the northern areas of Gallura and Sassari (see Jones (1988, 314) and Loi Corvetto (1982, 136)), which, like much of Gascon, show infinitive-clitic order. My analysis predicts that these infinitive-clitic languages should allow control with their equivalent of *if*; that is, they should differ minimally in this respect from their clitic-infinitive neighbors.

A complicating consideration is that some of these resemble Galician and European Portuguese in allowing both embedded clitic-infinitive and embedded infinitive-clitic order, depending on various factors. The prediction made with respect to such mixed languages is probably (since in all likelihood they have the type of leftward infinitive movement that will turn out to license control with *if* in Italian, Catalan, and Spanish) that they should allow it, too. According to Juan Uriagereka and Carlos Otero (personal communications), this is correct for Galician. In European Portuguese, control with *se* seems to be marginally acceptable, at least in contexts like (i):

(i)   Não sei se ir o não ir.
      NEG I-know if to-go or NEG to-go

(Brazilian Portuguese primarily has the order clitic-infinitive (see Parkinson (1988, 159), but note Renzi (1989, 365)); the few speakers I have asked do not accept control with *if*.)

62. The status of these subject clitics is not entirely clear. They are taken to be an instance of AGR by Brandi and Cordin (1989) and by Rizzi (1986b). They differ from AGR, however, in being obligatorily absent even from plural imperatives, much as French subject clitics are; one approach to French versus northern Italian subject clitics that distinguishes them less sharply than the AGR approach is given in Kayne (1983b).

63. Data from Luigi Burzio (personal communication), Nicoli (1983, 150), Paola Benincà (personal communication).

64. Judgment of Heidi Runggaldier, via Paola Benincà (personal communication).

65. And perhaps always; see footnote 61. Implicit, as usual, is the assumption (which should be checked to as great an extent as feasible) that the dozen or so Romance languages that I have information about (concerning control with *if*) are representative of the entire set. (A conservative estimate of the number of syntactically distinguishable Romance languages/

dialects would, I think, be in the hundreds; note the proportional implication for the number of syntactically distinguishable languages in the world (cf. chapter 1).

66. Presumably because I' there (all of whose segments dominate the infinitive) blocks c-command. There may well be an asymmetry here between functional and lexical categories (see Fukui (1989)).

67. *Se* asymmetrically c-commands the infinitive (see Chomsky (1981b, 134) and Rizzi (1990, 7)).

68. Alternatively, it could be that the notion "closer governor" is sufficient.

69. It is for this reason that it is advantageous to work with a set of closely related languages. much as in any experiment one tries to keep the number of variables as low as possible. In the future it should become possible to do the same with a set of (closely related) sets of closely related languages.

70. Based on work by Huang (1983).

71. This point was made very clearly by Battistella (1985) in his discussion of Chinese finite clauses, to which my proposal for Italian infinitives is quite close. He takes the position, as I have so far, that although some PROs are internally governed, in the sense at issue, many remain ungoverned. I will abandon this position later, when I propose that no PRO is ungoverned at all levels of representation.

72. Assuming that for every object position there is an associated subject position within the minimal complete functional complex to serve as potential antecedent. Otherwise, **John likes pictures (of) PRO* would incorrectly be permitted, as Hestvik (1990, 133) notes. Similarly, there must be no possibility of preposing V^1.

73. This was somewhat less straightforward under my (1990) approach involving infinitive adjunction to IP.

74. As extended to PRO in the way I have proposed; such an extension was not actually considered in *KL* (see p. 183 there), as far as I can tell.

75. It does not, however, provide an account of the contrast, within Italian, between *se* 'if' and *che* 'that'. Unlike *se*, *che* is normally incompatible with control, as in (i):

(i) Gianni vuole (*che) andare . . .
    Gianni wants (that) to-go

Perhaps the generalization is that *che* requires that its sister IP be tensed/finite (*che* does not occur with noncontrol infinitives either, even in Portuguese), for reasons that are unclear.

The *que* of (ii) and (iii) in Spanish is probably not the complementizer (C^0) *que* but rather an instance of *que* in spec of CP (like the *wh*-phrase *que*, in that respect), given the possibility of clitic climbing seen in (ii):

(ii) Lo tengo que hacer.
     it I-have QUE to-do

(iii) Hay que hacerlo.
      there-is QUE to-do it

(The impossibility of clitic climbing in (iii) is due to independent factors; see chapter 4, sect. 4.2.7.)

The *að* of Icelandic control infinitivals (see Sigurðson (1989) and references therein) might be in spec of CP or it might be, if Icelandic leftward infinitive movement were adjunction to I', a C^0. On the other hand, the *att* of Swedish control infinitivals must, since there is no infinitive movement there, be in spec of CP. This is compatible with Platzack (1986b), parallel to my discussion of French *de* in section 2.2.

76. More exactly, it assigns PRO qua anaphor a governing category that avoids a contradiction with that assigned to PRO qua pronoun. This point was also made by Battistella (1985).

77. As did Bouchard (1984) for certain PROs and, similarly, Koster (1987), both of whom take PRO to be able to be governed in a range of contexts completely different from those permitted in the text approach (which is much closer to that of *LGB*). As far as I can see, neither of their approaches (nor those of Bresnan (1982), Williams (1987), McCloskey and Sells (1988), Borer (1989), Huang (1989), or Hestvik (1990)) yields an account of the Italian-French contrast under study. (On the other hand, I have yet to clarify the degree to which similarities between antecedents of PRO and those of pro are significant.)

The text approach to control maintains the *LGB* account of **It seems (to me) to have understood* as a PRO theorem violation (since the governor *seems* is outside the infinitival IP). The grammaticality of the corresponding French and Italian sentences should be related to the grammaticality of the French and Italian equivalents of **I believe to have understood*, in terms of the ability of a certain class of verbs to take an opaque CP complement. For French and Italian 'seem', this must be in addition to the IP possibility suggested by the existence of subject raising.

One might wonder whether leftward adjunction of the infinitive to I' in Italian might not interfere with raising; it is perhaps worthy of note that raising with *seem* in Italian seems literary, and is completely absent (with infinitives (as opposed to small clauses); observation due to Luigi Burzio (personal communication)) in Piedmontese (similarly, it appears, in Paduan): I leave this question open.

Belletti (1990) has shown that in perception verb complements, as in (i).

(i)   Ho sentito i bambini piangere.
      I-have heard the children to-cry

infinitive movement takes place as elsewhere. Under my (1990) adjunction-to-IP approach, this would have forced me to deny that *i bambini* is in embedded subject position. Under the present adjunction-to-I' approach, this is not necessary (although I am led to claim that Case on *i bambini* must then come from within the embedded IP, as for English in Kayne (1981a, sect. 2.3.)). Infinitive adjunction to I' in the presence of a lexical subject seems definitely required for those speakers who accept (ii).

(ii)   ?Ho lasciato i bambini mangiare le mele.
       I-have let the children to-eat the apples

yet refuse the corresponding passive, again as in English (p. 35).

The question also arises whether the Binding Theory approach to PRO tells us anything directly about the difference between subject and object control. Manzini (1983b, 423) suggests that it should not, on the basis of cases where the choice between the two types of control is open. Although such cases are numerous, they are not typical (see the detailed study of Rooryck (1987)). It may be that obligatory object control involves a controller that is the subject of a small clause in the sense of Kayne (1981c, sect. 4.2) (also see Larson (1988)), with that small clause the governing category of PRO.

78. In French the S-structure infinitive does not govern PRO if only because it does not even m-command it, if my proposals in (9) and (14) are accurate. Sardinian is more interesting, given (83), if (15) is correct, since there the infinitive is in the head position whose maximal projection PRO is spec of, yet it must not govern PRO. Presumably head-to-spec government is possible only via agreement, if then; also see (the text to) footnote 66.

79. Thinking of Huang's (1982b) proposal that Chinese has *wh*-movernent at LF.

80. And similarly for English, although in English it might alternatively be *to* that at LF adjoins to I' and governs PRO.

If there is PRO in derived nominals (see Stowell (1989) for discussion), then there must be LF adjunction of N to NP, unless PRO is within N^{max} and a lexical category (see (text to) footnote 66) can govern its own subject PRO.

Recalling that the infinitive licensing PRO in Italian skips over the I whose single-bar projection it adjoins to, we might conjecture that a finite verb, which must move through each I position, could not so license PRO even in LF (for example, it may be that the trace of the verb adjoined to I' must be head-governed (by I) in Rizzi's (1990) sense (also see Frampton (1990)); or there might be a link to footnote 47). This would account for the lack of PRO with finite verbs in languages like English.

81. Rather than the embedded CP, which is not a complete functional complex in Chomsky's *KL* (p. 169) sense.

82. Note that in *John wants to be elected*, we can allow Principle B to apply to PRO at D-Structure since *John* will not be in the governing category then assigned.

83. This asymmetry, and my analysis in general, is predicated on the assumption that there exists a Principle B distinct from Principle A. It is not compatible with the attempt, pursued most recently and in most detailed fashion by Burzio (1989; 1992; 1996), to fully reduce Principle B to a kind of elsewhere case of Principle A. The at least partial independence of Principle B, in addition to being strongly supported by the way in which the (revised) PRO theorem accounts for the facts of control with *if* and the like is suggested by the phenomenon of nonintersecting reference (see Chomsky (1981a, 286)) and by assorted cases of noncomplementarity between anaphors and pronouns, as in Huang's (1983) original discussion of English and Chinese. The fact that Scandinavian (similarly, Russian) does show complementarity with possessives may be related to the fact that the anaphor is adjectival and/or to Hestvik's (1990; 1992) idea that Norwegian and English pronouns differ in X-bar status; his work also bears on the question, left open here, of the relation to all this of long-distance reflexives.

6

Italian Negative Infinitival Imperatives and Clitic Climbing

6.1. Infinitives in negative imperatives

Italian forms the negative 2sg. familiar imperative with the infinitive:

(1)   Non parlare! ('neg. to-speak')

This use of the infinitive is notable in several ways. First, there is the very fact that an infinitive is used in a root construction; second, the fact that it is limited to the negative imperative (i.e., the positive imperative corresponding to (1) would not have the infinitive). Third, and perhaps most striking, is the fact that clitics can precede the infinitive in this construction, although elsewhere in Italian, clitics invariably follow the infinitives they are associated with. An example with an ordinary infinitive would be:

(2)   Gianni ha deciso di farlo. ('G has decided *di* to-do it')

(3)   *Gianni ha deciso di lo fare.

With an infinitive in the negative imperative construction, the normal order is possible, but so is the other:

(4)   Non farlo! ('neg. to-do it')

(5)   Non lo fare!

It would not be terribly satisfying on general grounds to simply state that imperatives are an exceptional context as far as the relative order of infinitive and clitic is concerned. But there is in addition a more specific consideration which points to the same conclusion. The fact is that there appear to be no Romance languages with the reverse situation from Italian, that is, in which clitics normally precede infinitives but in which clitics exceptionally follow infinitives in negative imperatives. (Put another way, if a language has clitic-infinitive order in general and has infinitives in negative imperatives, then clitics will precede the infinitive there, too.[1])

Our proposal is that the unusual clitic-infinitive order that Italian displays in (5) is a hidden instance of clitic climbing, that is, that the clitic there is not adjoined to the infinitive at all[2] but is raised up to a phonetically unrealized modal licensed, at a first approximation, by the negation. This approach to (5) has the advantage of immediately accounting for the absence of 'reverse Italian', in that in a Romance language with clitic-infinitive order generally, the presence of a higher empty modal in imperatives could not possibly have an effect on the linear order of clitic and infinitive, whether or not the clitic moved up to the modal.

A second advantage is that postulating an empty modal makes it clear why there can be an infinitive in a root sentence here, the answer being that the infinitive is not actually the root predicate but is rather embedded under the empty modal.

A third consideration comes from a construction brought to our attention by Paola Benincà (p.c.):

(6)   Non lo prendere adesso e riportarmelo tra tre giorni!
      ('neg. it to-take now and to-return me it in three days')

The interpretation of this is as the prohibition of a conjunction of actions, that is, 'Don't [take it now and return it to me in three days]'.[3] That is, the negation *non* has scope over the entire conjunction. Since *non* (indirectly) licenses the infinitive in imperatives, it may not seem surprising that both verbs are in infinitival form, given that *non* has scope over both. On the other hand, *non* also indirectly licenses the order clitic-infinitive, in the sense that *non* licenses the empty modal, to which the clitic must raise if it is to precede the infinitive. In (6) the clitic precedes the first infinitive but not the second. Surprisingly, the second infinitive may not be preceded by its clitics:

(7)   *Non lo prendere adesso e me lo riportare tra . . . !

Our interpretation is as follows: If *non* somehow were able to license the preinfinitival clitic directly, the impossibility of (7) would be unexpected. The same would be true if *non* could license, in a conjoined structure, two empty modals, one in each conjunct. Let us propose, then, that in (6) there is only one empty modal, which is outside the conjunction (and hence to the left of the first infinitive), that is, the one empty modal takes the conjunction of infinitives as its complement. This is parallel to what we would propose for the overt modal counterpart (from our perspective) of (6):

(8)   (Non) lo devi prendere adesso e riportarmelo. . . .
      ('neg. it you-must to-take now and to-return me it')

We propose that (6) and (8) simply involve raising a clitic up to that one modal, whether empty or overt, out of the first conjunct. The apparent violation of the constraint against extraction from coordinate structures is probably akin to that found in English examples such as:

(9)   (?)John Smith, who I'm going to speak to tonight and then see his wife tomorrow, is an old friend of mine.
(?)John I AM willing to speak to tonight and then go home but Bill I'm not willing to speak to at all.

Although the question of the optimal theory of extraction will not be addressed here, these examples do make plausible the analysis suggested for (6), which involves treating the infinitival negative imperative as containing an empty modal counterpart of the overt one found in (8).

6.2.   Clitic climbing

Additional support for the postulation of an empty modal comes from another aspect of the phenomenon of clitic climbing seen in (6) and (8), and in particular from the fact that our presentation of (4) and (5) as being optional variants was an oversimplification. More specifically, it seems that (5), with the clitic preceding the infinitive, is more prevalent in the center and south of Italy than in the north, which prefers (4), with the clitic postinfinitival.[4] This geographical asymmetry recalls that found with standard instances of clitic climbing to an overt matrix verb, which are extremely robust in the center and the south, but not in the north.

This parallelism between clitic climbing to a matrix verb on the one hand and clitic moving to the left of the infinitive in the negative imperative construction on the other has been noted explicitly by Vizmuller-Zocco (1984), by Benincà (1989b, 15), and by Canepari (1986, 83). The existence of such parallelism is expected under the analysis just proposed, in which the negative imperative construction contains an empty modal and in which the pre-infinitival positioning of the clitic is in fact an instance of standard clitic climbing to the empty modal.[5]

6.3.   Licensing of the empty modal

The presence of the infinitive in Italian 2sg. negative imperatives, which we have claimed to depend on the presence of an empty modal, leads to the question of how exactly the empty modal is licensed. To say that it is allowed in negative, but not in positive, imperatives is not sufficiently precise, given the following facts:

(10)   Non parlare a nessuno! ('neg. to-speak to no one')

(11)   ?A nessuno non parlare!

(12)   *A nessuno parlare!

(13)   A nessuno parlo. ('to no one I-speak')

Preposing a negative phrase such as *a nessuno* in an infinitival imperative yields a reasonably acceptable result if the *non* remains but a sharply ungrammatical result if the *non* fails to appear, as in (12). This is the opposite of the state of affairs that holds in ordinary finite sentences, where a preposed negative phrase prefers to have *non* not appear, as in (13). We take this to indicate that the empty modal in this construction is licensed in Italian specifically by the morpheme *non*, rather than by negation in some more general sense.

One might be tempted to say for Romance in general that the licenser must be the X^0 negative element that is consistently preverbal,[6] but that would not be consistent with the facts of the Surmiran variety of Romantsch as described by Signorell et al. (1987). In Surmiran there is a negative morpheme *betg* that acts like French *pas* (rather than like French *ne*) in occurring to the right of finite verbs. Yet *betg* is compatible with the 2sg. infinitival imperative:[7]

(14) Betg am purtar chella roba! ('not me to-bring that stuff')

Nor does the requirement hold that the licensing negative element be to the left of the empty modal (and the infinitive), to judge by Bjerrome's (1957, 71n) citation of (15) and Olszyna-Marzys's (1964, 53) of (16):

(15) U fire pá! ('it to-do not' (vowel length omitted))

(16) Dìre pa a mè chen! ('to-say not to me that')

These last two examples of infinitival imperatives are notable in a second way, insofar as the dialects in question appear to have the order *pa*-infinitive in non-imperative contexts.[8] This suggests that (15) and (16) must involve a raising of the infinitive available only in negative imperative contexts. Under the analysis we have been developing, there is a natural proposal: In negative imperatives, the infinitive in these dialects raises up into the base position of the empty (finite) modal and then moves further left, as a finite verb would, across the matrix *pa*.[9]

Taken together, (10)–(16) show that the empty modal can be licensed either by an overt negative X^0 (*non*, in Italian) that projects NegP[10] or by the *betg*, *pa* type of negative morpheme, which, if Pollock (1989, 414) is correct, is a specifier of Neg^0. On the other hand, the very fact that both types of negative (and only those) can license the empty modal in question suggests that Pollock's (1989, 402) earlier idea that French *pas* could count as a head might be on the right track.[11] In (12), there is no element corresponding to either *non* or to *pas*,[12] so the empty modal is not properly licensed.

6.4. Overt modals in negative imperatives

The postulation of an empty modal in negative infinitival imperatives in certain languages is supported by the fact that there are many languages/dialects in northern, especially northeastern, Italy, that have a negative infinitival imperative construction with an overt modal (we have been using the term loosely—'auxiliary verb' would be more neutral) that seems to be licensed in much the same way that its empty counterpart is.

For example, in Paduan,[13] in the 2sg.:

(17)   No sta parlare! ('neg. aux. to-speak')

(18)   *Sta parlare!

In the negative imperative the infinitive is preceded by a form of *stare*,[14] one of the verbs corresponding to *be*. In the positive imperative, this construction is impossible, as seen in (18).

(19)   No sta parlarghe a nissuni! ('. . . to-him to no one')

(20)   A nissuni no sta parlarghe!

(21)   *A nissuni sta parlarghe!

These three examples contain an irrelevant doubled dative clitic *ghe*. Apart from that, they are essentially identical to (10)–(12). In the absence of *no*, the X^0 negative, the construction is impossible, even in the presence of a preposed negative phrase. (In a declarative with a preposed negative phrase, the dropping of *no*, while marginal, is clearly less bad than in (21).)

Thus, the overt *sta*, like the empty modal postulated earlier, must be licensed in Paduan by an overt *no* = X^0. Given the discussion of (14)–(16), we might expect there to be languages in which an overt modal/auxiliary like *sta* is licensed by the equivalent of *pas*. This seems in fact to be the case in the Piedmontese/Ligurian dialect of Cairo Montenotte studied by Parry (1984, 276), where *nent* is like *pas* in that it follows the finite verb:[15]

(22)   Sta nent a ciangi! ('*sta* not to to-cry')

Furthermore, returning to Paduan, there is an interesting fact concerning coordination:

(23)   No sta prenderlo uncò e (*sta) riportarmelo doman!
          ('neg. *sta* to-take it today and (*sta*) to-return me it tomorrow')

The negation *no* licenses one *sta* but cannot license two. This correlates well with our earlier claim that in (6) there is one empty modal, not two. (*Sta* here will therefore have as its complement a conjunction of infinitive phrases.) As for the question of why the negative element cannot license two modals/auxiliaries (whether overt or empty), it may be that the licensing in question here is mediated by head government in Rizzi's (1990) sense and that head government by *no(n)* of a second such modal/auxiliary would be precluded by the presence of the conjunction, which induces a minimality barrier.[16]

Our hypothesis that the Italian infinitival negative imperative involves an empty modal/auxiliary recalls to a certain extent Napoli's (1976, 320) and Delfitto's (1990, 89) proposals in favor of a deleted or abstract modal in Italian Wh infinitival constructions, even in the absence of negation (cf. Ambar's (1989) proposal of an abstract modal operator for certain root infinitives in Portuguese). Those proposals are not necessarily incompatible with ours, but whatever abstract element might be present in Italian Wh infinitival constructions must not have exactly the same status as that present in negative infinitival imperatives, given the absence in the former of pre-infinitival clitics. In other words, there is a clear contrast in general between the following:[17]

(24)   Non lo dire a nessuno! ('neg. it to-say to no one')

(25)   *Non so a chi lo dire. ('neg. I-know to who it to-say')

Various Northern Italian dialects that have the negative imperative construction with *sta* show or can show an *a* preceding the infinitive; examples from the Ventimiglia dialect given by Azaretti (1977, 208) are:[18]

(26)   Nu sta a mangià! ('neg. *sta* to to-eat')

(27)   Nu sté a vegnì! ('neg. *sta*$_{2pl.}$ to to-come')

If we are correct in analyzing the Italian negative 2sg. infinitival imperative as containing an empty counterpart to *sta*, the question arises as to why there can be no *a* in Italian:

(28)   *Non a mangiare!

A possible answer is that in the case of the empty modal, as in Italian, it is necessary for the infinitive to incorporate to it at LF and that such incorporation would be blocked by the presence of an intervening preposition. This abstract incorporation would be supported by the existence of an overt counterpart, which we have in fact already seen in (15) and (16).[19]

As seen in (27), the *sta* construction can have an agreeing form of *sta* for 2pl. (similarly for 1pl.). In the Italian construction with infinitive and empty modal, there can be no visible agreement, and furthermore, the interpretation cannot be 2pl. (or 1pl.). This can plausibly be attributed to the absence of any agreement morphology compatible with Italian infinitives[20] and to the impossiblity for an agreement morpheme to be suffixed to an empty auxiliary verb/modal. We might expect, though, that some Romance language would be able to combine an agreement suffix with an infinitive in a negative imperative. This possibility in fact exists in the Vallader variety of Romantsch,[21] as pointed out by Haiman (1988, 361) (cf. Ganzoni (1983a, 63, 90)), as in this example:

(29)   Nu'm scrivarai! ('neg. to-me to-write+AGR$_{2pl.}$')

Since this language does not appear to otherwise have agreeing infinitives, it is plausible to take the infinitive here to have raised up to the suffixal AGR position of the matrix via the modal position (cf. the discussion of (28)).

6.5. Conclusion

Italian negative 2sg. infinitival imperatives contain an empty modal/auxiliary. This construction, which is found in some dialects, too, requires the empty modal/aux to be licensed by a negative morpheme either of the *non* (Neg^0) type or of the *pas* type. A clitic originating in the infinitival clause may raise up to the empty modal/aux, yielding the linear order clitic-infinitive.[22] In addition, the infinitive itself may incorporate to the modal/aux position. In certain other dialects there is an overt aux element, *sta*, which corresponds very closely in syntactic properties to the empty element postulated for Italian.

NOTES

It is a great pleasure to dedicate this article to Nicolas Ruwet, who has taught me a great deal and whose friendship and support have been invaluable. For helpful comments on an earlier version of this article, I am grateful to Guglielmo Cinque and Raffaella Zanuttini.

1. As in, for example, Surmiran (Signorell et al. (1987, 111)); Vallader (Ganzoni (1983a, 63, 90)); the dialect of Bagnes (Bjerrome (1957, 71n)); and at least two of the dialects studied by Olszyna-Marzys (1964, 53, 82).

2. In particular, (5) is not comparable to French clitic + infinitive structures, as shown by the fact that adverbs and quantifiers in (5) must follow the infinitive as in Italian in general and may not precede it in the French fashion (e.g. *Non fare niente!* ('neg. to-do nothing'), **Non niente fare!*).

3. A similar interpretation appears to be possible for *non* followed by a conjunction of finite verbs: *Non lo prendo adesso e te lo riporto tra tre giorni* ('neg. it I-take now and to-you it I-return in three days'). This probably supports the possible generation of Italian *non* higher up than either Tense or AGR, as opposed to the cliticization approach of Belletti (1990, chap. 1), based on a proposal made for French by Pollock (1989, 414).

4. Berretta (1985, 211) notes that, in her corpus drawn from 23 educated Northern speakers, all the examples of negative imperatives had the clitic postverbal.

5. Luigi Rizzi (p.c.) notes that Marco Rizzi, in the course of acquiring Italian, passed through a stage in which he produced imperatives like (*)*Non lo farlo!*. From the text perspective, these are exactly like the widely attested instances of clitic reduplication in standard clitic climbing contexts, such as (*)*Lo voglio farlo* ('it I-want to-do it'). See chapter 4, note 37.

This reduplication phenomenon cries out for study, including those cases in which a matrix verb (even empty) does not seem to be involved, such as *Fó ló purtaló* ('*it-is-necessary it to-bring it*') from Ratel (1958, 32) (unless the first *ló* is in the matrix) or *No era tant facile de s'en catasenen una* ('neg. was so easy for/to self of-them to-buy self of-them one') from Andrews (1875, 50) (here the preposition may be crucial).

From the text perspective, the ungrammaticality of **Non lo darmi!* ('neg. it to-give to-me') and so on is parallel to that of **Non lo vuole darmi* ('neg. it he-wants to-give to-me').

On the status of such clitic splitting (possible in some Romance languages), see chapter 4, sect. 4.2.6, and chapter 5.

6. For the proposal that Romance preverbal negative morphemes are heads in the sense of X^0 theory, see chapter 4, sect. 4.2.2.

7. See Signorell et al. (1987, 111). See also Bernini (1987, 115), Bellosi and Quondamatteo (1979, 238) and Pelliciardi (1977, 174) for their respective dialects.

Cinque (1976) has *Mica prestargli soldi!* ('*mica* to-lend him money'), although *mica*, which normally follows finite verbs (apart from topicalization), is probably not comparable to *ne* or to *pas*. Note, too, the ungrammaticality of **Mica gli prestare soldi!*, which suggests that the initial example is either elliptical, as suggested to us by Paola Benincà (p.c.), and/or an instance of the impersonal infinitival imperative, such as *Non sporgersi dal finestrino!* ('neg. to-lean self from-the window'), **Non si sporgere dal . . .* , which also exists in French (unlike the 2sg. infinitival imperative) and is not as systematically tied to negation. See Rohlfs (1969, 87). For Luigi Burzio (p.c.), (12) is marginally possible as an impersonal.

8. See Bjerrome (1957, 140) and Olszyna-Marzys (1964, 80).

9. See (22).

10. We leave open the question of how best to express the difference between Italian on the one hand and Catalan, Spanish, Portuguese on the other, which lack the 2sg. infinitival imperative (they use the subjunctive) despite having a negative element that looks very much like Italian *non*.

11. With implications that go beyond the scope of this article.

12. As in note 10, we leave open the question of how best to express the fact that neither French nor Occitan *pas* licenses an empty modal. (Occitan negative 2sg. imperatives use the subjunctive or the indicative form; see Camproux (1958, 95).)

13. We are grateful to Paola Benincà for judgments and discussion.

14. Which looks specific to imperatives, in which case one would, from Zanuttini's (1996) perspective, be led to say that in this construction *sta* expresses Tense lexically. See Hornstein's (1990) idea that infinitives must undergo a sequence of tense rule dependent on the presence of a higher clause Tense.

15. We have simplified Parry's more phonetically accurate transcription to facilitate printing.

16. Alternatively to the text suggestion, one might, in the framework of Chomsky (1986a), think in terms of LF incorporation (cf. Baker (1988)) of the modal to the negation and antecedent government. In the case of (22), such incorporation would involve at least one extra step.

On government from outside being limited to the first conjunct, see also McCloskey (1986).

For a proposal in favor of an empty modal (not dependent on negation, however) in English, see Roberts (1985).

17. However, at least one speaker marginally accepts *?Ho capito che cosa gli dire* ('I-have understood what thing to-him to-say'). This recalls the fact that Bellosi and Quondamatteo (1979, 238) give clitic-infinitive (at least with reflexive clitics) as exceptionally possible in Romagnolo when the infinitive is preceded by *in do* ('where').

18. Who notes the similarity between the *sta* construction and the Latin *noli(te) cantare*, with what looks like incorporation of the modal ('want') into the negation; see note 16.

19. Conceivably, the infinitive might incorporate to the abstract modal before LF even in Italian, at least in some cases. Pre-LF incorporation would probably be predicted by Pesetsky's (1989) 'Earliness Principle'. Relevant is the status of sentences like **Non lo più fare!* ('neg. it no-more to-do'), which for some speakers are not as bad as expected. In coordinate structures like (6), incorporation would presumably affect only the first infinitive.

20. The fact that a 2sg. interpretation is possible is related to the fact that it is possible in simple positive imperatives despite their having no agreement morpheme either.

21. Entirely missing, on the other hand, is the possibility of combining to the same effect an infinitive and a subject clitic. This is related to the fact that subject clitics never occur with infinitives, gerunds, or participles in general. Nor do they (with the possible exception of an impersonal-looking subject clitic in Vallader and Puter (cf. Ganzoni (1983a, 89; 1983b, 90)) in the 1pl.; also, perhaps, Parry (1984, 276)) occur with noninfinitival imperatives. In this latter respect they differ sharply (in the plural) from agreement suffixes; this supports the idea that subject clitics, even in the North Italian dialects, originate in an A-position, as in Kayne (1983b, sect. 8) and Poletto (1990b) (vs. Brandi and Cordin (1989) and Rizzi (1986b)).

22. Our claim that the clitic-infinitive order possible in Italian negative imperatives is a result of the raising of the clitic up to a matrix empty modal/aux is neutral as to whether the clitic moves to the left or to the right of that modal/aux, a question beyond the scope of this article.

7

Toward a Modular Theory of Auxiliary Selection

The term 'auxiliary selection' is generally used to refer to a phenomenon found in a number of Romance and Germanic languages, in which the auxiliary in the nonpassive 'auxiliary + past participle' construction is not invariably *have*, as it is in English, but either *have* or *be*, depending on various factors. The term can also be thought of as encompassing the question of how best to distinguish languages like English and Spanish, with systematic *have*, from languages like French and Italian, which have either *have* or *be*.

In this essay, I will address both the language-internal auxiliary selection question and the cross-linguistic one and will attempt to integrate into the theory some of the Romance languages that have systematic *be* or else have a *have/be* alternation that looks quite different from the type familiar from French and Italian.

I will start from the assumption that we should expect the optimal theory of auxiliary selection to be highly modular, in a sense that goes back through much recent work to Chomsky's (1970) decompositional approach to the passive construction. From this perspective, the type of auxiliary selection rule proposed for Italian in Perlmutter (1983, 160; 1989, 82) or Burzio (1986, 55)[1] is akin to the rich and specific transformations of the sixties (and early seventies, as in Kayne (1975)).

The particular theory of auxiliary selection that I will propose here draws some of its inspiration from Benveniste (1966, sect. 15) and in particular from his idea that (the evolution of) auxiliary *have* and main verb (i.e., 'possessive') *have* should be thought of in parallel fashion. It is easy to see that an approach that attributes significance to the similarity between the two uses of *have* is less likely to be led to propose a rule specific to the 'auxiliary + past participle' construction, or even any property of *have* itself that makes specific reference to past participles. The analysis to be developed will contain no complex property of *have*, nor any auxiliary selection rule.[2]

If a proper understanding of auxiliary *have* depends on a proper understanding of main verb *have*, then it is essential to have a clear idea of the syntax of possessive constructions. Here, I shall take over the essentials of Szabolcsi's (1981; 1983) analysis of Hungarian possessive constructions, combining it with Freeze's (1992)[3] idea that *have* should be analyzed as an instance of *be* to which an abstract preposition has been incorporated. This will yield an analysis of possessive *have* that I will generalize to auxiliary *have*, in the spirit of Benveniste's diachronic proposal.

7.1. Possessive constructions

7.1.1. Hungarian

Szabolcsi (1981; 1983) argues that the Hungarian possessive construction (whose English counterpart would be *John has a sister*, etc.) contains a copula *van* plus a single DP itself containing a possessor DP whose D-structure position is to the right of and hierarchically below the D^0: . . . *van* [$_{DP}$ Spec D^0 [DP_{poss} . . .]]. If the larger DP is definite, then the possessor DP can remain in situ, appearing with nominative case, although it may also move up to the Spec position, then appearing with dative case. If it moves into the Spec position, it has the option of further movement out of the larger DP entirely, with the dative case being maintained. Evidence that the dative possessor in Spec originates in the lower DP_{poss} position comes from the fact that the dative possessor necessarily cooccurs with a postnominal AGR morpheme identical to the one that arguably licenses, or contributes to licensing, the nominative possessor.

If the larger DP is indefinite, then the possessor DP must raise up to Spec and proceed to move out of the larger DP entirely. Again, the possessor ends up with dative case (and the AGR morpheme appears): . . . $DP_{poss/dat/i}$ *van* [$_{DP}$ [e]$_i$ D^0 [[e]$_i$. . . .

Hungarian possessive sentences corresponding to *John has a sister* show a sharp definiteness effect, so in such sentences long movement of the possessor DP will always take place. Szabolcsi's claim that Hungarian possessive sentences contain at D-structure a copula plus a single argument can become intuitively clear to an English speaker if the Hungarian sentences are thought of as parallel to the almost acceptable English *There is (exists) a sister of John's*.

7.1.2. English

I would now like to claim that English possessive sentences such as *John has a sister* should be analyzed as substantially parallel to their Hungarian counterparts. This means that the D-structure should have a copula, to be noted 'BE', with a single DP complement: . . . BE [$_{DP}$ Spec D^0 [DP_{poss} . . .]], inside which is the possessor. I take English *'s* to be akin to AGR^0 (cf. Chomsky and Lasnik (1993) and references cited there), which is itself followed by NP (or QP, as in *John's three/many books*; cf. Giusti (1992)). Thus, a possessive sentence in English will have the fuller D-structure:

(1)   . . . BE [$_{DP}$ Spec D^0 [DP_{poss} [AGR^0 QP/NP]]]

I take the question of whether or not the DP_{poss} can remain in situ to be one of case. In both Hungarian and English, the possessive AGR^0 is not sufficient to license a DP in its Spec. In addition, a definite D^0 must be present.[4] Furthermore, for reasons that are not clear, this definite D^0 must, in English, always be phonetically unrealized: *John's sister* vs. **the John's sister*. (In Hungarian, the definite D^0 licensing the possessive DP can sometimes be overt.[5])

When D^0 is indefinite in Hungarian, DP_{poss} must raise to Spec, and then out of the DP entirely. In Spec, it picks up dative case, which it keeps under movement. English has from this perspective a notably different strategy for 'saving' the possessor DP when D^0 is indefinite. Namely, English moves QP/NP to Spec and inserts an overt preposition under D^0 to Case-license DP_{poss}:

(2) three sisters of John's / a sister of John's

The indefinite article *a* here must be of category Q, and not of category D, much as in Perlmutter (1970).[6] Assume, on the other hand, that *the* is necessarily of category D^0. Then the ungrammaticality of the following is straightforwardly accounted for:

(3) **the sister of John's

In effect, *the* and *of* would be competing for the same position.[7]

This analysis claims that *John's* in *a sister of John's* is not a constituent. Such nonconstituency is supported by the contrast between these two sentences:

(4) ??What woman were you talking to a friend of's?

(5) **What woman's were you talking to a friend of?

That *'s* is an instance of AGR may also be supported by the following: Assume that *'s* is not only AGR but actually substantially the same as the morpheme *-s* found on verbs and that, like the latter, it requires a singular antecedent.[8] Then its incompatibility with a plural possessor would become understandable:[9]

(6) **those kids's mother; *my sisters's common trait

The analysis proposed earlier of (2) has *of* playing a case-licensing role across a maximal projection (AGRP). In that respect, it resembles the standard account of *for there to be a solution*, etc., in which *for* case-licenses DP across a maximal projection. In earlier work (Kayne (1981e, Appendix 1)), I noted that English is unusual among the Germanic languages in having this *for* construction. To this can now be related the fact that the construction in (2) also seems to be limited to English.

If mainland Scandinavian lacks these two constructions and yet has pseudopassives to varying extents, the particular proposal should now be as follows: Pseudopassives depend on prepositions being able to withhold oblique case; this distinguishes English and mainland Scandinavian from Icelandic and Romance. Case-licensing by *for* and *of* across a maximal projection requires that (these) prepositions go a step further toward behaving like verbs and that they actually be able to license or play a role in licensing objective case;[10] this is possible only in English, of the languages under discussion.

7.1.3   Possessive *have*

If it is correct that English and Hungarian are substantially similar as far as the underlying structure of DPs containing possessives is concerned, the question arises as to whether English makes use of the specific movement-to-Spec strategy found in Hungarian, where the possessor DP moves to Spec and ends up with dative case. It is not surprising, given the lack of any dative case morphology in English, that English doesn't display any straightforward evidence of the same strategy being used. I will take the position, however, that English (and many other languages) have the property that they do allow recourse to the Hungarian movement-of-possessor-to-Spec strategy, but only in a more covert form.

Let us begin by asking how we can best state the fact that Hungarian, but not English, allows the possessor to appear in Spec as a dative. I suggest that it be thought of as a property of D^0, namely that Hungarian D^0 is capable of licensing oblique case in its Spec, but English D^0 never is.[11] This D^0 in Hungarian is sometimes overt, but when indefinite is, according to Szabolcsi's analysis, invariably nonovert. I would like to propose now that English has a nonovert D^0 that, while lacking the dative-licensing capability of its Hungarian counterpart, yet has something in common with it. Thinking of Chomsky's (1986a) notion of Spec-head agreement, of Szabolcsi's idea that (possessive) DP's are similar to CP's, and of my own earlier (Kayne (1981e)) proposal that English has an empty prepositional complementizer, I would like to adopt the idea that English has a nonovert prepositional (oblique) D^0 in possessive constructions, through whose Spec the possessor DP moves, much as in Hungarian.

More specifically, I take English to allow the DP_{poss} in (1) to move to Spec of this empty prepositional D^0, which will henceforth be represented as D/P_e.[12] In English, no case is assigned to the contents of this Spec, unlike Hungarian. Case-licensing of the possessor DP is achieved by the movement of that DP to a higher case-licensed position.

Consider again the structure at issue:

(7)   ... BE $[_{DP}$ Spec D/P_e^0 $[DP_{poss}$ $[AGR^0$ QP/NP$]]]$

Movement of DP_{poss} to Spec yields:

(8)   ... BE $[_{DP}$ $DP_{poss/i}$ D/P_e^0 $[[e_i]$ $[AGR^0$ QP/NP$]]]$

Movement of the possessor DP to Spec of the copula yields:

(9) $DP_{poss/i}$ BE $[_{DP}$ $[e_i]$ D/P_e^0 $[[e_i]$ $[AGR^0$ QP/NP$]]]$

If nothing further were said, this would incorrectly derive **John is a sister* instead of the desired *John has a sister*. There is reason to believe, fortunately, that (9) is not well formed as it stands. The reason is that it is plausible to take the Spec of D/P_e to be an A-bar position, following Szabolcsi's idea that this DP is significantly similar to CP. But if Spec of D/P_e is an A-bar position, then movement from it into Spec of

BE, an A-position, is illicit, that is, is an 'improper movement' violation. Let me suggest, then, that (9) is saved by the incorporation of D/P_e to BE, the idea being that, in the spirit of Baker's (1988) Government Transparency Corollary, the Spec of D/P_e becomes, as a result of incorporation, a derived Spec of D/P_e + BE and hence counts as an A-position:[13]

(10) $DP_{poss/i} \, D/P_{e/j}$ + BE $[_{DP} \, [e_i] \, [_{D/P} \, e \,]_j \, [[e_i] \ldots$

In essential agreement with Freeze (1992), I now take D/P_e + BE to be spelled out as HAVE (although I have diverged from his proposal as far as the exact source of P_e is concerned):[14]

(11)   John$_i$ has $[_{DP} \, [e_i] \, D/P^0 \, [[e_i] \, [AGR^0 \, 3 \, sisters]]]$

7.2.   Auxiliary + past participle

7.2.1.   English auxiliary *have*

The analysis proposed for possessive *have* can and should be generalized to auxiliary *have*. This can be accomplished by taking the BE-DP structure of (7) and carrying it over to the auxiliary + past participle construction. More precisely, what should be carried over is the initial subpart of the possessive structure, namely:

(12) $\ldots$ BE $[_{DP}$ Spec $D/P^0 \ldots$

The remaining part of (7), containing the possessor DP and the possessed QP/NP, should be replaced by a substructure appropriate for participles:

(13) $\ldots [_{VP} \, DP_{subj} \, [V \, DP_{obj}]]$

Example (13) incorporates the 'subject-within-VP' hypothesis,[15] Combining (12) and (13) yields:

(14) $\ldots$ BE $[_{DP}$ Spec $D/P^0 \ldots [_{VP} \, DP_{subj} \, [V \, DP_{obj}]]$

Example (14) can be thought of as representing a particular kind of nominalization, that is, a verbal (participial) structure embedded in a DP that is akin to a CP.

The basic idea will then be to claim that DP_{subj} raises to Spec of the larger DP, which as before is an A-bar position. Thus, further movement to Spec,BE would be barred by 'improper movement' unless Spec,DP can be assimilated to an A-position as a result of the incorporation of D/P^0 to BE. The result of moving DP_{subj} to Spec in (14) will be:

(15) $\ldots$ BE $[_{DP} \, DP_{subj/i} \, D/P^0 \ldots [_{VP} \, [e]_i \ldots$

The result of incorporation, plus further movement of DP_{subj}, is:

(16) $DP_{subj/i}$ D/P_e+BE $[_{DP}$ [e]$_i$ D/P^0 ... $[_{VP}$ [e]$_i$ V DP]

As before, D/P_e + BE is spelled out as HAVE, yielding, with V = *break* and DP_{obj} = *the window*:

(17)   John has broken the window.

In this way, then, auxiliary *have* is seen to be essentially the same as possessive *have*. More precisely, the two are the same in the sense that both correspond to D/P_e + BE.[16] (They differ, of course, in that *have* as an auxiliary has a DP complement containing a participial substructure, whereas possessive *have* has a DP complement containing a QP/NP substructure.)

From this perspective, the distribution of auxiliary *have* becomes partly a question of what kind of verbal structures can be embedded in a DP sister of BE and partly a question of what DP can move into the Spec of the larger DP, and when. One construction that normally never takes auxiliary *have* is the passive:[17]

(18)   John was/*had arrested by the police.

This might be related to the absence of *have* with adjectives:

(19)   John was/*had unhappy.

In both, the complement of *have* = D/P_e + BE would have no Tense interpretation, that is, neither an adjective nor a passive participle makes a Tense contribution/ is associated with T^0. It might then be that the kind of DP embedding/nominalization at issue requires Tense (cf. section 3.7).[18]

The idea that there is an indirect link between (17) and the Hungarian oblique possessive construction is itself indirectly supported by the facts of Classical Armenian discussed in a parallel diachronic context by Benveniste (1966, sect. 15). In that language, the subject of a transitive past participle appears as an oblique dative/ genitive (and the object as accusative). I take Benveniste to be correct in arguing that the construction at issue is not a passive. Therefore, there is a need for overt dativization/genitivization even in the context of a past participle, in my terms for a DP structure (perhaps accompanied in classical Armenian by a phonetically unrealized auxiliary) with a dativized Spec (licensed by D/P^0) into which the DP_{subj} of the participial VP can move.

7.2.2.   Unaccusatives with *have*

English *have* appears with unaccusative past participles as well as with transitive ones:

(20)   The window has broken.

I take the structure of such sentences to be essentially the same as that of the transitives, with the single difference that the VP contains one less argument:

(21) $DP_{subj/i}$ D/P_e + BE $[_{DP}$ $[e]_i$ D/P^0 ... $[_{VP}$ V $[e]_i]$

Spanish looks essentially like English with respect to auxiliary selection. Both transitives and unaccusatives take *have* (=*haber*) and not *be*. However, Spanish past participles differ from English ones in that they have a more complex morphology. The participial V is followed by a vowel (-*o* in the unmarked case, cf. Harris (1991)), which in turn can be (in passives) followed by a plural morpheme -*s*. In addition to showing number agreement, passive participles also show gender agreement, as reflected in the form of the vowel.

For the purposes of this essay, I will treat this vowel (called 'word marker' by Harris) and the plural morpheme as if they constituted a single AGR. Although they may well correspond to two distinct syntactic projections (cf. Picallo (1991); Bernstein (1991)), it will be sufficient for what follows if we agree that under no circumstances could those two projections license two distinct Cases.

I had suggested in earlier work that the participial agreement morphology corresponds to an AGR node.[19] Chomsky (1991, sect. 5) incorporates this idea into a more general claim about sentence structure to the effect that sentences will normally have, in addition to the familiar subject AGR_S, another AGR_O corresponding to object agreement. This will be true even in the absence of any overt morphology.

Let us, then, take the Romance participial agreement morphology to correspond to Chomsky's AGR_O. The fact that Spanish unaccusative sentences with auxiliary + past participle show no participial agreement:

(22)   María ha llegado/*a. ('M has arrived')

indicates that the DP *María* in moving from within VP up through the Spec of the larger DP, as in (21), does not pass through a Spec,AGR_O:

(23)   ... $[_{DP}$ $[e]_i$ D/P^0 AGR_O^0 $[_{VP}$ V $[e]_i]$

The agreement pattern of (22) is also seen with those French unaccusatives that both take *have* and for which the presence versus absence of agreement is morphologically detectable:[20]

(24)   La viande a cuit/*e. ('the meat has cooked')

On the other hand, there are Romance languages in which unaccusative past participles do show agreement in the presence of *have*. For example, Price (1967, 172–174) notes the existence of a dialect area in central France where the equivalent of (22) with agreement is found, at least with the past participle of *be* (i.e., 'M has been'). Similarly, in the dialect of Cori (about 50 km. SE of Rome) described by Chiominto (1984, 179),[21] auxiliary *have* is used in the 3pl. of the present perfect. With an unaccusative, past participle agreement takes place, to judge by his discussion and example:

(25)   Jésse èo ite a vedé. ('they$_{f.pl.}$ have gone$_{f.pl.}$ to see')

Giammarco (1973, 163) gives for the Aquila dialect in Abruzzo:

(26)   Au venuti. ('(they) have come$_{pl.}$')

Again, the past participle agrees with the (covert) subject of an unaccusative with auxiliary *have*.[22] (I return in section 7.2.8. to the question of how to distinguish the (22)–(24) type from the (25)–(26) type.)

7.2.3.   Transitives with *have*

In Italian (setting aside reflexive clitic sentences), transitives always take *have*:

(27)   Maria ha comprato i libri. ('M has bought the books')

(28)   *Maria è comprato/a i libri. ('M is . . .')

In (27), according to the analysis being developed, the subject *Maria* must have moved through Spec,DP, and incorporation of D/P^0 to BE must have taken place. Past participle agreement with the subject is impossible:

(29)   *Maria ha comprata i libri.

Therefore, *Maria* in (27) must not have passed through Spec,AGR$_O$ on its way to Spec,DP, essentially as in (22) and (24) (apart from the fact that (27) has an extra DP within the VP).

It remains to be shown why (29), displaying participial agreement with the subject, is ungrammatical. This fact recalls Chomsky's (1993) discussion of minimality, and more particularly his argument that the subject of a transitive VP cannot move through Spec, AGR$_O$, the reason for which is that if it did, the object would have no means of getting case.[23] Since the participial agreement at issue corresponds to AGR$_O$, the fact that the subject in (29) cannot agree with it apparently reduces to the general case discussed by Chomsky.[24]

There is a problem, however. Consider the dative reflexive clitic sentence corresponding to (27):

(30)   Maria si è comprata un libro. ('M refl. is bought$_{f.sg.}$ a book')

Here, the auxiliary is *be*, for reasons I will return to in section 7.2.6.[25] The directly relevant fact is that the past participle in (30) agrees with *Maria*, that is, AGR$_O$ is coindexed with an argument distinct from the object *un libro*$_{m.sg.}$ Consequently, for *un libro* to be case-licensed by AGR$_O$, LF movement of *un libro* must be able to override the overt indexing. But if that is possible in (30), why not also in (29)? Two possible solutions come to mind: First, the ungrammaticality of (29) might be attributed to AGR$_O$ being below the base position of the subject argument.[26] Second, if AGR$_O$ is above all the arguments of V (as in Chomsky (1993)), the LF overriding needed in (30) could be limited to structures in which there is a clitic locally coindexed with AGR_O (suggesting that the clitic moves not through $Spec,AGR_O$ but rather through a position of adjunction to $AGR_O{}^i$).[27]

7.2.4. Unergatives

In Italian, unergatives (apart, again, from reflexive clitic sentences) take *have*, just like transitives:

(31)   Maria ha dormito. ('M has slept')

(32)   *Maria è dormito/a. ('M is slept')

Furthermore, just as with transitives, past participle agreement with the subject is impossible:[28]

(33)   *Maria ha dormita.

The primary account given earlier of the ungrammaticality of the transitive counterpart of (33), that is, (29), followed Chomsky's (1993) idea that the subject of a transitive V could not move into $Spec,AGR_O$ because $Spec,AGR_O$ needed to be available for the object, in order for the object to receive case (locality conditions prohibit the object from getting case any higher up). The ungrammaticality of (33) can similarly be described by saying that the subject of an unergative cannot move to $Spec, AGR_O$. But that impossibility itself needs to be understood. From the perspective of Chomsky (1993) adopted for (29), there is one plausible explanation: (31) must contain a phonetically unrealized object that needs to be case-licensed by $(Spec,)AGR_O$. In other words, the similarity between transitives and unergatives with respect to past participle agreement leads, from this perspective, to the conclusion that unergatives are covert transitives.[29] (If AGR_O is below the base subject position, this conclusion is not necessary.)

7.2.5. Transitives and unergatives with *be*

The ungrammaticality of (28) and (32) in Italian is not representative of Romance. For example, in the Central Italian dialect described by Chiominto (1984, 179), both transitives and unergatives generally take auxiliary *be*:

(34)   Maria è magnato. ('M is eaten' = active ('has eaten'))

(35)   Nù simo magnato. ('we are eaten' = active)

(36)   Ntonio è rótta la bbròcca. ('Antonio is broken the jug')

(This phenomenon is quite common in Central/Southern Italy; see Tuttle (1986) for an overview.) Although the choice of auxiliary here is sharply different from that of Italian, the past participle agreement facts are actually the same as in Italian, in the sense that in this dialect, too, the active past participle of a transitive or unergative cannot agree with the subject argument:[30]

(37)   *Nù simo magnati. etc.

In (36), the participle obligatorily agrees with the object, unlike Italian.)

The lack of past participle agreement can be accounted for by saying that, for principled reasons, the subject argument cannot move through Spec,AGR_O. The question is, then, how to express the auxiliary selection difference between this kind of dialect and Italian. The solution I will propose will attempt to take advantage of the fact that, among the *be* dialects in question, it is very common for auxiliary selection to be sensitive to the person of the subject. For example, in Chiominto's dialect, in the present perfect, *be* is used everywhere except in the third-person plural, where one finds *have*. (It is common for *have* to be favored in the third person and *be* in the first and second.)

Sensitivity to the person of the subject suggests involvement of AGR_S. This suggests in turn that the skeletal structures I have been assuming for auxiliary + past participle constructions should be expanded to include an AGR_S projection above that of AGR_O:

(38)   ... BE [$_{DP}$ Spec D/P^0 AGR$_S$ AGR$_O$ VP]

Thus, these participial clauses are much like other full clauses, infinitival and finite, and can be taken now to satisfy the Extended Projection Principle.

The proposal concerning auxiliary selection is as follows: In Italian, this participial AGR_S is inert. Subjects of Italian transitives and unergatives, in moving up to Spec,DP, pass through Spec,AGR_S with no effect. After landing in the A-bar Spec,DP, those subjects will be able to move to Spec,BE if D/P^0 incorporates to BE, as before, yielding *have*.

In the dialects showing *be* with transitives and unergatives, on the other hand, the participial AGR_S is not inert. Rather, this kind of AGR_S can be activated by a DP passing through its Spec and having an appropriate set of person/number features.[31] When so activated (i.e. endowed with certain features), this kind of AGR_S can raise to adjoin to D/P^0 and convert that head into one compatible with an A-position (as opposed to A-bar position) Spec.[32] That in turn allows the subject DP to move through Spec,DP on up to Spec,BE without triggering an 'improper movement' violation and, crucially, without incorporation of D/P^0 to BE having been necessary. Consequently, BE is spelled out as *be*.[33]

In some of the dialects showing both *be* and *have* with transitives and unergatives, there is a notable difference in clitic behavior depending on which auxiliary is present. For example, in the dialect of Novara (Northern Italy, about 40 km. west of Milan) described by Turri (1973, 116–119), *be* seems to be the somewhat more usual auxiliary with transitives and unergatives in the first and second person, while in the third person *have* is preferred. What is of interest here is that if a clitic climbs up from the participial VP to the auxiliary, then the auxiliary must always be *have*, for example (p. 210):

(39) Mi i son mìa parlà. ('me I am not spoken')

(40) Mi i t'ò mài parlà. ('me I you$_{dat}$ have never spoken')

It is possible to make some sense of this asymmetry between *have* and *be* with respect to clitic climbing if we assume that in this dialect a clitic can reach an auxiliary out of a participial clause only via the D/P^0 position, much as I argue in chapter 4 that clitic climbing out of infinitival clauses has to pass through C^0. If D/P^0 itself raises/incorporates to the auxiliary, yielding *have*, as in (40), then the clitic can presumably move up with it.[34] No such raising/incorporation to the auxiliary need take place in (39) and arguably therefore cannot (cf. Chomsky (1991) on 'economy of derivation'). In this dialect, therefore, a clitic will have no way of raising up to auxiliary *be* (and evidently is not allowed to remain adjoined to D/P^0).[35]

In the dialect of Martinsicuro (Central Italy, on the Adriatic coast) studied by Mastrangelo Latini (1981), the present perfect has *be* in the first and second person and *have* in the third. There, too, clitic climbing from participle clause to auxiliary displays an asymmetry depending on choice of auxiliary. If the auxiliary is *have*, then the clitic can precede it. But if the auxiliary is *be*, the clitic must generally follow it:[36]

(41) Sillu dittę. ('(you$_{sg.}$)are-it said')

(42) (A) l'à dittę. ('(subj.cl.) it-(he)has said')

This paradigm can be accounted for in a way parallel to that of Novara. In (42), the clitic adjoins to D/P^0 and raises with it to precede the auxiliary. In (41), the clitic reaches the D/P^0 position (to which AGR$_S$ has adjoined) but can raise no further. However, in this dialect, unlike the preceding, the clitic can remain licitly in that adjoined position.[37]

7.2.6. Reflexive clitics with *be*

As is well known, Italian sentences with reflexive clitics have auxiliary *be*, even when the verb is visibly transitive, as in:

(43) Maria si è comprata un libro. ('M refl. is bought$_{f.sg.}$ a book')

(44) Maria se lo è comprato. ('M refl. it is bought$_{m.sg.}$')

The question is why *be* is permitted here, though normally excluded from transitive sentences in Italian.

I would like to relate this property of reflexive clitics to another, and that is to the fact that the sensitivity to person features that was discussed above for nonreflexive transitives and unergatives in certain dialects has a counterpart with reflexive clitics. What is surprising is that this sensitivity to person features is found not only in the dialects that display it with transitives and unergatives but also in many dialects in

Northern Italy, especially in the greater Veneto area, that otherwise invariably have *have* as the auxiliary with transitives and unergatives.

Moreover, the global preference for *be* with first- and second-person subjects and for *have* with third-person subjects that I mentioned earlier as holding (approximately) for the dialects that use *be* with transitives and unergatives is also found with reflexive clitics in the Veneto area. This suggests looking for a solution parallel to the one I have proposed for *be* with transitives and unergatives. Giupponi (1988) proposed for Trentino reflexive clitic sentences an approach based on identification via the participial agreement. This seems partly on the right track, but there is evidence that it is not the agreement morphology but rather the reflexive clitic itself that is central.

Graziella Saccon has brought to my attention the fact that in her dialect (that of Conegliano, about 50 km. north of Venice), the reflexive clitic for a second-person plural subject can be either *ve*, which is specific to second plural, as in Italian, or else *se*, which is also the reflexive clitic for third person.[38] When a second-plural subject co-occurs with the reflexive clitic *ve*, then the auxiliary is *be*, as it generally is with first or second person. However, when a second-plural subject co-occurs with *se*, then the auxiliary is *have*, as it is with third-person reflexive clitics. In other words, the generalization is clearly that the choice of auxiliary is keyed to the reflexive clitic and not directly to the person of the subject or to verbal agreement morphology.

Similarly, Paola Benincà has told me that in Paduan she prefers *be* with reflexive clitics with first-person singular and second-person singular or plural subjects but *have* with first-person plural and third-person subjects. However, the first-person plural reflexive clitic is *se* in Paduan, and the generalization is again clearly that the choice (in Paduan, a preference) of auxiliary is keyed directly to the reflexive clitic itself.

This points to the following proposal: It is the reflexive clitic adjoining to the participial AGR_S that activates AGR_S in such a way as to allow AGR_S to move to D/P^0 and turn Spec,DP into an A-position (thereby allowing movement through it to Spec,BE without any incorporation of D/P^0). In the languages that have *be* with transitives and unergatives, AGR_S can be activated by the appropriate features being present in its Spec; but in the Veneto dialects under consideration that is not sufficient; rather, adjunction to the head itself (of a coindexed element bearing the appropriate person features) must take place.[39]

It seems clear that it is the feature content of the reflexive clitic that is crucial and not simply the fact that it is coindexed with the DP that will pass through Spec,AGR_S. This is shown by a contrast from French:

(45)   ?Jean$_i$ me les lui$_i$ a fait rendre. ('J me them him$_{dat}$ has made to-give-back' = 'J made me give them back to him')

(46)   *Jean me les lui est fait rendre. ('. . . is . . .')

In complex causatives it is to some extent possible to have a dative clitic adjoined to the auxiliary that is coreferential with the subject of the causative. Yet, the auxiliary is *have* and not *be*, and the differential judgment seems to be sharp for all speakers.

This suggests, then, that the participial AGR_S can be activated by a clitic coindexed with the DP in its Spec only if that clitic bears an appropriate person feature.

Let us think of the fact that first/second-person reflexive clitics can activate AGR_S in this sense more readily than *se*, plus the fact that *lui* cannot at all, in the following terms: A necessary condition is that the clitic bear a person feature. The *l-* clitics of Romance bear no person feature.[40] *Se* bears the feature *0-person*, *me* the feature *1*-person, etc.[41] *0-person* is less strong than a 'positively numbered' person.

In Paduan, reflexive *se* licenses auxiliary *be*, that is, the feature *0-person* is sufficient (although, as mentioned earlier, *have* is preferred). However, impersonal *se* in Paduan does not license *be* at all:[42]

(47)   El se ze vardà. ('he refl. is looked-at')

(48)   Se ga balà tuta la note. ('refl. has danced all night')

(49)   *Se ze balà tuta la note.

I follow Cinque (1988, 573) and take Paduan impersonal *se* to be his [-arg] *si/se*, which (p. 535) does not head a chain. All other instances of *se* do head a chain. If so, then (47) versus (48) can be accounted for if a language like Paduan, which hesitates allowing *se* to activate participial AGR_S (compared with *me*, *te*), makes a further distinction and requires the potential activator of this AGR_S to be the head of its chain.

In Italian, all *si* licence *be* without exception (i.e., from this perspective activate AGR_S). Why Italian (like French and Piedmontese, cf. Burzio (1986, 123)) is freer in this respect than the Veneto dialects remains an open question.

7.2.7.   Sensitivity to tense

The suggestion about Paduan impersonal *se* correctly predicts that adding a reflexive *se* (which is the head of its chain) to (49) will improve it:

(50)   ??Se se ze visti. ('refl. refl. is seen')

Here, the reflexive *se* activates the participial AGR_S, which indirectly makes *be* possible (by removing the need for D/P^0 incorporation). What is of interest to this section is that the result improves still further, becoming almost perfect (Paola Benincà, p.c.), if the tense of the auxiliary is changed from present to imperfect, conditional, or future, such as in this example:

(51)   Se se gera visti. ('... was ...')

(In all these, auxiliary *have* would be perfect.)

The fact that auxiliary *be* is less good in this case in the present tense than in other tenses is not an isolated fact about Paduan, nor is it limited to reflexive clitic constructions. For example, in the Cori dialect discussed earlier, the auxiliary is generally *be*, whether with transitives, unergatives, unaccusatives or reflexives. However, in the third-person plural, *be* is impossible precisely in the present perfect (Chiominto (1984, 178)),[43] that is, only when the auxiliary is present tense, for all verb classes. In a third dialect area, distant from the other two, that of the northern part of the Swiss Jura, there is the Vermes dialect studied by Butz (1981, 78–79), in which *be* is excluded from reflexive clitic sentences only in the present perfect (apart from first-person singular).

This sensitivity of auxiliary selection to tense can be thought of, as a first approximation, in the following terms: Participial clauses, in addition to having a D/P^0 (comparable to C^0), an AGR_S and an AGR_O, have, as we might now expect, a T^0 in between the two AGRs. This T^0 is defective, like AGR_S, and in some languages must raise into the matrix clause (that of the auxiliary).[44] This must happen primarily when the auxiliary is present tense, presumably related to the fact that present tense is zero; see Giorgi and Pianesi (1997). But raising of T^0 is potentially inhibited by D/P^0, in particular when D/P^0 has not itself incorporated to BE, that is, when BE is spelled out as *be*, much as in the discussion of clitic climbing (cf. sect. 7.2.5.).

7.2.8.   Unaccusatives revisited

As noted earlier, Spanish (like English) has *have* with unaccusatives, just as with transitives. Similarly, the dialects described by Mastrangelo Latini (1981) and Chiominto (1984) treat all verb classes alike (although these dialects have a predominant use of *be*). On the other hand, as is well known, Italian and French distinguish unaccusatives from transitives and unergatives. Italian appears to have *be* with unaccusatives in a consistent fashion, and always has *have* with transitives (apart from reflexive clitic constructions, as mentioned above). French has *be* with certain unaccusatives, but with others not.[45]

Consider the skeletal structure of active auxiliary + past participle constructions that I have proposed (participial morphology omitted):

(52)   ... BE D/P^0 AGR_S T AGR_O V ...

Subjects of transitives move through Spec,AGR_S in all cases (and never through Spec,AGR_O). It is natural to claim now that, in languages like Spanish that treat all verb classes alike, the single argument of unaccusatives also moves through the participial Spec,AGR_S, at which point its further movement to Spec,DP becomes entirely parallel to that of transitive subjects (with the choice between *have* and *be* depending uniformly on whether or not incorporation of D/P^0 to BE takes place).

Furthermore, in languages, such as Spanish, that show no participial agreement with unaccusatives (cf. (22)), the unaccusative argument will not pass through Spec,AGR_O. In the languages that do, it will. When the auxiliary is *have*, we find both types of language. (See the discussion of (22)–(26).) Let me conjecture that this difference is keyed to the following:

(53)   a. Movement from Spec,AGR_O to participial Spec,AGR_S is prohibited

    b. Movement from Spec,AGR_O to Spec,DP is prohibited unless AGR_S raises to D/P^0

The idea (53)a might be derivable from Chomsky's (1991) 'last resort' principle. That of (53)b follows from his (1993) discussion of minimality (assuming Spec,TP not present). If both (a) and (b) are correct, then a language can have past participle agreement with unaccusatives with *have* only if its AGR_S can raise in this way (perhaps only if it can raise that way in the absence of a reflexive clitic).[46] From this perspective, the absence of such agreement in Spanish and French might follow from the fact that their auxiliary choice does not show sensitivity to person.

In Italian, past participle agreement with unaccusatives (with *be*) is obligatory:

(54)   Maria è arrivata/*o. ('M is arrived')

This is part of a broader generalization to the effect that all Romance languages with a *have/be* distinction according to verb class and independent of person/tense appear to show obligatory participle agreement with unaccusatives.[47] This is not expected under (52), since it is hard to see how to exclude the skipping of Spec,AGR_O, given that such skipping is possible (e.g., in Spanish and French) when the auxiliary ends up as *have*. Let me attempt to relate this to the basic question of how to ensure the proper *have/be* distinction for Italian, in particular how to prevent *be* from appearing with Italian transitives.

Assume that a projection headed by AGR_S (whether participial or not) can never function as an argument to a higher predicate. In other words, the counterpart to (52) but without D/P^0 is impossible.[48] Assume further that a transitive VP must be associated both with an AGR_O and an AGR_S.[49] Then a transitive participial VP will always appear in a structure like (52). (In Italian, this will imply auxiliary *have*, since Italian AGR_S cannot make Spec,DP into an A-position (except with reflexive clitics).)

An unaccusative participial VP with a single nonoblique argument on the other hand, will not need to be associated with an AGR_S, or consequently with a DP, and therefore will in some languages be able to be embedded under BE with an associated AGR_O only:[50]

(55)   ... BE AGR_O V ...[51]

BE will be spelled out as *be*, and the obligatoriness of participial agreement will reduce to that of adjective agreement.[52]

The contrasting nonobligatoriness of agreement with unaccusatives with *have* could be captured by saying that movement from within VP can skip Spec,AGR_O to land in Spec,AGR_S (which, followed by D/P^0 incorporation, will yield nonagreement with *have*) but not to land in Spec,BE. This might, in turn, follow, within the framework of Chomsky (1993), from the fact that the overt AGR_O (to which the participle has raised) can raise to abstract AGR_S, but not to overt BE.[53]

The obligatoriness of agreement illustrated in (54) is not invariably found with unaccusatives with *be*, as shown by the variety of Catalan spoken by Gemma Rigau (p.c.):

(56)   Sóc set vista. ('I-am been seen')

This variety of Catalan has *be* for all verbs, but only in the first and second singular.[54] In (56), the understood subject is feminine singular, as seen by the agreement on the passive participle *vista*. Yet the past participle of *be* remains in the default form, even though the highest auxiliary is itself *be*. The account is as follows: The passive participle *vista* corresponds to an AGR_O complement of *set* and so shows agreement. But the past participle *set* reflects the embedding under *sóc* of a full projection of D/P^0 that includes both AGR_O and AGR_S:

(57)   *sóc* D/P^0 AGR_S AGR_O *set* AGR_O *vista* $DP_{1f.sg.}$

The DP argument of *vista* moves through the lower Spec,AGR_O and then skips the upper Spec,AGR_O, landing instead in Spec,AGR_S. From there it moves into Spec,DP. AGR_S is capable of licensing Spec,DP as an A-position (as shown by the general sensitivity to person features in this variety of Catalan) and does so, raising to D/P^0, with the consequence that D/P^0 incorporation is unnecessary. In effect, what we see here is that (56) is substantially like the Spanish pattern of agreement, that is, no past participle agreeement with unaccusatives (cf. (22)), even though the auxiliary here is *be* and in Spanish is *have*. The movement pattern is identical here and in Spanish with respect to the skipping of Spec,AGR_O, but Spanish, lacking the appropriate kind of participial AGR_S, is forced to use D/P^0 incorporation and hence to have auxiliary *have*.

7.2.9. Reflexive clitics with *have*

The agreement variation studied earlier with respect to *have* and unaccusatives is found also with reflexive clitics. In Paduan (and similarly for Friulian), as discussed by Benincà (1984), reflexive clitics are on the whole compatible with either *be* or *have*. With *be*, past participle agreement is straightforwardly possible, but with *have* it is impossible:

(58)   La Maria se ze vestìa. ('the M refl. is dressed$_{f.sg.}$' = 'M dressed herself')

(59)   La Maria se ga vestìo/*a. ('. . . has . . .')

On the other hand, the version of (59) with participle agreement is grammatical (and obligatory) in the variety of Trentino studied by Gatti (1990, 174):

(60)   La Maria la s'ha vestìa. ('the M she refl. has . . .')

Following the analysis I have suggested for unaccusatives, let us say that in (60) *la Maria* has moved through Spec,AGR_O, and then directly to Spec,DP (allowable as a result of AGR_S having raised to D/P^0). Subsequently, *la Maria* raises to Spec,BE and D/P^0 incorporates to BE, yielding HAVE.

Let us now say that in Paduan, the raising of AGR_S to D/P^0 is incompatible with the incorporation of the latter to BE, so (59) with participle agreement is impossible. This approach may be supported by a fact from the variety of Veneto spoken by Cecilia

Poletto (from Mestre, between Padua and Venice), which differs from Paduan in not allowing (58) at all but which is similar to Paduan in disallowing participle agreement in (59) (which is grammatical without that agreement). Of particular interest here is the fact that (59) with agreement improves if the subject is a clitic rather than a full DP:

(61)   *La Maria se ga vista. ('the M refl. has seen$_{f.sg.}$')

(62)   ??La se ga vista. ('she . . .')

A possible account is that the clitic *la*, rather than moving to Spec,DP, adjoins to D/P^0 and facilitates the incorporation of D/P^0 to BE, that is, carries it along, even in the presence of a raised AGR_S.

7.2.10. *Have* for *be*

Consider again the skeletal structure I have proposed for the auxiliary + participle constructions at issue:

(63)   . . . BE D/P^0 AGR_S T AGR_O V . . .

If D/P^0 incorporates to BE, the result is HAVE. Until now, there has been no interaction between D/P^0 and the lower V at all. Consider now the following case: D/P^0 does not raise to BE, but the lower V itself raises (through the intervening functional heads) up to D/P^0, and furthermore the lower (participial) V is itself BE. This will yield a result in which, if the difference in order of adjunction can be ignored, there will be a constituent [D/P^0 + V] (ignoring the other affixes) comparable to the constituent produced by incorporating D/P^0 up to the higher BE.

In other words, if a language allowed the lower V to raise to D/P^0, then, if the lower V were BE, we should expect that 'BE D/P^0 . . . BE' would actually yield 'BE HAVE . . . [e]', rather than the familiar 'HAVE [e] . . . BE' (as in *John has been ill*). This kind of language seems to exist and thereby to support the analysis I have developed:[55]

(64)   I sö èvu mèlèd. ('I am had sick')

7.3. Conclusion

If the modular approach to auxiliary selection pursued in this essay is correct, then the proper way to understand the alternation between auxiliary *have* and auxiliary *be* is largely in terms of the participial clause that is their complement. Of course, *have* and *be* must differ from each other in at least one respect, and there I have taken over the position set forth for possessive *have* in Freeze (1992), namely that *have* is identical to *be* but for the incorporation of an abstract preposition. Apart from that, questions about the participial clause are central—whether it is a full clause, with a T^0, an AGR_S^0 and the equivalent of a C^0, or rather a reduced clause with nothing higher than AGR_O^0—whether AGR_S^0 raises or not, and, if so, what person features it is sensitive to—whether T^0 needs to raise or not—whether $Spec,AGR_O$ is moved through or not—how many arguments the V has that need to be case-licensed—and others, none of which involve a rule of auxiliary selection. Although the languages considered have been primarily Romance languages, including a number not traditionally taken into consideration, it is hoped that the basic approach will carry over to Germanic and to languages further afield.

NOTES

1. Fairly close to Burzio's formulation is that of Vikner and Sprouse (1988). For recent argument against purely aspectual approaches to the question, see Everaert (1992).

2. Nor will it have 'theta-deblocking/transmission' of the sort found in Hoekstra (1984, 282) or Haider (1985).

3. For related ideas, see Hoekstra (1995).

4. This recalls the idea, often put forth for the Germanic V-second languages, that C^0 plays a role in licensing Case on the subject DP. Note that Szabolcsi explicitly proposes a parallelism between D^0 and C^0.

5. This English-Hungarian contrast recalls that holding between French and Italian with respect to prenominal possessors: French (*le) mon livre ('the my book') versus Italian *(il) mio libro. For recent discussion, from a partially different perspective, see Authier (1992).

6. Unexplained under the present analysis are *John's a/no/any/each book, which contrast with Hungarian.

How best to state that of itself requires that Spec be filled by QP/NP—*of John's three books—is not clear. Perhaps a(n overt) prepositional D^0 is subject to a requirement like that of Rizzi's (1996) Wh-criterion.

7. The grammaticality of the sister of John's that I was telling you about now must be attributed to a raising analysis of such relatives (cf. Vergnaud (1974)), with indefinite sister of John's being raised from the position of object of about.

The movement of three sisters across John involves movement of a QP/NP across a DP and for that reason might not trigger a relativized minimality violation in Rizzi's (1990) sense. Alternatively, relativized minimality (or Chomsky's (1993) reinterpretation of it in terms of 'economy') might perhaps be irrelevant because John is in an A-position, while the Spec being moved to is an A-bar position.

8. In chapter 10, I argue that -s is not specified for person.

9. This leaves open the question of why plurals unmarked with -s are compatible with 's—those children's mother—but not with the verbal -s. Perhaps it is related to the fact that the verbal -s has a zero alternant, whereas 's normally does not (perhaps in the kids' mother, the -s is really the possessive one).

Adapting a suggestion of Tony Kroch's, it might be that in my/your/our/their/her/his book the pronoun has cliticized to AGR, with AGR itself having then to be spelled out as 's only when needed to license a null NP.

10. 'Play a role in' may be appropriate given two houses of John's/*John and similarly, from the text perspective, for John *(to be) happy.

11. The German dem Mann sein Buch ('the man_{dat} his book') construction (cf. Fiva (1984) for an analysis of a similar Norwegian one) may involve a comparable dative in Spec, though the German one seems unable to move out of the larger DP in the way available to the Hungarian dative. In German, this dative seems to depend on the presence of a possessive

pronominal/anaphor. On the perhaps similar French *un ami à moi* ('a friend to me'), see Fillmore (1968), Kayne (1975, sect. 2.20).

12. On empty prepositions, see also Kayne (1983c), Holmberg and Platzack (1995), Pesetsky (1995). The whole question of the relation between DP and CP needs to be further pursued (cf. in part Kayne (1982)). For a proposed prepositional status for complementizers in general, see Emonds (1985).

An example of an overt prepositional determiner might be the *de* ('of') of French and Occitan partitives.

13. How best to distinguish this case from that of I-to-C movement is not entirely clear.

The text incorporation proposal recalls in part Baker (1988, 489) on ECM constructions. Pursuing the parallel, one would say that C-to-V incorporation makes Spec,CP an A-position. There is also a similarity here to Pollock (1985).

14. From now on, the $_e$ of D/P_e will be dropped.

I am indebted to Michal Starke for calling my attention to the potential advantages of taking (9) to be the precise source structure under this incorporation approach (as opposed to having the incorporating P_e originate as sister of DP_{poss}, as in the oral presentation of this material (at the 1992 Going Romance conference in Utrecht) that led to his suggestion).

In English, the derivation in question requires $AGR^0 = \emptyset$ and is not possible with $AGR^0 = $ *'s* **John has 's three sisters*—cf. (4) and/or the possibility of a double-case violation. The fact that $AGR^0 = \emptyset$ is not normally possible in possessive constructions is presumably due to *'s* being essential for case-licensing; the specificity of (9)/(10) from this perspective resides in the fact that DP_{poss} there can get case in the matrix/verbal part of the structure, and so does not need *'s*.

Examples of *have* with a definite possessed DP such as

(i)   *John has your article (with him)*

might be analyzed as containing a substructure with a prepositional small clause (cf. in part Freeze (1992)) in place of QP/NP, but with D^0 still indefinite:

(ii)   ... Spec D^0 [DP_{poss} AGR^0 [DP [P DP]]]

if one could account for *'s* being incompatible with such a small clause:

(iii)   **John's your article (with him)*.

A plausible proposal would be that in the preceding example the DP *your article* would be unable to get case. The remaining question would then be how *your article* gets case in (i).

15. See Koopman and Sportiche (1991) and references cited therein. I shall set aside the question of the exact status of the participial suffix itself, for recent discussion of which see Belletti (1990) and Giorgi and Pianesi (1997).

16. The different behavior of the two instances of *have* with respect to V-raising in (most of) American English—*Have you seen him?* versus **Have you lots of friends?*, etc.—might indicate, if Pollock (1989) is right about the relevance of theta-roles, that BE actually does assign a theta-role to DP in the possessive/existential construction (but not in the participial one), though this would require an account of why existential *be* does allow raising—*Is there a solution?*—as well as an account of the varieties of English in which possessive *have* can raise (at least in the present tense).

English is the only language I know of that has a causative *have*—*John had Bill arrested*—recalling the text discussion of (2) and the *for* construction, and suggesting a case-licensing

role for D/P$_e$ across a maximal projection. From this perspective, the ungrammaticality of
*John had Bill angry as a causative could be related to note 10.

17. The question of English get is beyond the scope of this paper. The passives with
have in the Altamura dialect studied by Loporcaro (1988) and La Fauci and Loporcaro (1989)
are perhaps to be related to those with get.

18. This recalls the fact that adjectival and passive small clauses never take an overt
complementizer. Whether they can ever be associated with a CP projection is not clear. See
Mouchaweh (1985).

Similar to (18) and (19) is perhaps:

(i)   John is/*has reading a book.

If progressive -ing is aspectual rather than a form of Tense, this will follow; see also Bolinger
(1971). From this perspective, the infinitive of:

(ii)   *John has to leave*

must contain Tense. See Stowell (1982); also Haider (1985). Note also:

(iii)   *For there being a problem is normal.

(17) contrasts in addition with finite forms of V:

(iv)   *John has breaks the window. *John has saw the circus.

This is perhaps akin to *For John breaks the window is too bad, and, more important, to the
fact that (iv) remains bad with be in place of have.

19. Cf. chapters 2 and 3.

20. See Sportiche (1990).

21. I am indebted to Edward F. Tuttle for making this work and others available to me.

22. In both these dialects, the past participle with have seems to show no agreement
with the equivalent of They have eaten/written. Cf. also Loporcaro (1988) and La Fauci and
Loporcaro (1989).

23. Burzio's (1986, 369) example:

(i)   ?Maria li è andata a prendere ('M them is gone $_{f.sg.}$ to get')

might have the clitic li Case-licensed via the AGR$_O$ associated with the infinitive.

24. Note that (29) is ungrammatical in the dialects of (25) and (26), too.

25. This is probably not related at bottom to the agreement problem, which, for a number of speakers, reappears in the absolute construction studied by Belletti (1990), where there
is no auxiliary at all:

(i)   ?Compratasi un libro, Maria . . . ('bought$_{f.sg.}$ refl. a book')

In addition, the Romantsch dialect described by Ganzoni (1983a, 172) allows, with auxiliary
have and with disagreement between the direct object and the past participle:

(ii)   Ella s'ha lavada ils mans. ('she refl. has washed$_{f.sg.}$ the hands')

(This dialect, unlike Italian, also allows (p. 174) past participle agreement with a nonreflexive dative clitic in the presence of a direct object, raising the same problem.)

26. See Travis (n.d.) and references cited there.

27. This would mean, in turn, that the past participle agreement in (30) is directly triggered by *si* and not directly triggered by *Maria*.

28. The impossibility of past participle agreement with the subject of an unergative is seen also in contexts where there is no auxiliary at all. Cinque (1990b, note 25) gives as marginally acceptable:

(i)   ??Una volta parlato Maria, . . . ('one time spoken M, . . .')

Agreement is sharply out:

(ii)   *Una volta parlata Maria, . . .

The text discussion carries over to (ii) straightforwardly.

29. As far as verbs that take sentential complements are concerned, those that require auxiliary *have* and nonagreement with the participle must either have a sentential complement that itself moves to Spec,AGR_O to get case (vs. Stowell (1981)) or else must have an empty object that does, to which the overt sentential complement is linked.

30. Recall that this dialect does have past participle agreement with unaccusatives—v. (25).

31. Assume that this property of AGR_S is dependent in turn on AGR_S being able to license referential null subjects in the language in question. Then the text analysis makes the prediction that *be* with transitives and unergatives should not be found in French or closely related dialects, or in any of the Germanic languages. Both parts of the prediction appear to be correct.

32. See Rizzi (1991).

The AGR that occurs in possessive constructions must not have this property of AGR_S, since, otherwise, one could derive (the equivalent of) **John is a sister* as a possessive sentence.

Note that in the dialects under discussion (and in Italian), AGR_S is never phonetically realized. The participial agreement morphology corresponds to AGR_O, and not to AGR_S.

33. If the subject does not have the appropriate features, the derivation can in theory proceed exactly as in Italian, yielding *have* but cf. sections 7.2.8 and 7.2.9.

34. It may be that this mode of clitic raising is involved, too, in the 'clitic splitting' construction 'CL AUX V CL' (with both clitics originating in the lower VP) discussed in chapter 5, 5.1.3. If so, then the contrast between past participles and infinitives, which don't allow a comparable 'CL V V CL', would be due to a clitic being able to raise directly to D/P^0 but being unable to raise directly to an infinitival C^0. If the clitic-splitting dialects never allowed direct raising of CL to AUX, then the prediction would be that split clitics are impossible with auxiliary *be*.

Perhaps relevant is that 'avere'+ infin. needs an intervening *da* (**Gianni ha parlare* ('G has to-speak')).

35. The text discussion assumes that once a clitic is adjoined to some X^0, it cannot be detached from it by further movement. See chapter 5, 5.1.3. See also, however, note 37.

An alternative to the text proposal would be to say that D/P^0 creates a minimality barrier for clitic movement that is lifted by incorporation, perhaps most plausibly if Baker and Hale (1990) are correct.

36. This phenomenon is not to be assimilated to V-CL order in Portuguese, which is incompatible with preverbal negation, whereas, in the Martinsicuro dialect, preverbal negation is compatible with *be* + CL—Mastrangelo Latini (1981, 245).

37. Mastrangelo Latini (p. 248) does give two examples with a clitic preceding auxiliary *be*. Similarly, the Cori dialect described by Chiominto (1984) seems to have CL + *be* as a matter of course, e.g. (p. 157):

(i)   Ci só visti. ('you_{pl} (I) am seen' = 'I have seen you')

I am led to propose that in this kind of dialect (and to some extent in that of Martinsicuro) clitics can either skip over D/P^0 or else perhaps excorporate from it in the sense of Roberts (1991).

38. It is not uncommon in Northern Italy for *se* to allow a wider range of antecedents than in Italian, French or Spanish. For relevant discussion, see Burzio (1991).

39. If German *sich* and Dutch *zich* cannot adjoin to a head, then it will follow as desired that they are incapable of licensing auxiliary *be*. See Everaert (1986, 111) and Vikner and Sprouse (1988).

40. See Benveniste (1966, Part V) and Milner (1982, 227–244).

An alternative to the person feature requirement might be a requirement that the clitic be anaphoric.

41. It does not matter here whether first/second plural are *1/2–person* or, say *4/5-person* (to use *3-* at all would now be confusing).

The text analysis has the consequence that in a sentence like *Il se voit* ('he refl. sees') *il* and *se* do not match in person features. See Burzio's (1991) notion of 'pseudo-agreement' (although in attributing a *0-person* feature to *se*, and thereby grouping *se* with *me, te* (which is supported by all three lacking gender morphology and being incompatible with number morphology), the text analysis departs from his).

42. See Benincà (1984).

43. Similarly for the Altamura dialect studied by Loporcaro (1988, 279–284); for transitives and unergatives. For unaccusatives and *si* constructions, the facts are not entirely clear. Tuttle (1986, 268) refers to a similar reduced use of *be* in the present perfect only in two other dialects. In the Martinsicuro dialect studied by Mastrangelo Latini (1981, 242), *be* is again excluded, from the third person only in the present perfect.

44. Alternatively, T raising must take place uniformly across languages, and what differs is the degree to which D/P^0 exerts a blocking effect.

45. See Burzio (1986). Also Sankoff and Thibault (1977).

46. Note that in (25) and (26), this raising of (empty) AGR$_S$ must not inhibit the incorporation of D/P^0 to BE, perhaps suggesting that incorporation carries AGR$_S$ along.

47. In unaccusative sentences with expletive subjects, some languages seem to show participial agreement with the expletive. See Christensen and Taraldsen (1989). Examples in Romance are French and Paduan, the latter with an empty expletive—v. Benincà (1984). If the expletive originates in Spec,AGR$_O$ or higher (cf. Rizzi and Roberts (1989)), the text account of the auxiliary being *be* carries over.

If the expletive originates within VP, as the subject argument, then the auxiliary, following the text analysis, should be *have* (even if the language otherwise has *be* with unaccusatives). This appears to match the facts of Sardinian. See Jones (1993) and La Fauci and Loporcaro (1993).

48. See Kayne (1982), especially if AGR$_S$ implies the presence of T. See Raposo (1987b) and Chomsky (1993).

49. This might follow from participial Spec,AGR$_O$ being skippable only by a phrase

landing in the participial Spec,AGR$_S$ (cf. the discussion following (55)), combined with the fact that the subject of a transitive would have to do exactly such skipping, for reasons discussed earlier, following Chomsky (1993).

50. What is crucial here is the number of nonoblique arguments (one vs. more than one), and not the question of whether one of them is a subject argument. Consequently, if there are verbs that take two nonoblique nonsubject arguments, they will be incompatible with (55), and must take auxiliary *have* in Italian. See Belletti and Rizzi's (1988) claim about certain psych-verbs.

The appearance of *be* in Italian 'restructuring' contexts like:

(i)   Maria è voluta andare . . . ('M is wanted to-go . . .')

implies that the infinitival complement here needs no Case, i.e. does not count as an argument. The ungrammaticality of:

(ii)   *Maria è voluta comprare il libro. ('. . . buy the book')

implies that *il libro* cannot be Case-licensed within the non-argument infinitival complement, but only via the AGR$_O$ associated with the matrix. If this loss of case-licensing ability took place obligatorily in the complement of restructuring verbs that normally took *be*, then when the complement contained a direct object, the auxiliary would have to be *have*—this does not happen in Italian, but appears to in Gascon (cf. Rohlfs (1977, 224)):

(iii)   Qu'as anàt cuélhe aigo. ('that you-have gone to-get water')

(*go* in Gascon normally takes *be*). If Wh-infinitival complements must always receive Case, then (iv) is accounted for:

(iv)   Non avrei/*sarei saputo dove andare. ('neg. (I) would have/be known where to-go')

Similarly for infinitivals with *di* (vs. with *a*).

51. That Italian takes advantage of the possibility of (55) and Spanish does not is now statable as a property of Italian *be* vs. Spanish *be*, with the latter unable to take a 'bare' AGR$_O$/ participle complement; perhaps a property of the participle is involved. See Lois (1990), but also Delfitto (n.d.).

Whether the correlation proposed by Taraldsen (1991) and Lois (1990) between (in my terms) (55) and past participle agreement with (nonreflexive) object clitics is at all valid is unclear. Taraldsen notes (p. 263) the problem of Catalan. Conversely, there would appear to be speakers of French for whom past participle agreement with object clitics is absent in the spoken language, but *be* with (certain) unaccusatives still robust (similarly in part for the dialect described by Dupraz (1938, 289–294)).

Whether the correlations that Taraldsen discusses for Scandinavian can be reformulated in the perspective of the text analysis is left an open question.

52. If the Novara dialect is able to use the (55) structure, then it is not surprising to find an example of clitic climbing with *be* with an unaccusative contrasting with the pattern of (39)/(40)—Turri (1973, 220.26)—but further study is necessary, including with reflexive clitics.

53. Durand (1936) has discussed cases of nonobligatory adjective agreement.

In (some varieties of) French (cf. Kayne (1975: sect. 5.8)) and in Paduan, participial agreement with reflexive clitics with *be* is not obligatory, in contrast to unaccusatives.

The variation within French concerning *be/have* with unaccusatives could be described by saying that only certain French unaccusatives allow the bare AGR_O structure. For relevant discussion, see Vikner and Sprouse (1988) and Haider and Rindler-Schjerve (1988).

54. And only in the present tense, contrasting with section 7.2.7, for reasons unclear.

55. Example from Taverdet (1971). See also Butz (1981, 142). (The phenomenon is widely attested.) Taverdet notes that in some dialects the past participle now used in both *have* and *be* sentences is etymologically that of *be*; for such a dialect, the text analysis would have that participle now reflecting D/P^0 incorporation.

8

Person Morphemes and Reflexives in Italian, French, and Related Languages

Helke (1973), Pica (1987), Iatridou (1988), Safir (1996), and others have emphasized the importance of the internal structure of reflexives of the English *himself* type and the Italian *se stesso* type. In this essay, I would like to extend that line of thought to the apparently monomorphemic nonclitic reflexives found in French and Italian (and many other European languages). More specifically, I will argue that French *soi* and Italian *sé* are themselves bimorphemic and that each subcomponent makes a distinct syntactic contribution.

I will simultaneously argue that *soi* and *sé* form a natural class with (French) *moi/toi* and (Italian) *me/te*, the first- and second-person singular nonclitic pronouns. In all of these, there is a consonantal person morpheme *m-*, *t-*, or *s-* that is followed by a morpheme *-oi* (in French) or *-é* (in Italian) having the property 'singular'.[1]

The person morphemes *m-/t-/s-* themselves are arguably not intrinsically 'singular'. This is certainly true of reflexive *s-*, and perhaps even of *m-* and *t-*, as we will see later.

8.1.   *m-* and *t-*

8.1.1.   French possessives

Let us begin with French possessives. When the possessor is first- or second-person singular and the noun plural, we have:

(1)   mes tables ('my tables')

(2)   tes tables ('your tables')

131

Compare these with the corresponding definite article:

(3)   les tables ('the tables')

The definite article with feminine singular nouns beginning with a consonant is also very similar to the corresponding first- and second-person singular possessives:

(4)   ma table ('my table')

(5)   ta table ('your table')

(6)   la table ('the table')

It is natural to take these paradigms to indicate that possessive *mes* and *tes* should be analyzed as *m-/t-+-es*, where *m-* and *t-* are the first- and second-singular person morphemes and *-es* represents agreement with the plurality of *tables*.[2] The definite article *les* will then be analyzed as *l-* plus the same *-es*.

The possessives in (4) and (5) are then *m-/t-+-a*, with *m-* and *t-* again the person morphemes, and *-a* agreement with the feminine singular *table*. In (6), the definite article is the same *l-* as in (3) plus the *-a* of (4) and (5).

It is quite clear in these cases that the person morphemes are just the consonants *m-* and *t-*. With a masculine singular noun, things are a bit more complex:

(7)   mon livre ('my book')

(8)   ton livre ('your book')

(9)   le livre ('the book')

Comparing (7) and (8), we see that the person morphemes *m-* and *t-* are followed by a morpheme *-on* that does not appear with the definite article.[3] This *-on* is specific to possessives. A variant of it, *-ien*, occurs with possessives when there is no overt noun (in which case the possessive is preceded by the definite article):[4]

(10)   le mien ('the mine')

(11)   le tien ('the your(s)')

These examples have the understood noun as masculine singular. When the understood noun is feminine singular, we have:

(12)   la mienne

(13)   la tienne

and when the understood noun is plural (masculine/feminine):

(14)   les miens/les miennes

(15)   les tiens/les tiennes

The possessive forms in (10)–(15) are composed of the person morpheme *m-/t-* plus
-ien plus an agreement ending sensitive to the gender and number of the phonetically unrealized noun.

In light of (10)–(15) and (7)–(8), I will take (1)–(2) and (4)–(5) to also contain
a possessive morpheme (i.e., an abstract counterpart of *-on/-ien*), so all the possessive forms will consist of 'person morpheme + possessive morpheme + agreement'.[5]

8.1.2.   French nonpossessives

The person morphemes *m-* and *t-* occur as preverbal clitics:

(16)   Jean m'invite ('J me invites')

(17)   Jean t'invite ('J you invites')

When the verb begins with a consonant, there is an orthographic *-e* (a schwa that is
sometimes not pronounced):

(18)   Jean me voit ('J me sees')

(19)   Jean te voit ('J you sees')

I will take this *-e* to be not a separate morpheme but epenthetic, so the clitic is syntactically always just *m-/t-*.[6]

The epenthetic character of this *-e* may underlie the fact that it cannot appear
postverbally in positive imperatives, where it might be expected to:

(20)   *Invite-me! ('invite me')

(21)   *Invite-te! ('invite you(rself)')

This could not be attributed to final stress falling on the *-e*, since these examples
contrast with (22), which does have a final stressed *-e*:

(22)   Invite-le! ('invite him')

The *-e* of *le* must then not be epenthetic. It must rather be a masculine (singular) word
marker (in Harris's (1991) sense), so that *le* here is bimorphemic.[7]

The *-e* of *le* in (22) is thus parallel to the feminine singular *-a* of:

(23)   Invite-la! ('invite her')

In having -*a*, the third person accusative clitic of (23) is just like the definite article in (6) and (12)/(13). Both are *l*- + -*a*. The claim that the -*e* of (18)/(19) is distinct from that of (22) is therefore supported by the fact that there is no clitic in -*a* for *m*- and *t*-:

(24)   *Jean ma voit.

(25)   *Jean ta voit.

I will return later (cf. (77)) to this property of *m-/t-*.
   The way in which French expresses (20) is:[8]

(26)   Invite-moi! ('invite me')

and similarly for (21) (changing the verb to make it more natural):

(27)   Couche-toi! ('lie-down you(rself) = lie down')

The *moi* and *toi* (pronounced /-wa/) found here are identical to the form of these pronouns found in nonclitic environments, for example:

(28)   Jean parle de moi. ('J speaks of me')

(29)   Jean pense à toi. ('J thinks of you')

(30)   Moi, j'aime cela. ('me, I like that')

(31)   Toi, tu aimes cela. ('you, you like that')

   Thinking of Haiman's (1980, 215) analysis of pronouns in Hua and of the basic fact that *m*- and *t*- are person morphemes, I will take these to be bimorphemic, that is, to be *m-/t*- + *oi*.[9]
   In conclusion so far, *m*- and *t*- are person morphemes that in French sometimes occur with -*oi*, sometimes with a possessive morpheme, as in section 8.1.1., and sometimes alone, as in (16)–(19).

8.1.3.   Italian

The Italian counterparts of (28) and (29) are:

(32)   Gianni parla di me.

(33)   Gianni pensa a te.

In the spirit of the preceding discussion, I take these nonclitic *me* and *te* in Italian to be bimorphemic, that is, to be *m-/t*- + -*é* (cf. note 1). The clitic counterparts are (when no other clitic follows) *mi* and *ti*, as in:

(34)   Gianni mi vede. ('G me sees')

(35)   Gianni ti vede. ('G you sees')

I will take the vowel /i/ to be epenthetic, as suggested by Benincà (1998, note 11).

These object clitics take the form *me/te* when followed by another clitic (of a certain type):[10]

(36)   Gianni me lo dice. ('G me it says')

(37)   Gianni te lo dice. ('G you it says')

I take this alternation not to reflect any change in the syntactic status of the object clitic; since in (34)/(35) it is monomorphemic, that is, *m-/t-* with an epenthetic vowel, then it is in (36)/(37), too. The person morphemes in question are *m-* and *t-* in Italian, just as in French.

Italian possessives, while different from French in some interesting respects, also fit well with the idea that the person morphemes for first and second singular are *m-* and *t-*. Italian possessives cooccur for the most part with an article. Thus, the Italian equivalents of (4) and (5) are:

(38)   la mia tavola ('the my table')

(39)   la tua tavola ('the your table')

The final *-a* in each word is the feminine singular word marker. Its presence in *mia* and *tua* reflects agreement with the gender (and number) of the noun *tavola*.[11]

I take the fact that (38) has an *-i-* where (39) has a *-u-* to be an irregularity that is compatible with the analysis of *mia* and *tua* as trimorphemic, that is, as *m-i-a* and *t-u-a*. This is supported (looking ahead a bit) by:

(40)   la sua tavola ('the his/her table')

with the same *-u-*, but with *s-* instead of *t-*. Much as in the discussion of French in section 8.1.1., I take this *-i/u-* to be a possessive morpheme. Again, the person morpheme is just *m-/t-* (or *s-*).

8.1.4.   *m-/t-* and number

It is uncontroversial to say that French and Italian *m-* and *t-* are specified for person (first and second, respectively).[12] It is equally clear that they are not specified for gender. Somewhat less clear is their status with respect to number.

To say that they are singular is natural and perhaps correct. But it is worth pointing out a (cross-dialectal) way in which their singularity seems less rigid than their person feature. What I have in mind is the fact that in some Italian dialects the clitic form of *m-* can in some (accusative, more than dative) contexts also be first-person plural. Thus, in Milanese, as described by Nicoli (1983, 142, 146, 150, 358), the following are possible:[13]

(41)   El me véd nun. ('he me sees us' = 'He sees us')

(42)   La vegnarà a toeumm. ('she will-come to get-me' = 'She will come to get us')[14]

With the same initial *n-* as that of nonclitic *nun* in (41), Milanese also allows *ne* as a first-person plural clitic:

(43)   La ne dà . . . ('she us gives . . .')

In other words, Milanese has both *n-* and *m-* as object clitics for first person plural (again, I take the vowel of *ne* and *me* in (43) and (41) to be epenthetic).

    Now *me* is also the (only) object clitic for first person singular:

(44)   El me véd nò. ('he me sees not')

Thus, it seems that in Milanese, *m-* is to be characterized as first person, without rigid specification for number.

    Something rather similar is found in various French dialects, in the case of the subject clitic *je*, which in standard French is first-person singular.[15] In these dialects, (the equivalent of) *je* can occur in the first person in both singular and plural (with differing verb forms). The following is from the dialect described by Fougeu-Fontaine (1986, 52):[16]

(45)   J èm ('I love')

(46)   J èmô ('I love-1pl' = 'We love')

In these dialects, then, *j-* seems to be first person, without specification for number.

    We can now note an asymmetry between person and number, as far as *m-/j-* is concerned. Although in certain dialects the specification for singular can be suspended so that *m-* or *j-*, depending on the dialect, becomes compatible with both singular and plural, there does not seem to be any dialect that drops the specification for first person (which would have yielded, for example, neutralization between first and second person).

    It may be, then, that these morphemes are fundamentally specified for (first) person but not fundamentally specified for singular. In the languages (and contexts) in which *m-* or its variant *j-* is incompatible with plural, that must be a secondary effect.[17]

    The phenomena discussed in this section, where *m-* or *j-* is compatible with plural, have involved object or subject clitics. I do not know of any Romance language/ dialect in which something comparable is found with a nonclitic pronoun:

(47)   Hanno visto me. ('they-have seen me')

(48)   Ils ont parlé de moi. ('they have spoken of me')

In these two Italian and French examples, nonclitic *me* and *moi* are strictly singular. Assume that this holds across all of Romance without exception. The question then is: Why should there be such a difference between clitic pronouns (in which first person *m-/j-* can sometimes be neutralized for number) and nonclitic pronouns (in which (by hypothesis) first person *m-*(/j-) cannot be so neutralized)?

I would like to suggest that this difference is due to the bimorphemic character of the nonclitic first person pronouns in (47)/(48) (and in their counterparts in other Romance languages) versus the monomorphemic character of the corresponding clitics. The nonclitic forms are composed of *m-* combined with another morpheme (*-oi* in French and *-é* (cf. note 1) in Italian). The corresponding clitics are, on the other hand, monomorphemic, that is, *m-* plus at most an epenthetic vowel. The reason that the nonclitics always remain singular is that their second morpheme *-oi/-é/* is always itself specified for singular.[18] (This property of *-oi/-é* will play an important role in the later discussion of reflexives.)

8.1.5.   *n-/v-* in French

In French, first- and second-person plural are associated with the consonantal morphemes *n-* and *v-*.[19] The possessive forms with a singular noun (there is no visible agreement with the gender of that noun) are:

(49)   notre livre ('our book')

(50)   votre livre ('your book')

With a covert noun, there is a change in vowel:

(51)   le nôtre ('the ours')

(52)   le vôtre ('the yours')

If the noun is plural:

(53)   nos livres ('our books')

(54)   vos livres ('your books')

If the noun is plural and covert:

(55)   les nôtres

(56)   les vôtres

The subject clitic forms for first and second plural are *nous/vous*, and the object clitic forms are the same:

(57)   Nous partons. ('we leave')

(58)   Vous partez. ('you leave')

(59)   Jean nous voit. ('J us sees')

(60)   Jean vous voit. ('J you sees')

These are furthermore the same as the non-clitic forms:

(61)   Jean parle de nous. ('J speaks of us')

(62)   Jean parle de vous. ('J speaks of you')

In each of these pairs, the first-person plural form in *n-* is identical to the second-person plural form in *v-*, except for the *n-* versus *v-* difference itself.

This makes it plausible to take consonantal *n-* and *v-* to be first- and second-person plural morphemes. As in the case of *m-* and *t-*, each is specified for person and indifferent to gender. Number-wise, they seem to be less flexible than *m-* (perhaps because plural is more 'marked' than singular).

If *n-* and *v-* are separate morphemes, the question arises as to the status of the other parts of the words containing them. The *-ous* of (57)–(62) might be decomposable into a plural *-s*[20] and a morpheme *-ou-*, perhaps the plural counterpart of the singular *-oi* of (48). (The *-s* of *nos/vos/nôtres/vôtres* in (53)–(56), on the other hand, almost certainly reflects agreement with the possessed noun, rather than the plurality of the first/second person itself.) The other pieces are better understood, I think, by switching back to Italian.

8.1.6.   Italian *n-* and *v-*

First-person plural *n-* in Italian fails to appear in the object clitic, which is instead *ci*.[21] Apart from that irregularity, *n-* parallels the second-person plural *v-*. The nonclitic forms corresponding to French (61)/(62) are:

(63)   Gianni parla di noi.

(64)   Gianni parla di voi.

The final *-i* is plausibly the final plural *-i* found in all three words of a DP like:[22]

(65)   i ragazzi tristi ('the boys sad')

in which case the *-o-* of *noi/voi* would have the same status as the *-ou-* of the French examples.[23]

The feminine plural of the definite article and of many nouns and adjectives ends in -*e*:

(66)   le ragazze tristi ('the girls sad')

(67)   le ragazze piccole ('the girls small')

Noi and *voi* cannot end in -*e*. They retain their -*i* ending no matter what their referent:

(68)   *noe/*voe

This is in all probability part of the more general fact, to which I will return later, that first- and second-person pronouns in French and Italian never inflect for gender. The possessive forms with *n*- and *v*- in Italian are illustrated by:

(69)   la nostra tavola ('the our table')

(70)   la vostra tavola ('the your table')

The final -*a*s are the feminine singular word marker. The -*o*- is probably that of *noi/voi*, the -*s* an irregular (for Italian) plural morpheme. The -*tr*- might be a possessive morpheme like the -*i* and -*u* of (38)–(40), or it might be a reduced form of the root *altr*- ('other'),[24] in which case the possessive morpheme in (69)/(70) would be null.

8.1.7.   *m*-/*t*- versus *l*-

In preceding sections, I have claimed that *m*- and *t*- (and similarly *n*- and *v*-) are person morphemes that sometimes occur alone, as, for example, when they are object clitics (though there may be an epenthetic vowel). Sometimes they occur in combination with other morphemes, as in the case of nonclitic pronouns (and also possessives). To call these morphemes first and second person (singular and plural) raises by itself no severe problems.[25] But a question arises as to the term 'third person'.

Benveniste (1966) argued that what is standardly called third person is best thought of as 'nonperson'. Some third-person pronouns are illustrated for Italian in:

(71)   Gianni la vede. ('G her sees')

(72)   Gianni vede lei. ('G sees her')

These are the feminine singular forms, clitic *la* and nonclitic *lei*. The question can be phrased as follows: Do *la*, *lei* and the other third-person pronouns form a natural class with the first- and second-person pronouns discussed so far?

I think that Benveniste was right and that the answer to this question is negative. If so, then the term 'third-person pronoun' should be abandoned. I will (try to) use the term 'determiner pronoun' instead, thinking of Postal (1966) and later work that grew out of his.[26] The term 'determiner pronoun' is straightforwardly appealing for

French since the accusative 'third-person' clitics (*le, la, les*) are identical in form to the definite article:

(73)   Jean le/la/les voit. ('J him-or-it/her-or-it/them sees')

(74)   le livre, la table, les livres ('the book, the table, the books')

In Italian, the accusative clitics can likewise be paired with corresponding definite articles (although one form of the definite article (*il*) cannot appear as a clitic, and the clitic *li* corresponds only partially to the definite article *i*):[27]

(75)   Gianni lo/la/li/le vede.

(76)   lo zio, la tavola, i ragazzi, le ragazze ('the uncle, the table, the boys, the girls')

All the object clitics of (73) and (75) begin with an *l-*. So do the 'third-person' dative clitics of French (*lui*(3sg), *leur* (3pl)) and two of the three dative forms in Italian (*gli*(3msg/3pl), *le*(3fsg), *loro*(3pl)). The nonclitic 'third person' pronouns also show an *l-* for the most part. French has *lui*(3msg), *elle*(3fsg), *eux*(3mpl), *elles*(3fpl). Italian has *lui*(3msg), *lei*(3fsg), *loro*(3pl).

Is this *l-* to be grouped with *m-* and *t-* (and *n-* and *v-*)? Four specific reasons to think that it should not be (i.e., to think that Benveniste was right) are the following: First, the singular accusative *l*-clitics in French and Italian always have a word marker reflecting gender, as seen in French *le, la* and in Italian *lo, la*.[28] There is no corresponding gender distinction with first or second person, for example in French:

(77)   Jean me/*ma voit. ('J me sees')

The clitic *me* serves for both male and female speakers; there is no feminine object clitic **ma* (and similarly for *te, *ta*).[29]

French dative clitics do not show a gender distinction, but Italian dative clitics do (*gli* ('msg') versus. *le* ('fsg')); again, there is no gender distinction in the first or second person. In the nonclitic forms, French distinguishes *lui* (msg) from *elle* (fsg) (*lui* vs. *lei* in Italian). Neither language shows any gender distinction in the first- or second-person nonclitic pronouns. There is thus a consistent difference between the determiner pronouns in *l-*, which often show gender distinctions, and the first and second person forms in *m-* and *t-*, which do not.

Second, the determiner pronouns in *l-* often express plural by adding the usual plural morpheme. This is true for French accusative clitic *les*, nonclitic *elles* (fpl), and subject clitics *ils* (mpl) and *elles* (fpl), as well as for the Italian accusative clitics *li* (mpl) and *le* (fpl).[30] But *m-* and *t-* have the notable property that they never combine with plural morphemes to express first- or second-person plural:[31]

(78)   *Jean mes/tes voit. (French)[32]

(79)   *Jean parle de mous/tous. (French)

(80)   *Gianni ha parlato di mei/tei. (Italian)

Third, *l-* never combines with the possessive morpheme that can show gender agreement with the head noun. Thus alongside (7)/(8), repeated here as (81)/(82), one might expect to find (83) (with the meaning 'his/her book'):

(81)   mon livre ('my book')

(82)   ton livre ('your book')

(83)   *lon livre

The same is true of the covert noun cases of, for example, (12) and (13), repeated here, which have no counterpart with *l-*:

(84)   la mienne ('the mine')

(85)   la tienne ('the yours')

(86)   *la lienne

Similarly, Italian has, corresponding to (38)/(39), repeated here, no form in *l-*:[33]

(87)   la mia tavola ('the my table')

(88)   la tua tavola ('the your table')

(89)   *la lia/lua tavola

Fourth, in some Italian dialects, *m-* and *t-* act differently from *l-* with respect to accusative clitic doubling. For Trentino, Gatti (1990, 195n) has pointed out:[34]

(90)   I me vede mi ('they me see me')

(91)   I te vede ti ('they you see you')

(92)   I la vede (*?ela) ('they her see her')

Nonclitic *mi/ti* can cooccur in Trentino with clitic *me/te*, but nonclitic *ela* cannot cooccur with clitic *la*.[35]

It seems clear, then, that *m-* and *t-* belong to a natural class that does not include *l-* (although it does include reflexive *s-*, as we will see later).

As far as the clitic doubling facts of (90)–(92) are concerned, I think the difference in behavior seen there can be at least in part related to an Italian fact noted by Benincà (1993, 272): If the direct object of a psych verb is preposed (without there being a clitic double present), that direct object can be preceded by the preposition *a* if the direct object is first or second person:[36]

(93)   A me preoccupa il viaggio. ('to me worries the trip')

This *a* recalls the *a* that is found more widely in Spanish. The fact pointed out by Benincà can be interpreted as indicating that the appearance of this *a* with direct objects is favored by the object being first or second person.

For a number of speakers, at least in the north of Italy, this predilection of direct object *a* for first and second person is seen even with nonpsych-verbs:[37]

(94)   A me mi hanno visto. ('to me me they-have seen')

(95)   ??A lui lo hanno visto. ('to him him they-have seen')

The contrast seen in (90)–(92) can be linked to these if the doubling construction of (90)–(92) contains an unpronounced *a*.

That an unpronounced *a* may well be present in (90)–(92) is suggested by the fact that some North Italian dialects (e.g., Paduan and Venetian) allow sentences like:[38]

(96)   Ghe lo dago Giorgio. ('him$_{dat}$ it I-give George')

The proposal, then, is that (90)–(92) must have a similarly unpronounced *a*, which, like its overt counterpart in (93)–(95), is favored by first or second person.

As to why this *a* should be favored by first and second person, there may be a link to Sardinian, as characterized by Jones (1993, sects. 2.2.6, 5.1; 1996).[39] The Sardinian accusative *a* is basically limited to appearing before proper names and (some) pronouns.[40] Jones's proposal is essentially that Sardinian *a* is required before all accusatives that lack a determiner position. (Indefinites of various kinds are assumed to have a null determiner.) Those pronouns which take *a* are NPs. Those that do not are DPs. In the spirit of Jones's proposal, it may be that Italian *a* favors first- and second-person pronouns because those are not DPs, whereas Italian third person pronouns are DPs.[41]

If the locus of word markers is D, as suggested by Uriagereka (1995, note 4), then the absence of a feminine form for first and second persons seen in (77) would also follow from their non-DP status.

The general conclusion of this section, then, is that *l*- is separate from *m*- and *t*- (and *n*- and *v*-). This seems quite solid and leads the way to consideration of reflexive *s*-.

8.2.   *s*-

8.2.1.   Reflexive *s*-

Virtually everything that we have taken into account so far points to the conclusion that there is a reflexive morpheme *s*- that patterns strongly with *m*- and *t*- (rather than with *l*-).[42]

In French, alongside object clitic *m'/t'* (before vowels; cf. (16)/(17)), we have reflexive *s'*:

(97)   Jean m'invite. ('J me invites')

(98)   Jean t'invite. ('J you invites')

(99)   Jean s'invite. ('J refl. invites')

Before consonants:

(100)   Jean me voit. ('J me sees')

(101)   Jean te voit. ('J you sees')

(102)   Jean se voit. ('J refl. sees')

There is no feminine form:

(103)   *Jean ma voit.

(104)   *Jean ta voit.

(105)   *Marie sa voit.

And no plural in *-s*:[43]

(106)   *Jean mes voit.

(107)   *Jean tes voit.

(108)   *Jean et Marie ses voit. ('J and M refl.pl. see')

The nonclitic forms are entirely parallel in form (cf. (28)/(29)):

(109)   Quand on parle de moi, . . . ('when one speaks of me . . .')

(110)   Quand on parle de toi, . . . (' . . . of you')

(111)   Quand on parle de soi, . . . (' . . . of refl.')

This parallelism is found in Italian, too:[44]

(112)   Parla di me. ('he-speaks of me')

(113)   Parla di te. (' . . . of you')

(114)   Parla di sé. (' . . . of refl.')

None of these allow a plural morpheme to be added (v. (80)):

(115)   *Parla di mei.

(116)   *Parla di tei.

(117)   *Parlano di sei. ('they-speak of refl.pl.')

The parallelism in form carries over to the object clitics:

(118)   Gianni mi vede. ('G me sees')

(119)   Gianni ti vede. ('G you sees')

(120)   Gianni si vede. ('G refl. sees')

including to the vowel change dependent on a following clitic, as mentioned earlier ((36)/(37)):

(121)   Gianni me lo dice. ('G me it says')

(122)   Gianni te lo dice. ('G you it says')

(123)   Gianni se lo dice. ('G refl. it says')

Furthermore, the doubling facts of (90)–(92) group *se* with *me/te*, rather than with the determiner clitics. Thus, in Paduan:

(124)   El me ga visto mi. ('he me has seen me')[45]

(125)   El te ga visto ti. ('he you has seen you')

(126)   El se ga visto lu. ('he refl. has seen him')

(127)   *l lo ga visto lu. ('they him have seen him')

The contrast between these last two examples shows that the earlier discussion of (90)–(92) was incomplete, since it attributed the deviance of (92) and now (127) to properties of the doubled nonclitic pronoun, which is the same *lu* in the grammatical (126). It may be that in the reflexive clitic example (126) no (unpronounced) *a* is needed (as opposed to the nonreflexive examples), for reasons having to do with the unaccusative-like status of reflexive clitic sentences.[46] Alternatively, or in addition, the contrast between (126) and (127) may indicate that the choice of clitic itself plays a direct role in determining the acceptability of doubling, with the D-clitic *lo* somehow making doubling more difficult to achieve (in these dialects; cf. note 34) than the non-D-clitic *se*.

I note in passing that the doubling parallel between *me/te* and *se* extends to the intriguing case of doubling in the 'neg . . . *che*' construction.[47] In Paduan, one has:

(128)   Nol me vede che mi. ('neg he me sees than/but me' = 'he sees only me')

Burzio (1991, 90n) gives a comparable example with *se* for Piedmontese:

(129)   Giuanin a s guarda mac chiel. ('G he refl. watches only him')

I conclude that reflexive *s-* forms a natural class with the person morphemes *m-* and *t-*.

8.2.2.   Reflexive *s-* and number

It would be natural to think, in light of the following (Italian) examples, that *s-* is neutral with respect to number:

(130)   Gianni s'invita. ('G refl. invites')

(131)   Gianni e Maria s'invitano. ('G and M refl. invite')

And, in fact, it is perfectly true that reflexive clitics in Italian (and French) occur productively with both singular and plural antecedents. (When the antecedent is plural, a reciprocal interpretation is also possible.)

However, if we turn to Italian nonclitic *sé*, we find an asymmetry:

(132)   Il ragazzo ha parlato di sé. ('the boy has spoken of refl.')

(133)   ?I ragazzi hanno parlato di sé. ('the boys have . . .')

With a plural antecedent, *sé* is somewhat less good than with a singular antecedent, on the whole.[48] (I have found one speaker for whom (133) is impossible.)

That *sé* should tilt toward the singular is not entirely surprising, given its resemblance to nonclitic *me* and *te*. In particular, all three should be analyzed as X + é, where X is *m-*, *t-* or *s-* and *-é* is a morpheme (cf. note 1) whose properties will be discussed next. (Important also is the fact that this resemblance does not extend to the plural *noi* and *voi*.)

The obvious proposal, now, is that the tilt toward singular seen with *sé* (as opposed to the clitic *si*, which is neutral between singular and plural) is to be attributed to the morpheme *-é* that *sé* has in common with nonclitic *me* and *te* (and that clitic *si* lacks).[49] In other words, it is *-é* itself that is singular.

This would seem to lead us to expect (133) to be sharply unacceptable, which is not the case. My hypothesis is the following:

(134)   *Sé* can have a plural antecedent only via the intermediary of a(n abstract) distributor.[50]

As for the question where that abstract distributor is (in, for example, (133)), consider the following fact brought to my attention by Luigi Rizzi, namely that a plural antecedent for *sé* is unacceptable if the antecedent is 'long-distance'. An example would be:[51]

(135)   ?Il ragazzo mi ha convinto a parlare di sé. ('the boy me has convinced to speak of refl. = him')

(136)   *I ragazzi mi hanno convinto a parlare di sé. ('the boys . . .')

The fact that (136) is worse than (135) suggests that the abstract distributor needed in (136) must be 'local' with respect to both *sé* and the antecedent of *sé*.[52] Representing it as *DB*, this gives for (133):

(137)   I ragazzi hanno parlato *DB* di sé.

But, given the double locality requirement, there is no satisfactory position available in the long-distance case (136):

(138)   *i ragazzi mi$_i$ hanno convinto a PRO$_i$ parlare *DB* di sé

(139)   *i ragazzi mi$_i$ hanno convinto *DB* a PRO$_i$ parlare di sé

In (138), *DB* is too far from the antecedent *i ragazzi* (cf. the general locality requirement on floated quantifiers (Sportiche (1988)). In (139), *DB* is too far from *sé* itself.

The conclusion that the *-é* of *sé* is singular (and that it therefore can never have a nondistributed plural antecedent) is supported by the fact that *sé* cannot be a reciprocal (as opposed again to the monomorphemic clitic *si*). Thus, the contrast between (131) and (133) is mirrored by the (sharper) contrast (in interpretation) between:

(140)   Loro si amano. ('they refl. love')

(141)   ?Loro parlano di sé. ('they speak of refl.')

Whereas the first of these has a natural reciprocal interpretation (in addition to the reflexive one), the second is not possible as a reciprocal. The reason is that *sé*, because it contains *-é*, prohibits its antecedent from being a nondistributed plural. But a nondistributed plural antecedent is precisely what a reciprocal needs:[53]

(142)   They're (*each) in love with one another.

In conclusion, the singularity of -*é* has significant effects in the case of *sé*, much as it did in the case of nonclitic *me* (cf. the earlier discussion of (47)).

8.2.3.   Further restrictions on -*é*

To take nonclitic *me/te/sé* to form a natural class in Italian, representable as *m-/t-/s-* + *é* seems correct, yet there is clearly a difference that has so far been set aside, namely that the antecedent of *sé* can be a full DP, whereas the antecedent of *me/te* cannot be.[54] Assume not only that this restriction on the antecedent of *me/te* is a fact about *m-/t-* but that it carries over to -*é* itself. Then Italian must be analyzed as containing a small discrepancy between the -*é* of *me/te* and the -*é* of *sé* (which are otherwise identical). That is, the -*é* of *sé* must be allowed to waive the antecedent restriction that it might otherwise be expected to take over from the -*é* of *me/te*.

Italian is evidently capable of bearing the burden of this discrepancy. French is not. The French counterpart of *sé* is nonclitic *soi* (cf. nonclitic first/second person *moi/toi*). The antecedent of *soi* generally cannot be a full DP:[55]

(143)   Quand on parle de soi, . . . ('when one speaks of refl.')

(144)   Chacun a parlé de soi. ('each has spoken of refl.')

(145)   *Ce linguiste a parlé de soi. ('that linguist . . .')

For Jean-Yves Pollock, there is a clear contrast between (145) and:

(146)   A ce colloque, chaque linguiste a parlé de soi. ('at that conference, each linguist . . .')

as well as between the following two:

(147)   *Tous les linguistes parlent de soi. ('all the linguists speak of refl.')

(148)   Tout linguiste parle de soi. ('every linguist . . .')

Thinking of Szabolcsi (1994) and Bartos (to appear), it may be that *chaque linguiste* and *tout linguiste* differ from *ce linguiste* and *tous les linguistes* in that the former pair lack a DP projection. If so, then a specific requirement on the antecedent of *soi*, namely that it lack a DP projection, in fact falls together with the basic requirement on the antecedents of *moi* and *toi*, if first and second persons lack a DP projection, as discussed earlier ((text to) note 41).

I therefore take French -*oi* to be broadly consistent across *m-*, *t-*, and *s-* as far as choice of antecedent is concerned. Put another way, the restrictions on the antecedent of *soi* are now seen to be a property of its subcomponent -*oi*.

Since French clitic *se* lacks -*oi*, it is not surprising, either, that *se* (which just has an epenthetic vowel, when it has one at all) shows none of the restrictions to which *soi* is subject.

From this perspective, one might wonder if there is still not a discrepancy in French (smaller than in Italian) between *moi/toi* and *soi* concerning antecedents. Although *-oi* in all three cases has the property of needing an antecedent that is not a full DP, the antecedent taken by *moi/toi* is very particular and not narrowly extendable to the antecedents of *soi*. If we again associate the antecedent of *moi/toi* not only with *m-/t-* but also with *-oi*, the discrepancy in question is of interest to the present discussion.

French evidently tolerates this small discrepancy. But Piedmontese and various other North Italian dialects arguably do not.[56] They have a clitic in *s-*, but no nonclitic in *s-*. It may be that these dialects do not allow their counterpart of French *-oi* or Italian *-é* to be generalized from *m-/t-* to *s-* at all, for reasons having to do with uniformity of antecedent.

8.2.4. A restriction on reflexive *s-*

The preceding section considered certain restrictions on nonclitic *s-*forms in French and Italian and related dialects. Those restrictions were not shared by the corresponding clitic forms. There is, on the other hand, one class of restrictions that is common to both clitic and nonclitic French and Italian *s-*, having to do with the person feature of the antecedent.[57] In neither language can the antecedent be first or second person, as in these examples in Italian:

(149)   *Tu s'inviti. ('you refl. invite')

(150)   *Io parlo di sé. ('I speak of refl.')

Taking *m-/t-/s-* to be strongly parallel, *m-* to be first person and *t-* to be second person, it would be natural to say that *s-* is itself neither first nor second person and therefore does not admit an antecedent that is. This would suffice for French and Italian, but not in general, as shown by various North Italian dialects that are less restrictive than French and Italian. For example, Nicoli (1983, 151/2) gives:[58]

(151)   Nun se lavom. ('we refl. wash')

The question how to understand this kind of variation within Romance is complicated by the fact that some dialects sometimes allow sentences like:[59]

(152)   Mi a ma sa lavi i man. ('me *a* me refl. wash the hands' = 'I wash my hands')

Mi here is a (nonclitic) subject pronoun and *a* a subject clitic.[60] Though there is only one other argument with 'wash' apart from the direct object *i man*, there are two further object clitics, *ma* and *sa*.

How best to allow for this kind of 'doubling' (*ma* and *sa* together when we would expect just one of them) is not yet clear.[61] But the existence of (152) raises the possibility that in sentences like (151) the relation between *s-* and the first- or second-person subject is mediated by an abstract counterpart of the *ma* of (152).[62] If so, then it might be feasible to take *s-* never to directly have a first- or second-person antecedent. In

(152) (and (151)), it would be *ma* that has *mi* as antecedent. *Sa* would itself not have *mi* as antecedent, though it would be in a (quasi-)doubling relation with first-person *ma*.

8.2.5. Reflexive *s*- and Condition B

First- and second-person pronouns are normally assumed to fall under Condition B of the Binding Theory:

(153) *I photographed me exactly twice yesterday.

(154) *Why did you photograph you only twice yesterday?

If I have been correct in emphasizing the systematic parallels between *m-/t-* and *s-*, we would expect *s*-forms to be subject to Condition B, too.[63] In the case of clitic *s-*, it looks as if the expectation is not met, since the following (Italian) sentence is perfectly acceptable:

(155) Gianni si fotografa. ('G refl. photographs')

On the other hand, the same holds of clitic *m-/t-*:

(156) Io mi fotografo. ('I me . . .')

(157) Tu ti fotografi. ('you you . . .')

(156)/(157) show that there is no discrepancy here among *m-/t-/s-*.[64]
    Nonclitic *sé* does, however, display what I take to be clear Condition B effects. We can see this by taking, first, the following three sentences:

(158) Gianni ha parlato di me. ('G has spoken of me')

(159) Gianni ha parlato di te. (' . . . of you')

(160) Gianni ha parlato di sé. (' . . . of refl.')

All three are acceptable. Consider now the direct object counterparts of these:

(161) Gianni ha fotografato me. ('G has photographed me')

(162) Gianni ha fotografato te. (' . . . you')

(163) ??Gianni ha fotografato sé. (' . . . refl.')

The contrast between (163) and (160), which was pointed out by Giorgi (1984, 328), varies in sharpness depending on the speaker. Judgments on (163) range from somewhat marginal to fully unacceptable. Giorgi correctly attributed the contrast to the presence of the preposition in (160). I would like to propose that the deviance of (163) is to be interpreted as a Condition B effect (that can be neutralized by a preposition).[65]

I note in passing that the plural counterpart of (163) is sharply impossible:

(164)   *I ragazzi hanno fotografato sé. ('the boys have . . .')

The reason is that (164) combines the Condition B violation seen in (163) with the reluctance of *sé* to admit a plural antecedent seen in (133). More precisely, *sé* can have a plural antecedent only via the intermediary of a distributor, as stated in (134). The fact that (164) is appreciably less acceptable than (133) (with plural antecedent and preposition preceding *sé*) suggests that the required distributor is facilitated by the preposition (which perhaps provides a Spec position for the distributor that is unavailable in (164)).[66]

Returning to the contrast between (160) and (163), the idea that the preposition is playing a crucial role is suggested by the following judgments of Giuseppe Longobardi's: For him (160) itself is only acceptable in an 'elegant' stylistic register. In his colloquial Italian, he has (with coreference):

(165)   Gianni ha parlato di lui. ('G has spoken of him')

But he accepts (and prefers) *sé* when the subject is *ciascuno dei ragazzi*:

(166)   Ciascuno dei ragazzi ha parlato di sé. ('each of-the boys has spoken of refl.')

In other words, his colloquial Italian is (substantially) like French (cf. (text to) note 55). What is of primary importance here, though, is that he finds a sharp contrast between (165) and the following, which is impossible with coreference:[67]

(167)   *Gianni$_i$ ha fotografato lui$_i$.

Thus, the importance of the preposition seems clear.[68] (In the framework of Chomsky (1986b), one might take the PP to be capable, in Italian (and French, but not English), of counting as governing category for a pronoun.[69])

Given the contrast between (167) and (165), and the fact that the former is certainly to be considered a Condition B violation, it is virtually certain that (163) should be considered a (weaker) Condition B violation, too. In that case, *s-* is visible to Condition B, just as are *m-* and *t-*.

8.2.6.   Pronominal *s-*

Italian (and French) have in possessives a pronominal *s-*:

(168)   Io ho visto la sua tavola. ('I have seen the his/her table')

This *s-* is clearly not reflexive.[70] The question is whether this *s-* is closer to the *l-* of determiner pronouns or to the reflexive *s-*. One consideration has to do with the absence of *l-* in comparable possessives—**la lua tavola* (cf. (89)). If this absence is not accidental (it might be related to facts about compounding—*a pick-me-up* vs. **a pick-him-up*[71]), then the *s-* of (168) cannot have too much in common with *l-*.

A second consideration has to do with the distribution within Romance of such pronominal *s-*. Apart from possessives, where it is commonly found, pronominal *s-* is found in nonclitic (nonpossessive) forms in some dialects. Thus:

(169)   Qu'ei se que parlo. ('that it's him that speaks')

(170)   Ca ve de se. ('that comes from him')

(171)   I fau coqui per se. ('I do this for him')

(172)   I pèr sè ke d e travalò. ('it's for him that I have worked')

The first three are from the Limousin dialect studied by Chabaneau (1874, 453), the last from the Savoie dialect studied by Ratel (1958, 31).[72] In both of these dialects, this pronominal use of *se* seems to be limited to (some) nonclitic environments. In fact, with the one exception to be discussed shortly, pronominal *s-* seems never to occur as an object clitic.[73]

Taken together with the point of the previous paragraph, this suggests that the *s-* of (168)–(172) is, first, not at all a variant of *l-*, and, second, that it is in fact the same *s-* as the reflexive one. Put another way, *s-* is not intrinsically specialized as anaphoric.[74] It is primarily anaphoric in Romance but can also be pronominal.

The absence of any clitic pronominal *s-*, combined with my earlier proposals concerning the difference between (monomorphemic) clitics and (bimorphemic) nonclitics (in the case of *m-/t-/s-*) leads me to the more specific proposal that *s-* can be pronominal (nonanaphoric) only by virtue of amalgamating with a second morpheme, either *-é*, as in (169)/(172), or *-u*, as in possessives (or their counterparts in other Romance languages). (In effect, then, these morphemes *-é/-u* can be pronominal, at least in (168)–(172).)[75]

The antecedent of *se/sé* in the dialects illustrated in (169)/(172) seems to be limited to singular. Similarly, the antecedent of *su-* in (168) is necessarily singular. Thus, these pronominal instances of *s-* have the same bias toward singular that we saw in the case of reflexive non-clitic *s-* in section 8.2.2. This supports the idea that the two are basically the same *s-*,[76] in that both, when they combine with another morpheme, are restricted to combining with morphemes (*-é/-u*) that are inherently singular.[77]

8.2.7.   A further question

The bias toward singular found with nonclitic *sé* was attributed in section 8.2.2. to a property of the morpheme *-é* with which *s-* combines. In a similar way, the singular bias of *su-* could be attributed to a property of the possessive morpheme *-u-*. The contrast with clitics in *s-*, which show no bias toward singular in either Italian or French, was attributed to the fact that those clitics are monomorphemic, so if *s-* itself is neutral with respect to number, the contrast follows. There are, on the other hand, some dialects that seem to show some bias toward singular even in their reflexive clitics.

For example, Lepelley (1974, 113) gives clitic *s-* for dative reflexive singular and plural and for accusative reflexive singular, but not for accusative reflexive plural.[78] Thus, it may be that in that dialect *s-* itself is not entirely neutral with respect to number. Alternatively, it might be that the accusative reflexive in question is bimorphemic, contrary to those of Italian and French.[79]

8.2.8. Morphology and Anaphora

The main points that I have argued in this essay are that nonclitic reflexive *sé* and *soi* in Italian and French are to be analyzed as *s-* + *-é/oi* and that to a substantial extent this *s-* patterns with first- and second-person *m-* and *t-*. These claims bear on Burzio's (1991) proposal concerning the relation between morphology and anaphora. Burzio proposed that the morphological poverty (lack of phi-features) of forms in *s-* implied their anaphoric status.

However, if I am correct, the fact that *s-* cannot combine with number morphology (cf. (108), (117)) is a property shared by *m-* and *t-* (cf. (106)/(107)) and (115)/(116)). Consequently, incompatibility with number morphology cannot be a sufficient condition for anaphoric status.

Similarly, gender morphology cannot combine either with *s-* (cf. (105) or with *m-* and *t-* (cf. (103)/(104)). Thus, incompatibility with gender morphology cannot be a sufficient condition for anaphoric status, either.[80]

On the other hand, if we set aside complex reflexives of the English type (cf. Jayaseelan (1996) and Safir (1996) for recent discussion), then it still might be the case, in the spirit of Burzio's approach, that lack of number (and perhaps gender; cf. note 80) is a necessary condition for anaphoric status.[81]

This might account for the fact that *s-* has no plural counterpart in the way that *n-* and *v-* are plural counterparts to *m-* and *t-* (cf. (49)–(70)). Thus, no Romance language, to my knowledge, has, for example, a *z-* that is the plural counterpart of *s-*:

(173)   Il ragazzo si fotografa. ('the boy refl. photographs')

(174)   *I ragazzi zi fotografano. ('the boys refl.pl . . .')

(Related to this is the fact, discussed earlier (cf. (132)–(142)), that *sé* is singular, that is, that the morpheme *-é* with which *s-* combines to form a nonclitic is singular.)

Jayaseelan (1996, note 11) suggests that it might be only the person feature whose absence implies anaphoric status. If we take *s-* to be a person morpheme lacking specification for first or second person (cf. my earlier discussion and the zeroperson (distinct from nonperson) of chapter 7, sect. 2.6),[82] the question is whether that is sufficient to imply anaphoric status. If I am correct in taking some nonclitic *s-* forms to be nonanaphoric (cf. (168)–(172)), then the answer is, not exactly. The status of *s-* with respect to person may imply anaphoric status, but only in those (clitic) cases where *s-* combines with no other morpheme.

NOTES

To Paola, whose inspired work has made dialect syntax indispensable.

1. Italian writes *sé* with an accent and *me/te* without one. This is a purely orthographic difference; the vowel is all these nonclitic forms is the same (an open /e/). When referring to the vocalic morpheme by itself, I will use *-é*.

French second singular *toi* and related forms with *t-* are restricted to 'familiar'; second singular polite uses the plural *vous* and related forms in *v-*, some discussion of which can be found later in this essay.

2. See Haegeman (1993, 63) on West Flemish pronouns and Picabia (1997) on the consonantal noun class morphemes of the Bantu language of Grande Comore. It is possible that *-es* itself is composed of two morphemes, with the *-e-* corresponding to Harris's (1991) word marker and the *-s* to number; on the status of number in French, see Tranel (1981, chap. 6) and Bernstein (1991).

3. This *-on* also appears with feminine singular nouns beginning with a vowel:

(i)   mon intuition, ton intuition

4. For further details, see Kayne (1975, sect. 2.20).

5. It should be emphasized here that the agreement in question is with the head noun (which may be covert) and not with the possessor itself. For example, the difference between (4) and (7) (*ma table* vs. *mon livre*) with respect to the form of the possessive (*ma* vs. *mon*) depends solely on the gender of the noun and is entirely independent of whether the speaker is male or female.

6. On treating (some) schwas as epenthetic in French phonology, see Tranel (1981, chap. 8) and references cited there.

7. It should be noted that the usual French masc. sg. WM is zero, as it in fact probably is in:

(i)   Marie l'invite. ('M him invites')

Alternatively, (i) has an *-e* that has been deleted phonologically.

Morin (1979b, 310) notes that the *-e* of *le* in (22) is a front rounded vowel, rather than a schwa. (20)/(21) is impossible with that pronunciation, too.

The *l-* of (i) can also correspond to 'her', that is, to *la*, with the fem. sg. WM *-a* of *la* failing to appear, just as in (ii) with the definite article:

(ii)   l'amie ('the friend (fem.)')

8. Bare *m-* (and *t-*) can appear postverbally when followed by the clitic *en*:

(i)   Donne-m'en! ('give me (some)of-it')

Possible in certain varieties of French is:

(ii)   Donne-moi-z-en!

For interesting discussion, see Rooryck (1992) and Morin (1979b). See also Chenal (1986, 360).

9. *M-* is replaced by (monomorphemic) *j-* in the subject clitic form, as seen in (30).

10. The oft-stated view that *mi/ti* gives way to *me/te* only in the presence of an immediately following clitic beginning with a sonorant cannot be completely right, given (i) (acceptable to some speakers):

(i)   Me ce ne vorranno due. ('me there of-them they-will-want two' = 'I will need two (of them)')

11. As in French, this agreement morpheme does not and cannot reflect the gender of the speaker or hearer.
Many Italian dialects have the equivalent of 'la mi/tu tavola', with no agreement on the prenominal possessive. See, for example, Mattesini (1976, 190) and Pelliciardi (1977, 70).
12. Further analysis of the notions 'first person' and 'second person' is certainly warranted, thinking, for example, of:

(i)   I don't like you, said John to Bill.

For relevant discussion, see Postal (1970, 494), Nadahalli (1998), and Bevington (1998).
Note also (with a matrix subject interpreted as 'first person'):

(ii)   The person who is talking to you wants you to give him/*me some money.

13. See also the dialects studied by Lurà (1990, 160) and Spiess (1976, 206).
14. The double *mm* is an orthographic convention indicating a preceding short vowel, not a doubled consonant; v. Nicoli, p. 49.
15. See note 9 above.
16. See Butler (1962, 39, 42), Chauveau (1984, 190), Ditchy (1977, 21), Gesner (1979, 17), Hervé (1973, 51), Maze (1969, 41, 66, 83, 85) (who notes that *je* cannot invert and that *nous* can appear with inversion), Rouffiange (1983, 115), Vey (1978, 186), Villefranche (1978, 24), Féral (1986, 68, 73–5), Hauchard (1994, 137), and Hull (1988).
17. See Harris's (1997, 40) proposal that *m-* 'loses out' to the more highly specified *n-*. The details of Milanese will require further work.
18. See (78)–(80).
19. See the second paragraph of note 1.
20. See Harris (1997, 39) on Spanish.
21. The second-person plural object clitic *vi* may be synchronically parallel in a regular way to *mi* and *ti*, as in (34)/(35); alternatively, it may be more like *ci*—v. Corver and Delfitto (1993, 21).
22. This *-i* is normally incompatible with the word marker *-o* that appears in the singular:

(i)   ragazzo ('boy')

(ii)   ragazzi/*ragazzoi

The two do cooccur in possessive forms:

(iii)   i tuoi ragazzi ('the your boys')

(iv)   i suoi ragazzi ('the his/her boys')

suggesting that *-i* is a pure number morpheme that normally causes the word marker not to be pronounced. See Khim (1997) on Wolof.

23. Note that the two morpheme *-oi* sequence in Italian *noi/voi* is pronounced approximately as written, as opposed to the single morpheme *-oi* of French *moi/toi*, pronounced /wa/.

24. Compare Spanish *nosotros, vosotros* ('we others/you others' = nonclitic 'we/you'), and similarly in many Italian dialects.

25. See, however, note 12.

26. See also Hale (1973).

27. Cardinaletti and Starke (1994, note 65) note that these discrepancies might indicate that clitics have more structure than determiners.

28. In the plural, Italian *li, le* shows a gender distinction, but French *les* does not. Thus, the contrast with the first and second person plural (which never show gender; v. (68)) is a shade less striking than in the singular. I take the gender distinction in Spanish *nosotros, nosotras* to be a property of *otros, otras* ('others') and not a property of *nos*.

The word marker can fail to appear in some cases in both French (cf. note 7) and Italian.

29. Recall that possessive *ma, ta* in French are composed of *m-, t-* plus a word marker *-a* that reflects agreement with the head noun only. See the earlier discussion of (4)–(6).

30. The *-s* of the French forms is pronounced only in certain syntactic environments (cf. note 2). Plural *-s* on determiner pronouns is particularly robust in Spanish, which has accusative clitic *los, las,* dative clitic *les* and nonclitic *ellos, ellas*; Spanish supports the text discussion that follows in that it does not allow plural *-s* to combine with *m-* or *t-*.

31. This appears to contrast with Cantonese, in which *deih* is added to *ngóh* (I) to yield *ngóhdeih* (we) (and similarly for second person), as described by Matthews and Yip (1994, 79). It may be that in Cantonese and comparable languages, the plural morpheme in question is not a plural in the sense of French or Italian but rather something more like 'and company' (cf. Matthews and Yip (p. 83)), thinking of Taljaard et al.'s (1991, 12) characterization of Siswati (prefixal) *bo-*; for recent discussion, see Cheng and Sybesma (1999).

Malagasy *-re-* appears in the second person, but not in the first person, according to Zribi-Hertz and Mbolatianavalona (1997, 245).

32. The *-s* of French possessive *mes, tes* does not express plurality of first or second person but is rather an agreement morpheme reflecting the plurality of the head noun. See the earlier discussion of (1)–(3).

Italian does have:

(i)　Gianni mi/ti vede. ('G me/you(sg) sees')

But the *-i* here is not the plural morpheme, and the interpretation is not plural. On this *-i,* see the discussion of (34)/(35).

Some Walloon (cf. Remacle (1952, 243)) has a form *tès-ôtes*; see notes 24, 28 and 31, especially Tranel's (1981, 211) suggestion that plural /z/ in French might be a prefix on a plural noun or adjective.

33. Italian does have (without gender agreement):

(i)　la loro tavola ('the their table')

This *-or(o)* that combines with *l-* here must have a sharply different status from the *-on/-ien/-i/-u* of (81)–(89); that is, *-or(o)* could be a case/number ending but not a possessive morpheme.

34. See Burzio (1989) on Piedmontese. This contrast seems to hold for Paduan, too, as I have learned from discussions with Paola Benincà; see Benincà (1983, note 8). On the other

hand, it seems to be absent from the dialects studied by Nicoli (1983, 144, 359), Pelliciardi (1977, 93), Vassere (1993, 97, 102), Spiess (1976, 209), and Salvioni (1975, 31).

35. And similarly for the other *l*-pronouns. The absence of a comma before the nonclitic object pronoun in Gatti's examples indicates that the doubling in question is nondislocation doubling.

The text discussion does not imply that *l*-pronouns have nothing in common with *me/te/sé*. In particular, they all (as opposed to full DPs) require or allow *di* with certain prepositions:

(i)   contro di me/te/sé/lui ('against of me/you/refl./him')

(ii)   contro il professore ('against the professor')

On this, see Rizzi (1988, 522).

36. With a doubled clitic preceding the psych verb, *a* would not be limited to the first or second person; see also Belletti and Rizzi (1988, note 27).

37. Conversely (for Raffaella Zanuttini) (i) is very marginal, while (ii) is fine and (iii) intermediate:

(i)   ???Me, mi hanno visto.

(ii)   Lui, lo hanno visto.

(iii)   ?Noi, ci hanno visto.

This construction is compatible with past participle agreement:

(iv)   A me mi hanno vista.

The combination of past participle agreement with the presence of *a* (also found in Occitan and Gascon; Miremont (1976, 55) and Rohlfs (1977)) is not expected by Uriagereka (1995, note 70). See note 45.

Anna Cardinaletti (p.c.) points out that in Central and Southern dialects (95) is possible in addition to (94).

38. Clitic doubling with datives is usually obligatory in the North Italian dialects; see Vanelli (1998, 134).

On the fact that clitic doubling is more prevalent with datives than with accusatives, note Pollock's (1983b, 97) observation that dative clitic resumptives in French relatives (perhaps with an abstract dative *à*) are more possible than accusative.

Paola Benincà points out (p.c.) that Friulian has clitic doubling of the (90) sort but lacks the *a*-less (96).

39. Jones (1993, 202) observes that dative clitic doubling with a postverbal *a* is limited in Sardinian to first- and second-person pronouns. Whether this restriction can be integrated with the others under discussion remains to be seen.

There also appear to exist cases of a preposition *a* preceding subject pronouns. See Tuaillon (1988, 295), Baptista (1997, 241).

40. See Marcellesi (1986) on Corsican.

41. Although Sardinian accusative and dative clitics have *l*-, it is notable that the third-person nonclitic pronouns that take *a* (*isse, issa, issos, issas*) (which for Jones are NPs) do

not, although they are presumably related to the Sardinian definite article (*su, sa, sos, sas*), and perhaps to the (close to addressee) demonstratives *cussu, -a, -os, -as* (Jones (1993, 34)).

Probably relevant, too, is the contrast (also found in French) between Sardinian *nois átteros* ('we others'), *vois átteros* ('you others') and the impossible **issos átteros* ('they others'). See Jones (1993, 208).

For relevant discussion, see also Uriagereka (1995, sect. 4).

There may be a further link between the non-DP status of first- and second-person pronouns and their failure to trigger Hungarian object agreement. See Bartos (to appear).

On the special status of first and second person with respect to auxiliary selection, see chapter 7, and on the probably closely related person split with respect to ergativity, see Mahajan (1994), Nash (1997), and Manzini and Savoia (1998).

42. See Milner (1978) on Latin and Montaut (1997, 125) on Dravidian.

43. Recall that the vowel in object clitics is in general epenthetic. There is also no:

(i)   *Jean ms invite.

(ii)   *Jean ts invite.

(iii)   *Jean et Marie ss invite.

44. Recall that the *e/é,* difference is just orthographic; v. note 1.

45. Here, however (cf. note 37), past participle agreement (which is normally optional with first and second person in Paduan) does not go well with doubling:

(i)   ??El me ga vista mi.

Note that the auxiliary in (126) is 'have' (rather than 'be'); v. chapter 7 and references cited there.

46. See Bouchard (1984, 68), Kayne (1986b).

47. On which, see Azoulay-Vicente (1985).

In Paduan (and Venetian), at least, the doubling seen in (128) and (124)/(125) is obligatory, in the sense that removing the clitic would make the sentences ungrammatical. (The same is true of (126), though there for a different reason, thinking of (167).) This suggests that Paduan direct object nonclitic *mi* and *ti* are obligatorily preceded by an abstract *a*, in which case the need for the clitic may be linkable to the obligatoriness of dative clitic doubling (cf. note 38).

48. Lidia Lonzi tells me that for her *sé* with a plural antecedent is better in control structures such as (i):

(i)   Ho invitato i ragazzi a parlare di sé. ('I-have invited the boys to speak of refl.')

See perhaps the discussion of (160)–(167).

Probably related to (132) versus (133) is a judgment given by Cordin (1988, 596), namely that a nonreflexive (nonclitic) pronoun can be a direct object coreferential with the subject in certain contexts, but only when the pronoun is plural:

(ii)   Vestivano di pelli loro e le loro donne. ('they-dressed in furs them and the their wives')

49. Cf. Cardinaletti and Starke's (1994) idea (contested by Zribi-Hertz (1998)) that the extra structure associated with nonclitic 'third person' pronouns, as compared with their clitic counterparts, is responsible for the nonclitics' (relative) incompatibility with inanimate antecedents.

50. See Heim et al. (1991). Proposal (134) carries over to French *soi*; see Kayne (1975, chap. 5, note 4), although in French the distributor may have to be overt.

Whether the plural uses of *m-/j-* in (41)–(42) and (45)–(46) involve an abstract distributor is left an open question.

51. This fact is masked in the Italian of those who (unlike Giorgi (1984)) accept no long-distance reflexives at all.

It may be that (136) improves if *i ragazzi* is replaced by a coordination of singulars.

52. See also perhaps the locality effect pointed out by Burzio (1986, 199):

(i)   They gave John a dollar each.

(ii)   *They want John to give me a dollar each.

Malagasy *izy/azy* looks similar to Italian *sé* in that, as discussed by Zribi-Hertz and Mbolatianavalona (1997, 253), it allows a plural antecedent (and in their terms is a bound variable; p. 255) only under restricted conditions. Why the restrictions are less severe than with *sé* remains to be investigated.

53. Note that *all* and *both* (the latter for some speakers) are not necessarily distributors; see Dougherty (1970; 1971).

An interesting complication arises when we take into account:

(i)   Loro parlano di se stessi.

Here *sé* is accompanied by *stessi* ('same') (note that the accent on the *-é* is not used here). (On *stess-*, see Safir (1996), whose (p. 567) discussion of reciprocals suggests the potential relevance of (163).) *Stessi* is *stess-* plus the mpl. *-i*. (With appropriate antecedents, there are also *stesso, stessa, stesse*.) Example (i) remains impossible as a reciprocal, like (141) and (133). But unlike those two, (i) is fully acceptable, that is, there is no longer a problem with a plural antecedent (and a reflexive reading). It may be that the presence of plural *stessi* facilitates the licensing of a DB.

The singularity of *-é* in Italian is mirrored by the singularity of the *-eg* of Faroese *seg*, to judge by Barnes's (1994, 212) example:

(ii)   Tey nokta seg sekan ('they deny refl. guilty')

with the adjective *sekan* in the accusative masculine singular agreeing with *seg* (and not with the plural *tey*).

54. See, however, note 12.

55. See Kayne (1975, sect. 5.1) and Legendre (1997, 56). For Anne Zribi-Hertz (144) is not possible in spoken French (nor is (146) or (148)), as opposed to (143).

56. See Burzio (1991, 91); also the dialects described by Ditchy (1977, 22), Francard (1980, 209) and Remacle (1952, 223), among others.

57. Impersonal and middle *s-* (cf. Cinque (1988)) fall outside the scope of this article.

58. The first person plural nonreflexive object clitic in Milanese is *ne* (Nicoli, p. 149). Similarly, the Veneto and Friuli dialects discussed by Vanelli (1998, 122) have *se* for first

plural reflexive, but *ne* and *nus*, respectively, for first plural nonreflexive. See also Blinkenberg (1948, 96), Remacle (1952, 224), and, on Catalan, Picallo (1994, 279).

59. Example from Spiess (1976, 207). See also Nicoli (1983, 152), Lurà (1990, 161), Vassere (1993, 35, 48), and Salvioni (1975, 33).

Note that the -a of *ma* and *sa* in (152) is not a gender marker and in all probability corresponds to no separate morpheme.

60. On this *a*, see Poletto (1993; 1995; 2000).

61. For proposals concerning a perhaps comparable phenomenon in Catalan, see Bonet (1991) and Harris (1997, 43).

62. If so, the question arises whether some comparable abstract doubling is present in Slavic languages.

A related question is whether anything comparable to (152) could exist with a nonclitic *s*-form.

63. Much as Riny Huybregts suggested in Pisa in 1979 for Dutch *zich*. For recent discussion, see Jayaseelan (1996; 1998), among others.

64. On the question why there is no Condition B effect here (or in (126) or (129), with *s'* doubling an *l*-pronoun), see note 82 below; see also Kayne (1986b) and McGinnis (1998).

65. Fully acceptable, on the other hand, is:

(i)   Gianni ha fotografato se stesso. (' . . . refl. same')

Here there is no Condition B effect, probably much as in English *John photographed his children*, with the phrase *his children* (and similarly *se stesso*) counting as the phrase within which the pronoun *his/sé* has successfully failed to be bound. See Chomsky (1986b) and chapter 5.

The fact that (163) is not fully unacceptable to all speakers is perhaps to be attributed to the possibility of an abstract *stesso*, in turn perhaps related to the fact that the object pronouns in (161)/(162) are contrastive. Alternatively, see. Jayaseelan (1996, notes 9 and 18), who emphasizes a similarity between the Malayalam counterpart of *sé* and first- and second-person pronouns. A third possibility would be to look for some relevant property of *-é* that distinguishes it from the (different) morphemes that combine with *l-*.

66. See perhaps Kayne (1975, sect. 5.3) and Belletti (1982) on French and Italian (nonclitic) reciprocals.

67. The contrast between (165) and (167) holds, too, for Guglielmo Cinque and for Cecilia Poletto. Anna Cardinaletti accepts, though:

(i)   Gianni è così egoista: ha fotografato LUI, non noi. ('G is so egotistical—he-has photographed HIM, not us')

(ii)   . . . : ha fotografato solo lui. ('he-has photographed only him')

68. For those speakers who reject (165) (and accept (160)), such as Burzio (1991, 90), the effect of the preposition must be limited to the case of *sé*. Burzio (note 6) argues against the relevance of the preposition on the basis of (i) (from Zribi-Hertz (1980)):

(i)   Victor n'aime que lui. ('V neg loves but him')

Kupferman (1986) has shown, however, that this example, although acceptable, is not typical and that the direct object/prepositional object distinction is significant (datives pattern with direct objects; see also Authier and Reed (1992, 309)). Burzio's example given in (129) is important but is probably to be interpreted as showing that a doubled pronoun can receive special treatment; see note 64.

The presence of a preposition seems to matter, too, for overlapping reference. Thus, (ii) seems better than (iii):

(ii)   ?Avete votato per te. ('you$_{pl}$-have voted for you$_{sg}$')

(iii)   *Avete scelto te. ('you$_{pl}$-have chosen you$_{sg}$')

    69. See Kupferman (1986, 493).

    70. Some possessive s- may be reflexive. See Kayne (1975, chap. 2, note 154) on French.

    71. See Postal (1988).

That the s- of (168) has more in common with m- and t- than with l- has been seen by Nash (1997, note 9).

    72. See Bonnaud (1974, 29). Note that the demonstratives in (170)/(171) have a different consonant from se; in Ratel's (pp. 35–37) dialect, demonstratives are vowel-initial (initial c- was lost). Thus, it is not likely that these se are demonstratives.

Vey (1978, 191) seems to indicate that a form set can still be used for lui ('him') in the Limousin, Perigord, and Auvergne regions, but only as the object of a preposition or after être ('be'), a distribution that suggests that it is not a demonstrative.

    73. French prenominal possessives, although clitic-like in a number of respects (cf. Kayne (1975, sect. 2.20)), are bimorphemic (not even counting the agreement ending; cf. (text to) note (5)), whereas first- and second-person and reflexive clitics are monomorphemic, which is the heart of the matter.

The nonstandard Spanish use of clitic se for nonreflexive second plural os mentioned by Picallo (1994, 280) might have os—>se via dropping of the o- plus an epenthetic -e, as suggested by Jones's (1993, 213) discussion of Campidanese. That is, this se might just be the plural -s of os, and may be unrelated to the person morpheme s- that aligns with m- and t-.

Somewhat similarly, the Spanish spurious se (cf. Perlmutter (1971, chap. 2)) recently discussed by Harris (1997, 43–50) might not contain the s- of m-/t-/s- but may instead be an (expletive) locative parallel to that found in Sardinian (Jones (1993, 220)):

(i)   Bi l'appo datu. ('loc. it I-have given' = 'I gave it to him/her/them')

The impossibility of plural -s in (Spanish) (ii) may reflect the incompatibility of locatives with plural, as in (iii):

(ii)   Yo se(*s) lo doy. ('I se(+pl.) it give' = 'I give it to him/her/them')

(iii)   *I went theres.

    Harris discusses varieties of Spanish that allow (iv) to be interpreted as having a singular direct object and a plural indirect object:

(iv)   Yo se los doy. ('I refl. it + pl. give')

Here the -s apparently belonging to accusative los actually reflects the plurality of the dative argument.

Assume that (i) and (ii) have a phonetically unrealized dative clitic. Then a plausible proposal is that (iv) has a plural dative clitic realized only as (plural) -*s* (rather than as the full form *les*). This will carry over to the parallel Sardinian case, from Jones (p. 220):

(v) Narrabilos! ('tell + loc. + it + pl.' = 'tell it to them')

From this perspective, both (iv) and (v) have three clitics, in the order locative-accusative-dative.

In a proper subset of the preceding varieties, Harris notes, one can have *no-los* for an expected *nos-lo* ('us-it'). Perhaps the -*s* of this *no-los* is an instance of number agreement in a position lower than that of the first-person clitic.

That there is more syntax going on in (ii) and (iv) than meets the eye is also suggested by Roca's (1992, sect. 2.10) observation that spurious *se* has a blocking effect on any binding from above of an immediately following accusative (human) clitic.

74. This recalls the fact that clitic *m-/t-*, while normally pronominal, can also act as anaphoric, in (156)/(157); cf. note 82.

I am not following Burzio's (1991) attempt (cf. Reinhart (1983)) to reduce Condition B to a 'by-product' of Condition A. That attempt takes as its starting point the existence of reflexives. Alternatively, one can take the existence of reflexives as something in need of explanation and try to explain it as a 'by-product' of Condition B (whose independence is suggested by the phenomenon of overlapping reference; cf. note 68). The whole question is beyond the scope of this article.

75. I am leaving open the question how this amalgamation takes place, that is, what the internal structure is. For relevant discussion, see Rouveret (1991, 364ff.), Haegeman (1993, 62ff.), Cardinaletti and Starke (1994, sect. 6), and Zribi-Hertz and Mbolatianavalona (1997).

76. See Picallo (1994, 280).

77. Why exactly *s*- has this property (which it shares with *m*- and *t*; cf. the discussion of (47)/(48)) remains to be understood.

Although French is like Italian with respect to (168) allowing only a singular antecedent, Northern Italy has many dialects whose possessive *s*- can have either a singular or a plural antecedent. It may be that in sentences where the antecedent of possessive *s*- is plural, an abstract distributor is involved; see note 50. Similarly, for Spanish and Catalan; see Picallo (1994) (whose translation (p. 281, (48a)) makes it look as if Italian *su*- could have a plural antecedent).

I know of no Romance language having any *s*-form, whether pronominal or anaphoric, that takes only a plural antecedent.

A special case is the reciprocal *s'ente* (= *s*- + 'between/among') found in the Gallo dialect of French. The following are from Chauveau (1984, 203):

(i) I s'ente taient mordus. ('they refl. + betw. were bitten' = 'They had bitten each other')

(ii) On s'ente lë passët. ('one refl. + betw. it passed' = 'we were passing it back and forth to each other')

78. The coreferential clitic in the accusative plural is in *l*- (and is identical in form to the 'third person' dative plural clitic). See in part Cochet (1933, 37); also Barras (1979, 9), Coppens (1959, 58), Page (1985, 108), Reymond and Bossard (1979, 82).

79. That would leave open the possibility that a related dialect could have an otherwise similar pronominal *s*-form (which would be more like a 'weak pronoun' in the sense of Cardinaletti and Starke (1994)).

80. Although *m-* and *t-* cannot combine directly with a feminine word marker, as seen in (i), they can, in some Romance languages, sometimes trigger past participle agreement, as seen in (ii):

(i)   *Gianni ma vede. ('G me-fem. sees')

(ii)   Gianni mi ha vista. ('G me has seen-fem.')

(At least) in such cases, *m-* and *t-* presumably do have a gender feature, even though it cannot be spelled out on the pronoun itself.

S- can occur with past participle agreement, too:

(iii)   Maria si è vista. ('M refl. is seen')

Whether this requires *s-* to have a gender feature here is less clear than for *m-* in (ii), since the source of *-a* might be *Maria*; for relevant discussion, see chapter 7.

Note that none of *m-/t-/s-* have suppletive variants for feminine, either.

81. We would also have to set aside Malayalam *taan*; see Jayaseelan (1996). On the potential importance of number for argument status/independent reference, see Rizzi (1986a, 543), Kihm (1997), and Zribi-Hertz and Mbolatianavalona (1997). Rouveret (1997, 195) argues that number is not sufficient for independent reference.

For me, the number of the pronominal part of the English reflexive need not match the number of *self*:

(i)   If someone buys themself a new car, . . .

(ii)   (?)We should each get ourself a new car.

82. This difference in feature content between *s-* and *m-/t-* arguably allows *m-* and *t-*, but not *s-*, to be ordinary object clitics linked only to object position; see (text to) note 46. (In all probability, that in turn plays a role in various instances of special behavior of *s-*.) If *m-* and *t-* in reflexive clitic contexts are not ordinary object clitics, but rather more like *s-*, then sentences like (i) may not interact with Condition B in any simple way:

(i)   Je me vois. ('I me see')

9

A Note on Clitic Doubling in French

French normally has verb-object order:

(1) Jean connaît Marie. ('J knows M')

(2) Jean parle de Marie. ('J speaks of M')

In the prepositional example, the object can be replaced by a personal pronoun:

(3) Jean parle de moi. ('J speaks of me')

In the direct object example, the corresponding sentence is deviant:

(4) *Jean connaît moi. ('J knows me')

A clitic counterpart is well formed:

(5) Jean me connaît. ('J me knows')

In earlier work,[1] I took the deviance of (4) to directly reflect the obligatory character of the movement operation involved in the derivation of (5).

That approach did not attach syntactic importance to the difference in form between the *moi* of (3)/(4) and the *me* of (5). In chapter 8, on the other hand, I have argued that *moi* and *me* differ in that *moi* is bimorphemic and *me* is not. (The presence of this second morpheme in *moi* (= *m-* + *-oi*) has syntactic effects, if French, Italian, and dialects of France and Italy are taken into simultaneous account.)

If *moi* is bimorphemic and *me* monomorphemic (*m-* with a phonologically epenthetic *-e*), then it becomes difficult to think of (5) as simply corresponding to (4) plus movement, which might have been expected to yield, rather than (5), the sentence shown in (6):

(6)   *Jean moi connaît.

In this essay, I will not be concerned with the (important) question raised by (6) (why exactly is *-oi* incompatible with this movement?)[2] or with the question of (7) (why can the clitic form not appear in canonical object position?):[3]

(7)   *Jean connaît me.

I will focus rather on the question of how to exclude (4) if (4) is not the exact nonmovement counterpart of (5). If (4) does not 'underlie' (5), then it is no longer possible to interpret the deviance of (4) as simply reflecting the failure to apply the movement operation needed to derive (5).

9.1.   Cardinaletti and Starke (1994)

In the spirit of Chomsky's (1981a) 'avoid pronoun' proposal (and subsequent 'economy' proposals (cf. Chomsky (1995)), Cardinaletti and Starke (1994) develop the following approach to (4). First, *moi* is taken to have more structure associated with it than *me*. (I agree with this.) Second, the exclusion of (4) is attributed to the very availability of (5), through a principle that favors structure minimization. In general, only when the clitic (here, *me*) is independently excluded will the (less minimal) nonclitic (here, *moi*) be legitimate.

Since the clitic sentence (5) is in this case possible, the corresponding nonclitic sentence (4) is not legitimate.[4] As Cardinaletti and Starke point out (in their note 70), structure minimization of this sort has a transderivational character.

Cardinaletti and Starke's proposal concerning (4) and (5) is superior to my earlier one in that it is compatible with the idea that *moi* is bimorphemic. On the other hand, it leads to the expectation that from a given comparison set there should always emerge one fully acceptable sentence.[5] (As we will see, this expectation, in the case of clitics vs. nonclitics, is not always met.) In the present essay, I will be exploring another approach to (4) that differs both from theirs and from my own earlier one.

9.2.   Clitic doubling in French

The account that I will suggest will attempt to integrate into the analysis of (4) what I take to be a French counterpart of the more familiar Spanish clitic doubling. In addition to (4) and (5), let us consider (8):

(8)   Jean me connaît moi. ('J me knows me')

This sentence has stress on *moi* and no 'break' of the sort found with right dislocation.[6]

Example (8) is an example of clitic doubling in that it contains a clitic cooccurring with a corresponding nonclitic (nondislocated) postverbal object. French clitic doubling in this sense is much more limited than its Spanish counterpart in that even with dative clitics French allows this nondislocated doubling only with pronouns:

(9)   Jean me parle à moi. ('J me speaks to me')

(10)   Jean lui parle à elle. ('J her speaks to her')

(11)   *Jean lui parle à Marie.

With direct objects, clitic doubling in French generalizes from (8) to other pronouns, but again not to lexical DPs:

(12)   Jean la connaît elle. ('J her knows her')

(13)   *Jean la connaît Marie.

(possible as right dislocation is *Jean la connaît, Marie* and *Jean lui parle, à Marie.*)

9.3.   Proposal

The problem with (4) is, from the perspective I would now like to pursue, not that *moi* has failed to move nor that there is a similar well-formed sentence with a clitic instead of *moi*, but rather that *moi* has not been doubled.[7] The proposal is:

(14)   Pronominal arguments that are structurally case-marked[8] in French must be doubled by a clitic.

Let me consider that clitic doubling involves introducing clitic and corresponding nonclitic as a single complex constituent in argument position. Thus, a sentence like (12) will have a phrase '[elle la]' merged as the object argument of the verb.[9] Subsequent movement(s) will yield the word order seen in (12).[10]
Returning to (4), repeated here, what now makes (4) deviant is that it is missing the clitic imposed by (14):[11]

(15)   *Jean connaît moi. ('J knows me')

Put another way, French cannot have a direct object argument *moi*, but only one of the form *moi m(e)*, which would yield (16):[12]

(16)   Jean me connaît moi. ('J me knows me')

Similarly, the following contrasts with (9):

(17)   *Jean parle à moi. ('J speaks to me')

(18)   Jean me parle à moi. (= (9))

The deviance of (17) relative to (18) is interpretable in terms of (14)—dative (nonoblique) *moi* must be doubled.

The deviance of (17) can be alleviated by contrastive stress:

(19)   Jean parle volontiers à MOI (mais pas à mon frère). ('J speaks gladly to ME (but not to my brother)')

This is less true in the direct object case:[13]

(20)   *Jean connaît MOI (mais pas mon frère). ('J knows ME (but not my brother)')

The contrast between (19) and (20) recalls the fact that French topicalization applies more readily to datives (and other PPs) than to direct objects:[14]

(21)   A Marie, Jean ne parle jamais. ('to M, J neg speaks never')

(22)   *Marie, Jean ne critique jamais. ('M, J neg criticizes never')

This suggests, in the spirit of chapter 13, that (19) might actually be an instance of topicalization in which the usually visible effect of topicalization is masked by subsequent leftward movement of IP past the topicalized PP. If so, then the unavailability of (20) would follow from that of (22), on the assumption that (at least with nonoblique pronouns) contrastive stress is available in French only in conjunction with overt movement such as topicalization.[15]

From this perspective, the absence of a clitic in (19) would reduce to the absence of a clitic in:

(23)   A moi, Jean ne parle jamais. ('to me, J neg speaks never')

The question arises as to how (23) and (19) are compatible with (14). Thinking of Couquaux (1976; 1978) and Postal (1990), it may be that French topicalization (sometimes) licenses reinterpreting dative *à* as nondative *à*.[16]

9.4. Gapping

The dative versus accusative difference seen in (19) versus (20) has a counterpart in the realm of gapping:[17]

(24)   Jean lui a parlé à elle, et Jacques à sa soeur. ('J her has spoken to her, and J to her sister')

(25)   ?Jean l'a invitée elle, et Jacques sa soeur. ('J her has invited her, and J her sister')

Pronoun clitic doubling in the first conjunct of a gapping sentence is fine if the clitic is dative, less so if it is accusative. This recalls the often discussed fact that clitic doubling with quantified or focused lexical objects in Spanish is good with datives but not with accusatives.

Since the first conjunct by itself would be well formed in both (24) and (25), the distinction between them must rest on the second conjunct. I shall follow Johnson (1994) in taking the object in the second conjunct to have moved leftward, in which case, (24) can be thought of as involving a second conjunct with the (simplified) structure:[18]

(26)   . . . à sa soeur lui a parlé.

If the object (in the second conjunct) of a gapping sentence is necessarily focussed, then (26) is arguably akin to Spanish clitic doubling of a focused (or quantified) dative. Correspondingly, (25) is akin to one with clitic doubling of a focused (or quantified) lexical accusative, which is deviant (for reasons that need further elucidation).[19]

9.5.   Subjects

The deviance of (20) is diminished if one switches from a first- (or second-) person direct object pronoun to a third-person pronoun:[20]

(27)   ?Je connais LUI (mais pas son frère). ('I know HIM (but not his brother)')

This presumably reflects the fact that there is a closer link between third-person pronouns and lexical DPs than between first/second-person pronouns and lexical DPs.[21] Of specific interest here is the fact that a similar contrast exists with subject pronouns, as follows.

French lexical subjects do not need to appear with a subject clitic:[22]

(28)   Jean voit Marie. ('J sees M')

With this in mind, note the parallelism between (15)/(16) and the following pair:

(29)   *Moi vois Marie. ('me see M')

(30)   Moi, je vois Marie. ('me I see M')

Nonclitic *moi* (whose form is not sensitive to case distinctions) is not by itself a possible subject with a tensed verb. If it is doubled by the subject clitic *je*, the resulting sentence is fine. (Although it is written with a comma, (30) is plausibly ambiguous between left-dislocation (CLLD, in Cinque's (1990a) sense) and nondislocation doubling of the sort seen in (16).)

The ungrammaticality of (29) can be seen to follow from (14) (nominatives are instances of structural case).

Now (29) remains impossible even with contrastive stress on the pronoun:

(31)   *MOI vois Marie.

However, the third person counterpart of (31) is possible:[23]

(32)   LUI voit Marie. ('HE sees M')

(Without contrastive stress on *lui*, (32) would be deviant.) Although the contrast between (31) and (32) is stronger than that between (20) and (27), I take the partial similarity to support treating (29)/(30) as akin to (15)/(16).

From the standpoint of Cardinaletti and Starke (1994), the impossibility of (29) could be thought of as deriving from the availability of:

(33)   Je vois Marie. ('I see M')

(although this would still leave open the impossibility of (31)). Their proposal characterizes the deviance of (29) and (15) as resulting from the very availability of an alternative pronoun with a more minimal structure. While agreeing that (monomorphemic) *je* has less to it than (bimorphemic) *moi*, I do not think that the deviance of (29) can be derived directly from the availability of (33) via an economy principle favoring pronouns with less structure. (In imposing doubling when it does, my own proposal (14) actually imposes more (overt) structure.)

Their proposal runs into difficulty with cases in which neither type of pronoun (nonclitic or clitic) yields a fully well-formed sentence. One such case (see the discussion of (89)) is that of French gerunds:

(34)   Jean ayant résolu le problème, tout va bien. ('J having solved the problem, all
        goes well')

Replacing *Jean* by a first- or second-person pronoun yields deviance:

(35)   *Moi ayant résolu le problème, tout va bien.

A (contrastively stressed) third-person pronoun would be better, much as in (32):

(36)   LUI ayant résolu le problème, tout va bien.

The deviance of (35) is surely akin to that of (29). Yet here there is no clitic counterpart available at all:[24]

(37)   **J'ayant résolu le problème, tout va bien.

Consequently, the deviance of (35) cannot be attributed to an economy principle dependent on the availability of a more minimally structured pronoun.

On the other hand, on the assumption that the subject of French gerunds is in a structural case position, (14) will impose a clitic double on (35), thereby correctly characterizing (35) itself as deviant.

The resulting doubling sentence is sharply impossible, presumably for the same (not yet clear) reason as (37):[25]

(38)   **Moi j'ayant résolu le problème, tout va bien.

9.6.   More gapping

Appreciably better than (35) is:

(39)   Jean aime la physique et moi la chimie. ('J likes (the) physics and me (the) chemistry')

Here, *moi* is the subject of the second conjunct of a well-formed gapping sentence, despite the absence of any overt doubling clitic, which would in fact be impossible:

(40)   **Jean aime la physique et (moi) je la chimie.

The impossibility of clitic *je* in (40) is arguably identical to its impossibility in (35) and (38).

　　More surprising is the contrast between (35) and (39). The former violates (14), the requirement that pronouns with structural case be doubled by a clitic. The latter looks like it does, but it may be that its second conjunct contains a phonetically un-realized '. . . j'aime . . .'. That is, it may be that (39) does contain a subject clitic that is eliminated by whatever is involved in gapping (despite the fact that (39) contains no overt subject clitic in its first conjunct).[26]

　　Alternatively, the subject of the second conjunct of a gapping structure is not in a structural case position. This proposal is close to one made by Johnson (1994) (fol-lowing Siegel (1987)), and may fit well with Chomsky's (1998, 43) suggestion that what is primary in general is not structural case itself but rather the phi-features of T and *v* that it interacts with. Thus, if, as Johnson suggests, the second conjunct in gapping lacks a T layer and if (as is clear) the subject in that second conjunct is not drawn into the *v* layer of any higher predicate, then the second subject in gapping plausibly lacks structural case altogether, so that the pronoun *moi* in (39) is not af-fected by the doubling requirement expressed by (14).

　　The idea that the second subject in gapping structures lacks structural case al-lows an account of a striking fact brought to my attention by a question of Guglielmo Cinque's:

(41)   Jean ayant résolu le premier problème et moi le second, tout va bien. ('J having solved the first problem and me the second, all goes well')

This is an example of gapping in which the verb is gerundial. Yet, here, subject *moi* (in the second conjunct) is possible, in contrast to (35). The question is why the ap-parently empty gerund in the second conjunct does not induce a violation parallel to that of (35). The answer, I think, is essentially given by Johnson's proposal that the second conjunct lacks a T layer (and by extension in (41) a layer corresponding to gerundial morphology[27]), combined with Chomsky's idea on structural case. The *moi* of (41) is not in a structural case position (since the second conjunct lacks the relevant functional layer), whereas the *moi* of (35) is in a structural case position (and therefore subject to (14)).

For Jean-Yves Pollock, the following, with a past participle, have the same status as (34)–(37):

(42)   Une fois Jean parti, . . . ('one time J left, . . .' = 'Once J has left, . . .')

(43)   *Une fois moi parti, . . .

(44)   Une fois LUI parti, . . .

(45)   **Une fois je parti, . . .

The analysis given of gerunds carries over, assuming the case of *Jean* in (42) to be structural case, so that (43) falls under (14). Again, there is a contrast with gapping, that is, (46) is better than (43):

(46)   Une fois Jean entré et moi sorti, . . . ('one time J come-in and me gone-out, . . .')

As before, this will follow if the *moi* of (46) has no structural case, unlike the *moi* of (43).[28]

The object pronoun counterpart of (39) seems slightly less good (but better than (20)):

(47)   (?)Marie aime Jean et Anne moi. ('M loves J and A me')

If the second conjunct has a full *v* layer, we would expect the object *moi* to have structural case (unlike the subject *moi* of (46) and (41)) and hence to be excluded by (14), unless there is a phonetically unrealized clitic in the second conjunct, that is, a phonetically unrealized '. . . m'aime . . .' (whose inexact matching with the first conjunct might be the source of the slight deviance).

Straightforwardly acceptable is:

(48)   Marie n'aime que moi. ('M neg loves than me' = 'M loves only me')

As in Azoulay-Vicente (1985, chap. 3), this 'ne . . . que' construction probably contains a covert *autre* ('other'), so that the *que* in (48) is likely to be the *que* found in comparatives:

(49)   Marie connaît mieux Jean que moi. ('M knows better J than me')

It may be that, like (47), (48) and (49) contain, by virtue of involving a gapping-like derivation, a phonetically unrealized object clitic.[29]

9.7. Modified pronouns

I have proposed partially dissociating the deviance of (29) from the availability of (33), and similarly for the object case. This dissociation is further supported by the fact that 'modified' nonoblique pronouns remain quite deviant in the environments under discussion even though replacing the nonclitic pronoun by a clitic would lead to complete impossibility:

(50)   a. *Jean photographiait nous autres. ('J was-photographing us others')

   b. *Jean a vu vous deux ce matin. ('J has seen you two this morning')

In these examples, the (plural) direct object nonclitic *nous/vous* is modified by the word *autres* ('others') or by a numeral. Although perhaps slightly better than the corresponding sentences with a bare nonclitic, as in (51), they are clearly deviant:[30]

(51)   a. *Jean photographiait nous.

   b. *Jean a vu vous ce matin.

Cardinaletti and Starke's (1994) proposal is that the status of (51) results from the availability of a clitic alternative, illustrated in (52) (in the first-person and second-person plural/polite, nonclitic and clitic have the same form in French):

(52)   a. Jean nous photographiait.

   b. Jean vous a vu ce matin.

However, for (50) there is no available clitic alternative:

(53)   a. **Jean nous autres photographiait.

   b. **Jean vous deux a vu(s) ce matin.

(54)   a. **Jean nous photographiait autres.

   b. **Jean vous a vu(s) deux ce matin.

In (53) we see that the modifier cannot occur next to the clitic and in (54) that the modifier cannot occur stranded in postverbal position. Nonetheless, (50) is deviant (thereby contrasting with modified nonclitic pronouns that are oblique):

(55)   a. Jean parle de nous autres. ('J speaks of us others')

   b. Jean parle de vous deux. ('J speaks of you two')

The proposal that I have put forth in (14) is repeated here:

(56) Pronominal arguments that are structurally case-marked in French must be doubled by a clitic.

It claims that what is wrong with (50) is that (50) is missing the required doubling clitic. In this case, the presence of a doubling clitic is possible (as opposed to the subject clitic gerund case of (38)):

(57) a. Jean nous photographiait nous autres.

b. Jean vous a vu(s) vous deux ce matin.

The subject clitic doubling case corresponding to (57) is also possible:

(58) a. Nous autres, nous partions. ('us others, we were-leaving')

b. Vous deux, vous partiez. ('you two, you were-leaving')

Example (58) without the subject clitic would be impossible in colloquial French, although perhaps possible (and better than (50), for unclear reasons) in more literary French.[31] The dative counterpart of (57) is possible:

(59) a. Jean nous parlait à nous autres. ('J us was-speaking to us others')

b. Jean vous a parlé à vous deux. ('J you has spoken to you two')

Without the doubling clitic, these are deviant to some degree, with subtle variation in judgments:[32]

(60) a. ??Jean parlera à vous autres.

b. ?Jean parlera à vous deux.

c. Jean parlera à vous tous. ('J will-speak to you all')

The deviance of (60a,b) is expected (although the exact degree needs further elucidation). The fact that they are somewhat better than the corresponding direct object examples in (50) is probably to be related to the discussion of (23), that is, to the possibility of reanalyzing *à* as a nondative preposition (whereas the direct object examples have no preposition that could be so reanalyzed).

9.8. Quantifiers

The quantifier present in (60c) leads to many questions that are beyond the scope of this essay. Let me note, though, that although dative counterparts of (54) are also not possible, one can have sentences with *tous* (with both accusatives and datives) that contrast sharply with (54):

(61) Jean nous photographiait tous. ('J us was-photographing all')

(62)   Jean vous a parlé à tous. ('J you has spoken to all')

The separability of clitic and quantifier seen in (61) can almost certainly be assimilated to familiar English quantifier floating/stranding:[33]

(63)   We/The boys were all talking.

That is, (61) is not a case of clitic doubling of the sort under discussion.[34]

9.9.   Quantifiers with covert nonclitic pronouns

Somewhat similar to (60c) is:

(64)   Jean a parlé à tous. ('J has spoken to all')

The quantifier *tous* by itself (and without any clitic present) can follow *à*, as well as other prepositions. It cannot appear in the same fashion as direct object, however:

(65)   *Jean a invité tous. ('J has invited all')

This suggests that the object of *à* in (64) is not simply *tous*, but rather *tous* together with a covert nonclitic pronominal (limited to third-person interpretation).[35] The contrast between (64) and (65) is a result of the fact that although the clitic doubling imposed on (nonclitic) pronominals by (56) can be suspended in some cases with datives (as seen in (60c)) it cannot be in the case of direct objects. Consequently, we can take (65) (containing postverbal *tous* + covert nonclitic pronominal) to be excluded as a violation of (56).

One might ask if the covert nonclitic pronoun of (65) could be doubled by an overt clitic. If it could be, then a sentence like (66) could be analyzed as an instance of clitic doubling:

(66)   Jean les invitera tous. ('J them will-invite all')

Thinking of the limitation to third-person interpretation for the covert nonclitic pronoun in (64), we might expect a doubling analysis of this sort (with covert pronoun and *tous* forming a single constituent) to be available only with third-person clitics:

(67)   . . . les invitera tous *pro*.

If so, then the following, with a first-person clitic, could only be an instance of quantifier floating/stranding (i.e., without any *pro*), as in the discussion of (61):

(68)   Jean nous invitera tous. ('J us will-invite all')

Example (66) would then be analyzable in two ways, either as doubling or as floating/stranding.

The conclusion that *tous* linked to a third-person clitic has an extra analysis available to it as compared with *tous* linked to a first- or second-person clitic is directly supported by the French of (at least) some speakers. For Marlyse Baptista, there is a sharp difference between (69) and (70):[36]

(69) Elle a tous commencé à les insulter/apprécier. ('she has all begun to them insult/ appreciate' = 'she has begun to insult/appreciate them all')

(70) a. *Elle a tous commencé à vous insulter/apprécier. ('. . . you . . .')

      b. *Elle a tous commencé à nous insulter/apprécier. ('. . . us . . .')

For her, then, (69) must be available only as an instance of doubling, in which the clitic *les* is preceded by its double consisting of *tous* plus a covert pronoun (limited to third person).

Similarly for the nonstandard (71) versus the impossible (72), which were brought to my attention by Isabelle Haïk:[37]

(71) ??J'ai tous voté pour eux. ('I have all voted for them')

(72) *J'ai tous voté pour vous.

Normally *tous* cannot be linked to a nonclitic pronoun to its right; in standard French neither (71) nor (72) is possible. The contrast between them suggests that in some French a phrase consisting of *tous* plus covert pronoun can be linked to a nonclitic pronoun but that, as before, the covert pronoun can be only third person.

These in turn recall Ruwet's (1978, (218)):

(73) Les candidats, j'aurais tous voté pour . . . ('the candidates, I would-have all voted for . . .')

Again, there must be a phrase *tous* plus covert (third-person) pronoun, and, in this kind of example, another covert (third-person) pronoun following the preposition.[38]

9.10. More on the third-person restriction on covert nonclitic pronouns

This restriction is also visible in French with subjects:

(74) Tous chantaient. ('all were-singing-3pl.')

(75) *Tous chantiez. ('all were-singing-2pl.')

In (74), the subject phrase must be *tous* plus a covert nonclitic (third-person) pronoun. If such a covert pronoun could also be second person, then (75) would have been possible (with second-plural verb agreement), but it is not.[39]

The question arises as to how general this limitation to third person is. There may well be languages for which it does not hold. But it is fruitful to postulate it to hold in a general way in (at least) French, Italian, and the related dialects.[40]

The hypothesis that there are covert nonclitic pronouns that are in these languages restricted to third person would appear to imply a difference between, for example, the following two sentences:

(76)   Jean la voit. ('J her sees')

(77)   Jean me voit. ('J me sees')

The first, with a third-person clitic, could contain in addition a covert nonclitic pronoun. The second, with a first-person clitic, could not. (Put another way, (76) might contain a *pro* in addition to *la*, whereas (77) could not contain a *pro* in addition to *me*.[41])

This might provide a novel way of understanding the fact that some Romance languages (e.g., Catalan and some varieties of Italian) allow past participle agreement with third-person clitics but not with first- or second-person clitics:

(78)   Gianni li ha visti/*visto. ('G them has seen(m.pl.)/seen(no agr.)')

(79)   Gianni vi ha visti/visto. ('. . . you(pl.) . . .)'

In (78) (Italian) we see obligatory past participle agreement in the presence of an accusative (here, masculine plural) clitic. In standard Italian, the corresponding agreement with a second-person plural clitic is generally considered optional, as illustrated in (79). For some speakers of Italian, though, agreement in (79) is not possible. More generally put, some Romance languages have past participle agreement only with third-person clitics. No Romance language, to my knowledge, has such agreement only with first- and second-person clitics.

We can understand this as follows. Of the Romance languages/dialects that have past participle agreement with object clitics, some take that agreement to be triggered by the clitic itself (at some point in the derivation); in those, all accusative clitics trigger agreement. Others, however, take past participle agreement to be triggered by *pro*, that is, by the covert nonclitic pronominal double. Since a covert pronoun in these languages is limited to third person, it follows that for the relevant speakers the agreement itself is limited to sentences with a third-person clitic.

For Guglielmo Cinque, in whose Italian past participle agreement is usually possible with clitics of all persons, a contrast nonetheless appears in the particular case of clitic climbing:

(80)   Li ho potuti/*potuto criticare. ('them I-have could criticize')

(81)   Vi ho potuto/?potuti criticare. ('you I-have . . .')

In both (80) and (81), the object clitic has 'climbed' into the matrix. In (80), with a third-person (plural) clitic, past participle agreement (on the matrix verb) is obligatory. In (81), with a second-person (plural) clitic, past participle agreement is slightly off, and nonagreement is possible. This effect is stronger for him with matrix *finire* (probably because of the presence of complementizer *di*):

(82)   Li ho finiti di criticare. ('them I-have finished *di* criticize')

(83)   Vi ho finito/??finiti di criticare.

What this seems to suggest is that, in clitic climbing contexts, past participle agreement on the matrix verb cannot readily be triggered by the clitic itself. To the extent that it cannot, past participle agreement must be triggered by the covert nonclitic pronoun. Such a 'pro' can be called upon in the third person, as in (80) and (82), but not in the (first or) second person, as seen by the deviance of (81) and (83).[42]

9.11.   An extension to covert subjects

A similar point can be made for subjects. Consider (in Italian):

(84)   Parlavano. ('they-spoke')

(85)   Parlavamo. ('we-spoke')

The first is a third-person (plural) null subject sentence. By previous reasoning, it may contain a covert nonclitic pronoun. The second of these is also a null subject sentence, but in the first person (plural). It may therefore not contain a covert nonclitic pronoun. Consequently, the pronoun subject of (85) must be overt, that is, must be the agreement suffix *–mo*[43] (whereas the agreement suffix *-no* of (84) needn't be pronoun-like).

   A plausible strengthening of this conclusion (at least for the languages under consideration) is:

(86)   a. Covert nonclitic pronouns can only be third person.[44]

   b. An agreement suffix having the properties of a pronoun can only be first or second person.[45]

Given (86b), the agreement suffix in (84) must be nonpronominal. Therefore (84) must contain a covert nonclitic third-person pronoun (*pro*). That is, (84) and (85) differ in that (84) must, but (85) cannot, contain *pro*.

   Consider now a language having pronominal agreement suffixes but (for some reason, unlike Italian) no pure subject (referential) *pro*. Such a language would need overt pronominal subjects in the third person, although not in the first or second person (when the agreement suffixes were present). This corresponds by and large to Paduan and Venetian (and various other North Italian dialects), which require overt subject clitics in the third person but not in the first person or in the second person plural.[46]

There may be a correlation here with the fact that Venetian, according to Cecilia Poletto, also lacks the object *pro* discussed by Rizzi (1986a) for Italian. An Italian example is:

(87)   Questo costringe a parlare subito. ('this constrains to speak right-away')

(Venetian would add a second person singular object clitic,[47] just as English would add either *you* or *one*.[48])

9.12.   Soi

French has an anaphoric pronoun *soi* (cf., e.g., Italian *sé*, German *sich*, Russian *sebja*) that is related (see chapter 8) to the first singular pronoun *moi* and the second singular *toi*. *Soi* can be a long-distance anaphor in certain contexts; in those contexts it interacts in a striking way with clitic doubling. An example of long-distance *soi* (with antecedent *on*) is:[49]

(88)   Quand on$_i$ dit aux gens de parler de soi$_i$, . . . ('when one says to people to speak of *soi*, . . .')

A comparable example with direct object *soi* would be impossible:

(89)   *Quand on$_i$ dit aux gens de photographier soi$_i$, . . . ('. . . photograph *soi*, . . .')

This contrast follows directly from (56), which imposes clitic doubling on (89) but not on (88), on the assumption that *soi* is a pronoun with structural case in (89) (but not in (88)).

For reasons having to do with the syntax of reflexive clitics (that go well beyond the bounds of this essay), adding the expected clitic double *se* (parallel to first singular *me* and second singular *te*) does not yield a grammatical sentence:

(90)   *Quand on$_i$ dit aux gens de se photographier soi$_i$, . . .

Put another way, (56) excludes (89) on the grounds that (89) lacks a doubling clitic, even though French provides no admissible clitic in this case. That is, a violation of (56) is maintained even when the doubling counterpart is itself unacceptable. (The unacceptability of (89) is therefore not expected from the Cardinaletti/Starke perspective discussed earlier, at least not under the most straightforward interpretation of what is meant by having a corresponding clitic available.[50])

9.13.   Conclusion

The unacceptability of sentences like (89), (65), (60a,b), (51), (50), (35), (31), (29), (27), (20), (17) (15), and (4) can be attributed to the requirement, stated in (56), that French structurally case-marked pronouns must be doubled by a clitic. This requirement suggests that the subject in the second conjunct of a gapping sentence does not have structural case. The doubling requirement in question sometimes rules out nondoubling sentences whose doubling and clitic counterparts are also not acceptable; this poses a problem for Cardinaletti and Starke's (1994) structure minimization proposal for such sentences.

French nondoubling sentences with a clitic (and no corresponding nonclitic) can contain *pro* (in addition to the clitic) only in third-person cases, with implications for the null subject phenomenon in other languages, for past participle agreement, and for apparently bare quantifiers.

NOTES

To Cino, whose *Grande grammatica italiana di consultazione* has set the standard for traditional grammars of the future.

1. Cf. Kayne (1975, sects. 2.16, 2.17).
2. Some French clitics are bimorphemic, such as the *la* of (i) = *l-* + *-a*:

(i)   Jean la connaît. ('J her knows')

The *les* of (ii) is probably trimorphemic (*l-* + *-e-* + *-s*):

(ii)   Jean les connaît. ('J them knows')

An initial conclusion is that *-oi* has neither the number status of plural *-s* nor the word marker status of *-a* (and probably *-e*) in the sense of Harris (1991).

The challenge posed by *moi* (and similarly *toi* 'you$_{\text{fam.sg.}}$') does not arise for *nous* ('we/ us') or *vous* ('you$_{\text{pl./polite}}$'), which occur both in nonclitic and in clitic position.

3. Chomsky (1995, 337) makes an interesting proposal that may or may not be compatible with the syntax of clitic doubling.
4. Cardinaletti and Starke use the term 'strong pronoun' rather than nonclitic. This is related to their argument that pronouns come in three varieties, 'strong', 'weak', and 'clitic'. Since their 'strong'/'weak' distinction is not essential to what follows, I will continue to use the term 'nonclitic'.
5. In a way partially similar to work in OT; see various articles in Barbosa et al. (1998).
6. Following usual practice, right-dislocation is represented with a comma:

(i)   Jean me connaît, moi.

For relevant discussion, see Kayne (1994, sect. 7.3), Villalba (1999), and Cecchetto (1999; to appear).

7. See in part Postal (1990).

Note that (14) applies also to covert pronouns (that are structurally case-marked); see the discussion on (65), example (iii) of note 39, and (75).

8. I am taking dative here to be an instance of structural case (and the case of objects of prepositions other than (certain) *à* ('to') not to be).

Possible with postverbal *moi* is:

(i)   C'est moi. ('It's me')

The clitic is excluded:

(ii) *Ce/Ça m'est (moi).

Given (14), the postcopula pronoun in (i) may have no structural case; see the discussion of (41). Similarly, perhaps, for clefted direct object pronouns:

(iii) C'est moi qu'ils ont vu. ('it is me that they have seen')

To take (iii) to be parallel to (i) here is straightforward if (iii) involves empty operator movement (cf. Chomsky (1977)) or movement of a (third-person) *pro*, rather than movement of *moi* itself. If it is *moi* that is moved (as suggested for the general case by reconstruction effects; see Chomsky (1995, chap. 3)), then things are more complex.

Of note is the fact that both (i) and (ii) are possible in Walloon, at least in the third person; see Remacle (1952, 220).

9. See Kayne (1972, sect. 3) on French subject clitics and Belletti (1999), Bianchini, Borgato, and Galassi (1982) and Uriagereka (1995, 81) on object clitics.

An alternative that I will set aside without discussion (although it is surprisingly (and interestingly) difficult to find evidence distinguishing it from the text approach to clitic doubling) is proposed by Sportiche (1995a), who takes clitics to correspond to AGR-like heads interspersed in the main sentential projection line. For Sportiche, the nonclitic moves into the Spec of the corresponding clitic, sometimes overtly, sometimes covertly.

Covert movement is incompatible with chapter 13. It might be possible, however, to take *elle* in (12) to move overtly to Spec,*la*, if that movement were followed by further movement of *la connaît* to the left of *elle*, in the spirit of (the references given in) note 10 of chapter 13.

For further very interesting discussion of clitic doubling, see Aoun (1996) and Schmitt (1998).

10. In a way somewhat similar to the quantifier stranding of Sportiche (1988) and Shlonsky (1991).

11. In Italian (unlike French, or Paduan or Venetian; cf. chapter 8; also Shlonsky (1997, sect. 9.4.3) on similarities to Semitic), the counterpart of (15) is acceptable if the pronoun is stressed:

(i) Gianni conosce me.

It might be that Italian is different from these other languages with respect to (14) itself. On the other hand, Belletti (1993, 108) suggests a correlation with focalization differences; see perhaps the discussion of (19).

Another possibility is that Italian might be able to take nonclitic *me* in (i) to be a phrase [*me* X] headed by X such that *me* is oblique and not subject to (14)), where X is a phonetically unrealized intensifier. See Iatridou (1988) on clitic doubling with Greek reflexives.

12. It may be that the right-dislocated example (i) derives from essentially the same structure:

(i) Jean me connaît, moi.

If *moi* is stressed, we have (16). If *moi* is destressed, we may have (i), probably involving leftward movement of *moi*; see the references of note 6.

It is possible that (16) also involves leftward movement of *moi*, to a different position, perhaps Spec,FocusP. See Rigau (1988), Belletti (1999), and Aoun (1996).

13. See Kayne (1975, chap. 2, (319)–(322)). For some speakers, (20) is relatively acceptable.

14. It may be that French topicalization in the sense of Kayne (1975, chap. 2, (174), (205)) is equivalent to Cinque's (1990a) CLLD.

15. On clefts, see note 8.

16. Spanish is different here.

17. See Kayne (1975, chap. 2, note 41).

18. The fact that gapping can 'eliminate' clitic, auxiliary, and participle in (26) is not novel. See Johnson (1994) and (i):

(i)   Jean lui a offert un livre et Jacques un stylo. ('J her has given a book and J a pen')

Note in addition that (26) resembles (in part) Cinque's (1990a) CLLD.

19. For recent discussion, see Torrego (1998, 58).

20. See Kayne (1975, chap. 2, note 125) and Cardinaletti and Starke (1994).
In certain North Italian dialects, this contrast is particularly striking. See chapter 8.

21. For relevant discussion, see Ritter (1995); see also Koopman (1993).

22. In standard French, the presence of a co-occurring subject clitic implies dislocation of the lexical subject:

(i)   Jean, il voit Marie. ('J, he sees M')

23. See Kayne (1972, note 22).

24. Subject clitics (but not object clitics) are limited to tensed sentences. Probably related to (37) is the impossibility of subject clitics in imperatives.

25. There may be a link to the fact that verbal person agreement is by and large limited to tensed verbs. (On the idea that person agreement should be strongly assimilated to a clitic, see Taraldsen (1992), Ordóñez (1997), Alexiadou and Anagnostopoulou (1998), and Ordóñez and Treviño (1999). On the different status of number agreement, see chapter 11.)

It might be that subject clitics require nominative case (and similarly for person agreement clitics/affixes; see Raposo (1987b)) and that French gerunds assign a structural case to their (preverbal) subjects that is not nominative.

26. And similarly perhaps in (one-word) answers to questions. See Kayne (1975, chap. 2, note 13).

27. Which in French is closer to tense than in English. See Kayne (1975, sect. 1.3) and Pollock (1989, 408).)

28. According to Martineau and Motapanyane (1996, 162), Quebec French has:

(i)   Moi/*je avoir dit ça à mon père, il . . . ('me have(infin.) said that to my father, . . .')

The contrast with (43) and (35) remains to be understood.

29. It remains to be seen how best to integrate:

(i)   Elle connaît ?(et) moi et Jean. ('she knows and me and J')

See Kayne (1975, chap. 2, note 140).

30. As opposed to:

(i)   Jean a vu chacun de nous. ('J has seen each-one of us')

in which *nous* must be oblique, in a way related to the presence of *de*.

31. More colloquial than (58a) would be:

(i)   Nous autres, on partait. ('us others, one was-leaving')

The subject clitic *on* is what determines the third singular agreement here:

(ii)   **Nous autres partait.

32. See Kayne (1975, chap. 2, (342)).
33. For relevant discussion, see Kayne (1975, chap. 1), Sportiche (1988), Shlonsky (1991), and Bobaljik (1998).
34. See, however, note 10.
35. Relevant here are the following, from Ruwet (1978, (199)/(200)):

(i)   Tous/*toutes ces laiderons essaieront de séduire Antoine. ('all(masc.)/all(fem.) these ugly-women will-try to seduce A')

(ii)   Ces laiderons essaieront toutes de séduire Antoine.

The noun *laideron* is masculine in grammatical gender. It must take a preceding masculine quantifier but can be followed by a 'floating'/'stranded' feminine quantifier. This suggests that in (ii) *toutes* is really *toutes* plus covert feminine pronoun, so that the gender mismatch (cf. Ruwet (1967)) in (ii) is really between pronoun and antecedent (rather than between quantifier and antecedent).

See the discussion of (66)–(73).

Perhaps similar is the acceptability for some Italian speakers of (iii), with the feminine clitic *l(a)* in its use as second-person polite appearing to simultaneously trigger feminine agreement on *vista* and masculine agreement on *perso* (where the person addressed is male):

(iii)   ?L'ho vista perso. ('her = you I-have seen lost')

More likely agreement on *vista* is being triggered by *la* (whose vowel has dropped) and agreement on *perso* by a covert masculine pronoun.

In combination with the discussion of (78)–(83) (plus the assumption that (iii) can have only one *pro*), this would lead to the expectation that (iii) will be acceptable only to those speakers who accept past participle agreement in (79).

36. Similarly, she finds the following to contrast, though a bit less sharply (with the difference probably related to the presence vs. absence of *à*):

(i)   Elle aimerait tous les revoir. ('she would-like all them see-again')

(ii)   */??Elle aimerait tous vous revoir.

(iii)   */??Elle aimerait tous nous revoir.

37. See Kayne (1981b, note 13).
38. The order of pronoun and preposition is not important for the text point. Similarly it might be that the covert pronoun adjacent to *tous* in (69), (71), and (73) precedes it.

Relevant here is note 35.

39. In a pro-drop language (like Spanish), (75) could be possible with an analysis not parallel to that of French (74), namely with an analysis in which *tous* is 'floating'/'stranded' and the second-person pronoun is the verbal agreement suffix. See Taraldsen (1992).

The fact that (74) is much better than (65) should be related to the contrast between (32) and (27). Both contrasts require further study. That they are related is supported by the fact that in both cases acceptability drops sharply (setting aside 'pointing' contexts for (ii)) if the subject is postverbal as in 'stylistic inversion':

(i)   la fille à qui a parlé Jean ('the girl to whom has spoken J')

(ii)   *la fille à qui a parlé lui ('. . . he/him')

(iii) *la fille à qui ont parlé tous ('. . . have spoken all')

See Pollock (1998, note 37).

40. Beyond the scope of this essay is the question why it should hold at all in certain languages. Part of the answer is presumably that in those languages third-person pronouns are different in internal structure from first- and second-person pronouns. See Ritter (1995) and chapter 8 for relevant discussion.

41. What I am calling *pro* here is a covert doubled pronoun, entirely distinct from the trace of the clitic.

42. If I read them correctly, Hernanz and Rigau (1984) state that Catalan past participle agreement is not available in clitic climbing contexts where the matrix verb is *intentar* or *procurar*, even in the third person. Much remains to be understood here.

43. See Taraldsen (1992).

44. A plausible extension would be:

(i)   A covert clitic pronoun can only be third person.

This might be relaxed in certain cases where the covert clitic is locally identified by a c-commanding pronoun. Thus, in section 8.2.4 of chapter 8, I suggested a link between (ii) and (iii) (from Lombardy dialects):

(ii)   Nun se lavom. ('we refl. wash')

(iii) Mi a ma sa lavi i man. ('me *a* me refl. wash the hands' = 'I wash my hands')

Example (ii) arguably contains a covert first-person plural object clitic parallel to the *ma* of (iii):

(iv)   nun $CL_{1pl.}$ se lavom

If this covert clitic must be licensed by the identical (apart from case) features of *nun*, then we may have an account of the absence in French dialects (as brought to my attention by Yves-Charles Morin) of:

(v)   *Je se lavons. ('I refl. wash$_{1pl.}$')

This is absent despite the widespread *Je parlons* ('I speak$_{1pl.}$' = 'we speak'). See section 8.1.4 of chapter 8. The reason is that (v) would have to have the analysis:

(vi)   je *CL* se lavons

But since *je* is grammatically singular, the covert clitic would be possible only if it were singular, too, that is, if it were the covert counterpart of *me*, which in the relevant French dialects must not be compatible with first-person plural. (In effect, for (v) to be possible there would have to be a dialect in which both *je* and *me* were compatible with 1pl.)

45. See the discussion in chapter 8 of the fact that the *l-* of Romance third-person pronouns/clitics never appears within possessives. Nor does it ever seem to appear as part of an agreement suffix (as opposed to first-person *m-* and second-person *t-*, which sometimes do).

Presumably (86b) in part underlies the fact that in so many languages third-person singular agreement is zero.

(Beyond the scope of this essay is the question of null topics of the sort found in German or Portuguese; see the end of note 48 and also Farrell's (1990) argument that Brazilian Portuguese has a *pro* object limited to third person. Similarly for the question whether pronominal agreement suffixes can be covert.)

46. Venetian and Paduan both have an obligatory subject clitic in the second singular, whose presence must be due to other factors. See Poletto (1993; 1995; 2000). This clitic does not, however, appear in imperatives (cf. note 24). Related to this is the fact discussed by Zanuttini (1997, chap. 4) that Italian second singular imperatives lack any verbal agreement morphology, despite which they do not require an overt subject, for unclear reasons.

Like Paduan and Venetian with respect to null subjects is (to a significant extent) Hebrew; for recent discussion, see Shlonsky (1997).

47. Apparently less necessary in Paduan. Note that the text approach never has a person feature of *pro* identified by verbal agreement morphology, unlike Rizzi (1986a); at the same time, the text approach does not give an immediate account of the behavior of (what seems to be) *pro* in the aux-to-Comp constructions he discusses.

Controlled PRO does not seem to be sensitive to person features, reinforcing the familiar idea that it is distinct from *pro*. Its insensitivity to person features would be expected if it were really the trace of movement, as in O'Neil (1997).

48. English is usually thought not to have any *pro* (apart perhaps from imperatives; cf. note 46). But it does seem to with quantifiers, as in:

(i)   John would like to speak to both/all five.

The interpretation is only third person (i.e., equivalent to *both/all five of them*), as expected. This is supported by:

(ii)   Both/all five were behaving themselves/*ourselves/*yourselves.

These facts carry over to nonuniversals, again suggesting the presence of *pro*:

(iii)   Five/most/not very many were behaving themselves/*ourselves/*yourselves.

This indicates a link with Pollock (1998, section 5), exploration of which is beyond the scope of this essay.

The third-person restriction does not hold for telegraphic English:

(iv)   Am waiting for an answer.

which may, then, not involve *pro*, as suggested by:

(v)   *You know am waiting for an answer.

The Italian counterpart of (iii) is limited to third person, as in English:

(xii)   Quattro sono venuti. ('four are$_{3pl}$ come')

(xiii)   *Quattro siete venuti. ('four are$_{2pl}$ come')

However, unlike French, the Italian counterpart of (i) does not seem to be so restricted, for reasons that remain to be understood.

49. See Kayne (1975, sect. 2.16) and Pica (1984, 140).

50. Note that (90) with *soi* dropped is likewise impossible with *on* as antecedent of *se*. Possible is:

(i)   Quand on dit aux gens de vous photographier, ... ('... you ...')

where *vous* seems to be taking *on* as antecedent. See Kayne (1975, chap. 2, note 123). This *vous* cannot double *soi*, however:

(ii)   *Quand on demande aux gens de vous photographier soi, ...

In addition, this *vous* is freer than long-distance *soi* in that it is not limited to subjunctive or infinitive complementation contexts:

(iii)   Quand on parle trop et que les gens vous mettent à la porte, ... ('when one speaks too-much and that the people you put to the door, ...' = '... and people throw you out, ...')

Examples (89)/(90) raise for OT the problem of language particular ineffability discussed recently by Legendre et al. (1998). (Cf. (35).) Whether the OT expectation that from a given candidate set there should always arise (at least) one fully acceptable sentence is contentful or not will depend on how restrictive the notion of candidate set can be held to be (and on how restrictive the OT notion of constraint can be made). In the case at hand, one might perhaps attempt to add in (i)–(iii). Other challenging cases are discussed in Kayne (1975, sects. 2.16, 2.17) and Postal (1990).

II

ENGLISH

10

Notes on English Agreement

10.1. *-s* as a number affix

Let us begin by setting aside the verb *be*. Then English subject-verb agreement has the following well-known properties: In the past tense, there is none. In the present, there are two forms, for example, *like* and *likes*. The form with the *-s* suffix is standardly characterized as co-occurring with subject NPs that are third person, singular.[1]

Hill (1958, 153) has, on the other hand, made the point that characterizing the *-s* form in terms of two features, person and number, leads to the expectation that the present tense paradigm should really have six forms, given three values for person and two for number. He suggests, instead, that the English present tense agreement paradigm be characterized in terms of a single feature, that of gender, in the following way: The *-s* form co-occurs with those subjects displaying gender or capable of being replaced by a pronoun displaying gender, that is, *he*, *she* or *it*, the point being that in English first and second person pronouns, as well as third person plural pronouns, show no gender distinctions.

In agreement with Hill's primary hypothesis, we shall pursue the idea that taking the *-s* form to be third person, singular is not the optimal way to characterize English verb agreement and that a more parsimonious description is required. We shall not, however, adopt his gender-based analysis, since it does not seem entirely natural (given the complete lack of gender morphology with nonpronominal NPs) to attribute gender in English to singular nonpronominal NPs while denying it to plural nonpronominal NPs and since allowing verb agreement to be sensitive to whether or not a NP could potentially be replaced by a visibly gender-bearing pronoun would appear to entail considerable expansion of the set of possible agreement phenomena. In addition, taking *-s* to be a gender-sensitive suffix would go against a generalization that holds without exception in all of the Germanic and Romance languages, namely that nonparticipial verb forms may show person and number, but never gender, morphology.

Our own proposal is that the -s form in question is not marked for gender, and neither, contrary to the tradition, is it marked for person. Rather, it is marked only for number.

To achieve this result, we need to take two steps. Consider first the case of a second person subject NP, as in (1):

(1)   You sing well.

This contrasts with a third-person singular subject NP:

(2)   He sings well.

It seems as if the choice between *sing* and *sings* is determined by person. That is straightforwardly true, however, only if *you* in (1) is singular. Now, although *you* can certainly be interpreted as referring to a singular, we would like to claim that it is grammatically plural in all cases. If so, then the contrast between *sing* and *sings* can be taken to be one between plural and singular, that is, to be one of number.

The plausibility of analyzing *you* as grammatically plural in all cases is enhanced by considering French *vous*. *Vous* in French is the normal second-person plural pronoun (for all cases). French *tu* is another second-person pronoun, one that is restricted to singular (other case forms are *te*, *toi*). However, *tu* is further restricted to the familiar singular. The polite singular is rendered by *vous*. Thus, *vous* can be either plural (polite or familiar) or singular (only polite) in reference. Depending on the number of the referent, an adjective predicated of *vous* will be either plural or singular. This can be seen with certain adjectives, as in (3):

(3)   a.   Vous êtes loyaux. (you are loyal-pl.)

       b.   Vous êtes loyal. (you are loyal-sg.)

Although the adjective is sensitive to the number of the referent, the verb is not—it is *êtes* in both cases. The second-person singular verb form would be *es*, which occurs with *tu* but cannot occur with *vous* even when *vous* has singular reference:

(4)   Tu es loyal.

(5)   *Vous es loyal.

This discrepancy between verb and adjective agreement could be attributed to the fact that in (3b) the verb and adjective are, strictly speaking, not agreeing with the same NP, in the sense that the verb is agreeing with the lexical NP *vous*[2] whereas the adjective is (locally) agreeing with an empty NP in its subject position, so that one could say that although *vous* is grammatically plural in all cases, an empty category contained in an A-chain headed by *vous* can fail to agree in number with it, that is, can be singular in accordance with the number of the (intended) referent.[3]

Returning to English, we would like to claim that *you* is always grammatically plural, just like *vous*. There is of course one major difference, namely that English makes no grammatical distinction between polite and familiar, so that the use of grammatically plural *you* to refer to a singular holds even more generally than in French. The grammatically plural character of *you* is, from this perspective, the reason for *you* taking the same present tense verb form as *we* and *they*, even when *you* has a singular referent. The distinction in verb form between (1) and (2) can therefore be accounted for in terms of a plural versus singular distinction, without any reference to person.

The second step that must be taken if we are to fully achieve our goal of reducing the *sing/sings* distinction to one of number alone involves the first person pronoun *I* and the fact that it does not take the *-s* form, despite having singular reference. To call *I* grammatically plural seems substantially less plausible than in the case of *you*, for at least two reasons. First, there is a distinction between *I* and *we* that has no counterpart in the second person. Second, *you* takes the same verb form as *we* and *they* even with *be* (*you/we/they are/were*) and even when its referent is singular, as we would expect if it is invariably grammatically plural. *I*, on the other hand, does not (*I am/was*).

Let us suggest, then, that English treats *I* as being grammatically unmarked for number. Thus, *I* has in common with *you* the possibility of referring to a singular despite not being grammatically singular. At the same time, it differs from *you* in not being grammatically plural.

The picture of English non-*be* present tense agreement that we have arrived at so far is the following: The *-s* form occurs with grammatically singular NP subjects. The bare form occurs elsewhere. The set of grammatically singular subjects includes neither *you* nor *I*.

Our use of the term 'elsewhere' in the preceding sentence but one might seem unusual, in that agreement morphemes usually pick out their compatible NPs in a more positive way. We might conjecture, then, that the 'elsewhere' characterization of the bare form in English is to be related to the very fact that the form in question is 'bare'. This amounts to suggesting that the English grouping of *I* with the grammatical plurals as far as verb agreement is concerned is dependent on the fact that the verb form occurring with the plurals is bare and that there could not be a language that was exactly like English except that the two verb forms found in the present tense would each bear an overt agreement suffix.

To put things a bit more precisely, the *-s* morpheme in question must be coindexed with a grammatically singular NP.[4] As for the bare present tense verb form, we should, if the conjecture of the previous paragraph is on the right track, not expect there to be a positive coindexation requirement specific to it. Instead, we should look for an alternative along the following lines: The bare present tense verb form, like the past tense forms, is intrinsically free to cooccur with any subject NP. But there is a principle to the effect that given a choice between an inflected form and a bare form, one must take the inflected form.[5] This will have no effect in the past tense but will in the present exclude the bare form with any subject NP that is compatible with the inflected *-s* form. From this perspective, (6) is excluded not by virtue of any intrinsic property of the bare form but rather as a function of the availability of (7):

(6)   *John sing well.

(7)   John sings well.

10.2.   Verb agreement with a wh-phrase

This approach to the ungrammaticality of (6) may be supported by the nonstandard variety of English discussed in Kimball and Aissen (1971), in which (8) is possible in addition to the standard form:

(8)   the people who Clark think are in the garden

Although this variety of English allows a singular subject to cooccur with *think* (when the head of the relative/wh-phrase is plural), it does not allow a plural subject to cooccur with the *-s* form (even when the head of the relative is singular):

(9)   *the man who the girls likes

Kimball and Aissen's approach to the contrast between (8) and (9) depends in part on taking singular to be universally unmarked as compared with nonsingular. Although there may be some sense in which that is true, we shall not adopt their markedness approach to these facts, for two reasons. First, it is odd to think of the *-s* form in English as unmarked, since it bears an overt suffix that distinguishes it from its bare opposite number. Second, and potentially more significant, Kimball and Aissen's approach to (8) amounts to the claim that the existence of (8) has nothing to do with the fact that the 'plural' verb form is bare.

In the spirit of the second paragraph before last, we would like to make the contrary conjecture, namely that (8) is possible in some variety of English precisely because the relevant verb form is bare. Put another way, we conjecture that in a language in which there is an overt singular agreement suffix and a distinct overt plural agreement suffix (8) will never be found.

An analysis to account for (8), while excluding (9), will express this conjecture by taking advantage of the asymmetry between the *-s* form, which we took, like other overt agreement suffixes, to be specified positively for a particular value, here +singular, and the bare form, which we took to be unspecified for a particular antecedent and whose distribution we took to be determined by a kind of elsewhere principle. However, to make this account precise, and to allow it to integrate the contrast between (8), with a plural relative head, and (10), with a singular one, requires that we specify more carefully the syntactic reflex of the difference between *-s* form and bare form:

(10)   *the person who Clark think is in the garden

It seems fairly clear that, if we are to account in a satisfactory manner for (8)–(10), the diffference between *-s* form and bare form must be more than an accident of phonetic realization, that is, that it will not be sufficient to think of the bare form as bearing an agreement suffix just like the *-s* suffix except that the agreement suffix for the bare form happens to be phonetically unrealized. If the difference were that minimal, it would be hard to see why (8) and (9) should contrast as they do.

Of (8) and (9), the latter is of course the expected case. Example (8) is odd in that it appears to display verb agreement with the head of the relative rather than with the subject. In fact, there is reason to think that the unusual agreement of (8) is really with the wh-phrase, since (11) seems to have the status of (10) rather than that of (8):

(11)   *the people whose car John think is beautiful

And (12) seems to go with (8) rather than with (10) and (11):

(12)   the person whose cars John think are beautiful

Agreement with a wh-phrase is in fact a familiar phenomenon, in particular given Rizzi's (1990) recent extensive discussion. It is nonetheless unusual to find the verb doing so, rather than the complementizer. Let us therefore propose that in (8) and (12) AGR has raised to C, in which position it is coindexed with the wh-phrase.

Put another way, (8) and (12) are examples of a widely familiar type of agreement, that between a head and its specifier. The ungrammaticality of (11) follows in part from the fact that when moved to C, AGR has the wh-phrase as its specifier and not the head of the relative, and in part from the same principle that rules out (13):

(13)   *This car look beautiful.

In our earlier discussion of (6), we in effect considered that it and the equivalent (13) are excluded by virtue of the availability of (7) and (14):

(14)   This car looks beautiful.

Now the contrast between (11) and (12) does appear to be parallel to that between (13) and (14), but the former pair shows that the principle involved must be more carefully delineated if it is to exclude (13) and (11) without also excluding (in the relevant variety of English) (12), the problem being that a principle that simply said that the bare form is excluded whenever the -s form is available would fail to distinguish (11) from (12), since the -s form is possible in both. Our solution to this problem will aim to account at the same time for the ungrammaticality of (9), in which it is the -s form that agrees with the wh-phrase.

As far as the -s form is concerned, we follow the standard approach of saying that it involves the lowering of AGR onto V.[6] Furthermore, we assume that such lowering in incompatible with the raising of AGR to C. (Once lowered, AGR can no longer be dissociated from V.[7]) Hence the mechanism that we suggested above as being responsible for the possibility of (12) will never be available with the -s form. This accounts for the ungrammaticality of (9).

To allow (8) and (12), we take the bare form of English present tense verbs not to bear any suffix that would have needed to lower onto V, that is, to be without any agreement suffix at all. We assume that there is an AGR in sentences with bare verb forms but that it dominates no suffix at any level of representation, contrary to sentences with the -s form. This purely abstract AGR needs to be coindexed with an appropriately local NP, but it does not need to lower onto V or for V to raise up to it. Consequently, it, unlike the -*s* suffix, is free to raise to C, where it can be coindexed with the wh-phrase. This accounts for the availability of (8) and (12).

To exclude (11) and (13) (without excluding (12)), we need to say that this abstract AGR can be coindexed only with a NP that is incompatible with the -*s* suffix. In other words, our earlier discussion of the alternation between bare form and -*s* form carries over naturally, as long as we interpret the mechanism in question to pertain to AGR in a given position rather than to verb forms.[8] In effect, (12) is possible (in the relevant English) despite the availability of *thinks* because the abstract AGR has been coindexed with an appropriate NP (i.e., with one incompatible with -*s*)—the fact that there is another NP with which it might inappropriately have been coindexed (if it had not moved to C) is irrelevant.

To exclude (8) and (12) in standard English, we might simply say that standard English lacks the AGR-to-C option that the variety of English described by Kimball and Aissen (1971) makes use of. A potentially more interesting approach would be to interpret this variation in terms of case, noting that the agreement with the wh-phrase seen in (8) and (12) appears to deprive the subject NP of its case source, since it fails to agree there with anything. Thus it might be that the nonstandard English in question has relaxed the requirement on the licensing of subject NPs: Whereas standard English (apart from cases in which objective case is assigned to a subject NP) requires licensing via coindexation with AGR, this nonstandard English requires only that the NP occupy the subject position of AGR.[9]

It might be that this relaxation is in turn dependent on English NPs generally not showing any case morphology. If so, we might expect nominative pronouns to continue to need coindexation with AGR.[10] To our ear, such an expectation is borne out, in that (15) is appreciably worse than (8) or (12):

(15)   a. *the people who she think are in the garden

        b. *the person whose cars he think are beautiful

Thus, nominative case morphology does seem to be keyed to coindexation with AGR, as usually assumed, but in the absence of such morphology the licensing of a subject NP (even in the absence of objective case) need not be (i.e., can be purely configurational).

Kimball and Aissen (1971) note that accepting the construction exemplified by (8) does not imply accepting (16):

(16)   *the people who think that John know the answer

In other words, the presence of *who* in the next Comp up does not license the bare verb form in the embedded sentence. From our perspective, this follows from the fact that AGR-to-lower C does not put AGR into a head position of which *who* is the specifier, in addition, the lower AGR has no way of reaching the upper C. This is so in part because long movement of AGR would be prohibited by familiar constraints on head movement[11] and in part because from the lower C AGR could not move up any further, for reasons not entirely clear.[12]

Kimball and Aissen note further that those who accept (8) also accept cases like (17), despite rejecting (16):

(17)   the boys who Tom think(s) Dick believe(s) Harry expect(s) to be late

In (17), one, two or all three of the finite verbs can fail to have the -*s* form. For *believe* and *expect*, the bare form is being licensed by a *who* that is in a higher Comp, in apparent conflict with the fact of (16). The contrast between (16) and (17) follows, however, from the existence of successive cyclic applications of wh-movement.[13] The bare form of any of the three finite verbs will be licensed, under our analysis, as a result of the abstract AGR moving into C. AGR in C is in turn licensed by the presence, in the specifier position of that C, of (the trace of) a wh-phrase. Successive cyclic application of wh-movement makes available a wh-phrase trace in each Comp in (17), but not at all in the lower Comp in (16), exactly as desired.

The construction studied by Kimball and Aissen thus appears to provide strong support (especially if the problem of the next section is satisfactorily solved) for successive cyclicity, in combination with the AGR-to-C analysis just presented, and with the analysis of English bare verb forms as involving an abstract AGR that does not need to be merged with V at S-structure.

10.3.   Raised auxiliaries are below C

Recall that we earlier ruled out (9) by the requirement that the overt agreement suffix -*s* merge with V by S-structure. This prevents -*s* from moving to C, since V in (9) is not in C. A question that comes to mind is the following: Could sentences like (9) be generated by having V-to-AGR raising, then [V+AGR]-to-C? This question has three variants. First, could such a construction exist in Romance, where V-to-AGR is usual? Second, could it exist in English with those (auxiliary) verbs that do seem to raise to AGR? Third, could V+AGR end up in C in English even with lexical verbs—at the level of LF—subsequent to a raising of AGR to C followed by the lowering of AGR to V in the syntax?

We don't know of any case in Romance of a verb agreeing with a wh-phrase while failing to agree with its subject. Nor does English seem to allow this unusual agreement pattern with the -*s* form:

(18)   Which girls do the boy think should be invited?

(19)   *Which girl does the boys think should be invited?

Example (18) is based on an example given by Kimball and Aissen of the agreement pattern in question. (19), with the -*s* form, seems to us much worse. We could exclude (19) as well as its Romance counterparts by prohibiting in general the movement of a finite verb to C. If *does* in (19) does not move to C, then the locality necessary for coindexing -*s* with the wh-phrase will never hold.

The idea that a finite V never moves to C in Romance would be a bit controversial.[14] The idea that *does* in (19) cannot move to C, with its implication that *do* in (18) is not in C, would be very controversial, although Pesetsky (1989) has in fact proposed just that. His proposal is combined, however, with the idea that the wh-phrase itself is in the specifier position of the auxiliary, which is not compatible with our analysis. This is so, since for us to distinguish (18) from (19) as we earlier distinguished (8) from (9), it must be the case that *does* is not in the head position of which the wh-phrase is the specifier, and the same must then hold for *do* in (18). Put another way, for us to treat (18) as parallel to (8) and (12), (18) must have a structure in which AGR has moved to C and in which *do* occupies a head position below AGR. The status of the specifier position of the base position of AGR is unclear. Leaving this last question open, we turn to considerations bearing on the possibility of taking English auxiliaries never to raise to the highest functional head position (and hence never to C).

10.4.   English vs. French

Pollock (1989) has argued strongly that finite IP should be reinterpreted in terms of two projections, AGRP and TP.[15] Lexical verbs remain in their base position in English. Verbs that assign no theta-role such as *have* in some of its uses and *be* do raise out of their base position, moving through the lower functional head position (for Pollock, AGR) on up to the upper one (for Pollock, T). *Do* is generated in AGR and raises up to T. The modals are generated directly in T. Thus, for Pollock, the various auxiliary verbs, although originating in diverse positions, share the property, when finite, of all ending up in the upper functional head position, that is, in the head position of TP. In French, on the other hand, all finite verbs move up to that position, with the result that lexical verbs differ in French and in English. They move to the highest functional head position in French, but they do not in English.

An earlier version of this way of distinguishing French from English had been used by Emonds (1978) to account for certain facts concerning adverb placement. Pollock shows that this approach also accounts for the contrast between (20) and (21) (setting aside parenthetical intonation):

(20)   John probably likes linguistics.

(21)   *Jean probablement aime la linguistique.

An adverb like *probably* is generated, according to Pollock, in between T and AGR in both languages. The lexical V in French must move to T and in so doing must cross over the adverb. The English lexical V, on the other hand, remains in its base position.

Consider, however, the following:

(22)   The fact that John probably has made several mistakes is well-known.

(23)   *Le fait que Jean probablement ait fait plusieurs erreurs est bien connu.

Pollock (1989, 370n) notes the existence of sentences like (22), with a preauxiliary adverb, and suggests that English be taken to have an extra adverb position, as compared with French, whose counterpart, given in (23), is deviant. To our eye, the contrast between (22) and (23) is identical to that between (20) and (21). Yet Pollock's hypothesis that English auxiliaries raise to the higher functional head position (just like French verbs in general) makes it difficult for him to provide a uniform treatment of these two pairs.

In the same footnote, Pollock observes that *never* and *not* contrast as follows:

(24)   John never has.

(25)   *John not has.

He proposes a condition on *not* to exclude (25), but that condition establishes no relation at all between (25) and the similar (26), which he later accounts for in an entirely different (and particularly interesting) fashion:

(26)   *John not likes linguistics.

To our eye, (25) and (26) constitute a single phenomenon. Again, it is Pollock's hypothesis that auxiliaries raise to the upper functional head position that is the source of the difficulty.

On the other hand, sentences like (27) indicate that finite auxiliary verbs can raise in a way that lexical verbs cannot, in English:

(27)   John wasn't there.

Even then, a preauxiliary adverb is possible:

(28)   John probably wasn't there.

Abstracting away from the base position of the negation, this suggests that finite auxiliary verbs raise to the lower functional head position, but not to the upper one, and that adverbs like *probably* can occur in between the two (as well as[16] in between F2 and V): . . . F1 . . . probably . . . F2 . . . V . . . , with V raising in (28) to F2 but not to F1.

From this perspective, there are no adverbs base-generated to the immediate left of F1, just as there are none so generated in French. The reason is presumably that adverbs can be adjoined to maximal projections but never to nonmaximal projections. (Note that this constraint is unavailable to Pollock, insofar as he has *wasn't* in (28) in F1.) *Probably* in (28) must therefore be adjoined to the maximal projection of F2 (or of Neg; cf. next section).

10.5.   Negation and emphasis as heads

As for the *n't* of (28), let us in essence follow Pollock (1989, 397) in taking it to be a functional head[17] occurring below F1 but above F2. Contrary to Pollock, let us take *was*, subsequent to its move into F2, to adjoin to *n't*,[18] rather than to move into F1. Similarly, we take the auxiliary to adjoin to emphatic *so, too,* and *not*, themselves taken to be functional heads parallel to *n't*:[19]

(29)   John was SO/TOO/NOT there.

Adjunction here may seem odd, since it amounts to postulating the existence of inflectional affixes bearing emphatic stress, but in addition to expressing what appears to be a real parallelism, it captures the fact that they may not be separated from the preceding auxiliary:

(30)   a. ?John was SO/TOO certainly there.

       b. ???John certainly was SO/TOO there.

       c. **John was certainly SO/TOO there.

It also makes the following a single phenomenon (to which we return later):

(31)   a. *John'sn't there.

       b. *John's SO/TOO there.

Similarly for (32):

(32)   a. *John n't likes linguistics.

       b. *John SO/TOO likes linguistics.

The ungrammaticality of (32) could be treated as in Pollock (1989) or Chomsky (1991), with the negative head inducing a barrier effect.[20] Alternatively, (32) could be excluded parallel to (33), on the grounds that an affix may not remain unsupported:[21]

(33)   a. *John s like linguistics.

       b. *John is ing study linguistics.

       Consider now (34):

(34)   *John not likes linguistics.

If *not* can be an affixal head like *n't*, then such a *not* will be excluded in (34), just as *n't* and *so/too* are in (32).There is clearly another *not*, however, as suggested by the following:

(35)   a. John was probably not talking to Bill.

       b. John has probably not talked to Bill.

       c. John will probably not talk to Bill.

(36) *John did probably not talk to Bill.

We interpret the ungrammaticality of (36) as resulting from the fact that auxiliary *do* must, apart from inversion structures, be licensed by a negative/emphatic affix. The *not* of (36) cannot be that affix because there is an intervening adverb; see (30c).

The ungrammaticality of (37) is now interesting in two ways:

(37) *John probably not talked to Bill.

First, it shows that, contrary to Chomsky's (1991, sect. 3.1) suggestion, the ill-formedness of *do* in the absence of (inversion or) a negative/emphatic element cannot be entirely attributed to the fact that there exists another well-formed derivation. If that were all that was at issue, we would incorrectly expect (36) to be well formed with unstressed *do* by virtue of (37) being ill formed. Second, as far as (37) itself is concerned, its ungrammaticality shows that, if it is to be excluded as Pollock and Chomsky exclude (32), that is, via the head character of the negative element, then this other kind of *not* must also be a head, which would imply that in (38) there are two negative heads:

(38) He couldn't not have accepted.

Alternatively, it could be that the *not* of (38) and (35) is not a head but a specifier, as would be more consonant with section 4.2.2 not having analyzed French *pas* as a head (as opposed to *ne*, given that the two diverge sharply with respect to their effect on clitic movement). If *not* in (38) is the specifier of an abstract negative head, as in Pollock (1989, 421), then (37) can continue to be thought of as strongly parallel to (32), at least from Pollock and Chomsky's perspective. If the *not* of (38) is the specifier of some other category, then (37) must be excluded more as in Rizzi (1990).

To return to the main point of this section, we have tried to make plausible the claim that the syntax of negation in English is compatible with the idea, suggested in the previous section, that English auxiliaries never move to the higher functional head position of the two proposed by Pollock (1989). If that idea is correct, then it becomes more plausible to take the position we did in section 10.3., namely that English auxiliaries never move to C, even in inversion constructions.

10.6. Zero suffixes

In section 10.2. we analyzed the nonstandard agreement studied by Kimball and Aissen (1971) as involving movement of AGR to C. The further claim was made that such movement is possible only when AGR does not need to merge with V and so is not available when AGR dominates an overt affix. This aimed to account for the fact that in this nonstandard English, agreement with a wh-phrase is available only when the verb form is bare and never when it bears the -*s* suffix. In discussing the fact that standard English never allows comparable agreement with a wh-phrase, no matter what the verb form, we suggested that nonstandard English might have relaxed a certain case requirement that otherwise prohibits such nonagreement with the lexical subject NP. Another possibility that we have not considered so far is that the difference lies instead with AGR itself. For example, it might be that standard English requires AGR to merge with V even when AGR dominates no morphological material, that is, even in the case where nonstandard English allows it to remain independent of V and to move to C. This would amount to saying that the standard English present tense bare verb form has a zero (i.e., phonetically unrealized) agreement suffix, whereas the discussion of section 10.2. took it to have no agreement suffix.

A consideration bearing on this is the absence in English of any equivalent of the French or Italian causative construction with embedded passive-like infinitive:[22]

(39)   Jean a fait réparer la table par Paul. (J has made repair the table by P)

(40)   a. *John had/made repair the table (by Paul).

        b. *John had/made the table repair (by Paul).

As far as we know, all the Romance languages that have productive use of infinitives have (39) to some degree. Furthermore, the Germanic languages all seem to have either (40a) or (40b), with the exception of English.[23] We would like to analyze the absence of (40) in English as related to the absence in English of any infinitival suffix. This relation can be expressed by taking the infinitival suffffix -r in (39) (and similarly for the other languages that have (39) or (40)) to have the capacity to be an argument in the sense of Jaeggli (1986) and Baker, Johnson, and Roberts (1989), so that (40) is excluded in English by virtue of having no element to which the subject theta-role can be assigned.

This presupposes, however, that the embedded verb form in (40) has no zero suffix comparable to the overt infinitival suffix in (39). The unavailability of a zero suffix in (40) strengthens the idea that there is no zero agreement suffix in the English present tense forms.

An open question is whether there is a zero tense suffix in the English present parallel to that often visible in the past tense forms. A more general open question is what exactly determines the availability of zero suffixes. It is unlikely that there are none. For example, Romance frequently has zero for 3sg agreement.[24] Let us conjecture that a verb (agreement) suffix can be zero only if it is the head of the construction, that is, only if the verb raises up to it. If a verb (agreement) suffix lowers to V, then it may not be zero.

If this is correct, then we can say that the bare form in English lacks a zero agreement suffix because the overt agreement suffix -s lowers to V, rather than having V raise to it, as it generally would in Romance. This leads to the question of why -s does lower to V in English. Roberts (1985) and Pollock (1989) suggest that V can raise only if the language has sufficiently rich agreement and that English agreement is not sufficiently rich. What exactly does 'sufficiently rich' mean? Platzack and Holmberg (1989) argue that within the Scandinavian languages, both past and present, there is a strong correlation between the raising of V and the presence of person agreement. In particular, if a Scandinavian language has person agreement, then it has without exception the raising of V. Under the traditional analysis of English *-s* as 3sg, English has person agreement and is therefore an unexpected exception to their generalization as extended at least to the class of Germanic SVO languages. Under our analysis of *-s* as simply +sg, English lexical verbs never show any person agreement, and English ceases to be exceptional.[25]

Although English lexical verbs fail to raise, English auxiliary verbs do raise. Conceivably, this might be related to the fact that within the class of auxiliary verbs, there is arguably one instance of person agreement, namely *am*. This would fit into Platzack and Holmberg's generalization about Scandinavian if UG permitted treating the class of lexical verbs as significantly separate from the class of auxiliary verbs, that is, if the existence of some person agreement within the latter class could license raising among its members without there being any spillover to lexical verbs. Whether lexical verbs raise or not would then be affected by the presence or absence of person agreement within that class alone.

Alternatively, the raising of the auxiliary verbs in English could be tied directly to absence of theta-marking.[26] Absence of theta-marking could well be a necessary condition, although not a sufficient condition, given the identical behavior of auxiliaries and lexical verbs to each other with respect to raising in mainland Scandinavian.[27]

Granted that English auxiliaries do raise, the question arises as to the label of the node they raise to. For Pollock (1989), the F2 of our schematic . . . F1 . . . F2 . . . V . . . is AGR. His proposal interacts in interesting ways with the analysis of the English bare verb form that we have developed so far. Recall that earlier in this section we suggested that the bare form truly had no suffix, not even a zero suffix, as a consequence of the fact that overt AGR in English lowered onto V, combined with a prohibition against zero-suffixes that would not be the head of the [V AGR] constituent. To the extent that V raises, however, this conclusion does not hold, that is, the raising of auxiliary V to *-s* makes it possible for the bare auxiliary verb form in English to have a zero suffix, contrary to the bare lexical verb form. Recall further that our analysis of the nonstandard agreement pattern discussed by Kimball and Aissen (1971) made crucial use of the movement of AGR to C and that we explicitly claimed that such movement is possible only if AGR and V do not merge. Assume now that the raising of auxiliary V to AGR is obligatory, at least in nonstandard English. In that case, AGR-to-C should be impossible, and the prediction is made that the nonstandard agreement pattern in question should be unavailable with auxiliaries. The relevant cases are these:

(41)   the people who John think should be invited

(42)   a. the people who John have thought should be invited
        b. the people who John were thinking should be invited
        c. the people who John don't think should be invited

Example (41) is essentially from Kimball and Aissen (1971). Example (42c) is a clear case of raising, given the *n't*. Examples (42a) and (42b) are, also, if the assumption of obligatoriness is warranted. Our judgment on (42) is uncertain (and so we have not explicitly indicated any *), but it seems to us that at least (42b) is appreciably worse than (41) and that (42c) might conceivably be, too, if one abstracted away from the perhaps differently nonstandard use of *don't* with all subject NPs.[28]

Assume that (42) turns out to support Pollock's hypothesis that auxiliary V raises to AGR rather than to T, and consider, in the light of that assumption, (18), repeated here as (43):

(43)   Which girls do the boy think should be invited?

Assume further, with Kimball and Aissen (1971), that (43) has the status of (41) and, with our tentative judgment, that (44) has the status of (42c):

(44)   Which girls don't the boy think should be invited?

Then in (44), *do* must (uncontroversially) not be in the V position, whereas in (43) it (rather controversially) must be, in order to free AGR to move to C. Put another way, our analysis of (41) as involving AGR-to-C, plus the assimilation of (43) to (41), combined with Pollock's ... T ... AGR ... V ... structure leads to the surprising conclusion that *do* in (43) is in a V position, contrary to Pollock's (1989, 399) analysis of the *do* of '*do*-support' but consonant with his argument (p. 402) that the *do* found in imperatives is a main verb.[29]

10.7.   Contraction

If the *do* of (43) is in a V position, then its exclusion from infinitives becomes an issue, presumably one related to that of excluding modals from infinitives (cf. note 28). Pollock (1989, 398) suggests generating modals in T, higher than AGR and also higher than NegP, if one is present. On the other hand, if *do* is a V and if there is some significant degree of similarity between *do* and modals, we would expect modals, too, to originate in V. In this regard, we mention briefly some evidence that seems to go against the idea that modals originate in T:

(45)   a. He'll do it.
       b. He'd do it if you asked him.
       c. He's been there before.
       d. They've been there before.
       e. He'd been there before.

(46)   a. *He'll not do it.
       b. *He'd not do it even if you asked him.
       c. *He's not been there yet.
       d. *They've not been there yet.
       e. *He'd not been there before.

The '*'s of (46) are accurate for our English and are probably widespread among speakers of American English (some of whom find (46c–e) intermediate betweeen (46a–b) and (45)). On the other hand, Quirk et al.(1972, 375) give (46a,d,e) as acceptable without comment. We will have no proposal to offer to account for all the variation across speakers and will limit ourselves to commenting on the implications of the variety of English that our own judgments represent.

It seems to us impossible to make sense of (46), in particular of (46a,b), if modals are generated in T, to the left of the negative morpheme. More precisely, this seems impossible to understand if the contracted variants of the modals are generated in T as such or originate there as uncontracted modals. Rather, we should interpret the deviance of (46) as resulting from the blocking effect of negation, already seen in (34), repeated here as (47):

(47)   *John not likes linguistics.

Taking *not* in (46) and (47) to be a head (but see also the discussion of (38)) and taking the contracted forms of (45) and (46) to have the property of having to move into T, we can extend Pollock's (1989, 405) account of (47) to (46) by denying the contracted forms the ability to L-mark, so that NegP in (46) remains a barrier and induces an ECP violation with respect, crucially, to the trace of the contracted form, which must, consequently, have originated below NegP, most plausibly in V.[30]

Contrasting with (46) is (48):[31]

(48)   a. I'm not listening.
     b. He's not listening.
     c. They're not listening.

Let us suggest that *be* differs for us from *have* and from the modals for the reason that its trace can delete at LF, eliminating the potential ECP violation of (46), because *be* is superfluous with respect to interpretation. Those speakers who reject (46a,b) while accepting to some degree (46c,d,e) may be able to delete the trace of perfective *have*, too.[32]

Further contrasting with (46) is (49):

(49)   a. He won't do it.
     b. He wouldn't do it. etc.

As in our discussion of (27) and (28), we analyze these as involving not movement to T but rather adjunction of the auxiliary to the negative head, with the result that the barrier status of NegP does not come into play.

It might appear that we could take the ungrammaticality of (31), repeated here as (50), to be parallel to that of (46):

(50)   a. *He'lln't do it.
     b. *He'll SO do it. etc.

However, that would miss the contrast between (48) and (51):

(51)   a. *I'mn't listening.
       b. *He'sn't listening.
       c. *They'ren't listening.
       d. *I'm SO listening. etc.

These can be excluded, rather, by the previous assumption that the contracted forms must move to T, since *n't* (and *so*) will then be unsupported (cf. the discussion of (32)).[33]

10.8.   *Amn't*

Let us return to the verb *be*. In the past tense, there are two forms *was* and *were*, whereas all other English verbs have only one form in the past tense. Moreover, these two forms do not match up with the two present tense forms that English lexical verbs have, in that *was*, unlike the regular *-s* form, is used with *I*. Given our analysis of *-s* as +sg, we cannot then have *was* be +sg. *Were*, on the other hand, can be taken to be +plural (given that *you* is always grammatically plural). This leads to the suggestion that *was* is the 'elsewhere' form for the past tense of *be*, appearing wherever *were* is impossible.

   In the present tense, *be* has three forms, as opposed to two for every other verb. *Am* seems clearly to be marked for 1st person, and that marking may perhaps have syntactic consequences, as in the discussion in section VI. *Is* can then be taken to be +sg, like the *-s* form of all other verbs. *Are* might appear to be +plural, but, in the spirit of this article, it is more appealing to take it to be unmarked and hence usable wherever *am* and *is* are not. Put another way, this view of *are* claims that it fails to occur with *I* and *he* because there are more highly specified forms that can be so used, and not because of any inherent incompatibility between *are* and those subject NPs.

   There is a so far unexplained gap in the *n't* paradigm:[34]

(52)   *I amn't listening.

(53)   a. You aren't listening.
       b. He isn't listening.

There is an alternative available to (52), namely (48a), with *'m* (and *not*). However, there is no exactly parallel alternative to the absence of the inverted form:

(54)   *Amn't I listening?

(55)   *'m not I listening?

From the agreement perspective that we have been pursuing, it now makes at least informal sense that (56) is available (although not necessarily perfect):

(56)   Aren't I listening?

This is so, since *are* is not inherently incompatible with *I* but merely excluded from appearing with it because of the availability of *am*. The deviance of (57) is, from this perspective, related to the availability of (48a):

(57)   *I aren't listening.

Finally, we can now understand why (56) can stand in for (54)/(55), whereas (58) cannot:

(58)   *Isn't I listening?

The reason is that *is* requires a +sg subject and that *I* is unmarked for number, as in section 10.1.

NOTES

1. See Akmajian and Heny (1975, 197), Curme (1977 (1931), I, 238), Jespersen (1961, VI, 14), Kimball and Aissen (1971, 241), Lyons (1968, 240), Quirk et al. (1972, 366), Roberts (1985, 43)

2. The fact that Russian *vy* gives rise to a comparable discrepancy between verb and (long) adjective agreement (cf. Crockett (1976, 119)) suggests that the clitic status of French *vous* in (3) does not play a central role in the phenomenon at hand.

3. This description carries over to sentences like (i), in which the verb agrees with third-person, singular *on*, while the adjective agrees in number with the empty NP whose plurality matches that of the (first-person) plural referent:

(i)   On est loyaux. (one is loyal-pl.)

Sentences such as (ii) suggest that a floating quantifier can agree (and here, at least, must agree) with such an empty NP, perhaps along the lines of Sportiche (1988):

(ii)   On est tous loyaux. (one is all-pl. loyal-pl.)

(To what extent comparable nonagreement in gender within an A-chain is possible is unclear, cf. Ruwet (1967); for other relevant discussion, cf. Pollock (1983b)). The lack of person agreement in (iii) will require further analysis, in which the clitic status of *on* is likely to be crucial (cf. Kayne (1972, 95; 1983b, note 9)):

(iii)   Nous, on est loyaux. (us, one . . .)

4. This NP can be an empty NP variable, as in (i):

(i)   the man who I know sings well

5. This recalls McCloskey and Hale's (1984, 531) discussion of the fact that in the general case the existence of a synthetic verb form (i.e., one marked for agreement) in Irish precludes using what would be the corresponding analytic form (i.e., one lacking agree-

ment marking), as well as Di Sciullo and Williams's (1987, 11) discussion of pairs like (i) versus (ii):

(i)   This book is longer than that one.

(ii)   *This book is more long than that one.

(A problem is the existence in Irish and in the English comparatives of some doublets (e.g., with bimorphemic adjectives in -y) versus (but note the discussion of (8)) the absence of any with *sing/sings*.)

The English comparative case might be looked at in terms of Pesetsky's (1989) proposal that S-structure movement is favored over LF-movement if (i) is closer to the correct LF representation than (ii). The Irish and English agreement cases cannot be looked at in the same way if Chomsky's (1991) approach to agreement is correct.

6.   See Pollock (1989) and references cited there.

7.   See Baker (1988) and Chomsky (1991).

8.   We might take this choice to reflect a broader principle to the effect that when a choice is available, preference is given to an overt functional suffix over its abstract counterpart. The contrast with Chomsky's (1981a) 'avoid PRO' might be related to the difference between a word-level and a phrase-level element. The suggestion of this note is compatible with Chomsky's (1991) approach to agreement (vs. note 5).

9.   Assuming that accepting (8) and (12) does not imply accepting (i), we conclude, with Chomsky (1991, sect. 5), that (English) infinitives lack AGR entirely (at least lack AGR-S, in his terms):

(i)   *John to arrive now would be unfortunate.

This conclusion, if extended to Romance control infinitives, is incompatible with Belletti's (1990) proposal that Italian control infinitives move to AGR, as well as with the AGR-based proposal of section 10 of chapter 4.

10.   There is a point of similarity here with Klima's (1964b) analysis of the most colloquial (L4) of the varieties of English he discussed.

11.   See Chomsky (1986a) and references cited there.

12.   Perhaps any projection headed by AGR must have a specifier, so AGR could move only into a C the projection of which dominated a wh-phrase. See Chomsky's (1982, 10) Extended Projection Principle.

13.   See. Chomsky (1973).

14.   Finite V-to-C has been proposed recently by Ambar (1989) and by Rizzi and Roberts (1989). The former proposal will depend on how adverbs to the immediate left of the finite V are treated. The latter one has V-to-I-to-C yielding a grammatical result only when the subject is a nominative pronoun, so the special agreement pattern we are interested in would be in any case excluded by the case considerations brought to bear in the discussion of (15).

15.   The existence of an AGR projection is motivated also by considerations of past participle agreement. See chapters 2 and 3.

16.   That adverbs of the *probably* type can occur in either of two positions is supported by the marginal acceptability of (i), especially if its marginality is attributable to a purely interpretive constraint, as suggested by Jackendoff (1972, 87):

(i)   ?John probably could almost certainly have won, if he'd been better prepared.

17. As had been suggested by Kitagawa (1986, sect. 2.4.3) for Japanese and in chapter 4, sect. 4.2., for French and Italian *ne* and *non*.

18. See Zwicky (1970, 328) and Zwicky and Pullum (1983)'s argument that *n't* should be treated as an inflectional affix.

19. This parallel was seen by Pollock (1989, 421n), but at a point in his article where he was thinking of NegP having an empty head, so he suggested taking the emphatic particles as specifiers (of a projection of which we are suggesting they are the head).

20. In a way similar in part to the proposal concerning clitic movement that we have made in Section 4.2. of chapter 4.

21. This would require an account of the impossibility of lowering the negative/emphatic affix to the verb. It suggests also that a negative/emphatic head must be an affix.

22. See Kayne (1975, sect. 3.5), Burzio (1986, sect. 4.2).

23. See Taraldsen (1981; 1983), Coopmans (1985).

24. Compare the Portuguese inflected infinitive and future subjunctive. Also see Harris (1969, 67).

25. Absence of person agreement in Scandinavian does not completely preclude V raising, so we cannot take a stronger position and say that its absence in English follows directly from that of person agreement.

Although having person agreement seems to imply having V raising, Sigurdsson (1986) could be interpreted to mean that Icelandic can sometimes fail to raise V, which would bear on Chomsky (1991).

26. See Roberts (1985) and Pollock (1989).⁻

27. Consider the fact, in essence noted by Pollock (1989, 373), that colloquial French cannot move any infinitive across negative *pas*, even *être* or *avoir*.

It would be desirable to know if there are any Scandinavian dialects that have the English asymmetry in person agreement between auxiliaries and lexical verbs and, if so, whether there is any asymmetry with respect to V raising.

28. See Curme (1977 (1931), II, 54), who suggests an analogy with the lack of agreement in modals.

29. See also his (p.399) proposal that auxiliary *do* has/gets a theta-grid, as well as Pullum and Wilson (1977).

30. From Chomsky's (1991) perspective, we might be able to link (46) to (47) by denying to the contracted forms the ability to pass through AGR.

31. Also contrasting with (46) is (i):

(i)   a. ?He'll probably not do it.

   b. ?He'd probably not do it. etc.

These, however, exemplify the *not* of (35), which can be taken to be generated below the modal, i.e. in between the modal and the main verb. See (ii) vs. (iii):

(ii)   ?He wouldn't probably not do it.

(iii)   *He'd not probably not do it.

32. See Platzack (1986, 201) on its 'visible' deletion in Swedish.

33. The nonemphatic *not* of (48) must not be affixal.

34. Perhaps related to *am* being marked for person.

11

Agreement and Verb Morphology in Three Varieties of English

11.1. English has inflection for number but not for person

(1)   You sing well

(2)   He sings well

If one takes *you* to always be grammatically plural, somewhat as French *vous* (cf. (3)–(5)), despite sometimes referring to a singular, then, if one takes *I* to be nonsingular (there is clearly nothing that *I* is a true singular of), English *-s* can be considered to be a pure indication of number (+singular), rather than involving person in any way.

(3)   a. Vous êtes loyaux
          You-pl. are-2pl. loyal-pl.

      b. Vous êtes loyal
          You-pl. are-2pl. loyal-sg.

(4)   Tu es loyal
      You-sg. are-2sg. loyal-sg.

(5)   *Vous es loyal.
      You-pl. are-2sg. loyal-sg.

This reduces the morphology/syntax discrepancy (if English present tense lexical verbs agree in both number and person, why are there only two forms?).

It may have the further advantage of allowing the generalization to English of Platzack and Holmberg's (1989, 72) claim about Scandinavian: If a Scandinavian/

English language has person morphology on the verb, then it invariably has V-raising of the Icelandic type. Given Vikner's (1995) discussion of Faroese, I would probably be led to suggest that Faroese shows a three-way number distinction (+sing., +plural, and -sing./-pl.), with the last equivalent to what is usually thought of as 1st sg.

(6)   *John sing well

(7)   John sings well

For standard English, I will now say that -*s* is compatible only with a singular antecedent and that (apart from *be*) there otherwise is, in the present tense, just -*0*, which is compatible only with a nonsingular (-*0* = a phonetically unrealized agreement morpheme), as seen in (6).

11.2.   Num is contentful or expletive

In the spirit of Picallo (1991), Rigau (1991), Ritter (1991) and Shlonsky (1989), I take -*s* and -*0* to correspond to a functional head Num(ber). This may receive further support from Paddock's (1990) suggestion that the -*s* of (Vernacular) Newfoundland English, which occurs with all subjects, is the verbal counterpart to the plural -*s* found with nouns, that is, that the two are essentially the same morpheme.[1]

Paddock's suggestion can be generalized as follows: Num can be either contentful (as with nouns) or not (i.e., can either be present at LF or not). If it is not inherently contentful, then it is like an expletive element, which can agree with another phrase (as pronominal expletives do in French complex inversion)[2]—this is what we call number agreement, as with English verbs, or with Romance adjectives.

When Num is not inherently contentful, it can also fail to agree (as expletives usually fail to), as in nominativeless oblique subject constructions.

The contrast noted by Paddock between (8) and (9):

(8)   It bees cold here (*generalization/ multiple instances*)

(9)   'Tis cold here (*present time*)

could be interpreted as indicating that contentful number cannot be raised to Tense.

From this perspective, we should carefully distinguish Num from number agreement. The latter is a relation between Num and something else. Thus, to have a category label AGR for the -*s* morpheme would be mistaken in much the same way that it would be to have a category label Subj(ect). (The same point holds straightforwardly for gender agreement, although the suffix in question may be a word marker in Harris's (1991, 28) sense rather than belonging to any category Gen.)

Person agreement would then be thought of as a relation between a category Pers and something else, rather than as involving a category AGR. Pers may further be assimilable to a (clitic) pronoun, as in Taraldsen (1992).

11.3.   Extracted elements may adjoin to NumP

(10)   the people who the boy think are in the garden

There is a variety of nonstandard (American, at least) English (Kimball and Aissen (1971)) that allows (10) (without allowing *The boy think the people are in the garden). (11) is, however, impossible:

(11)   *the man who the boys thinks is in the garden

It is clear from the following that (10) involves some sort of unusual agreement with the wh-phrase, rather than with the head of the relative directly.

(12)   *the person who Clark think is in the garden

(13)   *the people whose car John think is beautiful

(14)   the person whose cars John think are beautiful

The next two examples show that successive cyclic wh-movement is needed to account for a broader paradigm.

(15)   *the people who$_i$ [e$_i$] think that John know the answer

(16)   the people who$_i$ the boy think the girl know [e$_i$] are in the garden

Kimball and Aissen give an example comparable to (16) as acceptable to speakers of this variety of English. The standard type of successive cyclicity involving Spec of CP would compel one to say that the unusual agreement is somehow triggered from Spec of CP.[3] I would prefer to suggest the following alternative:

The successive cyclicity at issue involves, instead, a NumP-adjoined position (I take English to have the relevant NumP below TP, much as in Pollock (1989), modulo the category label), and hence in (16) a (weak) subjacency violation.[4]

The unusual agreement in (10), (14), and (16) is determined by the trace of the wh-phrase in this NumP-adjoined position (cf. the proposal in section 3.1 of chapter 3) concerning past participle agreement with a wh-phrase in French,[5] determined by a trace in an adjoined position.)

Passage through an adjoined position (conceivably to VP, as long as the correct government relation with Num holds) may be supported by:

(17)   a. *the people who J all thinks are in the garden

     b. *the people who John both thinks are crazy

     c. ?the people who John all think are in the garden

     d. ?the people who John both think are crazy

     e. ?the people who John and Bill all think are crazy

(Example (17e) seems nonstandard only.) I take the stranded/floating quantifier in (17c–e) to be in the position that directly determines number agreement.[6]

11.4. Analysis

The fact that (17e) is nonstandard suggests that the -0 morpheme of standard English may not enter into a double agreeement relation. Generalizing, this yields:

(18)   A number (or person) morpheme cannot be in an agreement configuration with more than one phrase.

Or perhaps, if English distinguishes dual and plural:

(18')   A number morpheme cannot be in an agreement configuration with phrases differing in number specification.

In addition to excluding (17e) in standard English, (18) (or (18')) has the desired effect of excluding (17a,b) in both standard and nonstandard English.

    The contrast between (17a,b) and (17c–e) within nonstandard English can be traced back to a fundamental asymmetry between the $-s$ form and the bare verb form in this variety of English: Whereas the $-s$ form of the verb contains a number morpheme just as in Standard English, the bare form in this nonstandard English has no zero agreement morpheme at all. Rather, it co-occurs with an abstract Num which works as follows (in the present tense):

(19)   Spell out Num if possible (*nonstandard*)

The interpretation of (19) is that nonstandard Num is spelled out as $-s$ whenever there is no NP in the local environment of Num that is incompatible with $-s$.

    This contrasts with Num in standard English:

(20)   Spell out Num (*standard*)

(We could take (20) to be responsible for standard English having -0; recall that nonstandard English has only $-s$.)

    In (10), *the boy* (or its trace) is in Spec of Num and the trace of *who* is adjoined to NumP.[7] In other words, Num in (10) is in an agreement relation with two NPs. By (18) (or (18') and the fact that *who* and *the boy* differ in number), it follows that in (10) $-s$ is impossible. Hence, Num is, in nonstandard English by virtue of (19), not spelled out, and (10) is derived.

    In standard English (10) with the *wh*-trace adjoined to NumP, neither $-s$ nor -0 is possible, by (18) or (18'). In *the people who the boy thinks are in the garden*, I take the *wh*-phrase not to have adjoined to NumP at all, so that $-s$ is straightforwardly possible.

    In (11) in standard English, there is again an obvious violation, since $-s$ is incompatible with a plural NP. In the nonstandard English under consideration, (11) is impossible for precisely the same reason. The asymmetry in nonstandard between (10) and (11) is fundamentally a result of the asymmetry between the -s form, which contains a number morpheme, and the bare form, which does not, as reflected in (19) versus (20).

In effect, the nonstandard English under consideration shows that the reduced agreement system of standard English is actually not minimally different from that of mainland Scandinavian. Perhaps that of this nonstandard variety is.

NOTES

The text of this article/squib is identical, apart from minor editorial changes, to the handout distributed at the 7th Workshop on Comparative Germanic Syntax in Stuttgart in November 1991. The editors and I agreed that it was preferable to publish this short version (I have been unable to prepare a longer revised version), rather than no version. The bibliography and the notes were added in April 1994.

1. This might be related to the fact that English verbs have no morphology comparable to the thematic vowel of Romance, and/or to the fact that English infinitives have no suffix at all.

2. See Kayne (1983b, section 7).

3. See the proposal in chapter 10.

4. For me, both (16) and the people who the boy think highly of are appreciably worse than (10) and (14), suggesting that (for me) the variable position must be nominative, and that a locality constraint holds that does not hold for those who accept (16). Further work is clearly called for.

5. This proposal needs to be rethought in the light of my more recent argument (cf. Kayne (1994, ch. 3)) to the effect that a phrase adjoined to XP is not distinguishable from the Specifier of XP.

6. For me, this wh-linked quantifier is not limited to nominatives in the way that I noted special agreement to be in note 4, since I accept equally well ?these books, which I've both read twice (and also ?These books I've both read twice).

7. This is incompatible with Kayne (1994, ch. 3).

An alternative approach, thinking of Henry's proposal (1995) concerning an unusual (and different) agreement pattern in Belfast English (cf. also Montgomery (1988), would be that in (10) and (14) the wh-phrase passes through Spec-NumP and that the subject of think is case-licensed by Tense.

That the subject of think in such examples is not case-licensed by person agreement (AGRS) is suggested by the fact that a pronominal subject is not possible with nonstandard agreement: *the people who he think are in the garden, *the person whose cars she think are beautiful. (Cf. also Rigau (1994) on (a different construction in) Catalan.) For the possibility that pronouns quite generally raise higher than lexical DPs (the relevance of which here was pointed out to me by Teun Hoekstra), see Koopman (1993).

The alternative of this note does not immediately account for the ungrammaticality of (11). The text approach does, on the assumption that what is crucial is solely the presence of an -s suffix on thinks. There are two reasons to think that that assumption may not be correct.

First, Guglielmo Cinque has brought to my attention an example from Giorgio Bassani's Il giardino dei Finzi-Contini (Einaudi, 1962, 179–180) in which Italian shows a pattern of agreement similar to that of (10): . . . tutta la simpatia e la considerazione che la mia tenacia nel lavoro gli ispiravano ('. . . all the sympathy and the consideration that the my tenacity in work him$_{dat}$ inspired'). In this example, *wh*-movement has applied to a plural (coordinate) DP, which has apparently licensed a plural verb form, despite the subject itself being singular and, crucially, the verb having a number suffix (*-no*).

Second, there is some (marginal) evidence that the *-s* suffix on the subject in (11) may also be of importance. Replacing *the boys* in (11) by a plural subject without *-s* does not seem to yield any improvement: **the man who the children thinks is in the garden*. However, there is for some speakers a contrast between a plural subject with and without *-s* in sentences with inversion:

(i)   *Which man does the boys think should be invited to the party?

(ii)   ??Which man does the children think should be invited to the party?

The fact that this effect is perceptible only with inversion is probably related to the fact that *Which people do the boy think are in the garden?* is more widely accepted than (10). (A pronominal subject remains impossible: **Which people do he think are in the garden?*)

My impression, based on presentations of this work to several audiences in the Northeast of the United States, is that (10) has been acceptable to at least a third of the English speakers present.

The contrast between (i) and (ii) recalls the (stronger) contrast holding between **the boys's recent party* and *the children's recent party*. This might suggest the existence of a constraint prohibiting the head of a phrase from being the same (in a sense to be made precise) as the head of the specifier of that phrase (if plural *-s* is the head of *the boys*, i.e., if plural *-s* has *the boy* in its Spec). This would require that plural, possessive and verbal *-s* all be the same in the requisite sense. (A feature-based constraint of a similar sort has been proposed by Taraldsen (1994), related in part to an idea of Chomsky's.)

12

The English Complementizer *of*

In this squib, I will try to show that in some varieties of English the preposition *of* has a use in which it is strongly similar to the familiar *to* of infinitives:

(1)   John wants to leave.

Although the *to* of (1) and (2) differs in important ways from the *for* of (2), I will use the term 'complementizer' to informally refer to both, as well as to the *of* in question:[1]

(2)   John wants very much for Bill to leave.

This *of* appears in some varieties of English in sentences like (3):

(3)   John should have left.

For my (colloquial) English (but not only mine), this standard orthography is misleading: Under normal intonation, it is highly artificial for me to pronounce the third word of (3) as a full *have*, that is, with an initial /h/ and an unreduced vowel. Rather, the vowel must be reduced, and the /h/ must not be pronounced, as reflected in the alternative orthography given in (4):

(4)   John should've left.

This orthography conveys the idea that, along with its reduced pronunciation, *'ve* is a form of the verb *have*.

Although this may be an accurate characterization of some varieties of English, there is evidence that for others what is written as *'ve* would more accurately be written as *of*:

(5)   John should of left.

First, there are speakers for whom the third word of (3)–(5) can clearly be pronounced with no /h/ and with the vowel of the preposition *of* as it is pronounced, for example, in (6):[2]

(6)   Who are you thinking of?

There is thus some plausibility to the claim I will now make, namely that (5) faithfully reflects the syntax, for at least some varieties of English.[3] The modal is separated from the past participle by the preposition *of*, a prepositional complementizer, like the *to* of (1) and (2). Even more closely, this interpretation of (5) recalls the syntax of *ought*, which can occur followed by *to* at the same time that it displays modal behavior:[4]

(7)   Ought John to leave?

Put another way, the *of* of (5) is to past participles as the *to* of (7) is to infinitives.

A second piece of evidence in favor of taking the third word of (5) to be a true *of* comes from the colloquial English phenomenon whereby the /v/ of *of* drops, leaving just a reduced vowel. Thus, *a bunch of grapes* can be pronounced without the /v/; I will follow a common orthographic convention and write this reduced *of* as an *a* attached to the preceding word:

(8)   a buncha grapes

From the point of view of the syntax proper, it might be more straightforward to write *a bunch a grapes*. On the other hand, this convention is also well established for *to* in cases like *They want to leave/They wanna leave*.

The relevance of (8) lies in the fact that the third word of (5) allows the same reduction:[5]

(9)   John shoulda left.

Taking the third word of (5) to be the preposition *of* permits an immediate generalization across (8) and (9). That this generalization is a significant one receives support from an observation made by Jean-Yves Pollock (p.c.), namely that from the perspective of his British English both (8) and (9) are Americanisms (and not possible for him).

Since the *of* of (5) (and its reduced variant in (9)) is parallel to the *to* of infinitives, we would of course not expect to find it in finite contexts, that is, in place of finite *have*. Although there are varieties of English for which (5) accurately reflects the syntax (and almost certainly others for which (3) accurately reflects the syntax), no variety of English will have a finite *of*, just as none have finite *to*:

(10)   *The kids of told a lie.

(11)   *The kids to tell a lie.

It follows that in (12) the standard orthography is straightforwardly accurate:

(12)   a. The kids have told a lie

      b. They never have told us the truth.

This finite *have* can be reduced, dropping the /h/ and reducing the vowel:

(13)   a. The kids've told a lie.

      b. They never've told us the truth.

But here further reduction seems impossible, or at least very difficult:

(14)   a. *?The kidsa told a lie.

      b. *They nevera told us the truth.[6]

This suggests that although *of* can reduce to *-a*, *have* cannot,[7] in which case the contrast between (14) and (9) becomes understandable but only if (9) truly has *of*.

    A third piece of evidence in favor of the presence of a true *of* in (5) and a reduced *of* in (9) comes from the colloquial construction given in (15):

(15)   If you hadn'ta said that, . . .

It seems quite clear that the *-a* here is not a reduced form of *have*, given:

(16)   *If you hadn't have said that, . . .

Despite the impossibility of (16), a /v/ can be added back to the *-a* of (15),[8] which should obviously now be taken to be a reduced form of *of*:

(17)   If you hadn't of said that, . . .

Summing up so far, there seems good reason to take there to exist a complementizer *of* introducing past participial phrases in a way strongly similar to the way in which *to* introduces infinitive phrases.

    In further support of this parallelism, note that both *of* and *to* are compatible with VP-Deletion:

(18)   a. If you hadn't of, you wouldn't of gotten in trouble.

      b. If you hadn'ta, you wouldn'ta gotten in trouble.

(19)   a. If you want to, you can.

      b. If you wanna, you can.

Both can be followed by *all*:

(20)   If they hadn't of/hadn'ta all left at the same time, . . .

(21)   If they want to/wanna all leave at the same time, . . .

Both seem compatible with the following nonstandard inversion possibility, discussed by Johnson (1988) for the participial case:

(22)   %Should of/shoulda the kids left? (my choice of orthography)

(23)   %Oughtta he leave?

Neither is compatible with emphatic *so/too*:

(24)   *He should of/shoulda SO/TOO left.

(25)   a. *He ought to/oughtta SO/TOO leave.

         b. *He claims to SO/TOO be happy.

    Although one might think that the ungrammaticality of (24) and (25) results from the impossibility of *so/too* occurring within an infinitive phrase, I find the following to have a different status (in noncolloquial English):

(26)   *?He claims to have SO told the truth.

Here, there is (marginally), following *to*, a true nonreduced nonfinite *have*, followed by an emphatic *so* within an infinitive.

    The examples so far considered for which I have suggested that the past participle is preceded by *of* or its reduced variant *-a* have all involved modals. Thinking of (26), one can ask whether *of/-a* can itself be preceded by *to*. At least in the case of *ought*, the answer seems clearly to be positive:

(27)   He oughtta of/a said so before.

In particular, the possibility of having *-a* after *oughtta* (= *ought to*) indicates the presence of *of*, as opposed to *have*.[9] With a nonmodal in place of *ought*, the judgment with *-a* seems less clear:

(28)   ??He seems to a made a mistake.

It might be that *seem* + infinitive is not sufficiently colloquial; alternatively, there might be a problem with having two complementizers in succession (*to of*) after a nonmodal.[10]

    In my English, as I mentioned earlier, (3), repeated here as (29), is highly artificial with a true *have*:

(29)   (*)John should have left.

Somewhat surprisingly, however, the VP-deletion counterpart is natural with a full *have*:[11]

(30)   John should have.

Also acceptable to me is the following, with stress on *have*:

(31)   I should send it off. No, you should HAVE sent it off.

The generalization seems to be that (in my English) nonfinite *have* is possible as an auxiliary[12] only in contexts of the kind in which auxiliary *do* is possible. In other words, (29)–(31) is paralleled by:

(32)   *John does leave early.

(33)   John does.

(34)   John DOES leave early.

Thinking of Chomsky's (1995, 140) idea that (32) is excluded because auxiliary *do* is possible only when necessary, one might relate the possibility of (31) to the impossibility of (35) (similar, perhaps, to (24) and (25)):

(35)   I should send it off. *No, you should OF sent it off.

Problematic is the fact that (36) seems possible alongside (30):[13]

(36)   He really should of/shoulda.

But, if that problem can be solved, the impossibility of (29) in the relevant English might follow from the possibility of (37):

(37)   John should of/shoulda left.[14]

To say that nonfinite *have* is only possible when necessary, that is, when *of/-a* is not available, would not be to say that it is always possible then. For example, neither is possible with *-n't*:

(38)   *John should ofn't/shouldan't left.

(39)   a. *John should haven't left.

        b. *He claims to haven't told any lies.

Here there is of course a contrast with auxiliary *do*:

(40)   John didn't leave.

On the other hand, (38) patterns as expected with *to*:

(41)   *They want ton't/wannan't leave.

A common account of (38), (39), and (41) that distinguishes them from (40) while leaving intact the parallel under discussion between *do* and the nonfinite *have* would attribute the ungrammaticality of the first three to a property of *-n't* itself, namely the requirement that *-n't* be adjoined to by a finite head.[15]

The *of/-a* complementizer that I have argued can be found preceding (active) past participles in a way strongly parallel to the more familiar *to* that occurs with infinitives is also reminiscent of the infinitival complementizers *de* and *di* of French and Italian, respectively.[16] Exactly like *de* and *di*, *of* is identical in form to the preposition that occurs in possessive and related constructions in the three languages.[17] Given the existence of the complementizers *de* and *di* in French and Italian, the existence of a complementizer *of* in English is not an exotic property of English. What does remain specific to English is the use of an overt complementizer with active participial phrases under modals. Part of that specificity apparently lies in the fact that (some) English is able to embed participial phrases directly (abstracting away from the complementizer itself) under modals, without the intermediary of an auxiliary verb *have* whereas we normally think of English modals as requiring their complement to be infinitival (usually without *to*, apart from *ought*), rather than participial.

The present proposal claims that that normal way of thinking of English is mistaken (at least for some varieties). At least some English modals can also have their complement be a participial phrase (with the complementizer *of*). In this respect English does differ from French and Italian. But it does not differ from the Scandinavian languages, which robustly show (certain) modals embedding active participial phrases (with no overt complementizer). An example from Taraldsen's (1984) discussion of Norwegian is:

(42)   Vi skulle gjort det før. 'we should done it before'

Taraldsen states that relative to his discussion Swedish is similar to Norwegian. Faroese examples are given by Lockwood (1977, 141ff.) (cf. Einarsson (1945, 163ff.) on Icelandic). In Faroese, at least, a modal can even be followed by the participial form of *have* (Lockwood, p. 143):[18]

43)   Eg skuldi havt gjørt . . . 'I should had done . . .'

I take these Scandinavian facts to substantiate the plausibility of English allowing an active participle to be embedded under a modal directly.[19]

Although I will not pursue the Norwegian-English comparison in detail, it is perhaps noteworthy that the Norwegian counterpart of the questionable (28) is ungrammatical without (nonfinite) *have*. To the extent that English is significantly similar to Scandinavian here, we want the analyses to be substantially similar. Let me suggest the following:

(44)   The Scandinavian construction represented by (42) contains a phonetically
        unrealized complementizer comparable in other respects to English *of*.[20]

Conversely, it might be plausible to conclude, from the fact that many modals in Icelandic take infinitival complements preceded by an overt complementizer *adh*,[21] that all English (and Icelandic) modals have their infinitival complements introduced by a complementizer, which is sometimes phonetically unrealized in Icelandic and usually so (except for *ought*) in English. If this converse suggestion is correct, then modals in English are similar to the auxiliaries *have* and *be* (in English and other languages) in taking complements with more internal structure than was envisaged in the early years of generative syntax.[22]

My conclusion that (some) English has a complementizer *of* between modal and past participle might appear to be weakened by the following observation: In some cases English does have a nonfinite *have*, as discussed earlier. This nonfinite *have* can differ in syntactic behavior from nonfinite *be*. When it does so differ, nonfinite *have* can pattern instead with *of*.

For example, Curme (1977, 473) says ". . . we often hear in popular speech . . . '*if they had have said so*' . . . in other words, a *have* (frequently in the contracted form of '*a*' or *of*) is often inserted . . .". This construction is presumably closely related to (15). The two pronunciations given as frequent by Curme fit in straightforwardly, but not the pronunciation with *have*, which he seems to say is sometimes heard. Similarly, the construction from Johnson (1988) cited in (22) is given by him with the orthography *have*, suggesting that for some speakers the auxiliary verb *have* is possible here:

(45)   %Shouldn't have Pam remembered her name?

Along with this example, Johnson gives the following, with nonfinite *be*, as impossible:

(46)   *Shouldn't be Pam remembering her name?

Related to this, I think, is the fact that I have the following contrast, with respect to the position of *all*:

(47)   They should all speak up. No, they should (all) HAVE (all) spoken up.

Nonfinite *have* is possible for me with a following participial phrase when stressed (cf. (31)); it can be either preceded or followed by *all*. Stressed nonfinite *be* is also possible, but the position of *all* is not the same:[23]

(48)   They should all speak up. No, they should (all) BE (*all) speaking up.

The fact that *all* can follow *have* but not *be* groups *have* with *of/-a*, given (49):

(49)   They should of/shoulda all spoken up.

Although it would go beyond the bounds of this squib, the solution that comes to mind is the following: *have* resembles complementizer *of* more than *be* does because *have*, but not *be*, is a form of complementizer. That is so, since *have* results from the amalgmation of *be* with an abstract prepositional complementizer.[24]

NOTES

1. *To* was called a complementizer in Rosenbaum (1967, 24ff.) I adopt this terminology because I think that infinitival *to* has more in common with *for* than is currently thought (and than I thought in Kayne (1981e)), but I will not pursue this here. See also Lencho (1992).

2. As noted by Cheshire, Edwards, and Whittle (1993, 66), who state earlier: "*Should of* appears, then, to be widespread throughout Britain". See also Labov's (1972, 151) black English vernacular example: *It wouldn't of been nothing I could do.*

3. For relevant discussion, see Curme (1931, 403, 473) and Mencken (1937, 442–443; 1948, 366).

Akmajian, Steele, and Wasow (1979, 49) use *of* in cases like (5), but only to represent the *pronunciation* schwa+/v/. I use *of* to indicate a syntactic preposition, and do not use it to indicate the schwa+/v/ pronunciation of the (finite) verb *have*. See the discussion of (13).

4. See Pullum and Wilson (1977).

5. That the two reductions are similar was pointed out by Zwicky (1970, 328 n).

6. Note the contrast with *They would never a told us the truth*, with a reduction of *of*. Another case of reduction of *of* to *a* not adjacent to the modal itself is *Should he a left that soon?*; also *He shouldn't a left so soon.*

7. Reduction of finite *have* seems easier under (noninitial) inversion: *?Whya they been arrested?*, *?Whata you done with them?*.

8. When the participle begins with a consonant, the reduced form seems preferable here.

9. Randolph (1927, 4) states that in Ozark English one can find *could-a-of* and *might-a-of*. Conceivably, these are really *could/might-to-of*, with *to* following these modals as it does *ought*.

On the other hand, the Scots example *Ah would uh could uh done it* given by Miller (1993, 121) may well have two *of*s.

10. The Icelandic complementizer *adh* is compatible with infinitival V-raising when embedded under a non-modal control verb, but not when embedded under a modal verb; see Thráinsson (1984). See also the discussion of Norwegian in this essay.

Ken Safir points out a contrast between *I would like to a/uv been hiding behind the curtain when he said that* and *It was wrong of me to *a/??uv been hiding behind the curtain when he said that*; he suggests that the *of* complementizer may require an irrealis context and notes the relevance of *?He might claim to have SO of told the truth, but I doubt him* (vs. (26)) and *If John hasn't (*of) left, we might win this game.*

11. However, I don't think the following is possible (cf. (18a)): **If you hadn't have, . . . ,* suggesting that in the colloquial English that allows (18), nonfinite auxiliary *have* might be entirely absent.

12. Nonauxiliary *have* does not show the restriction under discussion: *John should have more time, John should have his car repaired*. Note also that auxiliary *having* is possible (although perhaps not in colloquial English): *Despite having made a mistake, . . .*

13. Cf. Wood (1979, 371, 373).

14. This economy calculation would have a global character to it, however.

15. On finiteness, see Lapointe (1980, 237) and Zwicky & Pullum (1983, 507). On adjunction to -n't, see chapter 10. This finiteness property of -n't may be related to what one finds in other languages, as noted by Payne (1985, 240); see Zanuttini (1996).

Scots has a bound negation -nae that resembles -n't in being incompatible with contracted auxiliaries (a property that may have a counterpart in Serbian/Croatian, as suggested by Wilder (1996, 174)) and in being excluded from contexts of VP-negation; see Brown (1991, 80, 84). (It differs from -n't in not inverting with an auxiliary (Brown p. 80).) Brown p. 78 mentions (based on a paper by MacAfee) a variety of Scots in which a modal followed by -nae can occur following used to: He used to widnae let me up the brae ('it used to be the case that he wouldn't let me go up the hill'). Either -nae in this variety is not subject to the finiteness requirement, or the embedded modal here is finite, or used to is adverbial, as suggested by Labov (1972, 56) for useta in BEV (which has p. 57, . . . to don't throw bottles and rocks).

16. For some relevant discussion of de and di, see chapter 5, sect. 5.2.2)—the Spec, CP proposal made there needs to be rethought.

17. For relevant discussion, see Kayne (1994).

18. This Faroese construction has a parallel in some Irish English. Harris (1993, 159) gives the example: I shoulda haven killed him (= 'I should have killed him').

19. Taraldsen notes that in Swedish the active past participle can be phonologically distinct from the passive participle. The former is sometimes called the supine in discussions of Scandinavian.

I leave open the question of why English does not allow the word-for-word equivalent of (42). Both (42) and Swedish (embedded) sentences with a 'missing' finite have (cf. Andersson & Dahl 1974) bear on chapter 7; for an interesting proposal accounting for the Swedish restriction to embedded contexts and for the fact that Norwegian does not allow finite have to be 'missing', see Taraldsen (1984).

20. This recalls the fact that at least some Scandinavian has 'zero' instead of of in phrases like the month of May, a pound of corn; see Holmes and Hinchliffe (1994, 451). See also the fact that English differs from Scandinavian in having both of and 's in a friend of John's, as well as differing from at least some in having of+lexical DP in all of my friends; see Strandskogen and Strandskogen, (1989, 129) and Holmes & Hinchliffe (1994, 452). Similarly, English, but not Scandinavian, has a complementizer for that licenses a lexical subject.

21. See Thráinsson (1994, 186). Faroese seems to have fewer (cf. Lockwood (1977, 146) but has a notable phenomenon of 'attracted supines' (p. 141) yielding cases of a supine preceded by the infinitival marker at; cf. perhaps Anward (1988).

22. See, for example, Chomsky (1957, 39). The text discussion recalls Ross (1967) and Pullum & Wilson (1977). On have and be, see chapter 7. How auxiliary do fits in here remains to be determined.

23. Judging by Pollock (1989, 382), at least some British English might allow (48). Like (47) versus (48) for me is (26) versus the worse *He claims to be SO telling the truth. See also Johnson (1988, 159) on VP-fronting and VP-ellipsis differences between nonfinite have and nonfinite be.

24. See chapter 7 and, with some important differences, den Dikken (1995c). This issue might be relevant to Zwart's (1996) discussion of the fact that Dutch does not allow *. . . hebben moet gelezen ('. . . have (infin.) modal read (past participle)').

III

UNIVERSALS

13

Overt versus Covert Movement

Klima (1964a, 285) analyzed the narrow-scope/wide-scope ambiguity found in an English sentence such as (1):

(1)   I will force you to marry no one.

In Kayne (1981a, sect. 1), I noted that there exist in English comparable examples with subjunctives:

(2)   She has requested that they read not a single linguistics book.

In this sentence, there is a narrow-scope reading according to which the content of the request is that they read not a single linguistics book. There is also a wide-scope reading (facilitated by having an initial *In all these years* or *Funnily enough*) according to which there have been no requests made for linguistics book reading.

I proposed in that article that the ambiguity in (2) (and (1)) be captured (in the spirit of Chomsky (1976) and May (1985)) by having covert (LF) movement apply to *no one, not a single linguistics book*, moving those phrases to a scope position either within the embedded sentence (short movement) or within the matrix (long movement). A phrasal movement approach to (2) has the advantage (compared with Klima's *neg*-incorporation) of allowing an account of the interpretive contrast between (2) and (3):

(3)   She has requested that not a single student read our book.

In (3), the narrow-scope reading is straightforwardly available, but the wide-scope reading is much more difficult than in (2). Covert movement of *not a single N* in these examples thus shows a subject-object asymmetry recalling that found with overt Wh-movement. This is expected if the principle determining subject-object asymmetries of this sort comes into play at LF, subsequent to covert movement, as I suggested then.

In the present essay, I would like to explore an alternative approach to such ambiguities. This alternative will agree with the earlier proposal in part, insofar as I will continue to interpret the type of narrow versus wide scope ambiguity just described in terms of movement and, more specifically, as before, in terms of a short-movement versus long-movement distinction. Furthermore, I will continue to take the movement operations in question to be movement of a phonetically realized phrase. However, I will now suggest that what is at issue is not covert but rather overt (pre-Spellout) movement.

Quite similar to the ambiguity in (2) is the narrow-scope/wide-scope ambiguity in (4) (cf. Longobardi (1992, 153ff.), Bayer (1996):

(4)   She has requested that they read only *Aspects*.

Another familiar scope ambiguity is found in English in sentences like (5):

(5)   At least one student has criticized each of the professors.

The reading of (5) in which *each* has wide scope relative to *one* is by now standardly treated in terms of covert movement. Covert movement is also widely assumed to be necessary to an account of antecedent-contained deletion (ACD), as in (6):

(6)   John read every book that Bill did.

The phrase headed by *every* is moved at LF in such a way that the deleted VP within the relative clause comes to be outside the VP that serves as antecedent.

Generalizing the analysis I will propose for (2), I will suggest that, while a movement approach to (4)–(6) is correct, it should be rethought in each case in terms of overt, rather than covert, movement. In each case, the phrase moved will again be a phonetically visible one.

13.1. Negation

13.1.1. Scandinavian

Let me begin with Norwegian, and in particular with Christensen's (1986) analysis of *ingen*,[1] which I take to be the counterpart of English *no*. Norwegian *ingen* is subject to restrictions that at first glance seem quite foreign to English:

(7)   Jon leser ingen romaner. ('J reads no novels')

(8)   *Jon har lest ingen romaner. ('J has read no novels')

Ingen romaner is possible after a finite verb, but not after a past participle. Christensen notes, however, that the correct generalization is not finite versus nonfinite, given (9):

(9)   *Dette er en student som leser ingen romaner. ('this is a student that reads no novels')

The correct generalization is, rather, that *ingen romaner* is a possible postverbal object only in verb-second contexts where the V in question moves to the C position. The finite nonembedded verb of (7) moves to C, under the standard analysis of Norwegian verb-second phenomena. The past participle in (8) is not subject to such movement (although the auxiliary is, irrelevantly). The finite verb in (9) is not subject to verb-second movement, either, this time because it is within a relative clause.

Christensen proposes that the reason for the sensitivity of postverbal object *ingen romaner* to verb-second is the following: *Ingen* is in effect the spellout of *ikke* + *noen* ('not + any/some'). The position of *ikke* is outside of VP, as seen in (10) and (11):

(10)   Jon har ikke lest noen romaner. ('J has not read any novels')

(11)   Dette er en student som ikke leser noen romaner. ('this is a student that not reads any novels')

The *ikke* . . . *noen* counterpart of (7) is (12), in which it can be seen that *ikke* and *noen* have come to be adjacent as a result of finite verb movement to C:

(12)   Jon leser ikke noen romaner. ('J reads not any novels')

Christensen then proposes that it is the derived adjacency of *ikke* and *noen* in (12) that permits (optional) spellout as *ingen*, yielding (7). Spellout as *ingen* in (10) and (11) is impossible because *ikke* and *noen* there are not adjacent.

In the framework of Chomsky (1995), two revisions to Christensen's analysis come naturally to mind. First, one can take *ingen* to be a lexical item (much as Chomsky does for inflected verb forms) and have it be required to be adjacent to an abstract negative head, rather than to the morpheme *ikke* itself. Second, one can re-interpret the relevant notion of adjacency to be a Spec-head relation. The essential requirement now is that *ingen romaner* overtly be in the Spec of NegP.[2]

From this perspective, (8) and (9) are impossible in Norwegian simply because *ingen romaner* is not in Spec, NegP. (I continue to make the standard assumptions that NegP is above VP and that Norwegian Neg⁰ precedes VP and in turn is preceded by Spec,NegP.) More precisely, (8) and (9) are excluded because *ingen romaner* does not overtly occupy Spec,NegP. Put another way, Norwegian requires of a phrase like *ingen romaner* that it move overtly to Spec,NegP, which it has clearly not done in (8) and (9).

The grammaticality of (7) must now be interpreted as indicating that *ingen romaner* has in that example moved overtly[3] to Spec,NegP. It can in fact readily have done so, despite the fact that it follows the verb in (7), given that the verb in (7) has itself raised to C. (In (8) and (9) on the other hand, the postverbal position of *ingen romaner* shows that it is not in Spec,NegP, since the verb has not raised.)

Christensen notes that in noncolloquial varieties of Norwegian one finds the following:

(13)   %Jon har ingen romaner lest. ('J has no novels read')

(14)   %Dette er en student som ingen romaner leser. ('this is a student that no novels reads')

I follow her in taking these to be obvious instances of movement. From the revised perspective I have given, these involve overt movement of *ingen romaner* to Spec,NegP.

In the varieties that accept (13) and (14),[4] this overt movement is indifferent to whether the lexical verb has been raised to C or not. In the varieties that reject (13) and (14), overt movement of *ingen romaner* is successful only in combination with the raising of V to C (in a way that recalls Holmberg's generalization (for the case of pronouns and definite DPs)).[5]

13.1.2.   English

As discussed, the basic contrast in (all varieties of) Norwegian is:

(15)   Jon leser ingen romaner. ('J reads no novels')

(16)   *Jon har lest ingen romaner. ('J has read no novels')

English does not have this contrast here:

(17)   John reads no novels.

(18)   John has read no novels.

Thus, the preceding discussion might appear to be irrelevant to English, especially given the sharp contrast between (16) and (18). More specifically, the acceptability of the latter in English, combined with the unacceptability of (19) and (20), could well be taken to indicate that English lacks the overt movement of negative phrases that is found in Norwegian:

(19)   *John has no novels read.[6]

(20)   *That's a student who no novels reads. (vs. (14))

That this might be a premature conclusion is suggested by the fact that English does sometimes show the contrast of (15) versus (16):

(21)   John is/was no Einstein.

(22)   *John became no Einstein.

Compare these with:

(23)   John isn't/wasn't an Einstein.

(24)   John didn't become an Einstein.

Although both (23) and (24) are possible, (22) is substantially less good than (21).

The contrast between (21) and (22) should, I think, be related to the well-known difference between *be* and *become* concerning verb raising. As illustrated, for example, by *Was John happy?* versus **Became John happy?*, *be* can raise in a way that *become* cannot. Consequently, *no Einstein*, although it has remained within VP in (22), can be taken to have raised overtly out of VP in (21). The fact that it follows *is/was* is due to *is/was* also having raised (to a position still further to the left).[7] We can then account for (21) versus (22) by saying that in English a negative predicate nominal like *no Einstein* must raise overtly (to Spec,NegP).

Similar facts seem to me to hold (somewhat surprisingly) for possessive *have*. Both *have* and *own* are straightforwardly possible in:

(25)   John doesn't have/own a car.

But with *no car*, the corresponding sentence with *have* seems more neutral than the one with *own*, which feels emphatic:

(26)   John has no car.

(27)   John owns no car.

This becomes sharper in examples where another phrase competes for emphasis:

(28)   The only person who has/?owns no car this year is John.

I think that the nonneutral status of (27) is not particular to *own* but is in fact shared by (17) and (18). This suggests that the neutral character of (26) is to be attributed to the raising of *have*, as opposed to *own*. More important for what follows, the neutral character of (26) appears to correlate with the overt movement of *no car* to Spec,NegP (which is made possible by *have*-raising).[8] (As we will see, however, overt raising of *no car* to Spec,NegP actually takes place with *own*, too. The crucial difference will, rather, turn out to involve VP-movement.)

Assume that I am correct in claiming that both (21) and (26) necessarily involve overt movement of *no Einstein* and *no car*, respectively. Then two possibilities arise: First, English might have overt negative phrase movement in just these special cases, but otherwise not. Second, English might uniformly have recourse to overt movement in all cases in which the negative phrase follows the verb. I will favor the second possibility, that is, I will explore the idea that, even in (27) and (17)/(18), English has overt movement of *no car* and *no novels*. Put another way, English, like Norwegian, consistently requires of its negative phrases that they move to Spec,NegP in the overt syntax.[9]

The idea that I will pursue for (27) and (17)/(18) is that, although they do not involve verb movement in exactly the way that (21) and (26) do, their derivation is very close to one involving verb movement. More specifically, the proposal will be that the derivation of sentences like (27) and (17)/(18) involves negative phrase movement (exactly as in (21) and (26) and as in Norwegian) plus verb phrase movement.[10]

The derivation of (17) proceeds schematically as follows:

(29)   John reads no novels → (neg phrase preposing)
        John no novels$_i$ reads t$_i$ → (VP-preposing)
        John [reads t$_i$]$_j$ no novels$_i$ t$_j$

The first movement places *no novels* in Spec,NegP.[11] The second movement takes the VP[12] (including the trace of *no novels*)[13] and moves it into a Spec position further to the left. (I return later to the question of the landing site of this second movement.)

From this perspective, the more emphatic, less neutral character of (27), as opposed to (26), must be correlated with VP-movement, and the deviance of (22) must involve some incompatibility between VP-movement and the negative predicate nominal.

13.1.3.   More complex VPs

The two movements illustrated in (29) have the combined effect, in that simple example, of leading to canonical English word order. That effect disappears, however, once we begin looking at more complex verb phrases, in particular verb phrases within which the negative phrase is accompanied by other material X. In that case, we would have (using NegDP as an informal abbreviation for phrases like *no novels*):

(30)   DP V NegDP X → (neg phrase preposing)
        DP NegDP$_i$ V t$_i$ X → (VP-preposing)
        DP [V t$_i$ X]$_j$ NegDP$_i$ t$_j$

The output of the two movements has X preceding NegDP, whereas in the input X followed NegDP.[14]

More generally, observe that, in a derivation such as (30), NegDP will come to follow all VP-internal material. Consider in this light (31)/(32):

(31)   John invited in no strangers.

(32)   John invited no strangers in.

Under the assumption that the particle *in* starts out within the VP, successive application of negative phrase preposing and VP-preposing will yield only (31):

(33)   John [invited no strangers in] →
        John no strangers$_i$ [invited t$_i$ in] →
        John [invited t$_i$ in]$_j$ no strangers$_i$ t$_j$

In order to derive (32), an extra movement operation is necessary, one that will re-move the particle from the VP and thereby allow VP-preposing to strand the par-ticle. To get the right word order, this movement of the particle must be to a position in between NegP and VP:[15]

(34) John [invited no strangers in] → (particle preposing)
      John in$_k$ [invited no strangers t$_k$] → (neg phrase preposing)
      John no strangers$_i$ in$_k$ [invited t$_i$ t$_k$] → (VP-preposing)
      John [invited t$_i$ t$_k$]$_j$ no strangers$_i$ in$_k$ t$_j$

I would like to propose now that this particle preposing is not an operation spe-cific to English but is rather to be assimilated to the already established predicate raising found in Dutch, in the sense of Koster (1994) and Zwart (1994, 399ff.; 1997, 43, 100ff.).[16] Koster and Zwart argue that small-clause predicates in Dutch obligato-rily raise leftward, to the specifier position of a projection they call PredP, located above VP.[17] (PredP must be below NegP.) It is predicate raising that is responsible for the Dutch word order property that has small-clause predicates preceding the verb (apart from V-2 effects). As Zwart (1997, 102) notes, this analysis is supported by the fact that the (raised) predicate (adjectival in (35)) is not necessarily adjacent to the verb but can be separated from it by a stranded preposition:

(35) de kwast waar Jan de deur rood mee verft ('the brush where/which J the door red
      with paints')

Particles in Dutch are themselves separated from a following (infinitival) verb by the infinitive marker *te*, as seen in (36), and can be separated from a following infinitive by a modal or certain lexical verbs, as seen in (37) and (38):[18]

(36) omdat hij mij probeert op te bellen ('because he me tries up to call' = 'because he
      tries to call me up')

(37) omdat hij mij op probeert te bellen ('because he me up tries to call' = 'because he
      tries to call me up')

(38) dat ik Jan de doktor op heb willen laten bellen ('that I Jan the doctor up have want
      let call' = 'that I have wanted to let Jan call up the doctor')

Taking particles to be a subtype of small-clause predicate,[19] it is natural to think that particles can raise in essentially the same way as adjectival small-clause predi-cates (cf. Zwart (1997, 43n). My more specific proposal for English, then, is that the first step of the derivation illustrated in (34) has the particle raising out of VP into the PredP projection, thereby making it possible for the VP-preposing illus-trated in the third step to prepose the VP without carrying along the particle. (For the purposes of subsequent discussion, little would change if particle prepos-ing were reinterpreted as head-adjunction to Pred^0,[20] rather than as movement to Spec,PredP.)

English, of course, differs from Dutch in that Dutch lacks VP-preposing, so Dutch ends up (apart from V-2 contexts) with the word order (and structure) displayed in the third line of (34).[21]

Although the derivation in (34) is given for a sentence with a NegDP followed by a particle, it is intended that the same should hold for sentences with NegDP followed by the predicate of an adjectival small clause:[22]

(39)   John [considers no linguist smart] → (predicate raising)
        John smart$_k$ [considers no linguist t$_k$] → (neg phrase preposing)
        John no linguist$_i$ smart$_k$ [considers t$_i$ t$_k$] → (VP-preposing)
        John [considers t$_i$ t$_k$]$_j$ no linguist$_i$ smart$_k$ t$_j$

In summary, then, English negative phrases such as *no novels* must move overtly to Spec,NegP. The fact that *no novels* ends up following the verb, rather than preceding it, in a sentence like *John reads no novels* is due to the subsequent application of VP-preposing.[23] VP-preposing itself has the effect of making the negative phrase follow all VP material. To derive a sentence like *John invited no strangers in/ John considers no linguist smart*, the particle or adjective phrase must (previously) be moved out of VP to the PredP level by predicate raising so that it can be stranded by VP-preposing.

13.1.4. *no* versus *some*

Recall, now, the Norwegian contrast:

(40)   *Jon har lest ingen romaner. ('J has read no novels')

(41)   Jon har ikke lest noen romaner. ('J has not read any novels')

The ungrammaticality of (40) occurs because *ingen romaner* has not moved overtly to Spec,NegP. A natural conclusion, then, is that *noen romaner* in (41) did not have to move out of VP in any parallel fashion. Transposing freely back to English and simplifying the examples slightly, we reach the conclusion that (42) and (43) must differ in that (42) involves obligatory overt raising of *nobody* (followed by VP-preposing), whereas in (43) *somebody* has not (or at least need not have) overtly raised:[24]

(42)   John saw nobody.

(43)   John saw somebody.

I think that this difference between *no*-phrases and *some*-phrases is what underlies the following contrast:

(44)   Nobody is bound to be there.

(45)   Somebody is bound to be there.

Whereas (45) has an interpretation that seems synonymous with that of (47), (44) cannot be interpreted as synonymous with (46):[25]

(46)   There is bound to be nobody there.

(47)   There is bound to be somebody there.

Put another way, (45) allows a narrow-scope interpretation for *somebody* (narrow relative to *bound*) that *nobody* in (44) cannot have.[26]

The narrow-scope interpretation for *somebody* in (45) has been analyzed in terms of 'quantifier lowering' (cf. May (1985)). The question, however, is why the same does not then also hold for (44). One possibility is that there's a kind of 'improper movement' effect ruling out the narrow-scope interpretation of (44). Assume that a narrow-scope reading for (44) would require there to be a NegP in the embedded sentence (but not in the matrix) and that *nobody* would have to move overtly through the Spec position of that NegP. Assume, further, that for EPP or case reasons, *nobody* in (44) must move into the Spec position of the matrix IP (or TP). If Spec,NegP is like an A-bar position, then *nobody* will have moved from an A-bar position to an A-position, yielding a violation akin to:[27]

(48)   *Who was wondered to get first prize?

In (48), *who* moves from subject position to Spec,CP (without getting case within the embedded sentence) and from there to Spec,IP (or TP) in the (passive) matrix. If (48) and the narrow-scope reading of (44) are excluded for similar reasons,[28] then we have an additional argument internal to English that converges with the earlier one based on Norwegian + English + (21)/(26), to the effect that English *no*-phrases (like their Norwegian counterparts) move overtly to Spec,NegP.

At the same time, this account of the contrast between (44) and (45) implies that *somebody* does not need to move to an A-bar-like position in the embedded sentence on its way up to the matrix Spec,IP/TP.

13.1.5.   Wide-scope negation

Recall Klima's example of a wide-scope/narrow-scope ambiguity:

(49)   I will force you to marry no one.

The derivation of the narrow-scope reading, from the perspective I have outlined, involves moving *no one* overtly to a Spec,NegP within the infinitive phrase and then moving the VP [marry $t_{no\ one}$] to the left of that:

(50)   ... to marry no one → (neg phrase preposing)
        ... to no one$_i$ marry t_i → (VP-preposing)
        ... to [marry t_i]$_j$ no one$_i$ t_j

Consider now the wide-scope reading of (49). Following the reasoning pursued so far, we must have *no one* moving overtly to Spec,NegP, but this time that movement must be longer distance than in any of the previous examples, since Spec,NegP in the wide-scope reading must be within the matrix part of the sentence. Subsequently, VP-movement takes place, but this time it must be of the matrix VP:

(51)   I will force you to marry no one → (neg phrase preposing)
I will no one$_i$ force you to marry t$_i$ → (VP-preposing)
I will [force you to marry t$_i$]$_j$ no one$_i$ t$_j$

That (somewhat) long-distance negative phrase movement illustrated in (51) is not unfamiliar. Some varieties of French allow movement of *rien* ('nothing') even out of finite subjunctives:[29]

(52)   Il n'a rien fallu que je fasse. ('it neg-has nothing been-necessary that I do')

The leftward movement of *rien* seen in (52) is more limited in one respect than the Scandinavian construction discussed earlier, in that the French counterpart of *no novel* (with a lexical noun) is not subject to such movement. A second difference is that movement of *rien* is paralleled by movement of *tout* ('everything') in the varieties of French in question,[30] unlike what holds for Icelandic, at least, to judge by Rögnvaldsson (1987, 42):

(53)   Il a tout fallu que je leur enlève. ('it has everything been-necessary that I them$_{dat}$ remove')

All varieties of French, as far as I know, allow *rien* to move out of (certain) infinitival embeddings:[31]

(54)   Jean n'a rien voulu faire. ('J neg-has nothing wanted to-do')

Here Icelandic is strikingly similar to French. Rögnvaldsson (1987, 44) and Jónsson (1996, 86) give (55) and (56), respectively:

(55)   Hann mun ekkert hafa getadh gert. ('he will nothing have could done')

(56)   Their hafa ekkert lofadh adh gera. ('they have nothing promised to do')

Despite differences in detail among the various languages under discussion, I take (52) and (54)–(56) to support the plausibility of overt long-distance negative phrase preposing in English, as in (51).

Let us now take Klima's example (49) and replace the embedded verb with a verb and particle:

(57)   I will force you to turn down no one.

(58)   I will force you to turn no one down.

Narrow scope for *no one* seems equally possible in both examples. Yet wide scope for *no one* (e.g., with the sentences introduced by *Over the next month, . . .*) seems more difficult in (58) than in (57). Adding a negative polarity phrase like *in all these years* to the matrix (which dampens the narrow scope reading) heightens the judgment:[32]

(59)   In all these years, they have forced us to turn down no one.

(60)   ?In all these years, they have forced us to turn no one down.

Why should the wide-scope reading be inhibited by a particle following the NegDP (but not by one preceding the NegDP)?

Consider the derivation of (60) (with a wide-scope reading):

(61)   . . . forced us to turn no one down $\rightarrow$ (particle preposing)
       . . . down$_k$ forced us to turn no one t_k $\rightarrow$ (neg phrase preposing)
       . . . no one$_i$ down$_k$ forced us to turn t_i t_k $\rightarrow$ (VP-preposing)
       . . . [forced us to turn t_i t_k]$_j$ no one$_i$ down$_k$ t_j

By assumption, wide scope requires *no one* to move overtly to Spec,NegP within the matrix. It is clear, then, that to produce the correct word order, VP-preposing must in this case be preposing of the matrix VP (to the left of *no one*). Now the particle *down* must, if it is to follow *no one*, be stranded by this preposing of the matrix VP. Consequently, *down* must itself have been previously preposed out of the matrix VP, as indicated in the first step of (61).

Let us now examine (61) for the cause of the deviance of (60). VP-preposing in (61) crosses both the particle and the negative DP, but that is no different from what happens in (34), in the derivation of *John invited no strangers in*. Similarly, the long-distance negative phrase preposing in (61) is no different from what must take place in the derivation of the wide scope reading of (59). We conclude, therefore, that the deviance of wide scope in (60) must be due to the long-distance particle preposing seen in the first step of (61).

In other words, the particle preposing to Spec,PredP (or perhaps Pred^0) that makes it possible for VP-preposing to strand the particle cannot readily apply out of an infinitival complement of the sort we have in (61), which is a case of object control.[33] The facts concerning subjunctives suggest that a particle cannot readily prepose out of a subjunctive:[34]

(62)   In all these years, they have requested that we turn down no one/no student.

(63)   ?In all these years, they have requested that we turn no one/no student down.

In (63), wide scope for *no one/no student* would require it to move to the matrix Spec,NegP,[35] which in turn would require the matrix VP to prepose. For the matrix

VP to be able to prepose yet strand *down* to the right of NegDP requires the prior preposing of *down* from within the embedded VP to the PredP above the matrix VP, which is evidently difficult.

This account of the deviance of (60)/(63) (in terms of the difficulty of overly long particle movement) implies that in (59)/(62), where the wide-scope reading is possible, long particle movement has not taken place:

(64)   ... requested that we turn no one down → (neg preposing)
        ... no one$_i$ requested that we turn t$_i$ down → (VP-preposing)
        ... [requested that we turn t$_i$ down]$_l$ no one$_i$ t$_l$

The derivation in (64) has the negative phrase in Spec,NegP within the matrix, as desired, and lacks long-particle preposing, again as desired.

In summary, then, wide-scope/narrow-scope ambiguities with negation in English can be expressed in terms of overt movement of the visible NegDP. Wide scope corresponds to overt movement to a matrix/higher Spec,NegP, and narrow scope corresponds to overt movement to an embedded/lower Spec,NegP.

The sensitivity of wide-scope negation to a following particle turns out to be a result of the fact that overt movement to Spec,NegP must, in English, be followed by VP-preposing that can strand the particle only if the particle has itself moved out of VP. In the wide-scope reading the particle must move a relatively long distance, which is not straightforwardly possible.[36]

13.1.6.   Subject-object asymmetry

The fact that in (65) the wide-scope reading is, for most speakers,[37] not possible can be accounted for in a way that is partially similar to and partially different from the approach I followed in earlier work (Kayne 1981a).

(65)   She has requested that not a single student read our book.

We can maintain the idea that the deviance of the wide-scope reading in (65) is closely related to the deviance found in many well-known cases of overt extraction from preverbal subject position (e.g., in Wh-constructions of various types). What changes is that (65) is no longer an instance of a covert LF movement construction and no longer constitutes an argument for covert movement. Rather, a wide-scope interpretation here would require overt movement of the embedded subject NegDP to the matrix Spec,NegP, which is not possible.[38]

13.2.   Only

13.2.1.   Similarities to negation

Longobardi (1992) showed that the subject-object asymmetry[39] found with wide-scope negation ((65) vs. (2), repeated here as (66)) is also found with wide-scope *only*:

(66) She has requested that they read not a single linguistics book.

More specifically (transposing to English), just as a wide-scope reading for *not a single* is much more difficult in (65) than in (66), so is a wide-scope reading for *only* much more difficult in (67) than in (68):[40]

(67) She has requested that only John read it.

(68) She has requested that he read only *Aspects*.

This suggests that wide scope for *only* be treated parallel to wide scope for negation.[41] Given the results of section 13.1. on negation, the conclusion must be that wide scope for *only* rests on overt movement, and not on covert LF movement.

The derivation of the wide-scope reading of (66) is parallel to those given earlier for the wide-scope readings of (51) (*I will force you to marry no one*) and (64) (*In all these years they have requested that we turn down no one/no student*). It runs as follows:

(69) ... requested that they read not a single linguistics book → (negative phrase preposing)
   ... not a single linguistics book$_i$ requested that they read t$_i$ → (VP-preposing)
   ... [requested that they read t$_i$]$_j$ not a single ling. book$_i$ t$_j$

The first step involves movement of an argument phrase out of the embedded subjunctive into the matrix. The second step moves the matrix VP to the left of the landing site of the first movement.

An entirely parallel derivation for a wide scope reading with *only* would be:

(70) ... requested that he read only one book → (*only*-phrase preposing)
   ... only one book$_i$ requested that he read t$_i$ → (VP-preposing)
   ... [requested that he read t$_i$]$_j$ only one book$_i$ t$_j$

In (70), movement of *only one book* corresponds to movement of *not a single book* in (69).

If we now transpose back to simpler cases, we can see the parallelism between *not a single* and *only* in the following way:

(71) John read not a single book.

(72) John read only one book.

The first of these has the derivation:

(73) ... read not a single book → (neg phrase preposing)
   ... not a single book$_i$ read t$_i$ → (VP-preposing)
   ... [read t$_i$]$_j$ not a single book$_i$ t$_j$

The second has:

(74)   ... read only one book → (*only*-phrase preposing)
       ... only one book$_i$ read t$_i$ → (VP-preposing)
       ... [read t$_i$]$_j$ only one book$_i$ t$_j$

These derivations produce a word order identical to that which would have resulted from applying neither preposing operation. As we saw earlier in the discussions of (31)/(32), (57)/(58), and (62)/(63), this apparent lack of word order difference is an artifact of the lack of complexity of the VP. Adding a particle brings out the fact that the derivation in (73) (like that in (69)) will produce the word order '... Prt NegDP'. To reach the word order '... NegDP Prt', an additional operation preposing the particle is necessary. This will now be true for the corresponding cases with *only*. Thus, replace *read* in (74) by *pointed ... out*:[42]

(75)   ... pointed only one book out → (*only*-phrase preposing)
       ... only one book$_i$ pointed t$_i$ out → (VP-preposing)
       ... [pointed t$_i$ out]$_j$ only one book$_i$ t$_j$

The result corresponds to the sentence:

(76)   John pointed out only one book.

To derive (77), there must be an additional operation, as illustrated in (78):

(77)   John pointed only one book out.

(78)   ... pointed only one book out → (particle preposing)[43]
       ... out$_k$ pointed only one book t$_k$ → (*only*-phrase preposing)
       ... only one book$_i$ out$_k$ pointed t$_i$ t$_k$ → (VP-preposing)
       ... [pointed t$_i$ t$_k$]$_j$ only one book$_i$ out$_k$ t$_j$

The extra step in the derivation of (77) as opposed to (76) appears to have little effect on acceptability (though (77) is perhaps a shade less natural).

A stronger effect is visible if we combine presence of a particle with wide-scope interpretation of *only*, much as in (62)/(63). The relevant examples are:

(79)   We've requested that he point out only one book.

(80)   We've requested that he point only one book out.

In a context favorable to wide scope for *only*, such as one in which 'he' is a bookseller to whom a single request has been made, (79) seems appreciably more natural than (80).

The reason is as follows. The derivation of (79) requires preposing of *only one book* plus preposing of the matrix VP:

(81)   . . . requested that he point only one book out[44]→ (*only*-phrase preposing)
   . . . only one book$_i$ requested that he point t$_i$ out → (VP-preposing)
   . . . [requested that he point t$_i$ out]$_j$ only one book$_i$ t$_j$

Crucially, given our approach based on overt movement including VP-preposing, (80) is derivable only via the introduction of the additional operation of particle preposing, which in this wide-scope example would have to move the particle out of the finite subjunctive:

(82)   . . . requested that he point only one book out → (particle preposing)
   . . . out$_k$ requested that he point only one book t$_k$ → (*only*-phrase preposing)
   . . . only one book$_i$ out$_k$ requested that he point t$_i$ t$_k$ → (VP-preposing)
   . . . [requested that he point t$_i$ t$_k$]$_j$ only one book$_i$ out$_k$ t$_j$

As we have seen earlier in the discussion of (63), such relatively long-distance particle movement is not readily available.

13.2.2.   An important difference between *only* and some negation

In the previous section, I have shown that one can extend the overt movement approach to *only* sentences, taking phrases such as *only one book* to prepose in a way entirely parallel to the overt preposing of *not a single book, no one*, and *no student* described in section 1 (with VP-preposing applying subsequently, in the cases under consideration). There is some reason to think, however, that 'entirely parallel (in the type of derivation)' is too strong a position to be taken consistently. What I have in mind is the behavior of these various elements with respect to prepositions.

   The negative phrases with *not a single* and *no* have so far been studied using examples in which they appear as part of the direct object (apart from the examples in which they are part of the subject). Also possible are prepositional examples:

(83)   John spoke to not a single linguist/no one/no student.

The status of examples with *only* is not always the same:

(84)   John spoke to only one linguist.

(85)   ?John spoke to only Bill.

As we see here, *only one linguist* does act like *not a single linguist*, etc., but *only Bill* does not. The '?' in front of (85) needs explication, however. It is meant to indicate not that speakers generally find this sort of example intermediate in acceptability but rather that speakers vary substantially in their judgments, ranging from fully acceptable to fully unacceptable.[45] For me, (85) is substantially less acceptable than:

(86)   John spoke only to Bill.

The general acceptability of (84) suggests that *only one N* (and similarly with other numerals) should in fact be treated as strongly parallel to *not a single N*, that is, as subject to phrasal movement of exactly the sort presented earlier.[46] Those speakers who find (85) fully acceptable might conceivably allow *only Bill* to be analyzed as a phrase subject to that movement, too. However, definitely for those who do not find (85) acceptable, and probably in fact for all speakers of English, I would like to suggest a different analysis: Whereas *only one linguist* is in fact merged into the derivation as a phrase, as I have assumed, that is not the case of *only Bill*.

13.2.3. Attraction by *only*

Put another way, *only* cannot be combined directly with a DP like *Bill*, despite the fact that (87) is acceptable:

(87)   John criticized only Bill.

The derivation of (87) will not involve merging *only* with *Bill*. Instead, *Bill* is merged into the VP in standard fashion,[47] after which *only* is merged with the whole VP (or perhaps some larger constituent). This amounts to claiming that (87) and (86) are derived from structures which resemble:

(88)   John only criticized Bill.

(89)   John only spoke to Bill.

The more specific claim is that *Bill* then raises up to *only*, after which VP-preposing applies, establishing the correct word order. This analysis treats (87) and (90) as having similar but not identical derivations:

(90)   John criticized only one linguist.

Bill in (87) and *only one linguist* in (90) raise in parallel fashion, except that the former raises to *only* and the latter, I now suggest, to a phonetically unrealized counterpart of *only*. VP-preposing applies in both, as we will see in more detail.

My idea concerning the rejection of (85) is that (85) is for the speakers in question a preposition-stranding violation (despite the fact that English allows preposition stranding in various other cases). To see this, let us consider first the derivation of (87), under the hypothesis that it involves movement of *Bill*. One basic idea will be that this movement is triggered by *only*, that is, that *only* attracts *Bill*, in Chomsky's (1995) sense, perhaps via a focus feature.[48] If so, then we expect that movement will be to Spec,*only* (and that *only* is properly taken to be a head).[49] Movement of *Bill* to Spec,*only* will, of course, not yield the word order of (87). Let me therefore postulate an operation that raises *only* to the next highest head position, reestablishing the correct order:

(91)   . . . only criticized Bill → (attraction by *only*)
    . . . Bill$_i$ only criticized t$_i$→ (raising of *only*)
    . . . only$_j$ Bill$_i$ t$_j$ criticized t$_i$ → (VP-preposing)
    . . . [criticized t$_i$]$_k$ only$_j$ Bill$_i$ t$_j$ t$_k$

I take *only* in English to have a feature +w (mnemonic for 'word order') that must be checked in the overt syntax by another head.[50] Consequently there must be a head just above it to which it can be attracted. I tentatively take this head (call it W) to be abstract, in the sense that it is not one of the familiar functional heads such as T. I furthermore take VP-preposing to move VP into the Spec of W (subsequent to *only* adjoining to W).

Example (86) must have a derivation like that of (91), except that what is attracted by *only* is a phrase of category PP:

(92)   . . . only spoke to Bill → (attraction by *only*)
    . . . to Bill$_i$ only spoke t$_i$ → (raising of *only* (to W))
    . . . only$_j$ to Bill$_i$ t$_j$ spoke t$_i$ → (VP-preposing (to Spec,W))
    . . . [spoke t$_i$]$_k$ only$_j$ to Bill$_i$ t$_j$ t$_k$

Example (85) would be derivable via a derivation like the preceding if *only* could attract *Bill*, stranding *to*. Let me suggest, then, that P-stranding under attraction to *only* is not available (for the speakers who reject (85)), just as P-stranding in English is generally not available in middles, or in the so-called heavy-NP shift construction:[51]

(93)   *That kind of person doesn't speak to very easily.

(94)   *I was speaking to about linguistics the same person you were.

Nor is it readily available for me in VP-subdeletion, which arguably involves leftward movement of the 'remnant' out of the VP to be deleted:[52]

(95)   He didn't speak to his mother, but he did *(to) his father.

Similarly for gapping itself:[53]

(96)   John will speak to your mother and Bill *(to) your father.

If we set aside pseudo-passives as being dependent on some form of Case suspension not present in any of the other cases at hand,[54] the generalization may be that English allows P-stranding only if the landing site is sufficiently high. For those who reject (85), 'sufficiently high' would mean above IP (so that P-stranding would be allowed in various subtypes of wh-constructions, topicalization, *tough*-movement[55]), and Spec,*only* would be below IP.

Those speakers who accept (85) must set differently the relation between the P-stranding 'barrier' and the location of Spec,*only*, either by lowering the barrier or by allowing *only*P to be higher than is allowed by those who reject (85). It may be that this split among English speakers corresponds to one found within Scandinavian with respect to negative phrase movement, which is possible with P-stranding in Icelandic, but not in Norwegian.[56]

Turning now to (84) (and similarly for (83)), let me suggest that the sentences at issue do not involve P-stranding at all, but rather pied-piping as in (92):

(97)   . . . spoke to only one linguist → (*only*-phrase preposing)
    . . . to only one linguist$_i$ spoke t$_i$ → (VP-preposing)
    . . . [spoke t$_i$]$_j$ to only one linguist$_i$ t$_j$

It seems plausible to take the landing site of the PP here to be the Spec of a phonetically unrealized counterpart of *only* endowed with the feature +w. This head will then raise to the head W above it, after which VP-preposing places the VP in the Spec of W.

13.2.4.   Attraction by Neg^0 and *not*

Attraction by a phonetically unrealized head seems appropriate also for (83) (and similarly for the parallel direct object cases):[57]

(98)   . . . spoke to not a single linguist → (neg phrase preposing)
    . . . to not a single linguist$_i$ Neg^0 spoke t$_i$ → (Neg^0 raising)
    . . . Neg^0_j + W to not a single linguist$_i$ t$_j$ spoke t$_i$ → (VP-preposing)
    . . . [spoke t$_i$]$_k$ Neg^0_j + W to not a single linguist$_i$ t$_j$ t$_k$

A natural question at this point is whether there are any cases of attraction of this sort by a visible negative head. A plausible candidate is:

(99)   I saw not John, but Bill.

The facts concerning prepositions are as with *only* (though perhaps sharper, on average):

(100)   I spoke not to John, but to Bill.

(101)   ??I spoke to not John, but to Bill.

Unlike the case of *not a single N*, which I have taken to be a possible phrase,[58] *not John* is not one. Thus, (99) has the derivation (ignoring, perhaps wrongly, the *but . . .* part):[59]

(102)   . . . not saw John → (attraction by *not*)
    . . . John$_i$ not saw t$_i$ → (raising of *not*)
    . . . not$_j$ + W John$_i$ t$_j$ saw t$_i$ → (VP-preposing)
    . . . [saw t$_i$]$_k$ not$_j$ + W John$_i$ t$_j$ t$_k$

The derivation of (100) is essentially similar, except that the category moved to Spec,*not* is a PP *to John*. Example (101) is derivable only as a violation of the constraint prohibiting P-stranding when the landing site is too low.

13.2.5. More on wide scope

To some extent, the construction exemplified by (99) and (100) seems able to display a wide-scope reading of the familiar sort, as in:

(103)   John has refused to read not Aspects but LSLT.

This example seems fairly natural with a wide-scope interpretation that contrasts two (potential) refusals (cf. *J has not refused to read Aspects, but he has refused to read LSLT*). I think this contrasts with:

(104)   John has refused not to read Aspects but LSLT.

Here, to the extent the sentence is acceptable at all, there seems to necessarily be only one refusal. From the perspective I have been developing, the wide-scope reading of (103) has a derivation in which *not* is actually in the matrix. (It has attracted *Aspects*, moved up to W, and then had the VP *refused to read* move past it into Spec,W.)

The reason that (104) has no wide-scope reading is that in (104) *not* cannot be part of the matrix, that is, there is no derivation using only attraction + *not*-raising + VP-preposing that can yield (104) with a matrix *not*.[60]

A clearer case of a similar sort (except that an abstract Neg^0 is at issue) can be constructed with *not a single*:

(105)   She has requested that they read not a single linguistics book.

(106)   She has requested that they not read a single linguistics book.

The first allows a wide-scope reading much more readily than the second.[61] (In fact, the second becomes hard to accept if prefaced with *Amazingly enough, in all these months, ...*) Example (105) has the derivation:

(107)   . . . requested that they read not a single ling. book → (attraction by Neg^0)
. . . not a single ling. book$_i$ Neg^0 requested that they read t_i → (raising of Neg^0 to W)
. . . Neg^0_j + W not a single ling. book$_i$ t_j requested that they read t_i → (VP-preposing to Spec,W)
. . . [requested that they read t_i]$_k$ Neg^0_j + W not a single ling. book$_i$ t_j t_k

No comparable derivation can produce (106).

The wide-scope reading of (105) is accounted for by a combination of overt movement operations and a matrix Neg^0. Example (106) cannot be derived that way; in addition, it must also be the case that (features of)[62] the embedded *not* in (106) not be able to raise covertly to a matrix Neg⁰. This would follow most strongly if there were no covert (feature) movement in syntax at all.[63]

Pursuing the parallelism between negation and *only* that has played an important role so far, consider now comparable facts with *only*:

(108)   She has requested that they read only Aspects.

(109)   She has requested that they only read Aspects.

The first of these has a wide-scope reading absent in the second.[64] Again, the wide-scope reading of (108) has a derivation in which *only* is actually in the matrix. (It has attracted *Aspects*, moved up to W, and then had the VP *requested that they read* move past it to Spec,W.)

In (109), on the other hand, *only* can only be within the embedded sentence. No derivation with matrix *only* of the sort under consideration can yield (109).[65] I further assume, as in the discussion of (106), that no covert movement of (features of) *only* is possible.

13.2.6.   Subject and pre-subject *only* and negation

We have not yet considered examples like these:

(110)   Only to John have they spoken the truth.

(111)   ?Not to John has she spoken, but to Paul.

It is straightforward to take these to involve preposing of *to John*. On the basis of the deviance of (101), I have taken this *not* not to form a constituent with (*to*) *John* that would be subject to movement, and I have taken the same position for *only* followed by (*to*) *John*. In other words, *only/not* and *to John* do not form a constituent.

Maximal integration with what has gone before leads to the proposal that here, too, there is attraction to *only/not*:[66]

(112)   only/not has she spoken to John → (attraction to *only/not*)
to John$_i$ only/not has she spoken t$_i$ → (raising of *only/not* to W)
only/not$_j$ + W to John$_i$ t$_j$ has she spoken t$_i$

The facts of (85) and (101) that led me to think that *only* and *not* are attractors here are sharpened in these cases of preposing out of IP:[67]

(113)   *To only John have they spoken the truth.

(114)   *To not John has she spoken, but to Paul.

These contrast with:

(115)   To only one person have they spoken the truth.

(116)   To not a single person have they spoken the truth.

As in the derivation of (97) and (98), these last two examples are instances of attraction not by overt *only/not* but by their phonetically unrealized counterparts. What is attracted is the phrase *to only one person/to not a single person,* which does contain *only/not,* in contrast to what is attracted in (110) and (111).

Since *only one N/not a single N* are phrases, it is unsurprising that they can appear as subjects:[68]

(117)   Only one person came to the party.

(118)   Not a single person came to the party.

Similar is:[69]

(119)   Only John came to the party.

The derivation here, in particular since *only John* is not a phrase, must be:

(120)   only John came to the party] → (attraction by *only*)
        John$_i$ only t$_i$ came to the party → (raising of *only* to W)
        only$_j$ + W John$_i$ t$_j$ t$_i$ came to the party

Let us make the plausible assumption that when *only* attracts something to its Spec, it is necessarily either that phrase or a subpart of it that is 'focused' by *only*.[70] From this it follows, as desired, that in (119) the only possible focus for *only* is *John.*

The fact that in, for example, (121) the focus of *only* can be the verb, either object, or the whole VP might then indicate that the (finite) VP has moved to Spec,*only* (with *only* subsequently raising further):[71]

(121)   John only gave Bill a book.

Recalling that (111) is less natural than (110), consider the fact that (119) has no direct counterpart with *not*:

(122)   *Not John came to the party.

Similar, I think, is the pair:

(123)   John shows his work only to Mary.

(124)   *John shows his work not to Mary.

In other words, especially if we set aside the cases of *not . . . but,* we reach the conclusion that *only* is a more 'powerful' attractor than *not,* despite the existence of many parallelisms between them. If, as a subcase of this, we said that *not* differed from *only* in that *not* could not attract a finite phrase to its Spec, we might (ultimately) be able to relate the ungrammaticality of (122) and (124) to that of (125), as opposed to the grammaticality of all of (119), (123), and (121):[72]

(125)   *John not gave Bill a book.

Consider now:

(126)   Not all his friends came to the party.

Not all X (contrary to *not a single person*, but like *not every X*) is not possible postverbally:[73]

(127)   *John invited not all his friends/not everybody to the party.

This may indicate that *not all/every X* cannot be a constituent.[74]

13.3.   Other elements related to *only* and negation

13.3.1.   *Even*

The fact that (119) does not have the same interpretive flexibility as (121) could be taken to imply, in addition to what has so far been claimed, that *only* cannot attract IP. The property of pre-subject *only* in question shows up in embedded contexts, too, in the sense that the following sentence cannot have the embedded IP focused by *only*:

(128)   John said that only he was hungry.

There is some evidence, however, indicating that attraction of IP is not systematically prohibited.
     Even is fairly similar to *only* as far as the phenomena discussed in this article are concerned. For example, the contrast between (110) and (113) is mirrored by:

(129)   Even to John they wouldn't tell the truth.

(130)   *To even John they wouldn't tell the truth.

And the fact that (119) and (121) differ in range of interpretation is mirrored by:

(131)   Even John came to the party.

(132)   John even gave Bill a book.

In the first of these, *even* can only focus *John,* whereas the second allows a range of possibilities. Focusing an embedded IP is as impossible with *even* as with *only* in (128):

(133)   John said that even he was hungry.

The natural conclusion is that *even* is an attractor, too.
Consider now, in colloquial English:[75]

(134)   John gave Bill a book yesterday, even.

This seems to allow a choice of (stressed) foci, in a way that looks a lot like what is possible in (132). Again, when *even* is sentence initial, the range of possibilities disappears, and only (part of) the subject can be focused:

(135)   Even John gave Bill a book yesterday.

Thinking of what was suggested in the discussion of (120), namely that focus is associated with (part of) the Spec of the attractor, I conclude that in (134) IP has moved to Spec,*even*.[76]
Yet, in (135) IP cannot have moved to Spec,*even*, otherwise the focus would not be limited to *John.* Of course in (135) IP does not look like it is in Spec,*even*. since it follows *even.* The way to make sense of all this, I think, is to conclude that although IP can be attracted by *even*, as seen in (134), *even* cannot subsequently raise past it to the next highest head (W).
On the other hand, *even* must have raised past the phrase it has attracted in other examples, namely VP in (132) and the subject DP in (135). Let me propose, then, that what is at issue is the possible position of W, the head to which *even* can raise. More specifically, assume a sufficient generalization of Larson's (1988) VP-shell hypothesis (which made into Specs (some) constituents previously thought to be complements, in the X-bar sense) to make plausible the following restriction on movement:

(136)   Specifiers and heads can be moved, but never complements.

Then, in (134), where IP has moved into Spec,*even*, IP must have been not the complement of *even* but rather the Spec of some other head, call it C.[77] Assume now that W, the head to which *even* moves when it precedes the phrase it has attracted, may not occur higher than C. Then, (135) cannot have IP as the attracted focus of *even*, as desired.

13.3.2.   *Too*

Like *even* in some respects is *too.* In particular, (137) is like (134) (but not necessarily colloquial):

(137)   John gave Bill a book, too.

On the other hand, *too* can never precede its focus:

(138)   *Too John gave Bill a book.

In the same vein, (139) has *Bill* as focus, never *a book*: ·

(139)   John gave Bill, too, a book.

Thus, *too* is an attractor that differs from *even* and *only* in never being able to raise past its Spec to a higher head W.

In (137), then, IP is in Spec,*too*, and IP or one of its subconstituents can be focused. In (139), *Bill* is in Spec,*too*, so that only it can be focused. Note the contrast between (139) and the following:

(140)   *John read Bill, too,'s book.

The unacceptability of (140) follows in part from the fact that XP + *too* is never a constituent,[78] that is, from the fact that *too* combines with its associated focus by attraction, not by merger, and in part from the fact that movement of a possessor (to Spec,*too*) is blocked by whatever generally blocks sentences like:

(141)   *Which linguist did John read's book?

Similarly, the following two sentences will he unacceptable for the same reason,[79] since both now involve (overt) movement:

(142)   *John read Bill's, too, book.

(143)   *Which linguist's did you read book?

Consider the contrast:

(144)   *John read Bill, even,'s book.

(145)   John read even Bill's book.

The former is excluded just like (140). The latter is acceptable with a derivation in which what moves to Spec,*even* is not *Bill* but rather *Bill's book* (followed by raising of *even*).

Example (139) differs from (137) in that in the former, but not in the latter, the focus must immediately precede *too*:[80]

(146)   *JOHN gave Bill, too, a book.

(147)   JOHN gave Bill a book, too.·

This follows from the fact that in (147) the whole IP *John gave Bill a book* has moved to Spec,*too* (thereby licensing focus on its subpart *John*), whereas in (146) it is *Bill* that has moved to Spec,*too*.

A question arises concerning the derivation of (139), since it is not plausible to think of *too* as being merged internal to VP. Let us instead take *too* to be merged here above VP (cf. *only* in (91)):

(148)   ... too Bill a book → (attraction to *too*)
         Bill$_i$ too gave t$_i$ a book → (VP-preposing)
         [gave t$_i$ a book]$_j$ Bill$_i$ too t$_j$

This does not yield the desired word order. Moreover, the output is unacceptable:

(149)   *John gave a book Bill, too.

The status of (149) has to do with some property specific to datives,[81] as can be seen by comparing it with (150), with the derivation (151):

(150)   John put on the table this book, too.

(151)   ... too put this book on the table → (attraction to *too*)
         ... this book$_i$ too put t$_i$ on the table → (VP-preposing)
         ... [put t$_i$ on the table]$_j$ this book$_i$ too t$_j$

To reach (139), (148) needs to be supplemented with an initial movement operation that extracts the direct object from VP (cf. (39)):

(152)   ... gave Bill a book → (dir.obj. preposing)
         ... a book$_k$ [gave Bill t$_k$] (merger of *too*)
         ... too a book$_k$ [gave Bill t$_k$] → (attraction to *too*)
         ... Bill$_i$ too a book$_k$ [gave t$_i$ t$_k$] → (VP-preposing)[82]
         ... [gave t$_i$ t$_k$]$_j$ Bill$_i$ too a book$_k$ t$_j$

Similarly, (153) will involve an initial step preposing *on the table*:

(153)   John put this book, too, on the table.

More generally put, any sentence in which *too* is followed by some part of the VP will have to have a derivation in which that part of the VP is initially raised out of VP so that it can be stranded by subsequent VP-preposing.

As we saw earlier in (78) and (82), comparable preposing of a particle can yield some degree of deviance. Thus, we are not surprised, from this perspective, to find the following contrast:[83]

(154)   John pointed Bill out, too.

(155)   John pointed out Bill, too.

(156)   ?John pointed Bill, too, out.

13.3.3. Focus

I have argued that the deviance of (156) should be understood as reflecting the application of VP-preposing (itself dependent on prior attraction to Spec,*too*; cf. note 82). VP-preposing (to the Spec of a functional head W above *too*) will, all other things being equal, carry along the particle, yielding (155). For (156) to be derived, the particle *out* must be raised out of VP (up to PredP; cf. the discussion following (34)) prior to VP-preposing:

(157)   . . . pointed Bill out → (particle preposing)
   . . . out$_k$ pointed Bill t$_k$ → (merger of *too*)
   . . . too out$_k$ pointed Bill t$_k$ → (attraction to *too*)
   . . . Bill$_i$ too out$_k$ pointed t$_i$ t$_k$—(VP-preposing)
   . . . [pointed t$_i$ t$_k$]$_j$ Bill$_i$ too out$_k$ t$_j$

Although I am not in a position to account for the precise degree of deviance of (156), the proposal is that it is the presence of particle preposing in the derivation of (156) that distinguishes it from the fully acceptable (155) (which does not involve such particle preposing).[84]

Assuming this is on the right track, we can use the kind of deviance observed in (156) as a probe into the derivation of other types of sentences. Consider in this light the notion of focus (on a DP). The term 'focus' has been used in a wide variety of ways, to the point that the phenomena that have been characterized by that term probably do not form a natural class. However, if we restrict our attention to certain instances of what has been called focus, I think we find effects reminiscent of (156). Take, in particular, focus in question-answer pairs, especially with an indefinite answer,[85] as in:

(158)   What is he looking up? He's looking up a linguistics term.

(159)   What is he looking up? ?He's looking a linguistics term up.

Similarly, I accept (160) as a kind of single-sentence counterpart to (158), but I find (161) appreciably less good:

(160)   What he looked up was he looked up a linguistics term.

(161)   ??What he looked up was he looked a linguistics term up.

I take these facts to indicate that this kind of focus is subject to (overt) attraction (by an abstract head Foc^0)[86] in a way parallel to the various cases of attraction by Neg^0 and by *only, even,* and *too,* discussed earlier. In (160), we have:

(162)   ... Foc^0 looked a linguistics term up $\rightarrow$ (attraction to Foc)

     ... a linguistics term$_i$ Foc^0 looked t_i up $\rightarrow$ (raising of Foc to W - cf. (102))

     ... Foc°_j + W a linguistics term$_i$ t_j looked t_i up $\rightarrow$ (VP-preposing)

     ... [looked t_i up]$_k$ Foc^0_j + W a linguistics term$_i$ t_j t_k

The derivation of the deviant (161) is:

(163)   ... looked a linguistics term up $\rightarrow$ (particle preposing)

     ... up$_i$ looked a linguistics term t_i $\rightarrow$ (merger of Foc)

     ... Foc^0 up$_i$ looked a linguistics term t_i $\rightarrow$ (attraction to Foc)

     ... a linguistics term$_j$ Foc^0 up$_i$ looked t_j t_i $\rightarrow$ (raising of Foc to W)

     ... Foc^0_k + W a linguistics term$_j$ t_k up$_i$ looked t_j t_i $\rightarrow$ (VP-preposing)

     ... [looked t_j t_i]$_l$ Foc^0_k + W a linguistics term$_j$ t_k up$_i$ t_l

As mentioned in note 84, the deviance must be a result either of particle preposing itself or of a locality effect induced by it.

13.3.4. Universal grammar

Assume that the kind of focus illustrated by (158)–(161) is necessarily subject to overt movement to Spec,Foc in English, as I have claimed. If so, then the following hypothesis is plausible (especially since the deviance of (159) and (161) is not visible in the primary acquisition data):

(164)   This kind of focus is subject to overt movement to Spec,Foc in all languages.

In some languages, such as English, this focus movement will be followed by VP-preposing, in others not.[87]

     Assume, similarly, that English has overt movement of negative phrases to Spec, Neg and overt movement (attraction) to Spec, *only/even/too*. Then it is plausible to think that (165) holds:

(165)   a. Negative phrases of the (standard) English sort are subject to overt movement to Spec,Neg in all languages.[88]

       b. Counterparts of *only, even, too* in other languages always attract phrases to their Spec overtly.

Again, VP-preposing will apply sometimes, but not always. For example, as mentioned in note 57, at least some Scandinavian has VP-preposing with *only,* but not with negation.

     For a language like Japanese, (165b) requires that DP-*even*, and so on not be a syntactic constituent (cf. note 78), despite the apparently affixal (suffixal) character of such elements in Japanese.[89]

     We have seen that English itself does not treat all such elements consistently, in the sense that *only* precedes, whereas *too* follows, the associated XP attracted to their Spec. (*Only* raises to W, but *too* does not, in my terms; *even* has mixed behavior.)

Yet it seems unlikely that 'everything goes'. For example, the following two conjectures are worth testing:

(166)   Conjecture: Languages that are like Japanese in being robustly head-final (in particular having little or no 'leakage' of arguments to the right of V) never have *only, even, too* raising to W (i.e., never have these elements preceding their associated XP).

(167)   Conjecture: Strict VSO languages (robustly head-initial) never have *only, even, too* following their associated XP (i.e., always have these elements raising to W).

The correctness of either of these conjectures (or of some minor variant of them) would support the idea that these elements are heads that, like other heads, are capable of attracting a phrase to their Spec.[90]

13.3.5.   Heavy-NP shift

My use of VP-preposing is obviously related to Larson's (1988; 1990) reinterpretation of Heavy-NP Shift in terms of V-bar preposing (cf. also note 10). The usual way of thinking about sentences such as (168) was as involving rightward movement of the 'heavy NP':

(168)   John put on the table the book that he had just bought.

Larson noticed that his VP-shell idea allowed one to dispense with rightward movement here in favor of leftward movement of a verbal constituent.

Den Dikken (1995a) proposed an analysis of Heavy-NP Shift that is like Larson's in having recourse to (overt) leftward movement of a verbal projection but differs from it in having the heavy NP move (overtly), too (to Spec,Agr-O).[91] In addition, den Dikken has the maximal projection VP moving (rather than V-bar). In these two respects, the derivations that I have proposed (e.g., for negative phrases and *only*) resemble den Dikken's analysis of Heavy-NP Shift more than Larson's.

Given this resemblance, the question arises as to whether it would not be possible to recast Heavy-NP Shift in exactly the form I have proposed for negation and others. One difference between den Dikken's proposal for Heavy-NP and mine for these lies in the landing site (of, e.g., the heavy phrase or the negative phrase), in his proposal Spec,Agr-O, in mine Spec,Neg/*only*, and so on. Of importance here is not so much the Agr-O label but rather den Dikken's proposal that the landing site for the heavy NP is an A-position, with the expectation that long-distance movement of the heavy NP out of a finite complement should be impossible. I have argued that such long-distance movement (of *not a single linguistics book, Aspects,* into the matrix, followed by movement of the matrix VP—v. (107)/(108)) is possible out of finite subjunctives in cases like:

(169)   She has requested that they read not a single linguistics book.

(170)   She has requested that they read only Aspects.

Corresponding subjunctive examples with Heavy-NP Shift would look like (171), which I find reasonably acceptable:

(171) ?She has been requesting that he return ever since last Tuesday the book that John borrowed from her just last year.

The derivation is (with *ever since last Tuesday* in the matrix):[92]

(172) ... requesting that he return the book that J borrowed ... ever since last Tues. →
(heavy-NP preposing)
... the book that J borrowed ... $_i$ H^0 requesting that he return t_i ever since last Tues. (raising of H^0 to W and VP-preposing)
... [requesting that he return t_i ever since last Tuesday]$_k$ H^0_j + W the book that J borrowed ... $_i$ t_j t_k

Thus, it does seem plausible to take Heavy-NP Shift to be significantly parallel to attraction to Neg, *only*, and so on.

I find that *John* in (171) can be the antecedent of *he,* whereas in the following it is more difficult to do so:

(173) He returned only yesterday the book that John borrowed last year.

That *John* can antecede *he* in the first is not surprising, given that *the book that John borrowed* ... is raised (overtly) out of the embedded sentence. Evasion of a Condition C violation is then comparable to what one sees in sentences like (cf. also note 35):

(174) Which of the books that John borrowed yesterday did he return today?

The different status of (173) then correlates with the fact that the landing site Spec,H is below the subject position, so in a simple sentence the Heavy-NP-shifted phrase will not raise past the (derived position of the) subject.

If Heavy-NP Shift is parallel to attraction to Neg,*only*, and so on, and involves subsequent VP-preposing of the same sort,[93] it is natural to ask if we find with Heavy-NP Shift cases in which VP-preposing strands a PP, as it does, for example, in:

(175) John introduced no one to Bill.

(176) John introduced only Paul to Bill.

One type of example of the desired sort that I think is reasonably acceptable is:

(177) ?John put on the table one of his favorite linguistics books about two days ago.

But there are simpler examples. Consider:

(178) John put the book that he was reading on the table.

This is usually considered to be an instance of a heavy object not being shifted. From the present perspective, however, there is an appealing alternative, illustrated in the following derivation (with PP-preposing akin to the predicate raising of (39), for example):

(179)   . . . put the book that . . . on the table → (PP-raising)
        . . . on the table$_i$ put the book that . . . t$_i$ → (merger of H and heavy-NP preposing)
        . . . the book that . . . $_j$ H^0 on the table$_i$ put t$_j$ t$_i$ → (raising of H to W and
            VP-preposing)
        . . . [put t$_j$ t$_i$]$_l$ H^0_k + W the book that . . . $_j$ t$_k$ on the table$_i$ t$_l$

In other words, (178) does involve preposing of the heavy NP(DP) (plus VP-preposing). This allows us to take heavy NPs to shift uniformly, thereby reinforcing the parallel with negative phrase preposing. The optionality seen when (178) is compared with (180) is now displaced:

(180)   John put on the table the book that he was reading.

Rather than being a property of heavy-NP movement, this double possibility is now statable as a fact about PP-raising.[94]

    If the overt leftward movement of a heavy NP is obligatory (and in English then followed by VP-preposing), as the analysis in (179) makes possible, we have a way of accounting for (181):

(181)   ?John picked the book that he was reading up.

The deviance of this kind of sentence can now be attributed to the fact that its derivation requires an application of particle preposing. As we saw earlier in the discussion of (163) and many other examples, particle preposing itself leads to some degree of deviance.[95]

    In Dutch and German, if we abstract away from V-2, a direct object always precedes its verb. Even a heavy object by and large does not follow the verb.[96] This is true of negative phrases and *only/even*-XP, also.[97] In present terms, this means that the set of preposings under study in this article (attraction to Neg, *only, even, too,* Foc, H) are never or only in very limited circumstances followed by VP-preposing in Dutch or German.[98]

13.3.6.   German *nur* (= *only*)

The contrast between (113) and (115) has a counterpart in German that has been studied by Bayer (1996):

(182)   *Er hat mit nur seinem Bruder gesprochen. ('he has with only his brother spoken')

(183)   Er hat mit nur einem Mann gesprochen. ('he has with only one man spoken')

Bayer proposes that the *nur*-construction without a numeral is subject to LF-movement of *nur* + DP and that the ungrammaticality of (182) can therefore be assimilated to the general prohibition against P-stranding in German, illustrated in (184):[99]

(184)   *Wem hat er mit gesprochen? ('who has he with spoken')

Bayer's assimilation of (182) and (184) in terms of movement and violation of P-stranding seems to me to be exactly right. But, from the perspective outlined earlier, the assumption that it must be LF-movement that is at stake in the former is not necessary. Let me propose instead that the P-stranding violation of (182) is one that is produced by overt movement (of *seinem Bruder*).

I take German *nur* to be an attractor like English *only*.[100] *Nur* can attract a DP that is a direct object:

(185)   Er hat nur seinen Bruder gesehen. ('he has only his brother seen')

Here *seinen Bruder* has moved to Spec,*nur,* and then *nur* has raised to the next head W. VP-preposing of the English sort does not take place. If, instead of a direct object, we have a PP, then the PP itself can be attracted by *nur,* which yields, with subsequent raising of *nur* to W:

(186)   Er hat nur mit seinem Bruder gesprochen. ('he has only with his brother spoken')

Since German does not allow P-stranding,[101] *seinem Bruder* alone cannot move to Spec,*nur* stranding the preposition *mit.* With subsequent raising of *nur,* that would have yielded:

(187)   *Er hat nur seinem Bruder mit gesprochen.

(To get (182) this would have had to be followed by further preposing of *mit.*) Example (183) is possible because *nur einem Mann* with a numeral can (unlike *nur seinem Bruder* without a numeral) be generated as a constituent, and that constituent can be the object of *mit,* in which case the entire PP *mit nur einem Mann* can be attracted to Spec of a phonetically unrealized counterpart of *nur* in a way quite parallel to the derivation of English (115).

13.3.7.   Scandinavian negation

Some of the Scandinavian languages have a variety of negative phrase movement that is particularly transparent in that the negative phrase ends up to the left of a non-V-2 verb form. I repeat here examples given earlier as (13) and (14):

(188)   %Jon har ingen romaner lest. ('J has no novels read')

(189)   % Dette er en student som ingen romaner leser. ('this is a student that no novels reads')

The '%' indicates that such sentences, taken from Christensen (1986), are acceptable only in certain varieties of Norwegian. Two Icelandic examples, given earlier as (55) and (56), from Rögnvaldsson (1987) and Jónsson (1996), are:

(190)   Hann mun ekkert hafa getadh gert. ('he will nothing have could done')

(191)   Their hafa ekkert lofadh adh gera. ('they have nothing promised to do')

I have argued extensively that the English counterparts of these should also be analyzed as involving overt negative phrase preposing:

(192)   John has read no novels.

(193)   He could have done nothing.

Although *no novels* and *nothing* in these examples appear not to have moved overtly, I tried to show that that is not the case. They have indeed moved overtly, but, in English, unlike in Scandinavian, that overt movement is masked by subsequent movement of the verb phrase.

In English examples like the following (= (51)), where there is a wide-scope/narrow-scope ambiguity, the claim is that the overt preposing of the negative phrase can target one of two landing sites:

(194)   I will force you to marry no one.

In the narrow scope reading, *no one* moves to Spec,NegP within the infinitival (followed by preposing of the lower VP). In the wide-scope reading, *no one* moves to Spec,NegP within the matrix (followed by preposing of the entire higher VP).

To judge by some initial data, it seems that one does not find ambiguities of the (194) sort in Scandinavian. If the negative phrase moves overtly to a landing site within the infinitival (recall that in Scandinavian there is no subsequent VP-preposing), then only the narrow-scope reading is available ((195) from Swedish, (196) from Icelandic):[102]

(195)   Hon har bett oss att inga böcker läsa. ('she has asked us to no books read')

(196)   Pabbi hennar mun neydha hana til adh giftast engum. ('father her will force her til to marry no one')

13.3.8.   Covert movement

Put another way, if the negative phrase is attracted to the embedded NegP, then its scope is fixed as narrow. This means, in turn, that there must be no covert means of extending its scope if it has moved overtly only as far as the embedded NegP. In Chomsky (1995, 265), covert (LF-) movement is limited to the raising of features. We thus need an answer to two questions:

(197) a. Why can covert feature movement not alter the scope of a negative phrase that has been moved overtly to some Spec,NegP?

b. Why must negative phrases (of the English sort) always move overtly to some Spec,NegP (cf. (165a))? That is, why can negative scope not be set covertly?

Taken jointly, these two questions suggest a strong limitation on the power of covert feature movement. A joint answer would then be either of the following:[103]

(198) a. Covert feature movement does not exist.

b. Covert feature movement is subject to locality restrictions at least as strong as those to which overt head movement is subject.

In addition, it must also be the case that movement of an empty operator of the sort proposed by Watanabe (1992) can neither alter scope already set by overt movement nor establish scope, as far as negative phrases (of the English sort) are concerned.

Consider, in this light, the fact that in the following West Flemish example (and similarly for Swiss German) the negative phrase necessarily has narrow scope, as discussed by Haegeman and van Riemsdijk (1986, 442ff.):

(199)   da Jan hee willen geen vlees eten ('that J has want(ed) no meat (to)eat')

This contrasts with English, in which wide scope in the following is possible:

(200)   John wanted to eat no meat/none of the meat.

The position of the negative phrase *geen vlees* to the left of the infinitive *eten* could a priori be interpreted in one of two ways. Either *geen vlees* is in the normal position for direct objects, or it has raised further within the infinitival embedding, to Spec,NegP.[104] In the former case (which would violate (165a), however), the question would have been why covert feature movement could not lead to a wide-scope interpretation as well as to a narrow-scope interpretation. In the latter, more plausible case, the question is exactly that of (197a). The answer is found in (198), again. It is essentially that there is no covert movement that is capable of spanning the required amount of structure.

Haegeman and van Riemsdijk (1986, 451) observe that multiple wh-questions act differently from negation, in that a wh-phrase found within an infinitival phrase of the sort seen in (199) can, contrary to a negative phrase, have wide scope. More specifically, it can be part of a multiple wh-question linked to a higher Spec,CP (example in West Flemish; again, Swiss German works alike):

(201)   K weten nie wien dan-ze goan willen voo wekken cursus anduden. ('I know not *whom* that-they go(= fut.) want *for which course* (to)appoint')

The PP *voo wekken cursus* is clearly within the infinitival embedding, yet can be linked to *whom*, which is in Spec,CP of the finite clause whose verb is *goan*.

A way to understand this contrast between negative phrases and wh-phrases (in multiple wh-questions), while continuing to follow the approach to the former outlined earlier, would be to consider that multiple wh-questions can have a derivation of the sort proposed by Watanabe (1992). The lower wh-phrase in (201) would contain an empty operator that would move in the overt syntax (as a phrase, not as a head). This is plausible, because Haegeman and van Riemsdijk (p. 450) have shown that overt extraction from within an infinitival clause of the relevant type is possible.

If so, the question is why overt movement of an empty operator could not allow wide scope in (199), too, that is, in the case of a negative phrase. The answer must be that, while compatible with a wh-phrase, an empty operator is not compatible with a negative phrase. This, too, is plausible, I think, if we take into consideration the following English paradigms:[105]

(202)   where, somewhere, anywhere, nowhere, everywhere, elsewhere

(203)   how, somehow, anyhow, nohow

Although English is obviously not perfectly regular here, the set of forms in (202), especially, does suggest that the (noninitial) *where* of multiple interrogation (and by extension other wh-words) could well be associated with an abstract counterpart to *some/any/no/every*, which would correspond to the empty operator under discussion.[106] The idea, then, would be that the empty operator, being of the series *some/any/no/every*, could not co-occur with one of those, that is, the empty operator could be associated with (form a constituent with) *where*,[107] but not with *nowhere*,[108] as desired.

13.3.9. German

Bayer (1996, 246) discusses a contrast in German that recalls the fact of (199):

(204)   weil mir der Hans niemanden zu grüssen versprochen hat ('because me the Hans nobody to greet promised has' = 'because Hans has promised to greet nobody')

(205)   weil mir der Hans versprochen hat niemanden zu grüssen

In the first of these, the negative phrase *niemanden* can have either narrow or wide scope. In the second (where it is clearly within the infinitival phrase), *niemanden* can have only narrow scope. Thus, (205) differs from the seemingly similar English example, for which a wide-scope reading is available:

(206)   because John has promised to greet nobody

In that reading of (206), *nobody* has overtly moved past *promised*, subsequent to which the VP *promised to greet t* has overtly moved past the landing site of *nobody*. The first of these two movements is what licenses the wide-scope reading.

The absence of wide scope in (205) correlates with the fact that German, like West Flemish and the Scandinavian languages, does not have its negative phrase preposing followed by VP-preposing. Put another way, the landing site of negative phrase preposing in non-English Germanic is not obscured by VP-preposing the way it is in English. Since the landing site in (205) is within the infinitive phrase (i.e., in the embedded Spec,Neg), only narrow scope is possible. As we saw for West Flemish, UG does not provide any covert means of extending the scope.

Bayer (1996, 215) notes similar facts with German *nur* ('only'). In the following example, *nur* has only narrow scope:

(207)   ... dass man uns gezwungen hat nur Spanisch zu lernen ('that one us forced has only Spanish to learn' = 'that they have forced us ...')

As before, English differs:

(208)   They forced us to learn only Spanish.

In this English example, a wide-scope reading is possible. From the perspective developed so far, this corresponds to a derivation in which *only* is merged into the matrix sentence. *Spanish* is attracted by *only*. VP-preposing (of *forced us to learn t*) to a position to the left of (the final position of) *only* yields the visible word order.

The absence of wide scope in German sentences like (207) again correlates with the absence of VP-preposing. Without VP-preposing, the postauxiliary position of *nur* can only mean that *nur* is within the infinitival sentence, and not within the matrix. From that, the limitation to narrow scope follows.[109]

13.3.10.   Scope ambiguities with two quantifiers

Bayer (1990, 184n) notes a fact about scope ambiguities with two quantifiers that recalls the facts of (207) and (205):

(209)   weil jemand versucht hat jeden reinzulegen ('since someone tried has everyone to-cheat')

In (209) *jeden* cannot have scope over *jemand*. Again there is a contrast with English:

(210)   (since) someone has tried to cheat everyone

An interpretation with *everyone* taking scope over *someone* is fairly natural in English.

It is not the case that German allows no sentences in which a lower quantifier takes scope over a higher one. Thus, Bayer (1990, 201) gives as having a reading in which *jeden* has scope over *irgendjemand*:

(211)   weil irgendjemand auf jeden gespannt ist ('since someone for everyone anxious is')

English has the same ambiguity:

(212)   Someone is anxious about everybody.

The ambiguity possible in (211) makes it plausible that the lack of ambiguity in (209) results from the fact that *jeden* there is within an extraposed infinitive.

I have interpreted the limitation to narrow scope in (207) and (205) to reflect the fact that covert movement cannot extend the scope of a phrase that is overtly within an embedded sentence. Since *jeden* in (209) is within the extraposed infinitive, the necessarily narrow scope for *jeden* there follows in the same way.

The possible scope ambiguity in (211) should probably be taken to be an instance of reconstruction (cf. quantifier lowering in May's (1985) sense), the idea being that *irgendjemand* there originates in a position below that of (*auf*) *jeden* (whereas *jemand* in (209) does not originate in a position below that of *jeden*).[110]

The remaining question is why (212) and similar examples are fairly natural in English:[111]

(213) At least one student has tried to fool every professor/each of the professors.

(214) At least one student has asked to see each of these new books.

If the *every/each* phrase is within the infinitival embedding, we would not expect wide scope for it to be available, given the discussion so far.

Let me propose, then, that the *every/each* phrase in (210), (213), and (214) has in fact raised overtly into the matrix.[112] The observed word order is produced by a subsequent application of VP-preposing (or preposing of some phrase containing VP). The English/German contrast reflects the fact that German does not allow VP-preposing in such cases, as we have already seen.

In the spirit of Brody (1990 on Hungarian and Beghelli and Stowell (1997) on English,[113] I take the landing site of the *every/each* phrase to be Spec,Dist^0 (for 'distributive') in the matrix sentence. DistP must clearly be above the position in which *someone/at least one student* originates (and perhaps above IP itself). After the *every/each* phrase is attracted to Spec.Dist^0, the matrix VP will move to Spec,W (W the head to which Dist^0 will have raised).

In many cases studied so far, we have seen that VP-preposing carries along all the material within VP (apart from the phrase previously attracted to Spec.Neg/*only*/*even*/*too*/Foc/H). This produced contrasts such as:

(215) He looked up only the shorter word.

(216) ?He looked only the shorter word up.

Attraction to Spec,*only*, plus raising of *only* to W, plus VP-preposing to Spec,W will yield (215). These three operations are also part of the derivation of (216), but for (216) an additional operation preposing the particle (prior to attraction to *only*) is required in order to get the correct word order. Particle preposing is usually associated with some degree of deviance.

If the derivation of (213)/(214) involves VP-preposing. then adding a particle should have an effect parallel to that seen in (215) versus (216). I think this is the case:

(217)   At least one student has tried to put down every professor.

(218)   At least one student has tried to put every professor down.

In the reading where *at least one student* has wide scope, these seem of approximately equal naturalness. But with wide scope attributed to *every professor*, (217) seems quite a bit more natural than (218).

Moreover, I find a comparable contrast in simpler cases, with no embedding:

(219)   At least one student has put down every professor.

(220)   At least one student has put every professor down.

Again, with wide scope for *at least one student,* acceptability is approximately equal. With wide scope for *every professor,* on the other hand, (219) seems appreciably more natural than (220).[114] This suggests that (overt) VP-preposing is necessary, even in simple sentences, if the object is to have scope over the subject. VP-preposing will produce the correct word order if it follows upon attraction of the *every*-phrase to Spec,Dist. I conclude that for the *every*-phrase to have scope over *at least one* in these examples, the *every*-phrase must move overtly to Spec,Dist.

The status of (220) recalls Hornstein's (1994, 459) observation:

(221)   At least one person considers every senator to be smart.

(222)   At least one person considers every senator smart.

Hornstein observes that wide scope for *every senator* in (221) is possible[115] but that it is (surprisingly, from a standard perspective) virtually impossible in (222). If I am right to claim that wide scope requires overt movement of *every N,* followed by VP-preposing,[116] then (222) is derivable only if movement of *every senator* is preceded by raising *smart* in a way parallel to the way the particle is raised in the wide scope reading of (220). My interpretation of Hornstein's judgment, then, is that, for him, raising of the AP causes (strong) deviance. (Either the AP raising is itself not available, or the raised AP acts to inhibit either the movement of *every senator* or that of the VP.)

That (221) is possible with wide scope for *every* (I agree with the thrust of Hornstein's judgments, although for me the difference is somewhat less sharp) means that preposing the *to* + infinitive phrase is more readily available than preposing the AP (either intrinsically so, or because the *to*-phrase does not create the same blocking effect on subsequent movement). In the end, I think that neither of these examples is as natural with wide scope as:[117]

(223)   At least one person has praised every senator.

Thus, for me, preposing the *to*-infinitive creates some deviance, though less than preposing the AP.

13.3.11.   A digression on particles

I have attributed the facts of (221)–(222) in part to the necessary application of AP preposing in the latter versus *to*-phrase preposing in the former. Since these operations have nothing specifically to do with quantification (nor does VP-preposing), we might expect to find a similar contrast elsewhere, even in a nonquantificational part of English syntax. Consider the contrast:[118]

(224)   (?)They're trying to make out John to be a liar.

(225)   *?They're trying to make out John a liar.

This pair can be related to the previous discussion as follows: Simple cases of 'V DP Prt' do not require particle preposing or VP-preposing. Simple cases of 'V Prt DP' in English do not involve particle preposing, but they do involve VP-preposing (which carries along the particle).[119] This implies that in 'V Prt DP', the DP (even when it is not subject to attraction by Neg/*only/even/too*/Foc/H/Dist), is, prior to VP-preposing, outside and higher up than the VP to be moved. To generate 'V Prt DP XP', where XP originates within VP, XP must be moved out of VP prior to VP-preposing. The status of (225) indicates in a by now familiar way that the preposing (from within VP) of a predicate nominal, like that of AP, produces substantial deviance. Example (224) shows that preposing an infinitival *to*-phrase yields only slight deviance.

13.3.12.   ACD

Returning to quantification and to the question of wide scope, which I have argued should be treated in terms of overt movement rather than covert movement, I would like to briefly focus on the status of Antecedent-Contained Deletion, which Chris Wilder suggested to me could advantageously be integrated into the preceding framework. Consider in particular ACD in combination with particles:

(226)   John will stare down everybody (that) Fred will.

(227)   ??John will stare everybody (that) Fred will down.

It seems clear that the second of these is decidedly less natural than the first.[120]

The deviance of (227) must be a result of the application of particle preposing, which in turn tells us that VP-preposing has applied. Given the observed word order of (227), if VP-preposing has applied, then *everybody (that) Bill did* must have raised out of VP prior to that (and VP-preposing landed in a Spec position to the left of the landing site of *everybody (that) Bill did*). In other words, we arrive at a proposal similar to Hornstein's (1994, 466ff.; 1995, 79ff.) (cf. also the earlier works he mentions), namely that ACD requires the phrase containing the deleted verb phrase (here *everybody (that) Bill did*) to move out of the containing VP.

There is one major difference. Since the particle preposing and VP-preposing operations I have been positing are overt movements, the movement of *everybody* (*that*) *Bill did* must be overt, too. Put another way, ACD sentences, while they do not (necessarily) contain a second quantified phrase as in (223), must, like (223), involve overt preposing.[121]

This yields a straightforward account of the following fact, discussed by Hornstein (1994) and the references he cites:

(228)   *John requested (that) everybody that Bill did read Aspects.

Movement of *everybody that Bill did* would yield an ECP-type violation.[122]

Taking ACD movement to be overt has, finally, the advantage of eliminating LF pied piping, which would seem to be necessary from the standard perspective, as Kennedy (1997, 684) shows.

13.4.   Conclusion

I have argued that, in a number of cases where covert phrasal movement had been postulated, it is possible and advantageous to dispense with covert movement (including feature raising—v. (197)/(198)) and replace it with a combination of overt movements.[123]

The strongest interpretation of this conclusion is that the cases explicitly considered in this essay are typical and that it is not accidental that those cases lend themselves to analysis in terms of overt movement. It is rather that UG leaves no choice: Scope must be expressed hierarchically,[124] there are no covert phrasal movements permitted by UG, and neither can the effect of covert phrasal movement be achieved by feature raising. Scope reflects the interaction of merger and overt movement.

This strong conclusion is compatible with (211) and (45) if UG in some cases allows scope to be computed 'under reconstruction', where reconstruction is not itself a movement operation but rather the option of taking into account the pre-movement position of some phrase.[125]

For this strong conclusion to hold, it will have to turn out that all cases of covert phrasal movement can be advantageously rethought in terms of overt movement. One particularly challenging case is the 'inverse linking' of May (1985):[126]

(229)   One person from every city voted for Smith.

Under standard assumptions about constituent structure, *every city* does not c-command *one person* without the application of covert movement (QR). If sentences like (229) are to be compatible with the strong claim that covert movement cannot be what underlies such scope phenomena, then certain such assumptions must be given up.[127]

NOTES

The core ideas of this article originated in class lectures at Harvard University in the fall of 1995 and were subsequently presented in class lectures at UCLA in January 1996, at the 1996 Girona Summer School, at the Graduate Center of CUNY in the fall of 1996, at Rutgers University in the spring of 1997, at the University of Venice in May 1997, and at the LSA Institute in the summer of 1997 and in talks at ZAS, Berlin, in November 1996 and at the University of Paris VIII/ENS and at GLOW, Rabat, in March 1997. I am indebted to all those audiences for stimulating comments and questions.

1. See also Christensen and Taraldsen (1989, 72ff.).

2. As in Jónsson's (1996, 86) proposal for comparable facts in Icelandic; see Haegeman (1995, chap. 4). For a recent argument in favor of NegP, see Potsdam (1997).

3. As suggested for the corresponding Icelandic construction by Rögnvaldsson (1987, 45); cf. Jónsson (1996, 92).

A similar point (concerning overt movement of an object masked by verb movement) is made for Italian *tutto* ('everything') by Belletti (1990, 77ff.), Rizzi (1996, 82ff.), and Cinque (1995, chap. 9) and by Pollock (1989, 369) and Déprez (1994, note 22) for French *tout/rien* ('everything'/'nothing').

4. Like these varieties of Norwegian is Icelandic, in which sentences like (13) are "completely normal", as Rögnvaldsson (1987) states in his discussion. See also Christensen and Taraldsen (1989, 72).

5. For recent discussion, see Holmberg (1999). It remains to be understood how best to express the variation within Scandinavian concerning (13) and (14), in particular since there seems to be no comparable variation in the case of pronouns and definite DPs, which can never appear to the left of the relevant verb. This contrast between negative phrase movement and pronoun movement in Scandinavian recalls the French contrast between movement of *tout/tous/rien* ('everything/all/nothing') and clitic movement, with the latter more restricted, in ways discussed in Kayne (1975; 1980a; 1981b).

6. This sentence is marginally acceptable in the irrelevant (though interesting) reading parallel to *I'm sure he has it read by now*.

7. I find examples with nonfinite *be* of intermediate acceptability (e.g. *?John has been no Einstein*, *?John will be no Einstein*). This is presumably related to the fact that nonfinite *be* seems to be able to raise, to some extent. Thus, some varieties of English (not mine) allow *John will be always happy* (cf. Pollock (1989, 382)), in addition to *John will always be happy*. This variation contrasts with the perhaps general acceptability of *John will be happy and Bill will be, too*, which might also depend on *be* raising (cf. Lobeck (1995, 150)). Also relevant may be, in a context with less parallelism, in my English, *John may be happy today, but he won't *(be) tomorrow*; this seems to go beyond the restriction discussed by Lasnik (1995a, 263ff.).

8. Possessive *have* is normally taken not to raise in American English, which does not normally allow *Has John a car?* or *John hasn't any car*. On the other hand, some degree of raising seems available, quite apart from (26), given (a) *I haven't the faintest idea*, (b) *Does John have any students this year? ?No, but he has had (in the past)* and (c) *Do you have a car? ?Of course I have!* vs. *Do you own a car? *Of course I own!*.

9. The overtness of the movement and the fact that it is a phonetically visible phrase that is moved are at the heart of this article. That the landing site should properly be labeled Spec,NegP (as opposed, for example, to Spec,FocP, or to Spec,*is* ('also'/Hungarian) as in Brody (1990, 118ff.)) should be taken as an additional, less central, claim.

(On the question of whether NegP should be taken to be a subcase of SigmaP or PolP, cf. Laka (1990) and Zanuttini (1997).)

10. This may be an instance of pied-piping in Chomsky's (1995, 262ff.) sense. The lexical verb in English cannot raise by head movement, yet it must move; consequently the whole VP moves. For a similar idea concerning Malagasy, see Pearson (1997b).

On VP-preposing and similar movements, cf., among others, Larson (1988), den Besten and Webelhuth (1987; 1990), Huang (1993), den Dikken (1995a; 1995c), Koopman (1993; 1997), Endo (to appear), Barbiers (1995), Costa (1997), Slack and Lebeaux (1996), Cinque (1999, chap.1), Duffield (1995), Hinterhölzl (1997), Koopman and Szabolcsi (1997), and Sportiche (1995b).

The contrast between English and the varieties of Norwegian that allow (13) and (14) (those examples show neither lexical verb movement nor verb phrase movement) remains to be understood.

Note that there is a sense in which VP-movement does not cross a 'negative island', since the VP moves into Spec,Neg + X (cf. (91)ff.); for recent discussion of negative islands, see Kuno and Takami (1997).

11. It is likely that before reaching Spec,NegP *no novels* passes through a case-licensing position. On English having overt Case-licensing movement for objects, see Johnson (1991).

From the perspective of Chomsky (1995, p. 232), movement to Spec,NegP would involve checking of a *neg* feature taken to be a variant of D, as he suggests for *wh*.

I will be setting aside the (ultimately important) question of how and when exactly the subject (*John* in (29)) is merged into the derivation. For relevant discussion, see den Dikken (1996).

12. Or perhaps some maximal projection (e.g., AspP) larger than VP.

13. In allowing a trace to be removed from the c-command domain of its antecedent by subsequent movement of a phrase properly containing that trace, I follow den Besten and Webelhuth (1987; 1990). For recent more detailed argument, see Müller (1998). See also Franks and Progovac (1994) and Androutsopoulou (1997); also Bianchi (1993, 362) on a suggestion by L. Rizzi that Italian has some VP-topicalization after V has raised; see Cinque (1999) on *Tutto bene a TUTTI dovrai spiegare* ('everything well to everybody you-will-have-to explain'). Relevant, too, are many of the references mentioned in note 10, as well as Longobardi (1985, 178) on Italian parasitic gaps.

Note that the German/Dutch remnant topicalization construction studied by den Besten and Webelhuth exists to some extent in English, in cases like:

(i)   (I thought he would speak to Mary) ?and spoken/speak he has to that beautiful woman.

This contrasts with the following, for reasons of preposition stranding (cf. (93)–(96))):

(ii)   . . . *and spoken/speak to he has that beautiful woman.

A proper binding condition on traces has been made plausible by the standard non-derivational approach to Binding Theory, which may itself not be right; see the last part of note 121.

14. If Chomsky (1995, 340) is correct in saying that precedence comes into play only at Spellout, then a more accurate way of putting things would be: The output of the two movements has X preceding NegDP, whereas in the absence of any movement, X would have followed NegDP.

15. For relevant discussion in the area of derived nominals, see Hoekstra (1996).

16. For relevant discussion, see Johnson (1994; 1996). Koopman (1995) has suggested that the Dutch particle moves qua VP (i.e., what moves is a VP containing the particle and the trace of V) to a lower position than PredP, which I think is compatible with the text discussion (conceivably the Dutch particle might have two options). Also important here, though more indirectly, is Svenonius (1996) on Scandinavian particles. For recent discussion of incorporated particles, as in *overrun*, see Vanden Wyngaerd (1996).

17. It is possible that PredP is not immediately above VP; see Kayne (1994, 52) on Dutch and German having V-raising to AGR-S. If PredP is separated from VP by some XP, then VP-preposing in the text might turn out to be XP-preposing. See note 12.

Predicate raising may be relevant to the prohibition against small clauses as objects of prepositions mentioned in Kayne (1985, 123), and may be in competition with Stowell (1991).

18. In a way that recalls clitic climbing in Romance.

The text examples are taken from van Riemsdijk (1978, 54) and Koopman (1995).

19. See Kayne (1985). For recent discussion of Scandinavian particle constructions, see Svenonius (1996).

20. See Pollock (1996).

21. Whether Dutch has VP/PredP-preposing in other contexts is a separate question. For relevant discussion, see Barbiers (1995).

Note that no Germanic language has the order 'Prt (Neg)DP V'. This follows if particles cannot move any further than PredP, a conclusion already reached (apart from some cases of topicalization) by den Besten and Webelhuth.

22. Left open is the question why (i) is not natural (except perhaps with strong stress on *no linguist*):

(i)   ?John considers smart no linguist.

Note that in (ii) the phrase *no linguist* in Spec,NegP asymmetrically c-commands the phrase *any smarter* . . . in Spec,PredP, so that the standard c-command configuration for *no . . . any* licensing continues to hold under this approach (and this is so independent of whether adjuncts are complement-like, thus neutralizing Larson's (1988) *any*-based argument in favor of treating adjuncts like complements; cf. Williams (1994, 180ff). A different approach to adjuncts was suggested in Kayne (1994, 147) but not pursued far enough there. See Sportiche (1995b, 378) and Barbiers (1995) for related proposals):

(ii)   You consider no linguist any smarter than yourself.

Similarly for (iii):

(iii)   John solved none of the problems any more quickly than we did.

Less clear is the proper characterization of:

(iv)   ?You consider no smarter than yourself any linguist who . . .

(v)   ?John solved no more quickly than we did any of the problems that came up the other day.

Given the proposed derivation for wide scope negation in section 1.5, the impossibility of (vi) reinforces the idea familiar from cases like *Anything has nobody done* that *no . . . any* licensing shows no reconstruction effects:

(vi)   *In all these years, they've requested that anyone revise no article.

Example (vii) seems less bad:

(vii)   ??They said they wouldn't do anything and do anything they won't.

Perhaps there can be an abstract NegP within the preposed constituent (cf. note 63), recalling Progovac (1993; 1994, 66ff.).

23. VP-movement around neg in English might be significantly similar to the movement of the complement of Neg⁰ (AspP; cf. note 12) to Spec,Neg proposed by Nkemnji (1995) for Nweh; see Koopman (1996). See also the Dutch dialect with a final negative morpheme mentioned in Haegeman and Zanuttini (1996, 162).

24. This is similar to distinctions made by Beghelli and Stowell (1997) (although theirs are in terms of LF movement, for English).

25. With respect to *any*, the question is whether (i) and (iii) can have the interpretation of (ii) and (iv):

(i)   I don't think anybody is bound to be there.

(ii)   I don't think there's bound to be anybody there.

(iii)   the only time when anybody is bound to be there

(iv)   the only time when there's bound to be anybody there

The judgment is not clear to me, however, in particular because (ii) and (iv) are themselves not very natural.

Since *every* is not compatible with *there*, one has to ask directly whether (v) has a narrow scope interpretation:

(v)   Everybody is bound to be there (by now).

I think it does, in which case we would conclude that (vi), like (43), need not involve overt raising of *everybody* plus VP-preposing:

(vi)   John saw everybody.

This may be related to the fact that the Japanese *-mo* that corresponds to English *every* precedes the case-marker in *Daremo ga . . .*—v. Nishigauchi (1992, 198ff.), Kawashima (1993, note 10).

Unlike (v), (vii) seems clearly not to have the narrow scope interpretation:

(vii)   Not everybody is bound to be there.

The conclusion is that if *not everybody* is a phrase, it has the behavior of *nobody* rather than the behavior of *everybody*. If it is not a phrase, then *not* must be unable to raise from embedded to matrix sentence with predicates like *bound* (cf. note 26).

A related but separate question is why (viii) does not allow 'reconstruction' below *not*:

(viii)   Everybody is bound not to be there.

This perhaps recalls French (cf. Kayne (1975, sect. 1.4), Bonneau and Zushi (1993)):

(ix)   *Il a essayé de tout ne pas dire. ('he has tried to everything neg not say')

Presumably (x) has two NegP, and similarly for (xi) (cf. note 83):

(x)   He did NOT see nobody

(xi)   ?He gave nobody nothing (but he did give several people very little).

I leave open the question of (xii), which is for me appreciably more difficult than (x):

(xii)   *Nobody did NOT see him.

26. Note that the facts are different for *seem*, that is, both *nobody* and *somebody* seem to allow narrow scope in:

(i)   Nobody seems to be there.

(ii)   Somebody seems to be there.

This must be related to the fact that *seem* is a 'neg-raising' verb (cf. Horn (1989)), that is, to the fact that the following are (virtually) synonymous:

(iii)   John doesn't seem to be there.

(iv)   John seems not to be there.

Whereas (v) and (vi) are not:

(v)   John isn't bound to be there.

(vi)   John is bound not to be there.

In the text terms, the apparent narrow scope reading of (i) must be compatible with a matrix NegP (and not require an embedded NegP).

27. For relevant discussion, see Jónsson (1996, 196).

28. The formulation in the text implies that in a sentence like *No linguist came to the party*, *no linguist* is either in Spec of some NegP or else has moved through it, though, in the latter case, there would be (cf. Jónsson (1996, 87)) a conflict with the proposed account for (44), unless the subsequent landing site was not an A-position.

29. See Kayne (1981b, note 7); whether the long-distance movement of (51)–(56) takes place successive cyclically remains to be determined. For an argument that it does not pass through Spec,CP (in the French examples), see section 2.2 of that article. (Roberts (1997, 441) suggests a way in which it might.)

On the other hand, Bayer (1990, 194) gives *It was required that we study only Spanish* as impossible with wide scope. It does seem as if wide scope there is more difficult than in (*In high school*) *they required that we study only Spanish*. If so, that suggests that successive cyclicity is involved (at least in subjunctive cases), thinking of somewhat similar contrasts discussed by Kayne (1980b, sect. 1).

30. It is probably significant that both *rien* and *tout* are monomorphemic in French, unlike their English translations. Whether the landing site for movement of *rien* is Spec,NegP is left an open question (cf. note 102).

31. See Kayne (1975, sect. 1.4).

32. Some speakers don't find a contrast between (59) and (60) (and similarly for (62) and (63)). It may be that those speakers have more extended possibilities for predicate rais-

ing, related perhaps to the more extended use of clefted predicates in Irish English; see Trudgill and Hannah (1994, 107).

33. As noted earlier in (38), particles in Dutch can raise out of certain infinitival complements. On the probably similar clitic climbing found in Romance, see chapter 4 and references cited there.

34. Just as clitics cannot raise out of finite embedded sentences in Romance (with the notable exception of the finite control case discussed by Terzi (1996)). On speaker variation, see note 32.

35. Note that in (i) it seems possible for *he* to take *John* as antecedent:

(i) In all these years, she's requested that he revise none/not a single one of the articles that John has written for her journal

This supports the idea that, in the wide scope reading, the NegDP (*none/not a single one of the articles that John has written for her journal*) moves into the matrix, past the embedded subject.

36. Thinking again of clitic climbing, we might expect wide scope negation in English to be possible with modals, even with a following particle. Thus (i) should be better with wide scope for *noone* than (60)/(63), which I think is correct:

(i) John could turn noone down.

In the wide-scope derivation of this example, *down* raises to the PredP above *could* (followed by *noone* raising to Spec,NegP above *could*, and then by preposing of *could turn t t* to a Spec position above that NegP).

37. Some speakers seem to allow it, for reasons that I do not understand. (Conceivably, there is an ECM effect of an unclear sort.)

38. I will set aside the (important) question of whether it is the ECP that is at issue, or some other (kind of) constraint.

Note that to reach the word order in (65), preposing of *not a single student* would have to be preceded by preposing of *read our book* to the matrix Spec,PredP. Cf. note 122.

39. In Italian, both with negation and with *only*, the contrast with objects holds for preverbal subjects, but not for postverbal subjects. See Longobardi (1992, 153–154), Rizzi (1982a, chap. 4); this does not bear on the text discussion.

40. See Bayer (1996, 60).

41. See Klima (1964a, 311).

42. The output order would be unaffected if we started with '. . . V Prt *only* . . .'.

43. Particle preposing is to be interpreted as a subcase of a more general phenomenon (cf. the discussion of (34)).

44. See note 42.

45. Jones (1993, 368, note 6) indicates a full * for (comparable examples with) *even*. Bayer (1996, 40 (note 15), 52) takes them to be 'marked' but well formed.

Bayer (p. 106) (cf. Longobardi (1992, 158)) notes that the Italian counterpart of (85) is unacceptable:

(i) *Gianni ha parlato con solo Maria.

Guglielmo Cinque has pointed out to me that (ii) is even worse:

(ii) **Gianni non ha parlato con che Maria. ('G neg has spoken with but/than M')

Thus (ii) must involve, in addition to the P-stranding violation of (i), some extra violation having to do with the special empty category associated with the *non . . . che* construction, on which see Azoulay-Vicente (1985).

46. Stephanie Harves tells me that Russian and Czech do not allow the counterpart of (84) with a preposition. (Rather, one has the equivalent of *J spoke only to one linguist.*) This suggests that, in those languages, *only* is (perhaps for case-related reasons) invariably a VP-external head in such examples, with a derivation like that in (92).

The closest Russian counterpart of *She spoke with no one* is (cf. Harves (1998)), abstracting away from the position of the verb:

(i)   Ona ni s kem ne govorila. ('she neg with whom neg spoke')

Impossible is:

(ii)   *Ona s nikem ne govorila.

This clearly indicates that in Russian *ni* and *kem* cannot form a constituent. (*Kem* is presumably parallel to the French and Chinese indefinites mentioned in note 102.) *Ni* is probably not a simple negative but rather two morphemes best thought of as similar to English *not even* (cf. Benmamoun (1996), Choe (1997), and Acquaviva (1995, note 9) on negation in Moroccan Arabic, Korean, and Vulgar Latin, respectively), so the attraction of *s kem* by *ni* in (i) would partially resemble (cf. also (100)):

(iii)   Not even to John would we have shown our article.

(iv)   *To not even John would we have shown our article.

Thinking of note 59, we see that in two respects *not even* does not act like a complex head:

(v)   *John not even likes linguistics.

(vi)   *Not even does John like linguistics.

Thus, it may be that the attracting element in (iii) is *not*, in which case the attracted phrase would be *even to John*, but that would take us too far afield.

47. Note that this does not imply that *Bill* is merged as complement of V. Also to be considered is a generalized Larsonian (1988) analysis, whereby every argument starts out in a Spec position, in which case, if that argument is above the lexical V, the S-H-C order of Kayne (1994) does not always directly translate as SVO even for simple VPs, contrary to what has sometimes been assumed; for relevant discussion, see Takano (1996).

48. See in part Haegeman (1996).

49. Barbiers (1995, 71) discussed sentences like (i), noting that (the Dutch counterpart of) *at least* seems to be a phrase rather than a head:

(i)   John spoke to at least ten linguists.

However, the text claim that *only* must be a head holds only for those cases in which *only* is an attractor generated above VP. If (ii) is to be analyzed as strongly parallel to (87), with *at least* outside VP and attracting *Bill*, then I must take *at least* in (ii) to be a head with internal structure, rather than a phrase:

(ii)   ?John criticized at least Bill.

The text account of (87) has in common with Barbiers's the idea that the phrase focused by *only* is in Spec,*only* at some point in the derivation. It differs from his in having that phrase move to Spec,*only* from within VP and in having that movement always be overt.
 50. Strictly speaking, I leave open the question whether the *only* that seems to be 'DP'—internal (as in (84)) has the same feature.
 Possibly, *only* has the feature +w only when it acts as an attractor.
 51. On P-stranding in middles, see Keyser and Roeper (1984, 400), who consider it marginally possible, however. On P-stranding with 'heavy-NP shift', see Bresnan (1976, 33). On the latter construction, see the discussion of (168).
 52. See Kayne (1994, 76) and Lasnik (1995b), for whom sentences like (95) are marginally acceptable.
 53. Which also involves leftward movement of the remnant, if Johnson (1994; 1996) is correct.
 54. Pseudo-passives also depend on some property highly specific to English prepositions (cf. chapter 7, sect. 7.1.2.).
 55. See Chomsky (1977).
 56. See Rögnvaldsson (1987) and Jónsson (1996, 83) on Icelandic and Christensen (1986, 29) on Norwegian.
 A fully satisfactory theory of P-stranding awaits future work.
 57. This derivation and the examples in (83) and (8)/(9)/(16) are unavailable in Scandinavian. Since (much) Scandinavian has negative phrase preposing, the locus of the difference may be the absence of +w on the Scandinavian abstract Neg^0.
 At least some Scandinavian has +w with *only*, i.e. has sentences like (87). Yet, it seems that no Scandinavian has *I have only John seen today*, in which *only* would have attracted *John* without VP-preposing subsequently coming into play. Why *only* differs in this respect from Neg^0 remains to be understood.
 As in note 50, we may want to say that English Neg^0 has the feature +w only when it is an attractor—but see later in this chapter.
 Jónsson (1996, 84) has an example of neg phrase movement of a PP:

(i)   María hefur um ekkert annadh taladh í meira en viku. ('M has about nothing else talked for more than (a) week')

 58. Obviously, negation and *a single N* do not always form a constituent—*J didn't speak to a single linguist*. See also *?He spoke not to a single linguist*.
 59. Apparently similar to these are:

(i)   I saw not only John, but Bill, too.

(ii)   I spoke not only to John, but to Bill, too.

(iii)   ??I spoke to not only John, but Bill, too.

These suggest that *not only* can be a complex head (cf. note 74). That it is a complex unit of some sort must be the case, given:

(iv)   *Only is John intelligent.

(v)   *Not is John intelligent.

(vi)   Not only is John intelligent, . . .

Another case of verb second apparently licensed by a preceding head is the Yiddish verb topicalization discussed by Davis and Prince (1986).

60. However, if matrix *not* attracted the entire infinitive phrase, one would get *J has refused not to read Aspects but to read LSLT*. If one in addition allowed 'gapping' there, one could perhaps reach (104) with matrix *not*.

61. Thinking of the preceding footnote, one can perhaps have *She has requested that they not read a single linguistics book, but rather listen to several concerts*, to the extent that *not* can attract a VP.

62. See Chomsky (1995, chap. 4).

63. See (198). Relevant is the question whether overt movement of *not* is actually possible in 'neg-raising' sentences such as *I don't think he's here* (cf. note 26) and (with a possible copy):

(i)   He's not here, I don't think.

(ii)   (He's going to tell secrets tonight.) Not about us he's not.

(iii)   He's not real smart, John isn't. (cf. Kayne (1994, 78))

Another kind of case where raising of neg might be attractive is:

(iv)   I don't think that to anyone else would he have been willing to tell the truth.

64. See Bayer (1996, 55) and the references cited there.

65. More precisely, this is true if *only* attracts *Aspects*. A derivation of the sort under consideration could produce (109) if matrix *only* could attract the embedded VP.

66. In the examples at hand, nothing moves into Spec,W, raising the question of what exactly triggers VP-preposing in cases discussed earlier.

As before, I omit consideration of *but*. . . .

Also left open is the question of how exactly to license auxiliary-raising. One possibility (not incorporated into (112) is that the auxiliary is actually attracted by *not/only,* to which it adjoins; after *not/only* attracts *to John* to its Spec, *not/only* excorporates (cf. Roberts (1991)), raising to W and stranding the auxiliary.

A problem for such excorporation is the sort of sentence discussed by Haegeman (1996):

(i)   ?On no account during the holidays will I do that.

I find this somewhat possible with left-dislocation of an argument:

(ii)   ?Not once, that book, has he praised it in public.

Similarly for wh-movement:

(iii)   ?What else, with no money to speak of, could he possibly have done?

(iv)   ??How often, that book, has he praised it in public?

Examples (ii) and (iv) are substantially worse if *it* is omitted.

67. Put another way, these show that *only John* (and *not John*) is not a constituent. Additional examples are:

(i)   *From only John would they steal any money.

(ii)   *On only John can you rely unconditionally.

(iii)   *On only Sundays are all the stores closed.

68. They are probably still in Spec,$\text{Neg}^0/\text{Only}^0$, where $\text{Neg}^0/\text{Only}^0$ is phonetically unrealized, although it is conceivable that they have moved further up (cf. note 28).

69. Note, however, the contrast between the following, reminiscent of an ECP effect:

(i)   ??Not John has she criticized, but Paul.

(ii)   *Not John criticized her, but Paul.

(Cf. Nelson (1997) on exclamatives.) It remains to be understood why there is no comparable effect with *only*, or with the other cases of *not* to be discussed later.

Despite the * of (ii), (iii) is acceptable:

(iii)   Not John, but Paul, criticized her.

As Klima (1964a, 303) has argued, *Paul* here is probably the immediate subject of *criticized* (despite the punctuation and intonation; see the discussion of RNR in Kayne (1994, 67)).

70. This is not meant to imply that any subpart whatsoever can be focused. For relevant discussion, see Brody (1990, 101), Koizumi (1993, 411), and Barbiers (1995 chap. 3) Note also Barss et al.'s (1992, 33) suggestion that contrastive (negative) focus does not involve extraction (in their terms, covert); in the text terms, focusing of a subpart does not (necessarily) involve movement of the subpart of any sort, as seems clear from examples like *John is only doing PRE-doctoral work this year.*

Note that the derivation in (120), combined with the idea that there can be only one Spec (phrasal adjunction) per head, as in Kayne (1994), accounts for the impossibility of (i):

(i)   *Only probably John came to the party.

(I assume that, once *only* raises to W, both it and W can move no further.) On adverbs as Specs, see Cinque (1999).

71. If this is the correct approach to (121), then raising V across *only* would be expected to be impossible, unless excorporation is permitted (cf. note 66). Whether it is possible or not is difficult to test in English. Benincà and Salvi (1988, 122) give examples that indicate that it is in Italian. For example, the following can have VP scope for *solo*:

(i)   La segretaria ha messo solo dei fiori sul tuo tavolo. ('the secretary has put only some flowers on-the your table')

72. This approach to (125) would differ from those of Pollock (1989, 405) and Chomsky (1995, chap. 2).

The negation element of the other Germanic languages would differ from *not* in this respect. Thinking of the negation element as a potential attractor of VP leads to the expectation that it might end up following VP in some nearby language. See note 23.

73. See Klima (1964a, 271–273), Postal (1974, 94ff.).

74. The impossibility of (127) would then in part be due to the fact that *not* (as usual) cannot be generated within VP, in part to the fact that *not all/every X* cannot be introduced as a constituent, and in part to some still to be understood incompatibility between attraction of *everyone* and VP-preposing.

On the other hand, (i) and (ii) seem less clearly bad than (113) and (114):

(i)   ??To not everybody has he told the truth.

(ii)   ??To not all his friends has he told the truth,

If these are better than (127), it may alternatively be that *not all/every X* can (sometimes) be a constituent, though incompatible with the VP-preposing derivation.

On the potential nonconstituent status of *not every/all X,* see also E. Kiss (1992, 122, 129) (who takes Hungarian *nem* ('not') to be adjoined to VP, however).

Catalan, as Manuel Español-Echevarría has brought to my attention, can have *Not every . . .* as *No pas tots . . .* (with two negative morphemes), perhaps suggesting that *no pas* can be a complex head. See note 59; alternatively, see the latter part of note 46.

75. The parallel sentence with *only* does not seem very possible (though note Barbiers (1995, 68–69) on Dutch), for unclear reasons. It is possible to have:

(i)   Only, he went to Paris.

but not with a focusing interpretation on any constituent of IP: (i) is perhaps to be related to:

(ii)   The only thing is, he went to Paris.

Anderson (1972, 899) has an example of apparent S focus:

(iii)   . . . and Harvard has even been holding pep rallies.

It may be that the focused constituent here does not include the auxiliary, in which case, given a VP-internal trace of the subject, (iii) might be an instance of VP-focus under reconstruction, that is, of VP moving to Spec,*even,* as in (132). Derivative from this, perhaps, is the possibility for the subject to be focused in:

(iv)   John could even have done it.

This is perhaps related to the possibility of taking the topicalized consituent as focus of *even* in:

(v)   John, they even consider intelligent.

Again, *only* is different; see Aoun and Li (1993, 206).

76. For some interesting cases of Italian *soltanto* ('only') that lend themselves to the text approach, see Longobardi (1992, note 25).

Strictly speaking, if some phrase lower than *John* is focused in (134), the phrase attracted could be smaller than IP.

77. Similarly, in (132) VP must be not the complement of *even* but rather the specifier of some functional head below *even*.

78. Just as *only Bill* (and similarly *even Bill*) never is; see the discussion of (85), as well as Brody's (1990, 114ff.) earlier proposal of the same sort concerning Hungarian XP + *is* ('also'). For an extension of this idea to Japanese *wa, ga* and *o*, see Kayne (1994, 143), Whitman (1999); a further extension might be to at least some *mo* and *ka* (cf. the references to Japanese cited in note 25).

I suggested there that *only one N* can be a constituent (and similarly now for *even one N* in cases like *John didn't speak to even one linguist*). *Too* doesn't seem to combine with numerals in this way.

79. See chapter 7, sect. 7.1.2.

80. Comparable facts hold for *even*.

81. See the 'heavy NP shift' example:

(i)   *John gave a book the same person I did.

This is not surprising since the derivations in (148) and (151) are very much like that proposed by den Dikken (1995a) for 'heavy NP shift'. On the question of landing site, see note 93.

As for the question why (149) and (*i*) are not possible, part of the answer is probably that extraction of the indirect object is in fact never possible in English from its position in between verb and direct object, but that is beyond the scope of this article. See Kayne (1983c, esp. note 9), den Dikken (1995b: 1995c).

82. The head W into whose Spec the VP raises does not have *too* raising up to it, contrary to the cases of *only* and neg discussed earlier.

83. Beyond the scope of this article is a systematic study of multiple occurrences of *only*, *even, too* (cf. the last part of note 25 on negation), which are sometimes possible, sometimes not (cf. Anderson (1972, 894, 904). Brody (1990, 114), and Longobardi (1992, 169)):

(i)   ?Only John speaks only French, here.

(ii)   ?He'd even only/*only even speak English, if he had to.

(iii)   *He gave only Bill only his first article.

(The contrast in (ii) recalls Brody (p. 95) on the Hungarian focus field having *is* ('also') and its associated phrase precede *csak* ('only') and its associated phrase.) Apparently different from (ii) is:

(iv)   ?John speaks only French even to Bill.

(v)   *John speaks even French only to Bill.

However, the left-to-right order is misleading. Example (iv) almost certainly involves merging *only* before *even* (and (v) merging *even* before *only*), so that (iv) is actually, hierarchically speaking, akin to the *even only* case of (ii).

The contrast between (i) and (iii) must be attributable to the fact that (iii), but not (i), involves two instances of VP-preposing (more exactly XP-preposing, where XP equals or contains VP—v. note 23).

84. I leave open the question whether it is particle preposing per se that yields the observed deviance or rather a locality effect (on either movement of *Bill* or movement of VP or both) induced by the presence of the moved particle in PredP.

85. And a particle that is not a true (compositional) locative: for example, the *away* of *throw away* seems to me to prepose more readily than the *up* of *look up* when it comes to what I am calling particle preposing:

(i)   What he threw away was he threw away an apple.

(ii)   (?)What he threw away was he threw an apple away.

Example (ii) seems to me to be better than (iv), with a non(-compositional) locative (in the sense of *choose*, e.g., in a fruit market):

(iii) What he picked out was he picked out an apple.

(iv)   ?What he picked out was he picked an apple out.

(It may be that specificity is also relevant.)
    The contrast in preposability is sharper still in the case of preposing of the topicalization sort: . . . *and away he threw it* vs. *. . . and up he looked it.*
    86. See Horvath (1995) and other articles in the same volume.
    87. Such as Hungarian; see note 86.
    I take VP-preposing to come into play in English in all cases of (this kind of) focus on an object. It may be that subject focussing of this kind does not involve VP-preposing. Relevant is the status of sentences such as:

(i)   ?What fell was an apple fell.

See also Gueron (1980); Sportiche (1995b, 391).
    88. On the landing site, see note 9. I take 'of the (standard) English sort' to mean at least phrases that convey negation without the presence of a negative morpheme on the verb or auxiliary. For recent discussion of one variety of English that does need such a negative morpheme, see Sells et al. (1996).
    For recent discussion of negation in Romance, see Bosque (1992). Zanuttint (1997), and Déprez (1997a; 1997b).
    It might be that an English type derivation is appropriate in Romance only for what Bosque calls echo negation and for long-distance negation (where 'long-distance' includes at the minimum cases that cross a finite clause boundary).
    89. For a good example of how much phonology and syntax can diverge in their treatment of affixes (i.e., where 'X-affix Y' has the affix phonologically grouped with X but syntactically grouped with Y), see Anderson (1984).
    90. Testability of these conjectures assumes prior identification in a given language of counterparts of *only* and similar words. This need not be straightforward, thinking, for example, of the very common French *ne . . . que* construction, which translates well using *only* but is syntactically more like *not . . . (other) than*; see note 45.
    91. Den Dikken points out, correctly, that the approach to Heavy-NP Shift taken in Kayne (1994, 71ff.) does not extend in any natural way to 'long-distance' cases like (i) (cf. Postal (1974, 92n)):

(i)   John has expected to find since 1939 the treasure that . . .

    92. H^0 is mnemonic for 'heavy': beyond the scope of this essay is the question how exactly to characterize 'heaviness' and why such a notion should be relevant to the syntax at all.

Also set aside is the question whether H should be identified with Foc; see Rochemont & Culicover (1990).

On the interaction between Heavy-NP Shift and preposition stranding, see Kayne (1994, 74) and the earlier discussion of (85)–(94).

93. Den Dikken (1995a) proposes for Heavy-NP Shift that VP-preposing lands in the Spec of a PP adjunct, following ideas of Barbiers (1995). That approach will not generalize, however, to the various cases discussed earlier, such as *John saw only Bill*, in which there is no PP present.

94. Perhaps there is a link here to the apparent optionality of scrambling.

95. Left open at present is the question why the degree of deviance here is greater (cf. Fraser 1966, 59)).

96. See Groos and van Riemsdijk (1981, 184) and Hirschbühler and Rivero (1983, 515).

97. On the latter, see Bayer (1990, 108ff.), who notes that this restriction does not apply to sentential adjuncts such as conditional *if*-clauses.

98. This would become a straightforward 'never' if apparent cases of postverbal DPs in Dutch and German turned out to all be linked to an invisible preverbal counterpart of *the following N*, thinking of English sentences like:

(i)   I'm going to introduce the following people to John: . . .

Left open is how best to allow for those various 'extraposed' phrases (including the . . . of (i) that do follow the (non V-2) verb in Dutch and German. If Barbiers (1995) is right, then VP-preposing might be at work in those cases; v. note 93.

99. Some varieties of German (like Dutch) allow P-stranding if what is moved is an R-pronoun, but this is not relevant to the text discussion.

100. See Herburger (1993), modulo her taking the landing site to be Spec.FocP, where FocP is selected by (various focussing elements like) *nur*.

101. For reasons related to its 'V-final' property; see Koster (1986).

102. I am indebted to Anders Holmberg and Thorbjörg Hróarsdóttir for the Swedish and Icelandic judgments, respectively.

In Icelandic, but not in Swedish, the infinitive itself raises past the landing site of the negative phrase; see Platzack (1986), Thráinsson (1986), and Rögnvaldsson and Thráinsson (1990, 19).

Minimally different from (195) is French (cf. Kayne (1981a, note 4)):

(i)   (?)Jean n'a envie de rien faire. ('J neg has desire to nothing do')

To judge by the position of the negative morpheme *n'*, *rien* ('nothing') would appear to have matrix scope, despite having moved overtly to a landing site within the infinitive phrase. The conclusion, I think, is that, in the presence of *n'* at least, *rien* is not a negative phrase and, more precisely, does not need to move to Spec,NegP; see Déprez (1997a; 1997b), as well as Cheng (1994; 1995) and Li (1992) on Chinese *shenme*; also note 30. (From this perspective, the best English gloss for *rien* in (i) would be 'thing'.)

Like (195)/(196) is, where negation has only narrow scope:

(ii)   ?They insist that not a single linguistics book should he give to his students.

103. The implications of these for expletives appear to favor an approach along lines proposed by Andrea Moro; see Moro (1997) and, for partially similar ideas, Hoekstra and Mulder (1990) and Basilico (1997).

An approach to quantifier scope stated in terms of indexing (cf. van Riemsdijk and Williams (1981) and Williams (1994, 69)) would raise the same kind of questions as (197) and lead to the same kind of answer as in (198).

Locality considerations of the sort alluded to in (198b) probably argue against van Riemsdijk and Williams's (1981) movement of French negative *ne*—see note 88—and similarly for Chomsky's (1973, 242) suggestion concerning movement of *not* in *not . . . many.*

On (198b), see in part Bošković (1998).

104. Recall from the last paragraph of section 13.3.5. that Dutch and German (and, by extension, West Flemish and Swiss German, I assume) do not use VP-preposing in the constructions under discussion. It is therefore clear that *geen vlees* in (199) is within the infinitive sentence.

105. See Postma (1994) on Dutch. Empty operator movement (from within the wh-phrase(s) not in Spec,CP) might be of interest for the similarity between *What did who put where?* and parasitic gaps discussed in Kayne (1983a):see Sportiche (1995b, 390). On the other hand, the fact that English lacks the wh-as-indefinite construction discussed by Postma might mean that English and Dutch have different analyses of multiple wh; for example, English, rather than (or perhaps in addition to) using an empty operator, might subject the wh-in-situ to focus movement; see the discussion of (158)ff. Relevant is the status of:

(i)   Now we know who put off who(m).

(ii)   ?Now we know who put who(m) off.

For additional argument against LF-movement for wh-in-situ, see Aoun and Li (1993), Simpson (1995).

The general question of empty operator movement and island constraints is beyond the scope of this essay; for relevant discussion, see Brody (1995).

The fact that (iii) has no multiple wh-interpretation might mean that the presence of an empty operator is incompatible with movement to a + wh Spec,CP:

(iii)   Who was asking where to go?

106. This empty operator must be a phrase, not a head, on grounds of nonlocality of movement. That *some/any/no* could well be phrases is suggested by the appearance of French *en* in (i), from the perspective of Juan Uriagereka's suggested generalization of the 'movement to Spec,*de/of*' analysis of chapter 7—v. Kayne (1994, 161):

(i)   Paul n'en a aucun, ('P neg of-them has no/none')

Note also that the French counterpart of *no* is *aucun,* which could well be bimorphemic, with the second being *un* ('one').

107. Worth considering is the possibility that so-called partial wh-movement, recently studied by Horvath (1997), involves movement of an overt counterpart to the empty operator in question. (In wh-in-situ in the Indo-Aryan languages—cf. Bayer (1996, chap. 7) and references cited there—empty operator movement out of an 'extraposed' sentence complement must be unavailable. The possibility of wh-in-situ in a post-V adjunct (Bayer, p. 282) may indicate that the adjunct is not embedded; cf. the second paragraph of note 22.)

Both German *was* ('what') (in partial wh-movement sentences) and the empty operator in multiple wh sentences have their movement blocked by negation; see Beck and Kim (1997, 344), where the constraint is, however, formulated in terms of LF movement.

Partial wh-movement may well be present in English, too, in sentences like (i), with an empty operator (counterpart of *what*) preceding the second auxiliary:

(i)   Where did he go, do you think?

The embedded verb would have as its argument the phrase [Op *where*], with that phrase moving to a -wh Spec,CP, followed by movement of Op (a maximal projection) to the higher + wh Spec,CP (followed by preposing of the entire embedded CP).

Bayer's (1996, 229) examples with an apparent copy, such as (ii), might then start out with a constituent [*wer wer*], part of which would, in the course of the derivation, be split off by movement:

(ii)   Wer glaubst du wer uns besuchen will? ('who think you who us to-visit wants' = 'Who do you think wants to visit us?')

108. I take this consideration to also exclude the kind of analysis of English adopted by Haegeman (1995, 185ff.), with an empty operator in Spec,NegP coindexed (without movement) with, for example, postverbal *nowhere*. (In addition, nonmovement coindexation might not be available in the first place, in a strongly derivational syntax; cf. the latter part of note 121.)

109. Having a matrix *nur* attract *Spanisch* would yield *. . . *dass man uns nur Spanisch gezwungen hat zu lernen*, which is presumably impossible, extrapolating from Bayer's (1996, 246) discussion of fairly similar examples. If so, that would be a fact about extraction possibilities from 'extraposed' infinitives (extractions of certain sorts are possible, though), and presumably orthogonal to the text discussion.

It is possible to have (i) (p. 215), with focal stress on *Spanisch:*

(i)   . . . dass man uns nur gezwungen hat Spanisch zu lernen

Here, *nur* is in the matrix and may have attracted the phrase *gezwungen hat Spanisch zu lernen*; see (121), (132), (134), and (147).

Bayer (p. 216) states that (ii) allows a wide scope interpretation:

(ii)   . . . dass man uns den Hans nur Spanisch zu lehren gezwungen hat ('that one us the Hans only Spanish to teach forced has' = 'that they have forced us to teach Hans only S')

If so, then in this kind of example, with a nonextraposed infinitive, *nur* and *Spanisch* must be in the matrix.

Bayer's approach to these facts in terms of directionality (cf. Kayne (1983a) and Koster (1986)) does not seem compatible with Kayne (1994) and the present essay; the much stricter constraints on preposition stranding found in the OV Germanic languages (as compared with English and Scandinavian), which seem to lend themselves to a directionality approach, are beyond the scope of this article.

110. See Johnson and Tomioka (1998). On the other hand, Honda (1997) has proposed that Japanese verb-final order is produced by preposing to Spec,IP a VP out of which the V had previously raised (to I^0) (cf. in part Hinterhölzl (1997)); from that perspective, the text suggestion about German reconstruction would need to be rethought.

111. As Hornstein (1994, 463–464) notes, there may be substantial variation with respect to the question of which matrix verbs allow wide scope here; he gives an example with matrix verb *want*.

The often supposed clause-boundedness of this kind of reverse scope effect is, for me at least, even more elastic. The following subjunctive example seems fairly acceptable with wide scope for *each*:

(i)   At least one person/somebody has asked that I photograph each of these houses.

With indicatives, a bound subject pronoun may be necessary to get equal acceptability:

(ii)   At least one man/some man thinks he's in love with each of these women.

    112. See also Johnson (1997).
    113. Beghelli and Stowell take the relevant movement in English to be covert (at LF), however.
    114. Similarly for:

(i)   A different student called up every professor.

(ii)   A different student called every professor up.

The 'multiple student' reading (cf. Beghelli and Stowell (1997), Johnson (1997)) seems much more accessible in (i) than in (ii).
    Beghelli and Stowell discuss the fact that in (iii) there is a natural reading with *one book* having scope over negation but under *every boy*:

(iii)   Every boy didn't read one book.

The following suggest that in such readings the indefinite must move overtly to their Spec,ShareP:

(iv)   Every student didn't look up one/some word.

(v)   ?Every student didn't look one/some word up.

    115. This contrasts with Williams's (1986, 271–272) judgment that (i) does not allow wide scope:

(i)   The judge wanted not a single criminal to be executed.

Williams notes that this is unexpected from an ECP perspective and that the generalization seems rather to be that wide scope is best with the quantified phrase in final position. Although I gave the opposite judgment on a similar sentence in Kayne (1981a, ex. (58)), I think that Williams's idea about 'final position' is on the right track. In fact, the text analysis has the consequence that *not a single N* will end up in final position modulo the prior extraction of some other phrase from within the VP (and setting aside sentential adjuncts). Williams's restrictive judgment here means that he does not allow the *to*-phrase to be so extracted; consider his (1977, 130) restrictive judgment on sentences like (ii), which involve a similar preposing of a subpart of VP (cf. (95)) and which he rejects:

(ii)   (John didn't see Mary but) he did Bob.

'Final position' also plays a role in Kuno (1973); there, too, I think the idea was on the right track and will be explicable in terms akin to the text proposals; see Kayne (1997a) and chapter 15.

116. On *?At least one person considers smart every senator*, which to me is deviant for (unexplained) word order reasons, but possible with wide scope for *every*, see note 22. Kennedy (1997, 666) has examples that with wide scope are more acceptable than (222), perhaps somehow related to the fact of their being embedded in an *if*-clause.

117. The fact that the Chinese counterpart of (223) does not allow wide scope for the object (cf. Huang (1982, chap. 3)) might indicate that Chinese lacks VP-preposing of the English sort. Alternatively, see Aoun and Li (1989) (but note Huang (1993)); their account of English, on the other hand, does not cover (222). Their interesting discussion of sentences like (i), which usually resist wide scope for the second object, must, from my perspective, be recast in terms of the otherwise attested (but not uniform) difficulty (e.g., in passives) in overtly moving that second object (cf. also den Dikken (1995c)):

(i)   Mary gave someone every book.

Obenauer (1994, 67) gives wide scope for a direct object *beaucoup de N* ('many (of) N') in comparable examples as more difficult than when *beaucoup de N* is the object of a preposition. This might correlate with other cases in French in which preposing a direct object is more difficult than preposing a PP; see Kayne (1994, 75).

118. From Kayne (1985, 113).

119. VP-preposing across DP = pronoun yields strong deviance:

(i)   *John picked up it.

The same is true of VP-preposing in the H^0 cases:

(ii)   *John put on the table it.

Heavy stress on *it* leads to improvement:

(iii)   (John didn't notice both Paul and the car.) ?He noticed only it.

Reconsideration of 'V DP Prt DP' is beyond the scope of this essay.

120. Thinking of (181), the deviance of (227) should be more severe than that of *?John will stare everybody (that) Fred knows down*, as I think it is.

121. Hornstein (1994, 468) notes that (222) on the wide-scope reading is appreciably worse than (i), which may be fully acceptable:

(i)   I consider everyone you do smart.

What this probably indicates is that the landing site for movement of the ACD phrase is lower than the landing site for a phrase needing to get wide scope relative to a subject phrase and that AP-preposing is sensitive to that difference. (Note that substituting a predicate nominal for AP in (i) seems to bring out some deviance: *?I consider everyone you do a genius.*)

Note that the landing site for ACD (which I agree with Kennedy (1997) is not an A-position), though it must be higher than VP, can be lower than negation, since (ii) can have a 'not > every' interpretation:

(ii)   John won't like everything that Bill will.

A difference in landing site might also bear on the fact that, in sentences like (223) (unlike ACD cases), the wide-scope reading for the object tends to be associated with an intonation pattern reminiscent of that of heavy-NP shift (which also involves VP-preposing; cf. the discussion of (168). This supports the idea that wide scope for the object in such sentences depends on (a particular combination of) overt movements including VP-preposing; if it were just a question of covert movement (whether of a phrase or of a feature), no effect at all on intonation would be expected.

Similarly, no intonation effect would be expected if (223), in the spirit of Kayne (1994, 96), Bobaljik (1995, 351), and Groat and O'Neil (1996) (whose general proposal to eliminate post-Spell-out syntactic operations finds support in this article) or Pesetsky (1997), involved no VP-preposing but only overt movement of *every senator*, with the trace rather than the antecedent pronounced. In addition, it seems unlikely that such an approach (or that of Aoun and Li (1989) or Kitahara (1996)) could account for the difference in interpretation between (223) and (222) or the many other similar facts discussed earlier.

A deeper objection might be that Chomsky's (1995, sect. 3.5) copy theory of movement, on which such an approach rests, is incorrect, being at bottom inconsistent with a strongly derivational theory of syntax (i.e., it is too 'representational').

Local reduplication would have to be provided for, though (cf. note 107 and Gulli (1997); if reduplication is limited to heads, the theory might exclude a copy-based approach to (223), yet allow a version of Roberts (1997).

If copying as a general property of movement is incorrect, then Binding Theory must be more derivational than usually thought (cf. note 13 and Kayne (1997b); also Higginbotham (1995). In addition, the analysis of internally-headed relatives in Kayne (1994) must be given up, perhaps in favor of an empty operator approach (cf. the discussion of (201)), relevant are Cole and Hermon (1994), Basilico (1996), and Murasugi (1994).)

122. See note 38. This violation does not seem to allow repair via an empty complementizer. This recalls the fact that overt leftward movement of French *tout* ('everything') cannot have an ECP-type violation repaired by replacing *que* with *qui*; v. Kayne (1981b). The generalization seems to be that only movement to Spec,CP can take advantage of this sort of repair strategy; see Rizzi (1990); also note 29.

The object counterpart of (228) is better than (228), as we would expect, but not as good as wide scope out of subjunctives with negation and *only* (cf. (169) and (170)), for unclear reasons:

(i)   ??John is requesting that she invite everybody that I am.

The status is improved with comparatives:

(ii)   *John requested that twice as many people as I did leave.

(iii) (?)John requested that twice as many people leave as I did.

(iv)   ?John requested that she invite twice as many people as I did.

If the 'deleted' VP can escape from the matrix VP via 'extraposition' of the relative or comparative, that might be sufficient. The question that arises is whether in (iii) the embedded subject must raise, too. The absence of a *de dicto* reading in (iii) and (v) makes it look as if it must, if Kennedy (1997, 675) is right:

(v)   ??John desires that everybody come to the party that I do.

If it must, then (v), for example, will (abstracting away from the relative) have a derivation in which the embedded VP *come to the party* raises out of the matrix VP, followed by raising of *everybody* further, followed in turn by VP-preposing of the matrix VP *desires that* $t_{everybody}$ $t_{come\ to\ the\ party}$ (cf. note 38). The sharper deviance of (ii) and (228) will then indicate that *twice as many people as I did* and *everybody that Bill did* are not constituents; see (text to) note 127.

123.   Huang (1982a, 146) has a similar proposal for the case of *I couldn't solve many of the problems,* in terms of 'restructuring' (but he allows restructuring also in LF (pp. 148–149) for sentences like *Someone loves everyone*).

124.   See Reinhart (1983, chap. 9), May (1985) and Huang (1982a, chap. 3).

125.   See Chomsky (1995, chap. 3); also Higginbotham (1995) on the possibility of cyclic interpretation.

126.   Thinking of Huang's (1982a, chap. 3) important discussion of scope differences between English and Chinese, it is notable that inverse linking is not found in Hungarian, according to E. Kiss (1992, 133).

For additional interesting use of covert movement in a rather different area of syntax, see Jayaseelan (1998).

The text conclusion, while favorable to the movement character of Bošković's (1997) approach to specificational pseudoclefts, leads one to look rather to overt movement, using doubling, that is, with *an apple what* a complex constituent in sentences like:

(i)   An apple was what he ate.

See Kayne (1994, 153, 155) on clefts and left-dislocation; also note 107. Alternatively, or in addition, pseudoclefts might involve deletion, thinking of (160).

Sportiche (1995b, 364) envisages a syntax without covert movement of the LF type, but with a much wider use of 'overt movement of a covert element' than I have allowed; see section 13.3.8.

127.   See in part Kayne (1997a) and chapters 14 and 15.

14

Prepositional Complementizers as Attractors

The main theme of this article will be the status of elements like the *de/di* found with infinitives in French and Italian:

(1) *Jean a   essayé de chanter.*
     John has tried   *de* sing-inf.

(2) *Gianni ha   tentato di cantare.*
     John   has tried   *di* sing-inf.

I will use the term 'complementizer' for these *de/di*, on the understanding that at the heart of this article is in fact the question: What is the constituent structure in (1)/(2), and what is the derivation of such sentences?

I will suggest that the standard view, according to which *de/di* and the following infinitive phrase form a constituent, is not correct and that the derivation of (1)/(2) involves more syntactic movement than is usually thought. The analysis will take as its starting point the approach I took in earlier work for (3) and for related constructions in French:[1]

(3) *friends of John's*

Two aspects of that approach will be particularly relevant in what follows: First, that the phrase *friends* is moved from a position after *'s* to the Spec of *of*, and, second, that neither *of John* nor *of John's* forms a constituent (as opposed to *of John's friends*, prior to movement, and *of John's t*, where *t* is the trace of *friends*, subsequent to movement).

It will be useful to separate the proposal that some phrase is moved to Spec,*of* (and to Spec,*de/di* in French/Italian) from the question of what exactly that phrase is. As we will see, there is a sense in which that question has two answers.

In the earlier work mentioned, I did not generalize the analysis of (3) to (1)/(2). In this essay, I will argue that (1)/(2) does involve movement into Spec,*de/di* and that *de/di* plus the following infinitive phrase is not a constituent in the usual sense. I will in addition suggest extending this approach to English *to*.

14.1. The nominal character of French and Italian infinitives

A familiar fact about complementizers is that they are often restricted to occurring with a particular subtype of sentential constituent. For example, French *de* requires an infinitival, and is not compatible with a finite phrase:

(4)   *Il est important de chanter.*
      it is important *de* sing-inf.

(5)   **Il est important de vous chantiez.*
      . . . you sing-subjunc.

With a finite embedding, French uses a different complementizer *que*:

(6)   *Il est important que vous chantiez.*

Italian *di* is likewise restricted:

(7)   *Gianni dice di aver capito.*
      John says *di* have-inf. understood

(8)   **Gianni dice di (lui) ha capito.*
                (he) has understood

(Note that (8) is ungrammatical whether or not the subject is expressed.)

At this point, two questions arise: What property do infinitival phrases have that finite phrases lack, such that only the former are compatible with *de/di*,[2] and what is the best way of expressing the 'selectional' relation between *de/di* and infinitives?

With regard to the second question, I will develop an analysis that expresses that relation via movement, recalling proposals by Koopman (1994) and Svenonius (1994), except that the movement at issue will be phrasal movement. (*De/di* will attract the infinitive phrase to its Spec.)

With regard to the first, which is the topic of this section, I will follow Raposo (1987a) in taking Romance infinitives to be nominal. More specifically, there will be an infinitival functional head (above the VP) with a nominal feature. In the terms of Chomsky (1995), the infinitive form of the verb itself will have a corresponding feature in the lexicon. Verb raising of a familiar sort (to the infinitival functional head) will check this feature. Attraction of the entire infinitive phrase to Spec,*de/di* will be sensitive to the same nominal feature. The lack of such a feature on finite verbs will draw the desired distinction.[3]

Raposo (1987a) has argued that the appearance of *de/di* with infinitives is related to syntactic case, given paradigms such as the following (French):

(9) *Jean désire chanter.*
     John desires sing-inf.

(10) *Jean est désireux *(de) chanter.*
     John is desirous *de* sing-inf.

(11) *le désir *(de) chanter*
     the desire *de* sing-inf.

The fact that *de* is obligatory with the noun *désir* and with the adjective *désireux* but does not appear with the verb itself can be understood in terms of case if the infinitive phrase needs case, which it would seem to if it were nominal, as Raposo suggests.

The idea that Romance infinitives are nominal appears to be further supported by the fact that in several Romance languages an infinitive phrase can be preceded in certain contexts by the definite article, for example, in Italian:[4]

(12) *il mangiare la carne il venerdì*
     ('the eat-inf. the meat the Friday')

As expected, then, there are no comparable examples with a finite verb:

(13) **il (Gianni) mangia la carne il venerdì*
     the (John) eats

The subject of the infinitive in (12) is null. Italian also allows infinitive phrases with lexical subjects to be embedded under a definite article, in the so-called aux-to-Comp construction studied by Rizzi (1982a, 86), from which the following example is taken:

(14) *l'esser la situazione suscettibile di miglioramento*
     the be-inf. the situation capable of improvement

A natural conclusion is that in this construction, too, the infinitive has a nominal feature.

A complication arises, however, when we put this conclusion together with Raposo's idea that infinitive phrases need case, given the (marginal) possibility of the following (from Longobardi 1980, 143):[5]

(15) *??Sono certo esser tu migliore.*
     I-am certain be-inf. you better

     'I am certain that you are better.'

In (15), the infinitive phrase, which shows the word order produced by aux-to-Comp movement, is itself the argument of an adjective, which does not otherwise assign Case.[6]

Similar to (15) is the problem posed by Italian ECM sentences. Although substantially less widespread than in English, they exist to some extent. For example, Rizzi (1981, 151) gives:

(16)   *?Ritenevo Mario essere una persona onesta.*
     'I-considered M be-inf. a person honest

Mario here is (somewhat marginally) able to get case, presumably via the matrix case-licensing position.[7] But then there seems to be no obvious way in which the infinitive phrase itself could get case, especially given the fact that Italian (like French) does not have double object constructions of the English sort.[8]

A third facet to this complication can be seen in Italian infinitival interrogatives, which can at least in some cases occur as arguments of derived nominals. The following example is from Fava (1991, 720):[9]

(17)   *la sua incertezza se andarsene o meno*
     the his uncertainty if go-inf. + 2clitics or less

     'his uncertainty as to whether he should go away or not'

It is hard to see how the infinitive phrase in (17) can be case-licensed. (Italian derived nominals cannot case-license a following DP any more than English derived nominals can.)

(Part of) the solution, I think, is to adopt the NP versus DP distinction developed by Abney (1987) (which Raposo (1987a) was not yet able to take into account) and to take infinitive phrases in French and Italian to be nominal in the sense of sharing a feature with NPs, without taking French/Italian infinitive phrases to be DPs. Taking infinitive phrases to be parallel to NPs makes immediate sense of the fact that they can (sometimes) be embedded under a definite article, as in (12) and (14). Furthermore, assuming that syntactic case is needed by DPs but not by NPs, we can allow for no case at all to be assigned to the infinitive phrase in (15)–(17). (In (12) and (14) syntactic case would be assigned to the containing DP, but not to the infinitive phrase proper.)

A further question is then whether syntactic case of the sort required by DPs is ever required by French/Italian infinitives. Consider (18):

(18)   **Sono certo essere migliore.*
     I-am certain be-inf. better

The marginal status of the aux-to-Comp example in (15) (cf. also note 5) contrasts with the sharper unacceptability of the control example in (18). Although it may be that (18) is excluded as a case filter violation, by virtue of the infinitive phrase having no way to be case-licensed, I will tentatively adopt a partially different view, namely that the *di* of (19) is not playing a case-licensing role in the strict sense:

(19) *Sono certo di essere migliore.*
      I-am certain *di* be-inf. better

I will instead take *di* (and other complementizers) to play a licensing role with respect to sentential phrases that is not identical to DP case.

This is supported by the basic fact that has led to the use of the term complementizer:

(20) *Jean a oublié ses gants.*
      John has forgotten his gloves

(21) *Jean a oublié *(de) mettre ses gants.*
                      put-on his gloves

Various verbs such as *oublier* that occur straightforwardly in French with direct objects nonetheless require a *de* (and similarly in Italian, with *di*) when their internal argument is infinitival.[10] Since *ses gants* in (20) receives case in ordinary fashion, the presence of *de* in (21) must be attributed to a factor that is not case. In the next section, I will address some aspects of this licensing of infinitive phrases by *de/di*.[11]

14.2.   French and Italian infinitives do not occupy DP positions

The nominal character of French and Italian infinitives does not imply that they occupy the same positions as DPs, though Italian infinitives almost certainly do when embedded under a definite article, as in (12) and (14). (More precisely put, the phrase consisting of definite article plus infinitive phrase occupies some typical DP position.) In fact, there is reason to think that when not preceded by a definite article, a 'bare' infinitive phrase cannot occupy a typical DP position.[12]

First, bare infinitives cannot be the object of a subcategorized preposition other than *à/a* or *de/di*. This was discussed by Cinque (1990a, 35), who concluded (correctly, I think) that those two are exceptional precisely because they are complementizers, even in some cases where they might appear not to be. Two of his examples are:[13]

(22) **Contavo su essere onesto.*
      I-counted on be-inf. honest

(23) **La sua fortuna consiste in avere molti amici.*
      the his (good)fortune consists in have-inf. many friends

In this respect, Italian (and French) infinitives contrast sharply with English gerunds (cf. note 11):

(24) *He was counting on being chosen.*

(25) *She's interested in studying physics.*

Second, bare infinitives are not fully acceptable in the pre-predicate subject position of a small clause:[14]

(26) *?Jean considère aller au cinéma absurde.*
John considers go-inf. to-the movies absurd

(27) *?Gianni ritiene andare al cinema assurdo.*
John considers go-inf. to-the movies absurd

Again, there is a clear contrast with English gerunds:

(28) *John considers going to the movies a waste of time.*

Third, a bare infinitive cannot be the subject in the following aux-to-Comp construction:

(29) *Gianni ritiene   non essere la linguistica molto importante.*
John   considers neg. be-inf. the ling.   very imp.
'John considers linguistics not to be very important.'

(30) **Gianni ritiene   non essere studiare la linguistica molto importante.*
John   considers neg. be-inf. study-inf. the ling.   very imp.
'John considers studying linguistics not to be very important.'

The subject of this aux-to-Comp construction (on which cf. Rizzi 1981; 1982a) can be an ordinary DP, as is *la linguistica* in (29), but not an infinitive phrase, as seen in (30).

I take the deviance of (30) to thus depend (in part) on the non-DP status of *studiare la linguistica*. Example (30) may also fall under Longobardi's (1980) double infinitive filter. On the other hand, that filter (whatever its ultimate explanation) is not relevant to:

(31) *Fosse la linguistica molto importante, . . .*
were the linguistics very important, . . .

(32) *??Fosse studiare la linguistica molto importante, . . .*
were study-inf. the linguistics very important, . . .

Again, the deviance of (32) relative to (31) reflects the non-DP status of *studiare la linguistica*.[15]

Fourth, a bare infinitive phrase is often rejected following the Italian comparative *di*:

(33)   *Sarà più interessante la fisica della chimica.*
       will-be more interesting the physics *di* + the chemistry
       'Physics is probably more interesting than chemistry.'

(34)   **?Sarà più interessante andare al cinema di studiare la chimica*
       will-be more int. go-inf. to-the movies *di* study-inf. the chemistry

Comparative (noncomplementizer) *di* takes ordinary DPs straightforwardly, but not infinitive phrases.[16]

Fifth, a bare infinitive phrase in French is more or less impossible as a postverbal subject in the Stylistic Inversion construction and also as a right-dislocated subject, as noted by Huot (1981, 47, 145).

The conclusion that infinitive phrases in French and Italian (when not embedded under a definite article) never occupy an ordinary DP position recalls, of course, Koster's (1978) argument that sentential subjects in English are not really in subject position (but rather are topics), as well as Stowell's (1981) case-resistance principle. In light of the preceding discussion, Koster's conclusion should be carried over to French and Italian sentences like:

(35)   *Aller au cinéma serait une bonne idée.*
       go-inf. to-the movies would-be a good idea

The infinitive phrase *aller au cinéma* (in this French example) should be taken to be a topic, and not to occupy the position that DP subjects occupy.

This analysis of (35) would seem to be supported by Raposo's (1987a, note 9) observation that subject infinitives such as that in (35) are somewhat less natural in French than in Portuguese. This difference may be related to the fact that if the infinitive is in a topic position, the subject position is then empty, which implies that (35) is a 'null subject' sentence, something that French otherwise usually disallows.[17]

In conclusion, then, French and Italian 'bare' infinitive phrases, despite having certain nominal properties, do not occur in ordinary DP positions.

14.3. Attraction to *de/di*

It is natural to relate the widespread appearance of *de/di* with French and Italian infinitives to the preceding conclusion. Infinitive phrases need to be licensed in a special way. Having them preceded by *de/di* is one way of providing that licensing.[18] Bare infinitive phrases cannot occur in an ordinary DP position, since, if they did, they could not have been licensed.

What we need is a more precise characterization of how this licensing takes place.

For the Italian case of (12), where the infinitive phrase is embedded under a definite article, one might think of simply saying that infinitival IPs can never be introduced into argument position by themselves but that a DP headed by a definite article and containing an infinitival IP can be. I think that this would be partly right and partly wrong. What is right is that a DP consisting of definite article plus infinitival IP can occupy standard argument positions. The problem is that the complementizer *di* (or *de* in French), as illustrated in (1, 2, 4, 7) and (21), for example, is also a possible licenser for infinitive IP, yet the combination *de/di* plus infinitive IP is still not possible in ordinary DP positions.

This is seen sharply in both French and Italian in the case of subcategorized prepositions. Although (22)/(23) is not possible, adding *de/di* does not help (and similarly in French):

(36) **Contavo su di essere onesto.*
      I-counted on *di* be-inf. honest

(37) **La sua fortuna consiste in di avere molti amici.*
      the his (good)fortune consists in *di* have-inf. many friends

Furthermore, in Italian, *di* plus infinitive cannot be a subject (cf. Cinque 1990b, sect. 3.6; Rizzi 1988, 516):

(38) **Di cercarlo comporta dei rischi.*
      di look-for-inf. + him implies some risks

Without *di*, (38) would be possible, like (35).

Note that it would not be possible to say that *di* plus infinitive is introduced in argument position and then obligatorily moved, since placing *di* plus infinitive elsewhere in the sentence in (36–38) does not result in improvement. This is particularly striking for (38), for which Cinque gives the following:

(39) **Di cercarlo, credo che comporti dei rischi.*
      di look-for-inf. + him I-think that (it)implies risks

(40) **Comporta dei rischi di cercarlo.*

Example (39) would be the result of preposing *di* plus infinitive from subject position of an embedded sentence, while in (40) *di* plus infinitive has been 'extraposed'. In neither case does the movement operation make the sentence acceptable.

It seems to me that the problem posed by (36–40) is an artifact of the familiar assumption that *di* plus infinitive phrase is a constituent (in the grammatical sentences containing that sequence). Let me propose more generally:

(41) Prepositional complementizers do not form a constituent with the infinitival IP they
      are associated with.

In the present essay, I will pursue this claim for French/Italian *de/di* and for English *to*. I would expect it to carry over (with interesting differences of detail) to comparable elements in similar languages, for example, to German *zu*. I think that it will carry over to the complementizers that go with finite sentences, such as French/Italian/

English/German *que/che/that/dass*, but that question will remain beyond the scope of this essay.[19]

In section 14.1. I discussed evidence suggesting that infinitive phrases in French and Italian are nominal. From that perpective, we can say that the IP associated with *de/di* must be endowed with a nominal feature. Put more neutrally, the grammar of French and Italian must express the fact that *de/di* can be followed by an infinitival IP but not by a finite one, as illustrated in (5) and (8).

Syntactic theory as presently constituted can state this kind of 'selectional' restriction as a property of the merge operation proposed by Chomsky (1995, chap. 4). That is, one could state that the *de/di* complementizer must be merged with a nominal IP and cannot be merged with a finite IP. Chomsky's theory allows, however, for a distinct way of stating 'matching requirements', namely via the operation 'attract' and feature checking. This feels like a redundancy that would justify:

(42)   All matching requirements must be expressed by 'attract' and feature checking (rather than via pure merger).

I will now propose an analysis the correctness of which would imply that (42) is true at least for the case of (prepositional) complementizers.

The analysis to be proposed will bring complementizer *de/di* closer to possessive *de/di* and to the other instances of *de* discussed in Kayne (1994, chap. 8) in the sense that all will now involve movement to Spec,*de/di*.[20]

Let us return, then, to the Italian example given as (2):

(43)   *Gianni ha tentato di cantare.*
        John has tried *di* sing-inf.

If *di* is not merged with the IP *cantare*, and if *cantare* must rather be attracted to Spec,*di*, what is the derivation of such sentences? I will adopt a type of derivation that I have argued for in a recent paper having to do with apparently different areas of syntax (negation and *only*, for example).[21] The basic properties of this kind of derivation as applied to the case of *di* are:

(44)   a. The infinitival IP is merged with the main verb, not with *di*.[22]

        b. *Di* enters the derivation subsequent to that.

        c. *Di* attracts the infinitival IP to its Spec.

        d. *Di* then raises to an immediately higher head W.

        e. (*Di*+)W then attracts VP to its Spec.

The derivation of (43) then looks like this (subsequent to the merger of *tentato* and the IP *cantare*):[23]

(45)   . . . *tentato cantare* → merger of *di*
        . . . *di tentato cantare* → attraction of infinitival IP by *di*

... *cantare*$_i$ *di tentato* t$_i$ → merger of W and attraction of *di* by W

... *di*$_j$ + W *cantare*$_i$ *t*$_j$ *tentato* t$_i$ → attraction of VP to Spec,W

... [*tentato* t$_i$]$_k$ *di*$_j$ + W *cantare*$_i$ t$_j$ t$_k$

14.4.   The preposition restriction

Consider now (36), repeated here:

(46)   **Contavo su di essere onesto.*
       I-counted on *di* be-inf. honest

This illustrates an exceptionless restriction in both French and Italian, to the effect that a subcategorized preposition can never be followed by *de/di* plus infinitive.[24] Assume that subcategorized prepositions must enter the derivation before complementizer *de/di*, as seems natural from the present perspective.[25] Then the derivation of (46) will have, prior to the merger of *di*, verb plus preposition plus infinitive phrase:

(47)   *contavo su essere onesto* → merger of *di*
       di contavo su essere onesto → attraction of infinitival IP by *di*
       [*essere onesto*]$_i$ *di contavo su* t$_i$ → merger of W and attraction of *di* by W
       di$_j$+W [*essere onesto*]$_i$ t$_j$ *contavo su* t$_i$ → attraction of VP to Spec,W
       [*contavo su* t$_i$]$_k$ *di*$_j$ + W [*essere onesto*]$_i$ t$_j$ t$_k$

The reason for the deviance of (46) is now clear. The second step of this derivation, attraction of infinitival IP to Spec,*di*, is an instance of preposition stranding in which the argument of the preposition *su*, namely *essere onesto*, has been preposed without *su* being preposed along with it. Italian (like French) generally does not allow preposition stranding:[26]

(48)   **Chi contavi su?*
       who were-you-counting on

Therefore, (46) is not possible.

It is worth noting explicitly that the impossibility of (46) does not reflect any general prohibition against sequences of two prepositions.[27] In fact, (46) contrasts minimally with:

(49)   *Contavo su delle persone affidabili.*
       I-counted on of-the persons trustworthy

       'I was counting on some trustworthy people.'

(50)   *Contavo su di lui.*
       I-counted on of him

In (49), *su* is followed by a *di* that has fused with the following definite article (as it normally does) in the so-called partitive construction. In (50), *su* is followed by the *di* that occurs when the object of certain prepositions is a simple pronoun (cf. Rizzi (1988, 523).

From the perspective of the present analysis, the grammaticality of (49) and (50) means that they do not involve attraction of the argument of a preposition to the Spec of a *di* merged above the VP containing that preposition.[28]

14.5. The subject restriction

Consider again (38), repeated here:

(51)   **Di cercarlo comporta dei rischi.*
        di look-for-inf. + him implies some risks

Corresponding to the object of a verb, *di* plus infinitive is widespread in Italian, with the derivation that I have proposed in (45). Why, then, is *di* plus infinitive not possible as subject? Let us make the natural assumption that if (51) were acceptable it would have to have a derivation parallel to that given for (43) in (45). Let us assume further that there is no intrinsic difficulty in merging an infinitive phrase as subject argument. To derive (51), we would then merge *di* above the VP and have *di* attract the infinitive phrase, parallel to what takes place in (45). This would yield:

(52)   *cercarlo*$_i$ *di* t$_i$ *comporta dei rischi*

This looks a bit like a *that*-trace effect, but I am following Chomsky (1995) in taking the government-based ECP not to be a possible syntactic principle, so an ECP-based account of (51) is not available (cf. note 28).

Continuing on, then, merger of W with the structure in (52) and attraction of *di* to W will produce:

(53)   *di*$_j$ + W *cercarlo*$_i$ t$_j$ t$_i$ *comporta dei rischi*

This looks like (51), yet (51) is ungrammatical. Put another way, the derivation so far seems to contain legitimate steps (relative to the analysis being argued for), yet, if allowed to stop here, it produces an ungrammatical result. Let me therefore propose:

(54)   Attraction to Spec,W is obligatory.

Thus, if the derivation stops at the stage indicated by (53), there is a violation of (54). This accounts for the otherwise surprising status of (51).

14.6. Topicalization, dislocation, and extraposition

It is important to note that the ungrammaticality of (51) is not due to the initial position of *di* followed by infinitive. As brought to my attention by Anna Cardinaletti, it is possible to have sentences like:

(55) *Di capire ha tentato tante volte.*
      di understand-inf. he-has tried many times

The contrast between (55) and (51) is obviously a result of the fact that (55) is a topicalized version of (43). More precisely put, (55) does involve the required movement to Spec,W, exactly as illustrated in (45). Subsequent to that movement, topicalization applies, moving the phrase beginning with *di* to the front of the sentence:[29]

(56) ... [*tentato* $t_i]_k$ di_j + W *cantare*$_i$ t_j t_k (= last line of (45)) → topicalization
      ... [di_j+W *cantare*$_i$ t_j $t_k]_l$ ... [*tentato* $t_i]_k$ t_l

Sentences similar to (55) can be constructed with a clitic (example from Skytte and Salvi (1991, 559):

(57) *Di invitarla, me l'ha consigliato lui.*
      di invite-inf.-her, me it has advised he

From the present perspective, this suggests a (partial) parallelism with topicalization. Dislocated (Cinque's (1990a CLLD) structures like (57) must then also involve movement of the constituent beginning with *di*.[30] Again, the contrast with the subject infinitive in (51) is a result of the fact that (51) is not related via topicalization or dislocation to any other structure that does allow *di*.

More complex is the question of 'extraposition', that is, of postverbal infinitives. Consider again the example given earlier as (40):

(58) *Comporta dei rischi di cercarlo.*
      implies some risks *di* look-for-inf. + him

It is clear that such cases of postverbal *di* plus subject infinitive (i.e. where the infinitive phrase bears a subject theta role) are, on the whole, deviant in Italian compared with postverbal object infinitives, as in (43), repeated here:

(59) *Gianni ha tentato di cantare.*
      John has tried *di* sing-inf.

At the same time a number of Italian speakers find (some sentences like) (58) less strongly deviant than the corresponding preverbal subject infinitive with *di* in (sentences like) (51). For example, Fava (1991, 540) gives as acceptable:[31]

(60) *Non lo sorprende di essere stato respinto.*
      neg him surprises *di* be-inf. been rejected

      'Having been rejected doesn't surprise him.'

Given the analysis so far presented, we might expect (58) to be perfectly acceptable, if attraction of *comporta dei rischi* to Spec,W can apply in (53). Of relevance is the French vs. Italian contrast:[32]

(61)   *Il est possible de comprendre cette question.*
       it is possible *de* understand-inf. that question

(62)   **È possibile di capire quella domanda.*
       it is possible *di* understand-inf. that question

The Italian example (62) is like (58). The French example (61) is, on the other hand, perfectly acceptable. More generally put, postverbal subject infinitives in French require *de*:

(63)   **Il est possible comprendre cette question.*

Postverbal subject infinitives in Italian, on the other hand, are fine without *di*:

(64)   *È possibile capire quella domanda.*

The grammaticality of (61) in French suggests that a derivation of the sort indicated in (53), involving a subject infinitive and attraction to W, is not precluded in any general way:

(65)   *comprendre cette question est possible* → merger of *de*
       de comprendre cette question est possible → attraction of infinitive phrase to Spec,*de*
       [*comprendre cette question*]$_i$ *de* t$_i$ *est possible* → merger of W and attraction of *de* to W
       de$_j$ + W [*comprendre cette question*]$_i$ t$_j$ t$_i$ *est possible* → attraction to Spec,W
       [t$_i$ *est possible*]$_k$ *de*$_j$ + W [*comprendre cette question*]$_i$ t$_j$ t$_k$

Abstracting away from the question of expletive *il*, this yields (61).

As far as *il* is concerned, it might be inserted/merged in a position above any of those indicated in the last line of (65). Alternatively, it might be a double of the infinitive phrase (i.e., what would be merged as subject of (*est*) *possible* would be *comprendre cette question—il*) that would be stranded by movement of the infinitive phrase to Spec,*de*.[33]

A plausible hypothesis is that the difference between (63) and (64) concerning *de*/*di* is related to the presence of *il* in the former versus the absence of any expletive in the latter. Thus, if the infinitive phrase needs nominative case here, it might be able to get it in Italian, where there is no potentially competing expletive, but not in French, where *il* has nominative case.[34] That the presence of expletive *il* is responsible for the ungrammaticality of (63) is made less plausible, however, by the following French versus Italian contrast:

(66)   *Je crois possible de comprendre cette question.*
       I believe possible *de* understand-inf. that question

(67)   *Ritengo possibile capire quella domanda.*
       I believe possible understand-inf. that question

In these small-clause contexts, French continues to need *de*:

(68) **Je crois possible comprendre cette question.*

This is so, even though in (65)/(68) there is no *il* or other visible pronoun.[35]
    The derivation of (66) is:

(69) *je crois comprendre cette question possible* → merger of *de* and attraction to
     Spec,*de*
     [*comprendre cette question*]$_i$ *de je crois* t$_i$ *possible* → merger of W and attraction of
     de to W
     de$_j$ + W [*comprendre cette question*]$_i$ t$_j$ *je crois* t$_i$ *possible* → attraction to Spec,W
     [*je crois* t$_i$ *possible*]$_k$ *de*$_j$ + W [*comprendre cette question*]$_i$ t$_j$ t$_k$

In this derivation, the AP *possible* is carried along by the final movement to Spec,W.
It will therefore, barring some special mechanism allowing it to be left behind, necessarily precede the infinitive phrase itself, which is in a lower Spec,*de*. This is why
(70) is ill formed:[36]

(70) **Je crois de comprendre cette question possible.*

No recourse to 'obligatory extraposition' is necessary, nor is any specific constraint
against complex internal constituents needed.[37]
    It remains to be understood why Italian, but not French, allows a postverbal
subject infinitive without *de/di*, as we have seen in (64) and (67) as opposed to (63)
and (68). As already noted, (68) shows that a general account cannot be based on the
presence of an expletive pronoun linked to the infinitive, since in (68) there is none,
and yet *de* is required. One might alternatively think nonetheless of the 'pro-drop'
difference between Italian and French, hoping that the fact that French looks 'pro-
drop' in (68) itself (with respect to the subject of the small clause) might not prove
an insurmountable difficulty. However, although being a pro-drop language may well
turn out to be a necessary condition for allowing postverbal complementizerless
subject infinitives, I do not think it is likely to be a sufficient condition.
    For example, Sardinian is a pro-drop language, yet, to judge by Jones (1993,
262ff.), its postverbal subject infinitives normally require a complementizer (usually *a*). Somewhat similarly, Occitan, also pro-drop, seems to use *de* more than Italian.[38] This recalls the cross-Romance distribution of control sentences with the equivalent of English *if*:

(71) *Gianni non sa se andare al cinema.*
     John neg knows if go-inf. . . .

(72) **Jean ne sait pas si aller au cinéma.*
     John neg knows not if go-inf. to-the movies

Italian, but not French, allows control with *if*. But Sardinian and at least some Occitan
do not.[39] This may indirectly correlate with the fact that Sardinian and Occitan seem

to have less 'free inversion' of subject DPs than Italian.[40] With this as background, I would like to suggest that the Italian versus French difference with respect to postverbal complementizerless subject infinitives be (indirectly) related to inversion of subject DPs.

More specifically, let us recall sentences in Italian and French that contain a preverbal subject infinitive:

(73)   *Andare al cinema sarebbe possibile.*
      go-inf. to-the movies would-be possible

(74)   *Aller au cinéma serait possible*
      go-inf. to-the movies would-be possible

Following Koster (cf. the discussion of (35)), I took these to have the infinitive phrase in a pre-subject topic position. Let me suggest now that (75) is related to (73) via the preposing of *sarebbe possibile* to a Spec position higher still than the topic position in which the infinitive phrase is found:

(75)   *Sarebbe possibile andare al cinema.*

The intent is to have this be at least partially similar to the derivation of Italian sentences like:[41]

(76)   *Ha bevuto il latte un gatto.*
      has drunk the milk a cat

Comparable preposing of a VP or IP-like constituent is normally not possible in French:[42]

(77)   **A bu le lait un chat.*
      has drunk the milk a cat

If this discussion is on the right track, then to this is related:

(78)   **Serait possible aller au cinéma.*

(79)   **Il serait possible aller au cinéma.*

From this perspective, the derivation of (66) is:

(80)   *ritengo capire quella domanda possibile* → topicalization
      [*capire quella domanda*]$_i$ *ritengo* t$_i$ *possibile* → IP-preposing
      [*ritengo* t$_i$ *possibile*]$_j$ [*capire quella domanda*] $_i$ t$_j$

A comparable derivation in French would not be available, given the lack of IP-preposing in French. For that reason, (68) is ungrammatical.[43]

This approach to (73, 75) and (67/80) amounts to claiming that topicalization is an alternative means of licensing infinitive phrases in Italian (and similarly for (74) in French), alternative, that is, to licensing via attraction to Spec,*de/di*. If so, then such sentences contain no covert counterpart of *de/di*, except insofar as Top[0] itself might be considered one.[44] Somewhat similarly, there is the question of sentences with object infinitives that lack an overt complementizer, e.g.:

(81)   *Gianni detesta andare al cinema.*
        John detests go-inf. to-the movies

(82)   *Jean déteste aller au cinéma.*
        John detests go-inf. to-the movies

Many of these are instances of 'restructuring',[45] whereas others are not. I will leave open the question whether some or all of them contain a phonetically unrealized counterpart of *de/di*.

In conclusion, so far, I have argued that the complementizer *de/di* should be taken to enter the derivation above VP and to combine with the associated infinitive by attracting that infinitive to its Spec. Subsequent raising of *de/di* to W, followed by the preposing of VP to Spec,W, yields the observed word order in French and Italian.[46] I have in addition argued that sense can be made from this perspective of (at least) a good part of the specific distribution of *de/di* in these languages.

14.7. English *to*: similarities

Although I will not in this essay address the question of the (unusual)[47] English *for* complementizer, I would like to take up English *to* and reinterpret the differences between *de/di* and *to* that I discussed in earlier work.[48] It is of course not logically necessary that *to* be analyzed as parallel to *de/di*, that is, as an element that (when a complementizer) attracts an infinitival phrase to its Spec.[49] On the other hand, in the interest of achieving a theory of UG that is sufficiently restrictive, it would be highly desirable to severely limit the space of possible analyses that UG makes available.

In addition, there are some similarities between English *to* and *de/di* (in addition to the basic fact that all are incompatible with a finite IP)[50] that point in the direction of seeking a (largely) common approach. One is the preposition restriction, repeated here from (46):

(83)   **Gianni contava su di vincere.*
        John counted on *di* win-inf.

(84)   **Jean comptait sur de gagner.*
        John counted on *di* win-inf.

(85)   **John counted on to win.*

A second is the restriction concerning pre-predicate small clause subjects, from (70):[51]

(86)   *Gianni ritiene di vincere possibile.
        John considers di win-inf. possible

(87)   *Jean considère de gagner possible.
        John considers de win-inf. possible

(88)   *John considers to win possible.

This suggests that a grammatical sentence with complementizer to, such as (89), has the derivation shown (partially) in (90):[52]

(89)   John tried to sing.

(90)   ... tried sing → merger of to
        ... to tried sing → attraction of infinitive phrase to Spec,to
        ... sing$_i$ to tried t$_i$ → merger of W and raising of to
        ... to$_j$ + W sing$_i$ t$_j$ tried t$_i$ → movement of VP to Spec,W
        ... [tried t$_i$]$_k$ to$_j$ + W sing$_i$ t$_j$ t$_k$

The deviance of (88) is a result of the fact that this kind of derivation will not produce it:

(91)   ... considers win possible → merger of to
        ... to considers win possible → attraction to Spec,to
        ... win$_i$ to considers t$_i$ possible → merger of W and raising of to
        ... to$_j$ + W win$_i$ t$_j$ considers t$_i$ possible → movement of VP to Spec,W
        ... [considers t$_i$ possible]$_k$ to$_j$ + W win$_i$ t$_j$ t$_k$

Rather than (88), what is produced is:

(92)   *John considers possible to win.

Why this is unavailable, as compared with French (66), is not entirely clear to me.[53] To generate (88) itself, one would need to scramble the AP out of VP prior to merger of to, which is evidently not straightforward (cf. note 36).

    The preposition restriction seen in English in (85) can be understood in exactly the same way as in the discussion of the corresponding French and Italian restriction, illustrated in (47):

(93)   ... counted on win → merger of to
        ... to counted on win → attraction of infinitive phrase to Spec,to
        ... win$_i$ to counted on t$_i$ → merger of W and raising of to

... to_j + W win$_i$ t$_j$ *counted on* t$_i$ → movement of VP to Spec,W

... [*counted on* t$_i$]$_k$ to_j + W *win*$_i$ t$_j$ t$_k$

The movement of *win* to Spec,*to* is an instance of preposition stranding, in this case. I take that to be the source of the ungrammaticality of all of (83–85). Of course there is a twist here, in that English allows preposition stranding in various Wh-constructions and in pseudo-passives. On the other hand, English does not allow preposition stranding in the Heavy-NP Shift construction:

(94)   *John put something on two minutes ago the table that I was telling you about.

I thus take the position that (85) and (94) form a natural class.[54]

14.8.   English *to*: differences

To is compatible with a preposed Wh-phrase, unlike *de/di*:[55]

(95)   *John knows where to go.*

(96)   **Jean sait où d'aller.*

(97)   **Gianni sa dove di andare.*

The derivation of (95) must be (trace of *where* omitted):

(98)   ... *knows go where* → Wh-movement

   ... *knows where go* → merger of *to*

   ... *to knows where go* → attraction of subpart of infinitive phrase to Spec,*to*

   ... *go*$_i$ *to knows where* t$_i$ → merger of W and raising of *to*

   ... *to*$_j$ + W *go*$_i$ t$_j$ *knows where* t$_i$ → movement to Spec,W

   ... [*knows where* t$_i$]$_k$ *to*$_j$ + W *go*$_i$ t$_j$ t$_k$

The key point here is that, to derive (95), we need to let *to* attract not the whole infinitive phrase but rather the infinitive phrase minus the Wh phrase in its high Spec position.[56]

Assume that such subextraction (stranding the Wh phrase) is not allowed in French or Italian.[57]

Then the ungrammaticality of (96) and (97) follows. (I return later to why this might be the case.)

Notice that if *to* in (98) could have attracted the whole infinitive phrase including the Wh-phrase, we would incorrectly have derived:

(99)   **John knows to where go.*[58]

(100)   *Jean sait d'où aller.

(101)   *Gianni sa di dove andare.

This suggests that Wh-movement is movement to Spec of an interrogative head (as usually assumed) and that that interrogative head does not have a (nominal) feature attractable by complementizer *to/de/di*.[59]

To is compatible with subject-to-subject raising, whereas *de/di* are not:

(102)   John seems to be happy.

(103)   Jean semble (*d') être heureux.

(104)   Gianni sembra (*di) essere felice.

To account for this in a way parallel to the account of (95–97), the derivation of (102) must be:[60]

(105)   ... seems John be happy → merger of *to*
        ... to seems John be happy → attraction of subpart of infinitive phrase to Spec,*to*
        ... [be happy]$_i$ to seems John t$_i$ → merger of W and raising of *to*
        ... to$_j$ + W [be happy]$_i$ t$_j$ seems John t$_i$ → movement to Spec,W
        ... [seems John t$_i$]$_k$ to$_j$ + W [be happy]$_i$ t$_j$ t$_k$ → raising of *John*[61]

Assuming again that subextraction from the infinitive phrase is not permitted in French or Italian, the ungrammaticality of (103) and (104) with *de/di* is accounted for.

If movement to Spec,*to* were to carry along *John* in the second step of this derivation, we would end up with (cf. 99):

(106)   ... [seems t$_i$]$_k$ to$_j$ + W [John be happy]$_i$ t$_j$ t$_k$

As it stands, this presumably corresponds to a Case violation, in that *John* is not Case-licensed:

(107)   *It seems to John be happy.

(108)   *Il semble de Jean être heureux.

(109)   *Sembra di Gianni essere felice.

We also need, however, to be sure that (106) is not available as a possible input to the raising of *John* to Spec,IP. The unwanted effect of this would not be detectable in English but would be in French and Italian, since, if raising could apply to the French or Italian counterpart of (106), then the ungrammatical versions of (103) and (104) (with *de/di*) would become derivable. This suggests (keeping in mind that we are trying to avoid an ECP-like use of government) that (106) is itself illegitimate. This would follow in turn if the attraction to Spec,*to* of *John be happy* is precluded, in a fashion parallel to what was suggested above for (99–101). This would be accomplished if *John* in *John be happy* is necessarily in the Spec of a projection higher than the one bearing the (nominal) feature that *to* is attracting (and similarly for French and Italian).[62]

14.9. English *to*: negation

The impossibility of having a lexical subject or a Wh-phrase between *to/de/di* and the infinitive verb in (107–109) and (99–101) contrasts with the following, in which a negative morpheme or morphemes can be so placed:

(110)   *John promised to not do it.*

(111)   *Jean a promis de ne pas le faire.*
       John has promised *de* neg not it do-inf.

(112)   *Gianni ha promesso di non farlo.*
       John has promised *di* neg do-inf.-it

It seems clear that to derive the correct word order, what must move to Spec,*to/de/di* is the infinitive phrase, including negation (i.e. *not do it*, *ne pas le faire*, *non farlo*), for example:

(113)   ... *promis ne pas le faire* → merger of *de*
       ... *de promis ne pas le faire* → movement to Spec,*de*
       ... [*ne pas le faire*]$_i$ *de promis* t$_i$ → merger of W and raising of *de*
       ... *de*$_j$ + W [*ne pas le faire*]$_i$ t$_j$ *promis* t$_i$ → movement to Spec,W
       ... [*promis* t$_i$]$_k$ *de*$_j$ + W [*ne pas le faire*]$_i$ t$_j$ t$_k$

If this is so, then the (nominal) feature attracted by *de* must remain visible in the presence of negation. This means that, if the presence of *ne pas* indicates the presence of a NegP,[63] and if attraction can see only the highest projection, the relevant infinitival feature must raise to Neg^0.[64]

    In English, (110) is less normal than:[65]

(114)   *John promised not to do it.*

In French and Italian, on the other hand, placing the negation before the *de/di* results in ungrammaticality:

(115)   **Jean a promis ne pas de le faire.*

(116)   **Gianni ha promesso non di farlo.*[66]

The derivation of (114) must be:

(117)   ... *promised not do it* → merger of *to*
          ... *to promised not do it* → movement to Spec,*to*
          ... [*do it*]$_i$ *to promised not* t$_i$ → merger of W and raising of *to*
          ... *to*$_j$ + W [do it]$_i$ t$_j$ *promised not* t$_i$ → movement to Spec,W
          ... [*promised not* t$_i$]$_k$ *to*$_j$ + W [do it]$_i$ t$_j$ t$_k$

As in (98) and (105), what is moved to Spec,*to* is a subpart of the infinitival argument of the matrix verb. *Do it* is moved, stranding *not*.

Assuming for the third time, then, that such subextraction is not available in French or in Italian, we have an account of (115) and (116).

As for the question why English should differ from French and Italian in precisely this way, there may be a link with the fact that of the three only English allows VP-Deletion with *have* and *be* (and *to* itself), but I will not pursue this further here.[67]

Within English, on the other hand, there is an intriguing link with VP-preposing. VP-preposing of the sort seen in (118) can strand sentential negation, as shown in (119):

(118)   *He said he would do it and do it he will.*

(119)   *He said he wouldn't do it and do it he won't.*

Consider now what is often called 'constituent negation', that is, the second negation in:

(120)   *He won't not do it.*

VP-preposing does not seem to be able to strand constituent negation:

(121)   **He said he wouldn't not do it and do it he won't not.*

Now the *not* of (114) feels like sentential (ordinary) negation, while the *not* of (110) feels like constituent negation. In derivational terms, we see furthermore that the sentential negation of (114) is stranded by movement to Spec,*to* (of *do it*), as indicated in (117). Whereas the constituent negation of (110) is carried along by movement to Spec,*to* (of *not do it*), as indicated implicitly in (113).

In (121) we saw that constituent negation cannot be stranded by VP-preposing. Let us make the natural assumption that that property carries over to movement to Spec,*to*, that is, that movement to Spec,*to* could not strand constituent negation (although it does (and almost certainly must) strand sentential negation in (117)).

In the derivations considered so far, we have been starting with ... *promised not do it*, where *not* could be one or the other type of negation. To force an unambiguous instance of constituent negation, we can start instead (on the plausible assumption that there can be only one sentential negation per clause) with:

(122) . . . *promised not not do it*

Here the second *not* must be constituent negation, then. The first *not* can be of either type. Introducing *to*, we have:

(123) . . . *to promised not not do it*

What are the options concerning movement to Spec,*to*? If both *not*s are constituent negation, they should both be carried along:

(124) . . . [*not not do it*] *to promised* . . .

Raising of *to* to W and preposing *promised* . . . to Spec,W will yield the awkward but not impossible:

(125) ?*John promised to not not do it.*

If in (123) the first *not* is sentential negation and the second constituent negation then movement to Spec,*to* should carry along the second while stranding the first, yielding:

(126) [*not do it*] *to promised not* . . .

Raising *to* to W and preposing *promised not* . . . will yield:

(127) ?*John promised not to not do it.*

What should be impossible, starting from (123), is to strand both *not*s, since by assumption the second must be constituent negation, which is not strandable. Thus the following should not be available as an intermediate step:

(128) *[*do it*] *to promised not not* . . .

From this it follows, correctly, that (129) is ungrammatical, since (129) could only have been derived via (128), given our assumptions:

(129) *John promised not not to do it.*

This supports the idea that movement to Spec,*to* is involved in the derivation of (110), (114), (125) and (127), and by extension in other sentences with complementizer *to*.

14.10. Conclusion

The prepositional complementizers *de/di/to* in French, Italian, and English enter the derivation above the VP, and not as sister to the IP they are associated with. The relation between complementizer and IP is expressed by having the IP move to the specifier position of the complementizer. That movement can be thought of in terms of Chomsky's (1995, chap. 4) notion of attraction. Subsequent raising of the complementizer (to a head W), followed by phrasal movement to Spec,W, produces the observed word order in these languages. This kind of derivation is similar to those proposed in chapter 13 for various constructions involving negation, *only/even/too*, focus, scope and antecedent-contained deletion. Many syntactic relations that could at first glance be expressed in terms of merger (sisterhood) turn out to be better expressed in terms of attraction (Spec-head).[68]

NOTES

The core idea of this article originated in class lectures at the University of Venice in May 1995. I am grateful to the audience there, and to others subsequently at the University of Paris/ Nanterre, University of Essex, SOAS, Harvard, the Scuola Normale Pisa, UCLA, the University of Rome 3, the LSRL conference in Mexico City, the 1996 Girona Summer School, the Graduate Center CUNY, Rutgers University, the University of Padua, and the 1997 LSA Institute for stimulating comments and questions, as well as to Guglielmo Cinque for insightful and helpful comments on the written version.

1. Cf. chapter 7 and Kayne (1994, chap. 8).

2. Spanish *de* (unlike French and Italian) can be followed by *que* + finite clause, although not by a finite clause without *que*. This may be related to French having . . . *de ce que* + finite clause, with *ce* a demonstrative/pronominal of some sort. For recent discussion, see Pollock (1992).

3. If AGR is pronominal (cf. Rizzi 1982a, chap. 4) and if pronominal implies having nominal features, then AGR cannot be the head of a finite clause. For different interpretations of what AGR is, see Chomsky (1995, chap. 4) on the one hand and Taraldsen (1992) and Ordóñez (1997) on the other. *De/di* is also impossible with French *-ant* and Italian *-ndo* forms, which are presumably also not nominal. (In French, the *-ant* forms generally pattern with finite verbs, rather than with infinitives, as far as negation is concerned; see Kayne 1975, sect. 1.3 and Pollock 1989, 408).

4. Example from Bottari (1991); see Skytte and Salvi (1991, 559–569).

On the different behavior of (contemporary) French, see Pollock (1994, note 18), whose suggestion that French infinitives have lost most of their nominal properties may or may not be compatible with the text discussion.

Parallel to (13) is (i), with the *-ndo* form (cf. note 3):

(i)   *il mangiando la carne il venerdì*
       the eating the meat the Friday

5. Longobardi gives as less marginal an example with wh-movement:

(i)   *?Ecco l'uomo che sono certo aver vinto la gara.*
       here-is the man that I-am certain have-inf. won the competition

6. Similarly, Gross (1968, 88) has for French:

(i)   *J'avertis Jean y être allé.*
       I warn/inform John there be-inf. gone

       '. . . that I have gone there'

In this example, the verb *avertis* assigns objective case to *Jean*, apparently leaving no further case available for the infinitive phrase (French does not have double object constructions of the English sort). The similarity between (i) and (15) supports Déprez's (1989, 446n) proposal that such infinitives, despite not having a lexical subject, involve a French counterpart of Italian aux-to-Comp movement.

It may be that the *that* of (ii) is not a DP, and/or there may be a phonetically unrealized preposition:

(ii) *?That I'm sure.*

   7. See Postal (1974).
   8. See Kayne (1983c). On the French counterparts of (16), see Pollock (1985)
   9. See this French example from Huot (1981, 58):

(i) *As-tu fait attention où déposer ce dossier?*
     have you paid attention where leave-inf. that dossier

Similarly, Jones (1993, 293) gives an example from Sardinian with an infinitival interrogative as the object of an adjective:

(i) *Non so sicuru (*de) comente lu fákere.*
     neg I-am sure (*de*) how it do-inf.

10. Conversely, such verbs do not allow *de* when the object is an ordinary DP or pronoun:

(i) *Jean a oublié (*de) cela.*
     John has forgotten (*de*) that

Other verbs allow *de* with both infinitive phrase and DPs (e.g. *convaincre* 'convince'); see Cinque (1990a, 36).

11. I will not address the question why the infinitival complementizer is sometimes (much less often; cf. Long 1976) *à/a* ('to'); for interesting ideas on *à* versus *de*, which may be compatible with those of the text, see den Dikken (1996).

Infinitival interrogatives, as in (17), never have the infinitive preceded by *de/di*:

(i) **la sua incertezza se di andarsene*

Why (i) is impossible will be discussed later. The fact that (17) and (ii) are fine without *di* may indicate that the wh-element itself is a licenser for infinitives (and similarly for aux-to-Comp in (14) and (15)):

(ii) *So dove andare.*
      I-know where go-inf.

The aux-to-Comp infinitives seem to generally be incompatible with *di* (cf. Rizzi 1982a, 167, Cinque 1995, 201), though there is an example in (the text of) Belletti (1977, 283ff.):

(iii) *... motivato dal fatto di essere il ne la ...*
       motivated by-the fact *di* be-inf. the *ne* the ...

Why *di* is impossible in (16) will also be taken up below. The fact that ECM infinitives are good without *di* may be related to (ii).

English gerunds contrast with French/Italian infinitives as far as (ii) vs. (iv)/(v) is concerned:

(iv)   *I wasn't aware of what (John('s)) having said.*

(v)   *John remembers where having gone.*

Since English gerunds are almost certainly nominal, it may be that they differ from Fr./It. infinitives in that English gerunds must (almost) always be embedded within a DP (whose D may be phonetically unrealized) and that D is incompatible with an interrogative (nominal) Spec; see (vi):

(vi)   *John remembers where (his) trip.*

Huot's (1981, 66) example, given as (vii), contrasts well with (iv)/(v):

(vii)   *Je ne me souviens pas à qui avoir confié ce papier.*
        I neg. refl. remember not to whom have-inf. entrusted that paper

The impossibility of (viii) may similarly depend on the DP status of the English gerund phrase (contrasting with Western Shoshoni; see Crum and Dayley (1993: 188ff):

(viii)   *the man John's having seen*

Prepositional complementizers seem to be absent in Russian; it may be that Russian infinitives are not nominal.

12. By specifying 'bare' infinitives, I am setting aside here the question of the position of infinitives introduced by an interrogative phrase or involving 'aux-to-Comp'; see note 11.

13. French is the same as Italian here. The equivalent of (22) was noted by Long (1976, 60), Gross (1975, 73), and Togeby (1983, 205).

14. As opposed to the following (and similarly for Italian), for not entirely clear reasons:

(i)   *Jean considère étudier la linguistique la chose la plus absurde qu'on puisse imaginer.*
      John considers study-inf. the linguistics the thing the most absurd that one can imagine

It may be that (i) and (26)/(27) should be considered derivative from 'V XP DP' (where XP is predicative) via 'heavy-NP shift' of XP. (On 'V XP DP', cf. Rizzi (1986c, 81ff.)

15. Without inversion of *fosse* and with an overt *se* ('if'), the sentence is better:

(i)   *Se studiare la linguistica fosse molto importante, . . .*

Better than (32) is:

(ii)   (?)*Essendo studiare la linguistica molto importante, . . .*
       being . . .

But this gerundial subcase of aux-to-Comp may also allow a dislocated phrase to follow the preposed gerund.

16. Guglielmo Cinque has pointed out to me that (34) is improved with a longer infinitive phrase. This recalls note 14, as well as:

(i)　*That's the car of John.*

(ii)　*That's the car of the student who you were looking for yesterday.*

It remains to be understood what exactly underlies these 'heaviness' effects.

17. Probably related to (35) is (i), with a nonclitic subject pronoun (and no subject clitic):

(i)　*Lui partira le premier.*
　　he will-leave the first

In the singular this is possible only with a third-person pronoun (cf. Kayne (1972, note 22; 1975, sect. 2.4; and chapter 9):

(ii)　**Moi partirai le premier.*
　　I will-leave the first

It remains unclear why sentences like (35) are sometimes less than fully natural in Italian, see Skytte and Salvi (1991, 540).

18. See note 11.

19. As will the natural extension to (grammatical) prepositions in general. I will likewise set aside the implications of (41) for the phonetically unrealized prepositional complementizer posited for participial clauses in chapter 7.

Similarly for the question of *if/si/se*. The incompatibility of French *si* with control means that *si* cannot have exactly the same analysis as *de*. The extent to which the analysis of *if/si/se* and control given in chapter 5 needs to be rethought is unclear; what is clear is that the text proposals make unnecessary the analysis of *de* as a Spec element given there in section 5.2.2.

20. Notable in this regard is Hoekstra's (1999) argument that Dutch derived nominals should receive parallel treatment. Transposed back to English, his conclusion is that in *the destruction of the city*, *destruction* has moved into Spec,*of*.

21. See chapter 13.

22. In such cases, then, the argument of the verb is not a DP, contrary to the strongest interpretation of Longobardi (1994, 620). The fact that the complementizer is not part of the argument of the verb is what underlies the (no longer surprising) fact that complementizers show no case morphology, even in languages where they might have been expected to, such as German, Icelandic, or Russian.

23. I set aside the (ultimately important) question of how the subject argument of the main verb fits in, and similarly the question of the auxiliary.

24. Adjunct prepositions, which sometimes allow *de/di*, fall outside the scope of this essay.

25. If *di* could be merged before *su*, then (46) would show that *su* and other subcategorized prepositions cannot attract to their Spec a (nonmaximal) constituent headed by complementizer *di*.

26. There are exceptions discussed by Rizzi (1988, 524), but these all involve movement of a phrase that itself begins with a preposition. For example:

(i)　*A questa legge, voterò contro.*
　　to this law, I-will-vote against

Whatever the correct analysis of these, it seems unlikely that it will prevent aligning (46) with (48), both of which lack a corresponding second preposition.

27. This is not to say that there are no restrictions; there are some (cf. Rizzi 1988, 515), but they do not seem directly relevant to (46).

28. What the correct analysis is in these two cases is left open here.

Similar to (46) versus (43), on the other hand, is (i) versus (ii) in French:

(i)   *Jean ne peut pas compter sur d'amis.*
       John neg can not count-inf. on of friends

(ii)   *Jean n'a pas d'amis.*
       John neg has not of friends
       'John does not have any friends'

This *de/d'* should be analyzed parallel to complementizer *de/d'* in French—that is, in terms of a non-ECP-based account (as opposed to that of Kayne (1981d)—in a way that I hope to spell out shortly.

29. As given here, this topicalization step involves movement of a nonmaximal projection. If that sort of movement is disallowed (cf. Kayne 1994, 17), then there must be at least one additional functional head above W to the Spec of which the VP can move prior to topicalization. (Alternatively, it might be that (54) is not correct, in which case (55) could have *di* introduced above IP entirely, followed by attraction of the infinitive and raising of *di* to W. The ungrammaticality of (51) would then be attributed to the impossibility of attracting an infinitive out of (VP-internal) subject position, which would look like an ECP effect.)

The fact that French marginally allows the equivalent of (51) (cf. Huot 1981, 45n) may perhaps be treatable in a way partly similar to (55), given the well-formedness of *de* with postverbal subject infinitives, as discussed later—v. (61).

If topicalization as in (55) requires an additional functional head above W, and if some languages are less free than Italian in allowing the presence of one, then we would expect those languages not to allow the equivalent of (55). This may lead to an account of the absence of (most) such topicalization in Sardinian (cf. Jones 1993, 144 ff.), and of the fact that at least some speakers of Catalan don't accept (55). See Bayer (1996, 299) on Hindi and Bengali; on English, see note 55.

30. See Kayne (1994, 82); also note 29.

31. Guglielmo Cinque tells me that, for him, (60) is better with dislocation intonation, that is, with '*di* plus infinitive' right-dislocated. This recalls the French contrast (cf. Kayne (1976, 291):

(i)   *Ça/*Il amuse Jean que tu sois là*
       that/it amuses J that you be here')

32. Fornaciari (1974) characterizes some literary examples of (62) in Italian as being due to French influence.

33. See Kayne (1972, 90 ff.; 1997).

34. See Raposo (1987a, 243 ff.). On nominative for subject clitics, see Napoli (1981a).

35. In fact, there cannot be one:

(i)   *Je le crois possible (de) comprendre cette question.*

The reason for this contrast between French(/Italian) and English (which carries over to the finite counterparts of (i) and (ii)) is unclear:

(ii) *I consider it possible to understand that question.*

36. See Gaatone (1992, 250).

The AP could be left behind by movement of XP to Spec,W if it were scrambled out of VP past the infinitive phrase prior to the latter's moving to Spec,*de*. That kind of derivation is discussed at length (for other areas of syntax) in chapter 13. While not readily available here with AP, it is at least sometimes available with PP, as in the following, where (i) is the most natural order (produced by a derivation akin to 69), alongside (ii), with the more complex derivation given in (iii):

(i)   *Paul a dit à Jean de danser.*
      Paul has said to J *de* dance-inf.

(ii) *Paul a dit de danser à Jean.*

(iii)   ... *dit danser* à J → scrambling of *à Jean*
        ... [*à Jean*]$_i$ *dit danser* t$_i$ → merger of *de*
        ... *de* [*à Jean*]$_i$ *dit danser* t$_i$ → attraction of infin. to Spec,*de*
        ... *danser*$_j$ *de* [*à Jean*]$_i$ *dit* t$_j$ t$_i$ → merger of W and raising of *de*
        ... *de*$_k$ + W *danser*$_j$ t$_k$ [*à Jean*]$_i$ *dit* t$_j$ t$_i$ → attraction to Spec,W
        ... [*dit* t$_j$ t$_i$]$_l$ *de*$_k$ + W *danser*$_j$ t$_k$ [*à Jean*]$_i$ t$_l$

37. Whether the text account of (70) will extend to the whole range of cases discussed by Kuno (1973) remains to be determined.

38. See Miremont (1976, 166 ff.).

39. Cf. chapter 5, sect. 5.2.4.

40. See chapter 5, (text to) note 28.

41. See Ordóñez (1997, sect. 3.6).

42. In contexts of 'Stylistic Inversion', French allows VOS order if the object is idiomatic (cf. Kayne (1972, note 11), but nowhere near as readily as Italian. Whether this instance of VOS in French is produced in the same way as VOS in Italian remains to be seen. Certain registers of French have the possibility of VOS combined with *ne ... que* ('neg ... but' = 'only'); see Pollock (1985, 303).

43. Also relevant may be the fact that French allows topicalization (much) less readily than Italian. I am using the term 'topicalization' here loosely, leaving open the question of English topicalization versus Italian topicalization (in Cinque's 1990a sense) versus his CLLD; for related discussion, see Engdahl (1997).

With verbs like *tentare* that take an infinitive preceded by *di* (cf. 43), *di* must be introduced into the derivation before topicalization has a chance to apply, as shown by the need for *di* in (55). See Cinque (1990b, note 22).

44. On Top^0 see Rizzi (1997).

45. For recent discussion, see Cinque (1998).

46. It may be that 'final complementizers' in head-final languages involve attraction of IP to their Spec, without either of the other two operations coming into play.

IP-movement to Spec of C in head-final languages would, from this perspective, have a clearer basis than it did in Kayne (1994, 53): IP moves to Spec,C (in all languages, in fact) because that is the only way for IP to be related to C (given that IP cannot be merged directly with C).

47. See chapter 7, sect. 7.1.2.

48. See Kayne (1981e).

49. I will assume here that the fact that English infinitives have no suffixal morphology, unlike those of French and Italian, is for the most part orthogonal to the text proposals. For an interesting consequence of the lack of suffix in English, see Guasti (1990), Roberts (1993, 287).

50. Thus, parallel to (5) and (8) is:

(i)   *John claims to have/*has solved the problem.*

51. The judgments here are not as uniformly strong as in the preposition case, for reasons given in the discussion of (69) (scrambling of AP could make a derivation possible). Like (88) is (i) (vs. (ii)):

(i)   **They've made to smoke cigars legal.*

(ii)   *They've made smoking cigars legal.*

The text account of (88) and (i) will carry over to (iii) if *legalize* is derived from . . . *-ize* . . . *legal* . . . (cf. Baker 1988):

(iii) **They've legalized to smoke cigars.*

Another possible source for (iii) is also unavailable (cf. 92):

(iv)   **They've made legal to smoke cigars.*

Why (v) is ungrammatical remains to be determined:

(v)   **They've legalized it to smoke cigars.*

52. In (89), *tried* does not c-command *to*. Extrapolating to *want*, this means that the 'contraction' seen in (i) cannot depend on government (cf. Aoun and Lightfoot 1984), as we would expect if Chomsky's (1995) position is correct:

(i)   They wanna leave.

Lack of c-command between matrix verb and following complementizer is also part of Zaring's (1993) analysis (which has *de* + infinitive phrase as sister to V-bar); the constraint on adjunct extraction that she discusses bears on the question of exactly how high up *de* is introduced, from the text perspective.

53. If (i) is improved, compared with (92), then there may be a link with 'Heavy-NP Shift' facts:

(i)   *??John considers possible both to understand physics and to put it to practical use.*

More specifically, French is more generous than English when it comes to 'Heavy-NP Shift' (which involves leftward, not rightward movement; cf. chapter 13 and Larson (1988; 1990) of not very heavy phrases:

(ii)   *That's what made unhappy the poor boy.*

(iii)   *?C'est ça qui a rendu malheureux le pauvre garcon.*

    (Italian is still freer; cf. Rizzi (1986c, 82 ff.)
    The derivation of (iv) is beyond the scope of this essay:

(iv)   *John considers it possible to win.*

    54. As to what might underlie the difference between allowed and disallowed preposition stranding, see chapter 13.
    Somewhat similar to the text discussion is the fact that the Scandinavian languages allow a great deal of preposition stranding, yet forbid it sharply in the case of pronoun shift/definite object shift; see Holmberg (1986, 199; 1999). On the other hand, Scandinavian allows the equivalent of (85), perhaps via the use of an abstract pronoun (as suggested to me by John Whitman), thinking of languages like German and Russian.
    55. English *to* is compatible with subject infinitives, contrasting with Italian (51):

(i)   *To do that now would be a mistake.*

    It might be that English can suspend (54) in such cases. Less good than (i) are topicalized infinitives (as opposed to topicalized DPs):

(ii)   *To do the dishes he forgets quite often.*

(iii)   *His keys he forgets quite often.*

    On this, see the last paragraph of note 29.
    On the fact that *to* is necessary in (i), see Pollock (1994). On the fact that its apparent counterpart is not in Swedish, see Holmberg (1990).
    56. Consequently, (i) is not an instance of preposition stranding (unlike (85/93):

(i)   *John is thinking about where to go.*

    The relevant part of the derivation is (trace of *where* omitted):

(ii)   ... *to thinking about where go* → movement to Spec,*to*
         ... *go*$_i$ *to thinking about where* t$_i$

    The moved infinitive phrase is not the object of *about*.
    57. This account of (95–97) will carry over to (i–iii) if the *easy-to-please* construction involves Wh-movement as in Chomsky (1977):

(i)   *The children are difficult to photograph.*

(ii)   **Les enfants sont difficiles de photographier.*

(iii)   **I bambini sono difficili di fotografare.*

    On the other hand, locality restrictions here are stronger in French and Italian than in English, which led me (in chapter 4, note 50) to suggest that a clitic-like movement was involved in French/Italian. Whether (some form of) that idea is compatible with the text proposal remains to be determined.

Possible are:

(iv)   *Les enfants sont difficiles à photographier.*

(v)   *I bambini sono difficili da fotografare.*

These prepositions are not compatible with overt Wh-phrases:

(vi)   **Jean sait où à aller.*

(vii)   **Gianni sa dove da andare.*

For relevant discussion, see Kayne (1976, 283ff.) and den Dikken (1996).

58. Not to be confused with (i), where the first *to* is not the complementizer under discussion (and similarly for French and Italian):

(i)   *John knows to what city to go next week.*

59. If the head to whose Spec the Wh-phrase moves is a focus head, the point would not change. For relevant discussion, see Rizzi (1997).

60. Similar to (102–104) are the following ECM facts:

(i)   *John considered Bill to be an intelligent person.*

(ii)   *?Gianni riteneva Bill (*di) essere una persona intelligente.* (cf. 16)

In (i), we have the simplified derivation:

(iii)   ... *to considered Bill be an intelligent person* →
        ... *[be an intelligent person]$_i$ to considered Bill t$_i$* →
        ... *to$_j$ [be ...]$_i$ t$_j$ considered Bill t$_i$* →
        ... *[considered Bill t$_i$]$_k$ to$_j$ [be ...]$_i$ t$_j$ t$_k$*

Movement of *be an intelligent person* from within the larger phrase *Bill be an intelligent person* is parallel to the movement in (105) of *be happy* from within the larger *John be happy*. The impossibility of *di* in (ii) (and of *de* in the closest French counterparts—see Pollock 1985) reflects the fact that Italian (and French) do not allow such subextraction.

61. I leave open the question whether *John* moves to a position within the phrase that has moved to Spec,W or rather to a position higher than the W projection. If the latter, then this bears on the proper understanding of the 'Left Branch' constraint (cf. Corver (1990).

62. We are led to conclude that in the grammatical version of (103)/(104) (without *de/di*) there is no phonetically unrealized counterpart of *de/di*, at least not one with similar feature-checking properties. Beyond the scope of this essay is the question of what and where controlled PRO must be, from this perspective.

63. See Kitagawa (1986, sect. 2.4.3), Pollock (1989), Zanuttini (1997) and sect. 4.2 of chapter 4.

64. See also Grimshaw (1991).

65. In my English, *to* can be separated from the verb by floating quantifiers and certain adverbs, e.g.:

(i)   *They're trying to all talk at the same time.*

(ii) *He claims to still be able to run three miles.*

In the text terms, this means that *all* and *still* can be carried along by movement of the infinitive to Spec,*to*, parallel to (113).

In Dutch and German, *te/zu* cannot be separated from the infinitive verb by any adverb or argument. As in the discussion of (107–109), this would follow if the feature attracted by *te/zu* could not project high enough to dominate (a Spec containing) any adverb or argument (or separable particle).

66. This is to be distinguished from (i), in which *non* has matrix rather than infinitival scope, and which is not relevant to the text point:

(i)   *Gianni ha promesso non di farlo ma di rifarlo.*
      John has promised neg *di* do-inf.-it but *di* redo-inf.-it

Nor is the English counterpart of (i):

(ii) *John promised not to do it but (rather) to redo it.*

Rizzi (1997, 309) points out:

(ii) *Gianni pensa, il tuo libro, di conoscerlo bene.*
      John thinks, the your book, *di* know-inf.-it well

From the text perspective, this indicates that Italian does allow attraction into Spec,*di* to strand a left-dislocated phrase.

67. Another relevant factor might be the lack of infinitival suffix in English; see note 49.

The analysis of Kayne (1981e) expressed the French/Italian versus English differences by stating that French and Italian lacked an element equivalent to English *to*. The present approach may be able to cut deeper.

68. See in part Sportiche (1995b, sect. 4). Many details need to be filled in, of course. For example, how is the choice of phrase to be moved to Spec,W determined? Why can only certain prepositions be attractors for infinitive phrases?

15

A Note on Prepositions, Complementizers, and Word Order Universals

In earlier work, I suggested an analysis of (1) that is illustrated in (2):[1]

(1)   friends of John's

(2)   friends$_i$ [of [John's t$_i$]]

The material preceding *of* is moved into Spec,*of* from a lower position. *of John's* is not a constituent prior to that movement, nor is it one subsequent to that movement if we take the trace into account. In other work, I proposed generalizing this kind of analysis to French possessive constructions with *de*, as in *les amis de Jean* ('the friends of J').[2]

More recently, I argued that the type of analysis shown in (2) should be extended to the French/Italian complementizer *de/di*, seen in sentences such as:[3]

(3)   Jean a essayé de chanter. (Fr: 'J has tried *de* sing-inf.')

(4)   Gianni ha tentato di cantare. (It: same)

Just as *of* in (1)/(2) enters the derivation after the phrase *John's friends* has been put together, so does *de* in (3) enter the derivation above the verb phrase *essayé chanter* (and similarly for Italian). These prepositional complementizers are not merged directly with the infinitival IP they are associated with. The relation between complementizer and IP is established rather by movement (attraction).

Here, I will explore some further consequences of the view that prepositional complementizers, and prepositions and complementizers more generally, are introduced above the VP rather than merged directly with what we think of as their complements.

15.1. Prepositional complementizers

The analysis I proposed for (3)/(4) takes French and Italian infinitive phrases to be nominal (cf. the fact that *de/di* never attract finite IPs),[4] without taking them to be DPs (except in Italian when preceded by an overt determiner). The derivation, which resembles those I have proposed for negation and *only*,[5] has the following properties:

(5) a. The infinitival IP is merged with the main verb, not with *de/di*.

    b. *de/di* enters the derivation subsequent to that.

    c. *de/di* attracts the (nominal) infinitival IP to its Spec.

    d. *de/di* then raises to an immediately higher head W.

    e. (*de/di*+)W then attracts VP to its Spec.

    The derivation of (4), for example, then looks like this (subsequent to the merger of *tentato* and the IP *cantare*):

(6)   ... tentato cantare $\rightarrow$ merger of *di*
      ... di tentato cantare $\rightarrow$ attraction of infinitival IP by *di*
      ... cantare$_i$ di tentato t$_i$ $\rightarrow$ merger of W and attraction of *di* by W
      ... di$_j$ + W cantare$_i$ t$_j$ tentato t$_i$ $\rightarrow$ attraction of VP to Spec,W
      ... [tentato t$_i$]k di$_j$ + W cantare$_i$ t$_j$ t$_k$

15.2. *of*

(7) a picture of John

Given the proposal for (1)/(2) and (3)/(4), it would be natural to take *of* in (7), too, to have some phrase move into its Spec. Yet, *of* is usually taken to be a (case-) licenser for *John* in such examples, and *John* does not appear to be in Spec,*of*. This paradox can be resolved by taking *of* to enter into two attraction operations, much as for *di* in (6):

(8) John a picture $\rightarrow$ merger of *of*
    of [John a picture] $\rightarrow$ attraction of the possessor to Spec,*of*
    John$_i$ of [t$_i$ a picture] $\rightarrow$ merger of W and raising of *of* to W
    of$_j$ + W John$_i$ t$_j$ [t$_i$ a picture] $\rightarrow$ attraction to Spec,W
    [t$_i$ a picture]$_k$ of$_j$ + W John$_i$ t$_j$ t$_k$

In this case, the phrase moved to Spec,(*of*+)W is a small-clause-like constituent [t$_i$ a picture],[6] rather than a VP.

    The question arises whether there might not exist derivations in which the phrase moved to Spec,(*of*+)W is, in fact, a VP, as in (6). I would like to propose that the answer is positive (in a way that makes attraction of *John* by *of* a bit more (in such derivations) like attraction to a nominative or objective case-licensing position):

(9)   ... admiring [John a picture] → merger of *of*
    ... of admiring [John a picture] → attraction to Spec,*of*
    ... John$_i$ of admiring [t$_i$ a picture] → merger of W and raising of *of*
    ... of$_j$ + W John$_i$ t$_j$ admiring [t$_i$ a picture] → movement to Spec,W
    ... [admiring [t$_i$ a picture]]$_k$ of$_j$ + W John$_i$ t$_j$ t$_k$

The proposal is, then, that *of* can enter the derivation above VP and still attract the possessor *John*. Subsequent raising of *of* to W prepares the way for VP movement to Spec,W.

Note that, as a consequence of this derivation, we have a representation for (10) in which *a picture of John* is not a constituent:

(10)   Bill was admiring a picture of John.

This is relevant to the question of sentences such as:

(11)   Who was Bill admiring/?destroying a picture of?

Chomsky (1977), based in part on Bach and Horn (1976), had proposed that such apparent subextraction depends on the prior application of a 'readjustment' rule. This assumes that the following is true (although it's not a primitive):

(12)   Preposition stranding is not allowed out of a constituent of the form 'D N *of* XP'

In those cases in which (11) is possible, the readjustment rule would have applied to break up the object phrase.

    While taking (12) to be correct, I take Chomsky's (1977) readjustment rule to no longer be necessary. Its effect follows instead from the above-VP introduction of *of* illustrated in (9).[7]

    When *of* is introduced above VP, as in (9), the last step in the derivation illustrated, that is, the movement of VP to Spec,W, will have the effect of carrying all the material within VP to the left of *of John*. This ensuing final position of *John* means that no simple derivation of the form (9) can yield:

(13)   A picture of John just arrived in the mail.

Thus, in (13) *a picture of John* must, barring extra complexities, be a constituent. From (12) the expectation then arises that extraction of *John* should be degraded:

(14)   *Tell me who a picture of just arrived in the mail.

Put another way, the subject-object contrast between (14) and (11) can now be understood without recourse to 'government' or to 'L-marking'.[8]

Similarly, we now expect that, barring extra complexities, even object cases corresponding to (11) should be degraded if other VP material follows *of*:

(15)   Tell me who you're touching up a picture of.

(16)   ??Tell me who you're touching a picture of up.

In (15), *touching up a picture* has moved to Spec,*of*(+W). To derive (16) from the present perspective would require a derivation that includes the following step:

(17)   [touching up a picture] → particle preposing
       up_i [$_{VP}$touching t_i a picture]

Movement to Spec,*of*(+W) would then apply to the VP containing the trace of the particle and would strand the particle in a position to the right of *of*.

The marginal status of (16) can be interpreted as reflecting either the marginal status of particle preposing per se or the difficulty of preposing VP across the particle.

The apparently stronger deviance of (14) can be interpreted as follows: If *of* + W attracts VP, then (14) cannot be derived at all, since, in it, the VP follows *of*. The only remaining possibility would be to allow *of* to be introduced above IP and to have VP prepose in a way parallel to the particle preposing of (17):

(18)   [who a picture] arrived in the mail → VP-preposing
       [arrived in the mail]$_i$ [[who a picture] t_i] → merger of *of*
       of [arrived in the mail]$_i$ [[who a picture] t_i] →
       who$_j$ of [arrived in the mail]$_i$ [[t_j a picture] t_i] →
       of$_k$ + W who$_j$ t_k [arrived in the mail]$_i$ [[t_j a picture] t_i] → IP-preposing to Spec,W
       [[t_j a picture] t_i]l of$_k$ + W who$_j$ t_k [arrived in the mail]$_i$ t_l

This seemingly implausible derivation yields a representation in which *a picture of who* is not a constituent, as desired if (14) is to be generated. That this derivation should be available, despite the deviance of (14), is suggested by the fact that for some speakers the violation in (14) is weak, as it is for me in:

(19)   ?Tell me which door the key to is missing.

Note, in addition, that (18) has the surprising property that the closest c-commanding phrase to the verb is the phrase following *of*. This may lead to an understanding of the unexpected agreement pattern seen in:[9]

(20)   ?The identity of the participants are to remain a secret.

15.3.   Extraposition

Beyond obviating the need for a readjustment rule, the above-VP introduction of *of* appears to make unnecessary PP-extraposition. If parallel to (9), we start out with 'showing [John a picture] to me', we have:

(21)   . . . showing [John a picture] to me → merger of *of*
        . . . of showing [John a picture] to me → attraction to Spec,*of*
        . . . John$_i$ of showing [t$_i$ a picture] to me → merger of W and raising of *of*
        . . . of$_j$ + W John$_i$ t$_j$ showing [t$_i$ a picture] to me → movement of VP to Spec,W
        . . . [showing [t$_i$ a picture] to me]$_k$ of$_j$ + W John$_i$ t$_j$ t$_k$

That is, we derive (22) without any specific operation of PP-extraposition:

(22)   They were showing a picture to me of John.

    Similarly, we can derive (23) without PP-extraposition, as in (24):

(23)   A picture just arrived in the mail of John.

(24)   [John a picture] arrived → merger of *of*
        of [John a picture] arrived → attraction to Spec,*of*
        John$_i$ of [t$_i$ a picture] arrived → merger of W and raising of *of*
        of$_j$ + W John$_i$ t$_j$ [t$_i$ a picture] arrived → movement of XP to Spec,W
        [[t$_i$ a picture] arrived]$_k$ of$_j$ + W John$_i$ t$_j$ t$_k$

(It may be that XP here is larger than VP and that *of* is introduced correspondingly
higher.)
    Since material included in VP will be carried along to Spec,W, we correctly expect
the following to be less straightforwardly acceptable than (23):

(25)   ?A picture just arrived of John in the mail.

    In the absence of other factors, we would expect *John* in (23) and (22) to be
extractable, since *a picture of John* in those is clearly not a constituent. The expectation seems to me to be met to some extent:

(26)   ?Who did a picture arrive of yesterday?

(27)   ?Who were they showing a picture to you of? [best with stress on *you*]

What the other factors are is left open. The presence of *yesterday* in final position
requires an analysis of the sort I have given elsewhere for sentences like *Mary saw
only John yesterday* (cf. the discussion of (16)).
    This reinterpretation of PP-extraposition can be generalized to relative clause
extraposition if the relative clause complementizer (in at least some languages) can
be introduced above VP and attract the relative clause (out of the containing NP/DP,
perhaps through an internal Spec position not indicated in (28)), in a way parallel to
the way in which above-VP-*of* attracts *John* (out of the NP/DP *John a picture*) in
(21) and (24):[10]

(28)   . . . showing [a picture I like] to me → merger of *that*
　　　. . . that showing [a picture I like] to me → attraction of the relative (trace of object
　　　within relative not indicated) to Spec,*that*
　　　. . . [I like]$_i$ that showing [a picture t$_i$] to me → merger of W and raising of *that*
　　　to W
　　　. . . that$_j$ + W [I like]$_i$ t$_j$ showing [a picture t$_i$] to me → attraction of VP to Spec,*that*
　　　+ W
　　　. . . [showing [a picture t$_i$] to me]$_k$ that$_j$ + W [I like]$_i$ t$_j$ t$_k$

This corresponds to:

(29)   They were showing a picture to me that I like.

I have been taking the above-VP introduction of *of* to be an option, not a neces-
sity, that is, I have been taking *a picture of John* in *We were admiring a picture of
John* to be ambiguously analyzable as either a constituent (if *of* is introduced prior to
merger with V) or a nonconstituent (if *of* is introduced above VP). Especially if we
stick to indefinites, the possibility arises that *of* is always introduced above VP. This
leads to many complexities that I will leave aside. The point of interest, if we think
back to the discussion of (14), that is, to the observation that VP (or XP) movement
to Spec,W leaves *of John* in final position (barring extra movements of the sort required for *yesterday* in (26)), is that, if *of* is necessarily introduced above VP, the
expectation is generated that deviance will result if *of John* is not final.
　　With *of*, there is for me a real, if subtle, effect of the sort expected:

(30)   We still haven't been able to dig up a picture of John.

(31)   ?We still haven't been able to dig a picture of John up.

On the other hand, some speakers find (31) fully acceptable. For them, *of* is presumably not necessarily merged above VP (even with indefinites).
　　The effect is stronger for relative clauses:[11]

(32)   I just picked up a book that you'll like.

(33)   *I just picked a book that you'll like up.

If *that* must come in above VP in (32)/(33) (and if particles cannot (readily) avail
themselves of the extra operation open to *yesterday* in (26)), then the unacceptability
of (33) follows.
　　From this perspective, the unacceptability of (33) (i.e., the reluctance of certain
'heavy' phrases to appear in certain sentence-internal positions) is accounted for
directly in terms of the way in which complementizers function in a derivation. The
reason this 'heavy phrase' has special behavior is, from this perspective, that it (*a
book that you'll like*) is not in fact a phrase.

A conjecture at this point would be:

(34)   The kind of account just suggested for (33) will generalize to all restrictions on (multiple) center embedding.

15.4.   Word order universals

Some Greenbergian universals have turned out not to be right, while some do look right or largely right. One that seems exceptionless (Dryer (1992, 102)) is:

(35)   If a language is complementizer-final, then the language is OV.

We can think of this universal as excluding:[12]

(36)   *V IP C

Given the existence of large numbers of languages of mixed headedness (i.e., with some heads initial and others final), the question is: Why should the internal order within CP be in any way universally keyed to the internal order within VP. I think that an answer is forthcoming only if, as I have done earlier, we give up the idea that CP is a constituent of the familiar type.

Generalizing from prepositional complementizers to all complementizers, assume:

(i)   C is an attractor of IP (and cannot be merged directly with IP).

(ii)   C comes in above VP, that is, above where V and IP have been combined. (If nothing further happened, then, by antisymmetry,[13] C would precede VP (and V).)

(iii)   V can (apart from incorporation, which is not directly relevant here) end up preceding C only via VP-movement (and not via V-movement)

Then this is how V (*tried*) comes to precede C (*to*) in English, as already seen in (6) for Italian:

(37)   ... tried sing $\rightarrow$ merger of *to*
        ... to tried sing $\rightarrow$ attraction of infinitival IP by *to*
        ... sing$_i$ to tried t$_i$ $\rightarrow$ merger of W and attraction of *to* by W
        ... to$_j$ + W sing$_i$ t$_j$ tried t$_i$ $\rightarrow$ attraction of VP to Spec,W
        ... [tried t$_i$]$_k$ to$_j$ + W sing$_i$ t$_j$ t$_k$

The third line of (37) is of the form 'IP C V'. Raising C to W and then having C + W attract VP (containing V) yields 'V C(+W) IP' (as desired for Italian and English). Assume, on the other hand, that, after attracting IP, C could attract VP to a higher Spec without first raising to W. If that were possible, then we could, starting from

'IP C V', derive *'V IP C' incorrectly. Put another way, under the preceding assumption we would, undesirably, have a way of reaching (36). The conclusion is, then, that UG prohibits such a derivation:

(38)   Attraction to a second and higher Spec is prohibited by UG.

(either because second attraction can only go to a lower Spec (cf. Richards (1997)) or because heads can have only one Spec (antisymmetry)).[14]

    This completes the account of (35)/(36). In essence, (35)/(36) is true because of (38) plus the core proposal that C and IP are not merged as one constituent (but rather that IP is attracted by C, which enters the derivation above VP).[15]

    Note that C in this discussion is not intended to cover all Q-particles. The Chinese Wh *ne*, which is limited to root contexts (cf. Li (1992)), actually does fit in, because a final Q-particle in a root context has no matrix V to interact with and is therefore compatible with (36). In fact, if Chinese *ne* is introduced above the matrix VP (when there is one), then its impossibility in embedded postverbal contexts, that is, in '*V IP *ne*' follows from the proposal I have made (as a subcase of (36)).[16]

    Dryer (1992, 83) notes that the following is largely true (although here there are exceptions, unlike the case of complementizers):

(39)   If a language is postpositional, then it is OV.

Let me restate this as:[17]

(40)   *V DP P

(where P is a postposition and not an English-like particle, the analysis of which is left open). This will follow much as (36), if P is an outside-VP attractor. Schematically, we have:

(41)   P [V DP] $\rightarrow$ attraction by P
      DP_i P [V t_i]

(Whether this stage corresponds exactly to what transpires in postpositional verb-final languages is left open; cf. Pearson (1997a).)

    To reach (40), that is, to get V to the left of P, we would need (setting aside incorporation languages) to move VP. But VP cannot be attracted by P, given (38), unless P first raises to W:

(42) P_j + W DP_i t_j [V t_i] $\rightarrow$ attraction of VP
      [V $t_i]_k$ P_j + W DP_i t_j t_k

This derivation, however, produces 'V P DP' (as in English). Thus we have an account of (40), too (in a way strongly parallel to the account of (36)), although we still need to understand the exceptions (perhaps in those languages 'V DP P' is really 'V P DP P' with a phonetically unrealized additional preposition and a final P that is nominal. See Starke (1993) on (counterparts of) *inside (of)*).

15.5.   Further word order universals

Dryer (1992, 83) observes that, in his terms and in his sample, there are ten times as many genera with prepositional languages that are VO as there are genera with prepositional languages that are OV. Let me convert this to:

(43)   *P DP V

This formulation covers VO languages, too.[18] Within the universe of VO languages, the Chinese family seems to be the only exception. (That exception would disappear if the P's in question were actually V's in a serial verb construction; alternatively, Chinese might be like German, but with a different treatment of direct objects.) Among OV languages, nearby exceptions are German, Dutch, Pashto, and Persian. It may be that they are really 'V X P DP Y', with V raising to some high head position and 't_v X P DP Y' then raising to some still higher Spec position, as in Hinterhölzl (1997) for German.

Why should (43) be (largely) true? Consider the following derivation, which mimics those already discussed, except that it stops in time to (incorrectly) yield (43):

(44)   P [V DP] → attraction by P
DP$_i$ P [V t$_i$] → merger of W and raising of P to W
P$_j$ + W DP$_i$ t$_j$ [V t$_i$]

This derivation can be excluded, as desired, if we adopt (setting aside questions about determiners):[19]

(45)   Functional heads must always attract something overtly to their Spec.

Proposal (45) may also be relevant to the following contrast, where P is an ergative preposition:

(46)   V P$_{erg}$ DP . . . (Tokelauan[20])

(47)   *P$_{erg}$ DP V . . .

Although there are some ergative VSO languages (like Tokelauan) in which ergative 'case' is expressed via a preposition, there do not seem to be any SVO languages of that sort. The type (46) can be derived, in the spirit of the preceding, by having the ergative preposition enter the derivation somewhere higher than the subject DP. The ergative preposition will then attract the (transitive) subject DP and will subsequently itself raise to W. P$_{erg}$ + W will then attract VP (or some larger projection such as TP), which other material will have vacated. By (45), the derivation may not stop just prior to the VP-attraction step, from which the impossibility of (47) follows.

The case (47) is related to a broader generalization to the effect that there are no SVO ergative languages at all (cf. Schwartz (1972), Mahajan (1994)). A postpositional ergative SVO language would have:

(48) *DP P_{erg} V . . .

SVO languages are generally prepositional as far as verbal complements are concerned—v. (40). Thus, (48) may follow from:

(49) All simple grammatical (nonnominal) adpositions in a given language must have uniform behavior with respect to (raising to) W.

Like (43) is:

(50) *C IP V

In traditional terms, CP's that normally precede V are normally not C-initial. In my terms, the account of (43) carries over directly to (50) (and similarly for the question of exceptions).

15.6. Conclusion

Prepositions are not merged with their object DP, nor complementizers with their associated IP. Both are introduced above VP and attract DP or IP. Introduction above VP is also appropriate for certain *of* in English that may seem to be DP-internal and perhaps also for certain *that*, with implications for extraposition. Certain word order universals can be made sense of on the assumption that P and C are introduced above VP.[21]

15.7. Epilogue

These conclusions seem to go against a long-standing intuition about constituent structure. To take the case of prepositions, the derivation I have proposed appears to claim that P and object DP do not form a constituent:

(51) P [V DP] $\rightarrow$ attraction by P
      DP_i [P [V t_i]] $\rightarrow$ raising of P to W
      P_j + W [DP_i [t_j [V t_i]]] $\rightarrow$ attraction of VP
      [V t_i]$_k$ [P_j + W [DP_i t_j t_k]]

P(+W) and DP would form a constituent here were it not for the presence of t_j and t_k.

Assume that the long-standing intuition is correct, that it is at least partly a syntactic (as opposed to phonological) one, and that my conclusions about how P and C are introduced are correct. In a representational theory of syntax, and in a derivational theory with traces/copies, the traces t_j and t_k must be syntactically present. Therefore, if the preceding tripartite assumption is correct, syntax must be derivational, but without traces (and thus with cyclic interpretation[22] and no 're-construction'[23]).

NOTES

To Noam, who, taking nothing for granted, has set the standard.

1. See chapter 7, sect. 7.1.2.
2. See Kayne (1994, 101ff.).
3. See chapter 14.
4. See Raposo (1987a)
5. See chapter 13; also in part Barbiers (1995).
6. It is possible that the internal structure is [a picture t_i], and that this constituent has a phonetically unrealized head that is not indicated.
7. Why the acceptability of (11) is sensitive to choice of verb and to choice of article remains to be understood.
8. See Chomsky (1986a).
9. I find (i) equally possible, which might suggest a phonetically unrealized *of*:

(i)   ?The participants' identity are to be kept a secret.

Worse is:

(ii)   *Their identity are to be kept a secret.

For additional discussion, see den Dikken (1999).
    The contrast between (i) and (ii) recalls another that appears to hold for most of those who accept (iii) (on this construction, cf. Kimball and Aissen (1971) and chapters 10 and 11):

(iii)   ?the people that John think should be invited

(iv)   *the people that he think should be invited

10. Examples of relative clause extraposition in which the relative contains a Wh-phrase rather than *that* presumably require an abstract counterpart of *that*. The degraded status of (i) remains open:

(i)   ??We just put a book on the table the kids have been dying to read.

11. See Fraser (1976), Kroch (1979).
    If (33) is better without *that*, I would be led to say that relatives with no overt complementizer or Wh-phrase can fail to involve an abstract counterpart of *that* introduced above VP.
12. Formulation (36) goes further than (35) in that it also excludes (as far as I know, correctly) OV languages that would have postverbal sentential complements with a final complementizer (as opposed to German or Hindi, which have postverbal sentential complements with an initial complementizer).

13. See Kayne (1994).

14. Another proposal with broad import would be:

(i) A head cannot attract its own complement.

15. Also essential is the general antisymmetry claim that the order is always S-H-C. In addition, it must be the case that W can attract some XP (here, VP) only if some head (here, C) has adjoined to W. This may indicate, in attraction terms, that in (37) *to* is a double attractor (and similarly for other complementizers and prepositions).

From this perspective, W has the specific property of being an attractor of heads, and the presence vs. absence of such W the property of perhaps being the primary way in which UG expresses word order variation.

16. Contrasting with Chinese is Nweh (cf. Nkemnji (1995)) (vs. some other related languages (cf. Watters and Leroy (1989, 445)), whose final Q can be embedded and therefore must be able to be introduced below V.

17. This formulation goes beyond (39) in that it also excludes OV languages with postverbal 'postpositional phrases'.

It is to be understood as abstracting away from Wh-movement, so English sentences like
(i) do not fall under it:

(i) Which table did you put the book on?

Similarly for other A-bar movements and for:

(ii) You're being taken unfair advantage of.

18. Dryer (1992, 92) notes that 'PP' is generally on the same side of the verb as O.

This would be expected if direct objects always have an abstract preposition (if they don't have an overt one, as in Spanish *Veo a Juan* ('I-see *a* John')), as suggested by Starke (1993, 66). In my terms, direct objects, too, are plausibly attracted by P (further discussion is beyond the scope of this essay).

19. Note, though, that the Papago determiner *g* may fit in straightforwardly, in that it can never be sentence-initial (cf. Zepeda (1983, 13)) (nor is it a second-position clitic).

English sentences like (i) will not be a problem if the preposition has attracted some phrase to its Spec prior to topicalization and if that phrase has been stranded by topicalization; cf. the discussion of Italian in chapter 14, sect. 14.6.):

(i) To John they said nothing.

Guglielmo Cinque (p.c.) points out that certain functional heads may have in their Spec an AdvP that does not originate lower down (cf. Cinque (1999)). If so, then (45) could be revised to the following without affecting the exclusion of (44) (assuming 'merge' to be a subpart of 'move'):

(ii) Functional heads must always merge something overtly to their Spec.

Jacqueline Guéron (p.c.) raises the question of how (45) can be compatible with VSO languages. The answer is probably that the initial position of the V is a result of phrasal movement (rather than of head movement), as in Lee's (1998) analysis of Zapotec.

20. See Hovdhaugen et al. (1989); Chung (1978).

21. Left open is the question why adpositional agreement seems to be absent from SVO languages (a question no longer as straightforward as it seemed in Kayne (1994, sect. 5.3)). Part of the answer is presumably that such agreement is to be thought of in terms of cliticization and clitic doubling, as is complementizer agreement.

22. See Higginbotham (1995).

23. See Kayne (1997b).

REFERENCES

Abney, S. (1987) "The English Noun Phrase in Its Sentential Aspect." Ph.D. dissertation, Massachusetts Institute of Technology, Cambridge, Mass.

Acquaviva, P. (1995) "Operator Composition and Negative Concord." *Geneva Generative Papers*, 3, 72–104.

Aissen, J. L., and D. M. Perlmutter (1983) "Clause Reduction in Spanish," in D. M. Perlmutter (ed.), *Studies in Relational Grammar 1*, University of Chicago Press, Chicago, 360–403.

Akmajian, A., S. M. Steele, and T. Wasow (1979) "The Category AUX in Universal Grammar." *Linguistic Inquiry*, 10, 1–64.

Akmajian, A., and F. Heny (1975) *An Introduction to the Principles of Transformational Syntax*, MIT Press, Cambridge, Mass.

Alex, P. (1965) *Le patois de Naisey, Canton de Roulans, Arrondissement de Besançon* (Collection de linguistique bourguigonnne et comtoise. Série comtoise. Tome 1, Pierre Voisin, Paris.

Alexiadou, A., and E. Anagnostopoulou (1998) "Parametrizing AGR: Word Order, V-Movement, and EPP-Checking." *Natural Language and Linguistic Theory*, 16, 491–539.

Alvarez, R., H. Monteagudo, and X. L. Regueira (1986) *Gramática Galega*. Biblioteca Básica da Cultura Galega, Galaxia, Vigo.

Ambar, M. (1989) "Para uma sintaxe da inversao sujeito verbo em português." Ph.D. dissertation, University of Lisbon.

Anderson, S. R. (1972) "How to Get *even*." *Language*, 48, 893–906.

Anderson, S. R. (1984) "Kwakwala Syntax and the Government-Binding Theory," in E.-D. Cook and D. B. Gerdts, (eds.) *Syntax and Semantics. Vol. 16. The Syntax of Native American Languages*, Academic Press, New York, 21–75.

Andersson, A.-B., and O. Dahl (1974) "Against the Penthouse Principle." *Linguistic Inquiry*, 5, 451–453.

Andrews, J. B. (1875) *Essai de grammaire du dialecte mentonnais*, Nice.

Androutsopoulou, A. (1997) "On remnant DP-movement in modern Greek." M.A. thesis, University of California at Los Angeles.

Anward, J. (1988) "Verb-Verb Agreement in Swedish." *McGill Working Papers in Linguistics. Special Issue on Comparative Germanic Syntax*, 1–34.

Aoun, J. (1986) *Generalized Binding: The Syntax and Logical Form of Wh-interrogatives*. Foris, Dordrecht.

Aoun, J. (1996) "Clitic-Doubled Arguments." Ms., University of Southern California.

Aoun, J., and Li, Y.-H. A. (1989) "Scope and Constituency." *Linguistic Inquiry*, 20, 141–172.

Aoun, J., and Li, Y.-H. A. (1993) "*Wh*-elements in Situ: Syntax or LF?" *Linguistic Inquiry*, 24, 199–238.

Aoun, J., and D. W. Lightfoot (1984) "Government and Contraction." *Linguistic Inquiry*, 15, 465–473.

Authier, J.-M. P. (1989) "Arbitrary Null Objects and Unselective Binding," in O. Jaeggli and K. J. Safir (eds.), *The Null Subject Parameter*, Kluwer, Dordrecht 45–67.

Authier, J.-M. (1992) "Is French a Null Subject Language in the DP?" *Probus*, 4, 1–16.

Authier, J.-M., and L. Reed (1992) "On the Syntactic Status of French Affected Datives." *Linguistic Review* 9, 295–311.

Azaretti, E. (1977) *L'evoluzione dei dialetti liguri*. Edizioni Casabianca, San Remo.

Azoulay-Vicente, A. (1985) *Les tours comportant l'expression* de + *adjectif*. Droz, Geneva.

Bach, E., and G. M. Horn (1976) "Remarks on 'Conditions on Transformations.'" *Linguistic Inquiry*, 7, 265–299.

Baker, M. C. (1985) "Incorporation: A Theory of Grammatical Function Changing." Ph.D. dissertation, Massachusetts Institute of Technology, Cambridge, Mass.

Baker, M. C. (1988) *Incorporation: A Theory of Grammatical Function Changing*. University of Chicago Press, Chicago.

Baker, M. C. (1996) *The Polysynthesis Parameter*. Oxford University Press, New York.

Baker, M., and K. Hale (1990) "Relativized Minimality and Pronoun Incorporation." *Linguistic Inquiry*, 21, 289–297.

Baker, M., K. Johnson, and I. Roberts (1989) "Passive Arguments Raised." *Linguistic Inquiry*, 20, 219–251.

Baltin, M. R. (1982) "A Landing Site Theory of Movement Rules." *Linguistic Inquiry*, 13, 1–38.

Baptista, M. (1997) "The Morpho-syntax of Nominal and Verbal Categories in Capeverdean Creole." Ph.D. dissertation, Harvard University.

Barbiers, S. (1995) "The Syntax of Interpretation." Ph.D. dissertation, Holland Institute of Generative Linguistics.

Barbosa, P., et al. (1998) *Is the Best Good Enough? Optimality and Competition in Syntax*. MIT Press, Cambridge, Mass.

Barnes, M. P., with E. Weyhe (1994) "Faroese," in E. König and J. van der Auwera (eds.), *The Germanic Languages*, Routledge, London, 190–218.

Barras, C. (1979) *Etude d'un patois Couètsou*. Mémoire de licence, University of Fribourg (Switzerland).

Barss, A., K. Hale, E. T. Perkins, and M. Speas (1992) "Logical Form and Barriers in Navajo," in C.-T. J. Huang and R. May (eds.), *Logical structure and linguistic structure, Cross-linguistic Perspectives*, Kluwer, Dordrecht, 25–47.

Bartos, H. (1999) "Object Agreement in Hungarian—A Case for Minimalism," in G. Alexandrova (ed.) *The Minimalist Parameter*, John Benjamins, Amsterdam.

Basilico, D. (1996) "Head Position and Internally Headed Relative Clauses." *Language*, 72, 498–532.

Basilico, D. (1997) "The Topic Is 'There.'" *Studia Linguistica*, 51, 278–316.

Battistella, E. (1985) "On the Distribution of PRO in Chinese." *Natural Language and Linguistic Theory*, 3, 317–340.

Bayer, J. (1983) "COMP-Node in Bavarian Syntax." *Linguistic Review*, 3, 209–274.

Bayer, J. (1990) "Directionality of Govenment and Logical Form: A Study of Focusing Particles and Wh-Scope." Ph.D. dissertation, Universität Konstanz.

Bayer, Josef (1996) *Directionality and Logical Form. On the Scope of Focusing Particles and Wh-in-situ.* Kluwer, Dordrecht.

Bec, P. (1968) *Les interférences linguistiques entre gascon et languedocien dans les parlers du Comminges et du Couserans.* Presses Universitaires de France, Paris.

Beck, S., and S.-S. Kim (1997) "On WH- and Operator Scope in Korean." *Journal of East Asian Linguistics,* 6, 339–384.

Beghelli, F., and T. Stowell (1997) "Distributivity and Negation: The Syntax of *Each* and *Every,*" in A. Szabolcsi (ed.), *Ways of Scope Taking,* Kluwer, Dordrecht, 71–107.

Belletti, Adriana (1977) "Alcuni aspetti della struttura interna del sintagma nominale italiano." Thesis, Università degli Studi di Pisa.

Belletti, A. (1981) "Frasi ridotte assolute." *Rivista di grammatica generativa,* 6, 3–32.

Belletti, A. (1982) "On the Anaphoric Status of the Reciprocal Construction in Italian." *Linguistic Review,* 2, 101–138.

Belletti, A. (1988) "The Case of Unaccusatives." *Linguistic Inquiry,* 19, 1–34.

Belletti, A. (1989) "Agreement and Case in Past Participial Clauses in Italian." Ms., University of Geneva.

Belletti, A. (1990) *Generalized Verb Movement. Aspects of Verb Syntax.* Rosenberg and Sellier, Turin.

Belletti, A. (1993) "Case Checking and Clitic Placement." *GenGenP,* 1, 101–118.

Belletti, A. (1999) "Italian/Romance Clitics: Structure and Derivation," in H. van Riemsdijk (ed.), *Clitics in the Languages of Europe,* Mouton de Gruyter, Berlin.

Belletti, A., and L. Rizzi (1988) "Psych-Verbs and θ-Theory." *Natural Language and Linguistic Theory,* 6, 291–352.

Bellosi, G., and G. Quondamatteo (1979) *Le parlate dell'Emilia e della Romagna.* Edizioni del Riccio, Florence.

Benacchio, R., and L. Renzi (1987) *Clitici slavi e romanzi.* Quaderni Patavini di Linguistica, University of Padua and C.N.R., Padua.

Benincà, P. (1983) "Il clitico *a* nel dialetto padovano," in *Scritti linguistici in onore di G. B. Pellegrini,* Pacini, Pisa, 25–35 (reprinted in Benincà [1994]).

Benincà, P. (1984) "Uso dell'ausiliare e accordo verbale nei dialetti veneti e friulani." *Rivista italiana di dialettologia,* 8, 178–194.

Benincà, P. (1986) "Punti di sintassi comparata dei dialetti italiani settentrionali," in G. Holtus and K. Ringger (eds.), *Raetia Antiqua et Moderna: W. Theodor Elwert zum 80. Geburtstag.* Niemeyer, Tübingen, 457–479.

Benincà, P. (1989a) "Friaulisch: Interne Sprachgeschichte. Grammatik. Evoluzione della grammatica," in G. Holtus, M. Metzeltin and C. Schmitt (eds.), *Lexikon der Romanistischen Linguistik.* Vol. 3, Niemeyer, Tübingen.

Benincà, P. (1989b) "Note introduttive a un atlante dialettale sintattico," in G. L. Borgato and A. Zamboni (eds.), *Dialettologia e varia linguistica per Manlio Cortelazzo* (Quaderni patavini di linguistica, Monografie 6), Padua.

Benincà, P. (1993) "Sintassi," in A. Sobrero (ed.), *L'Italiano: le Strutture,* Bari, Laterza.

Benincà, P. (1994) *La variazione sintattica. Studi di dialettologia romanza.* Il Mulino, Bologna.

Benincà, P. (1996) "Agglutination and Inflection in Northern Italian Dialects," in C. Parodi, C. Quicoli, M. Saltarelli, and M. L. Zubizarreta (eds.), *Aspects of Romance Linguistics.* Georgetown University Press, Washington, D.C., 59–72.

Benincà, P. (1998) "Between Morphology and Syntax. On the Verbal Morphology of Some Alpine Dialects." Ms., University of Padua (earlier version appeared as Benincà [1996]).

Benincà, P., and Salvi, G. (1988) "L'ordine normale degli elementi nella frase semplice," in

L. Renzi (ed.), *Grande grammatica italiana di consultazione*. Vol. I. *La frase. I sintagmi nominale e preposizionale*. Il Mulino, Bologna, 119–129.

Benmamoun, E. (1996) "Negative Polarity and Presupposition in Arabic," in M. Eid (ed.), *Perspectives on Arabic Linguistics VIII*. John Benjamins, Amsterdam, 47–66.

Bennis, H., and T. Hoekstra (1984) "Gaps and Parasitic Gaps," *Linguistic Review*, 4, 29–87.

Benveniste, E. (1966) *Problèmes de linguistique générale*. Gallimard, Paris.

Beretta, C. (1984) *Contributo per una grammatica del milanese contemporaneo*, II Edizione, Edizioni del Circolo Filologico Milanese. Virgilio, Milan.

Bernini, G. (1987) "Morfologia del dialetto di Bergamo," in G. Sanga (ed.), *Lingua e dialetti di Bergamo e delle valli*. Lubrina, Bergamo, 83–118.

Bernstein, J. (1991) "DP's in French and Walloon: Evidence for Parametric Variation in Nominal Head Movement." *Probus*, 3, 101–126.

Berretta, M. (1985) "I pronomi clitici nell'italiano parlato," in G. Holtus and E. Radtke (eds.), *Gesprochenes Italienisch in Geschichte und Gegenwart*. Narr, Tübingen, 185–223.

Bevington, B. (1998) "Indexical Expressions: Syntax and Context," Ph.D. dissertation. City University of New York.

Bianchi, V. (1993) "An Empirical Contribution to the Study of Idiomatic Expressions." *Rivista di Linguistica*, 5, 349–385.

Bianchini, S., G. Borgato, and R. Galassi (1982) "Raddoppiamento del pronome in basso-mantovano/ferrarese," in D. Calleri and C. Marello (eds.), *Linguistica contrastiva. Atti del XIII Congresso internazionale di studi, Asti, 26–28 maggio 1979*. Bulzoni, Rome, 371–389.

Bjerrome, G. (1957) *Le patois de Bagnes (Valais)*. Almqvist and Wiksell, Stockholm.

Blinkenberg, A. (1948) *Le patois de Beuil (Acta Jutlandica. Aarsskrigt for Arhaus Universitet XX, 3(H34))*. Ejnar Munksgaard, Copenhagen.

Bobaljik, J. D. (1995) "Morphosyntax: The syntax of verbal inflection." Ph.D. dissertation, Massachusetts Institute of Technology, Cambridge, Mass.

Bobaljik, J. D. (1998) "Floating Quantifiers: Handle with Care." *Glot International*, 3.6, 3–10.

Boillot, F. (1929) *Le français régional de la Grand'Combe (Doubs)*. Presses Universitaires de France, Paris.

Bolinger, D. (1971) "A Further Note on the Nominal in the Progressive." *Linguistic Inquiry*, 2, 584–586.

Bonet, E. (1991) "Morphology after Syntax: Pronominal Clitics in Romance Languages." Ph.D. dissertation, Massachusetts Institute of Technology, Cambridge, Mass.

Bonnaud, P. (1974) *Nouvelle grammaire auvergnate*. Cercle d'Auvergne, Clermont-Ferrand.

Bonneau, J., and M. Zushi (1993) "Quantifier Climbing, Clitic Climbing, and Restructuring in Romance," paper presented at the LSA annual meeting.

Bordelois, I. (1986) "Parasitic Gaps: Extensions of Restructuring," in I. Bordelois, H. Contreras, and K. Zagona (eds.), *Generative Studies in Spanish Syntax*, Foris, Dordrecht, 1–24.

Borer, H. (1984) *Parametric Syntax*. Foris, Dordrecht.

Borer, H. (1986) "I-Subjects." *Linguistic Inquiry*, 17, 375–416.

Borer, H. (1989) "Anaphoric AGR," in O. Jaeggli and K. J. Safir (eds.), *The Null Subject Parameter*. Kluwer, Dordrecht, 69–109.

Bošković, Z. (1997) "Pseudoclefts." *Studia Linguistica*, 51, 235–277.

Bošković, Z. (1998) "LF Movement and the Minimalist Program." *Proceedings of NELS*, 28, GLSA, University of Massachusetts, Amherst, 43–57.

Bosque, I. (1994) "La negación y el principio de las categorías vacías," in V. Demonte (ed.), *Estudios de gramática española, número especial monográfico de la Nueva Revista de Filología Hispánica* 6. El Colegio de México, 167–199.

Bottari, Piero (1991) "Structural Representations of the Italian Nominal Infinitive," in E. Fava (ed.), *Proceedings of the XVII Generative Grammar Meeting—Trieste, February 22–24, 1991*. Rosenberg and Sellier, Turin.

Bouchard, D. (1984) *On the Content of Empty Categories*. Foris, Dordrecht.

Bourciez, E. (1967) *Eléments de linguistique romane (cinquième édition)*. Klincksieck, Paris.

Boysen, G. (1977) "L'emploi des verbes auxiliaires *essere* et *avere* avec les verbes modaux en italien." *Studia Neophilologica*, 49, 287–309.

Brandi, L., and P. Cordin (1989) "Two Italian Dialects and the Null Subject Parameter," in O. Jaeggli and K. J. Safir (eds.), *The Null Subject Parameter*. Kluwer, Dordrecht, 111–142.

Bresnan, J. W. (1976) "On the Form and Functioning of Transformations." *Linguistic Inquiry*, 7, 3–40.

Bresnan, J. (1982) "Control and Complementation." *Linguistic Inquiry*, 13, 343–434.

Brody, M. (1990) "Remarks on the Order of Elements in the Hungarian Focus Field," in I. Kenesei (ed.), *Approaches to Hungarian. Vol. Three. Structures and Arguments*. Jate, Szeged, 95–121.

Brody, M. (1995) *Lexico-logical Form. A Radically Minimalist Theory*, MIT Press, Cambridge, Mass.

Brown, K. (1991) "Double Modals in Hawick Scots," in P. Trudgill and J. K. Chambers (eds.), *Dialects of English. Studies in Grammatical Variation*. Longman, London, 74–103.

Burzio, L. (1981) "Intransitive Verbs and Italian Auxiliaries." Ph.D. dissertation, Massachusetts Institute of Technology, Cambridge, Mass.

Burzio, L. (1986) *Italian Syntax. A Government-Binding Approach*. Reidel, Dordrecht.

Burzio, L. (1989) "Work in Progress." Ms., Harvard University.

Burzio, L. (1991) "The Morphological Basis of Anaphora." *Journal of Linguistics*, 27, 81–105.

Burzio, L. (1992) "On the Morphology of Reflexives and Impersonals," in C. Lauefer and T. Morgan (eds.), *Theoretical Analyses of Romance Linguistics; Selected Papers from the Nineteenth Linguistic Symposium on Romance Languages (LSRL XIX)*. John Benjamins, Amsterdam.

Burzio, L. (1996) "The Role of the Antecedent in Anaphoric Relations," in R. Freidin (ed.), *Current Issues in Comparative Grammar*. Kluwer, Dordrecht, 1–45.

Butler, A. S. G. (1962) *Les parlers dialectaux et populaires dans l'oeuvre de Guy de Maupassant (Publications romanes et françaises LXXII)*. Droz, Geneva, and Minard, Paris.

Butz, B. (1981) *Morphosyntax der Mundart von Vermes (Val Terbi)*. Francke, Bern.

Calabrese, A. (1988) "I pronomi clitici," in L. Renzi (ed.), *Grande grammatica italiana di consultazione. Vol. I. La frase. I sintagmi nominale e preposizionale*. Il Mulino, Bologna, 549–592.

Camproux, C. (1958) *Etude syntaxique des parlers gévaudanais* (Publications de la Faculté des Lettres de l'Université de Montpellier, XX). Presses Universitaires de France, Paris.

Canepari, L. (1986) *Lingua italiana nel Veneto* (2nd ed.), CLESP, Padua.

Cardinaletti, A., and M. Starke (1994) "The Typology of Structural Deficiency: On the Three Grammatical Classes." *Working Papers in Linguistics* 4. University of Venice, 41–109.

Cecchetto, C. (1999) "A Comparative Analysis of Left and Right Dislocation in Romance." *Studia Linguistica*, 53, 40–67.

Cecchetto, C. (to appear) "Doubling Structures and Reconstruction," *Probus*.

Chabaneau, C. (1874) "Grammaire limousine (suite)." *Revue des Langues Romanes*, 5, 171–196, 435–481.

Chauveau, J.-P. (1984) "Le gallo: une présentation." Faculté des Lettres de Brest, Université de Bretagne Occidentale (Section de Celtique).

Chenal, A. (1986) *Le franco-provençal valdôtain*. Musumeci, Aoste.

Cheng, L. L.-S. (1994) "Wh-words as Polarity Items." *Chinese Languages and Linguistics*, 2, 615–640.

Cheng, L. L.-S. (1995) "On *dou*-quantification." *Journal of East Asian Linguistics*, 4, 197–234.

Cheng, L. L.-S. and R. Sybesma (1999) "Bare and Not-So-Bare Nouns and the Structure of NP." *Linguistic Inquiry*, 30, 509–542.

Cheshire, J., V. Edwards, and P. Whittle (1993) "Non-standard English and Dialect Levelling," in J. Milroy and L. Milroy (eds.), *Real English. The Grammar of English Dialects in the British Isles*. Longman, London, 53–96.

Chiominto, C. (1984) *Lo parlà forte della pora ggente*, Biblioteca di Cultura 243. Bulzoni, Rome.

Choe, H.-S. (1988) *"Restructuring Parameters and Complex Predicates—A Transformational Approach."* Ph.D. dissertation, Massachusetts Institute of Technology, Cambridge, Mass.

Choe, H.-S. (1997) "Two Functions of Negation: Negating and Licensing." Ms M.I.T./ Yeungnam University.

Chomsky, N. (1957) *Syntactic Structures*. Mouton, The Hague.

Chomsky, N. (1970) "Remarks on Nominalization," in R. A. Jacobs and P. S. Rosenbaum (eds.), *Readings in English Transformational Grammar*, Ginn, Waltham, 184–221.

Chomsky, N. (1973) "Conditions on Transformations," in S. R. Anderson and P. Kiparsky (eds.), *A Festschrift for Morris Halle*, Holt, Rinehart and Winston, New York, 232–286.

Chomsky, N. (1976) "Conditions on Rules of Grammar." *Linguistic Analysis*, 2, 303–351.

Chomsky, N. (1977) "On Wh-movement," in P. W. Culicover, T. Wasow, and A. Akmajian (eds.), *Formal Syntax*, Academic Press, New York, 71–132.

Chomsky, N. (1980) "On Binding." *Linguistic Inquiry*, 11, 1–46.

Chomsky, N. (1981a) *Lectures on Government and Binding*. Foris, Dordrecht.

Chomsky, N. (1981b) "Markedness and Core Grammar," in A. Belletti, L. Brandi, and L. Rizzi (eds.), *Theory of Markedness in Generative Grammar. Proceedings of the 1979 GLOW Conference*, Scuola Normale Superiore, Pisa, 123–146.

Chomsky, N. (1982) *Some Concepts and Consequences of the Theory of Government and Binding*. MIT Press, Cambridge, Mass.

Chomsky, N. (1986a) *Barriers*. MIT Press, Cambridge, Mass.

Chomsky, N. (1986b) *Knowledge of Language*. Praeger, New York.

Chomsky, N. (1991) "Some Notes on Economy of Derivation and Representation," in R. Freidin (ed.), *Principles and Parameters in Comparative Grammar*, MIT Press, Cambridge, Mass., 417–454 (reprinted as chapter 2 of Chomsky (1995)).

Chomsky, N., (1993) "A Minimalist Program for Linguistic Theory," in K. Hale and S. J. Keyser (eds.), *The View from Building 20. Essays in Linguistics in Honor of Sylvain Bromberger*, MIT Press, Cambridge, Mass. (reprinted as chapter 3 of Chomsky (1995)).

Chomsky, N. (1995) *The Minimalist Program*. MIT Press, Cambridge, Mass.

Chomsky, N. (1998) "Minimalist Inquiries: The Framework." *MIT Occasional Papers in Linguistics*, 15, MITWPL, Cambridge, Mass.

Chomsky, N. (1999) "Derivation by Phase," ms., Massachusetts Institute of Technology.

Chomsky, N., and H. Lasnik (1993) "Principles and Parameters Theory," in J. Jacobs, A. von Stechow, W. Sternefeld, and T. Vennemann (eds.), *Syntax: An International Handbook of Contemporary Research*, Walter de Gruyter, Berlin (reprinted as chapter 1 of Chomsky (1995)).

Christensen, K. K. (1985) "Complex Passive and Conditions on Reanalysis." *Working Papers in Scandinavian Syntax*, 19, Trondheim.

Christensen, K. K. (1986) "Norwegian *ingen*: A Case of Post-syntactic Lexicalization," in

O. Dahl and A. Holmberg (eds.), *Scandinavian Syntax*, Institute of Linguistics, University of Stockholm, 21–35.

Christensen, K. K., and Taraldsen, K. T. (1989) "Expletive Chain Formation and Past Participle Agreement in Scandinavian Dialects," in P. Benincà (ed.), *Dialect Variation and the Theory of Grammar*, Foris, Dordrecht, 53–83.

Chung, S. (1978) *Case Marking and Grammatical Relations in Polynesian*. University of Texas Press, Austin.

Chung, S., and J. McCloskey (1987) "Government, Barriers, and Small Clauses in Modern Irish." *Linguistic Inquiry*, 18, 173–237.

Cinque, G. (1975) "The Shadow Pronoun Hypothesis and 'Chopping' Rules in Romance." *Linguistic Inquiry* 6, 140–145.

Cinque, G. (1976) "'Mica.'" *Annali della Facoltà di Lettere e Filosofia*, Università di Padova, 1, Olschki, Florence, 101–112.

Cinque, G. (1988) "On *Si* Constructions and the Theory of *Arb*." *Linguistic Inquiry*, 19, 521–581.

Cinque, G. (1990a) *Types of A'-Dependencies*, MIT Press, Cambridge, Mass.

Cinque, G. (1990b) "Ergative Adjectives and the Lexicalist Hypothesis." *Natural Language and Linguistic Theory* 8, 1–39 (reprinted in Cinque (1995))

Cinque, G. (1995) *Italian Syntax and Universal Grammar*. Cambridge University Press, Cambridge.

Cinque, Guglielmo (1998) "On Clitic Climbing and Other Transparency Effects," paper presented at New York University.

Cinque, G. (1999) *Adverbs and Functional Heads. A Cross-Linguistic Perspective*. Oxford University Press, New York.

Cochet, E. (1933) *Le patois de Gondecourt (Nord)*. Droz, Paris.

Cole, P., and Hermon, G. (1994) "Is There LF *Wh*-movement?" *Linguistic Inquiry*, 25, 239–262.

Collins, C., and H. Thráinsson (1993) "Object Shift in Double Object Constructions and the Theory of Case," in C. Phillips (ed.), *Papers on Case and Agreement II, MIT Working Papers in Linguistics* (vol. 19), Cambridge, Mass., 131–174.

Comrie, B., ed. (1987) *The World's Major Languages*. Oxford University Press, New York.

Coopmans, P. (1985) *Language Types: Continua or Parameters?* Doctoral dissertation, University of Utrecht.

Coppens, J. (1959) *Grammaire aclote. Parler populaire de Nivelles*. Fédération wallonne du Brabant.

Cordin, P. (1988) "I pronomi riflessivi," in L. Renzi (ed.), *Grande grammatica italiana di consultazione. Vol. I. La frase. I sintagmi nominale e preposizionale*, Il Mulino, Bologna, 593–603.

Corver, N. (1990) *The Syntax of Left Branch Extractions*. Doctoral dissertation, Tilburg University.

Corver, N., and D. Delfitto (1993) "Feature Asymmetry and the Nature of Pronoun Movement." *OTS Working Papers*, Research Institute for Language and Speech, University of Utrecht.

Costa, J. (1997) "On the Behavior of Adverbs in Sentence-final Context." *Linguistic Review*, 14, 43–68.

Couquaux, D. (1976) "Une règle de réanalyse en français." *Recherches linguistiques*, 4, Université de Paris VIII—Vincennes, 32–74.

Couquaux, D. (1978) "Sur une incompatibilité de pronoms clitiques en français." *Lingvisticae Investigationes*, 2, 211–214.

Couquaux, D. (1979) "Sur la syntaxe des phrases prédicatives en français." *Lingvisticae Investigationes*, 3, 245–284.

Crockett, D. B. (1976) *Agreement in Contemporary Standard Russian.* Slavica, Cambridge, Mass.

Crum, B., and J. Dayley (1993) *Western Shoshoni Grammar (Occasional Papers and Monographs in Cultural Anthropology and Linguistics. Vol. 1),* Boise State University.

Crystal, D., ed. (1987) *The Cambridge Encyclopedia of Language.* Cambridge University Press, Cambridge, England.

Curme, G. O. (1977 (1931)) *A Grammar of the English Language. Vol. II: Syntax.* Verbatim, Essex, Conn.

Dansereau, D. M. (1985) *Studies in the Syntax of Central Languedocian.* Doctoral dissertation, University of Michigan.

Davis, L. J., and Prince, E. F. (1986) "Yiddish Verb-topicalization and the Notion 'Lexical Integrity'." in A. Farley and K.-E. McCullough (eds.), *Papers from the 22nd Regional Meeting,* Chicago Linguistic Society, 90–97.

Delfitto, D. (1990) *Generics and Variables in Syntax.* Tesi di Perfezionamento, Scuola Normale Superiore, Pisa.

Delfitto, D. (n.d.) "For a Diachronic Approach to Past Participle Morphology and Auxiliary Selection." Ms., University of Utrecht.

Den Besten, H., and Webelhuth, G. (1987) "Remnant Topicalization and the Constituent Structure of VP in the Germanic SOV Languages" (abstract). *GLOW Newsletter,* 18, 15–16.

Den Besten, H., and Webelhuth, G. (1990) "Stranding," in G. Grewendorf and W. Sternefeld (eds.), *Scrambling and Barriers,* Academic Press, Amsterdam, 77–92.

Den Dikken, M. (1995a) "Extraposition as Intraposition, and the Syntax of English Tag Questions." Ms., Vrije Universiteit Amsterdam/HIL.

Den Dikken, M. (1995b) *Particles. On the Syntax of Verb-particle, Triadic, and Causative Constructions.* Oxford University Press, New York.

Den Dikken, M. (1995c) "Copulas." Ms., Vrije Universiteit Amsterdam/HIL.

Den Dikken, M. (1996) "How External Is the External Argument?" paper presented at WECOL 1996, Vrije Universiteit Amsterdam/HIL.

Den Dikken, M. (1999) "The Syntax of Features." Ms., Graduate Center, City University of New York.

Déprez, V. (1989) *On the Typology of Syntactic Positions and the Nature of Chains.* Doctoral dissertation, Massachusetts Institute of Technology, Cambridge, Mass.

Déprez, V. (1994) "Parameters of Object Movement," in N. Corver and H. van Riemsdijk (eds.), *Studies on Scrambling. Movement and Non-movement Approaches to Free Word-order Phenomena,* Mouton de Gruyter, Berlin, 101–152.

Déprez, V. (1997a) "Two Types of Negative Concord." *Probus,* 9, 103–143.

Déprez, V. (1997b) "Subject/Object Asymmetries in Negative Concord. Ms., Rutgers University.

Di Sciullo, A. M., and E. Williams (1987) *On the Definition of Word.* MIT Press, Cambridge, Mass.

Ditchy, J. K. (1977) *Les acadiens louisianais et leur parler.* Slatkine Reprints, Geneva (Droz, Paris, 1932).

Dobrovie-Sorin, C. (1989) "Auxiliaries and Sentence Structure in Romanian," in J. Mascaró and M. Nespor (eds.), *Grammar in Progress,* Foris, Dordrecht, 101–111.

Dobrovie-Sorin, C. (1990) "Clitic Placement and the Rule of Verb Preposing." Ms., CNRS-Université de Paris 7.

Doniol, H. (1877) *Les patois de la Basse Auvergne: leur grammaire et leur littérature.* Société pour l'étude des langues romanes, Montpellier (Maisonneuve, Paris).

Dougherty, R. C. (1970) "A Grammar of Coordinate Conjoined Structures: I." *Language,* 46, 850–898.

Dougherty, R. C. (1971) "A Grammar of Coordinate Conjoined Structures: II." *Language*, 47, 298–339.

Dryer, M. S. (1992) "The Greenbergian Word Order Correlations." *Language*, 68, 81–138.

Duffield, N. (1995) *Particles and Projections in Irish Syntax*. Kluwer, Dordrecht.

Dupraz, J. (1938) "Notes sur le patois de Saxel (Haute-Savoie), en 1941." *Revue de linguistique romane*, 14, 279–330.

Durand, M. (1936) *Le genre grammatical en français parlé à Paris et dans la région parisienne*. Bibliothèque du "français moderne," Paris.

E. Kiss, K. (1992) "Logical Structure in Syntactic Structure," in C.-T. J. Huang and R. May (eds.), *Logical Structure and Linguistic Structure. Cross-linguistic Perspectives*. Kluwer, Dordrecht, 111–147.

Einarsson, S. (1945) *Icelandic. Grammar, Texts, Glossary*. Johns Hopkins Press, Baltimore.

Emonds, J. E. (1976) *A Transformational Approach to English Syntax. Root, Structure-Preserving, and Local Transformations*. Academic Press, New York.

Emonds, J. (1978) "The Verbal Complex V'-V in French." *Linguistic Inquiry*, 9, 151–175.

Emonds, J. E. (1985) *A Unified Theory of Syntactic Categories*. Foris, Dordrecht.

Endo, Y. (1996) "Right Dislocation," in M. Koizumi, M. Oishi and U. Sauerland (eds.) *Formal Approaches to Japanese Linguistics: Proceedings of FAJL 2* (MIT Working Papers in Linguistics #29).

Engdahl, E. (1997) "Relative Clause Extractions in Context." *Working Papers in Scandinavian Syntax*, 60, 51–79.

Engver, K. (1972) *Place de l'adverbe déterminant un infinitif dans la prose du français contemporain*. Studia Romanica Upsaliensia, 7, Uppsala.

Epstein, S. D. (1984) "Quantifier-pro and the LF Representation of PRO$_{arb}$." *Linguistic Inquiry*, 15, 499–505.

Everaert, M. (1986) *The Syntax of Reflexivization*. Doctoral dissertation, University of Utrecht.

Everaert, M. (1992) "Auxiliary Selection in Idiomatic Constructions." Ms., University of Utrecht.

Fabra, P. (1981) *Gramatica catalana*, 10th ed., Teide, Barcelona.

Farrell, P. (1990) "Null Objects in Brazilian Portuguese." *Natural Language and Linguistic Theory*, 8, 325–346.

Fauconnier, G. (1974) *La coréférence: syntaxe ou sémantique?* Editions du Seuil, Paris.

Fava, E. (1991) "Interrogative indirette," in L. Renzi and G. Salvi (eds.), *Grande grammatica italiana di consultazione. Vol. II. I sintagmi verbale, aggettivale, avverbiale. La subordinazione*, Il Mulino, Bologna, 675–720.

Féral, R. (1986) *Le patois de Saussey*. Association Bourguignonne de Dialectologie et d'Onomastique, Fontaine lès Dijon.

Fillmore, C. J. (1968) "The Case for Case," in E. Bach and R. T. Harms (eds.), *Universals in Linguistic Theory*, Holt, Rinehart and Winston, London, 1–88.

Fiva, T. (1984) "NP-Internal Chains in Norwegian." *Working Papers in Scandinavian Syntax*, 14.

Flutre, L.-F. (1955) *Le parler picard de Mesnil-Martinsart (Somme)*. Droz, Geneva, and Giard, Lille.

Flutre, L.-F. (1970) *Le moyen picard d'après les textes littéraires du temps (1560–1660)*. Musée de Picardie (Collection de la Société de linguistique picarde, Tome XIII), Amiens.

Fornaciari, R. (1974 (1881)) *Sintassi italiana*. Sansoni, Florence.

Fougeu-Fontaine, M. (1986) *Le patois de Chaumont Le Bois*. Association Bourguignonne de Dialectologie et d'Onomastique, Fontaine lès Dijon.

Foulet, L. (1968) *Petite syntaxe de l'ancien français*. Honoré Champion, Paris.

Frampton, J. (1990) "Parasitic Gaps and the Theory of WH-Chains." *Linguistic Inquiry*, 21, 49–77.

Francard, M. (1980) *Le parler de Tenneville: Introduction à l'étude linguistique des parlers wallo-lorrains* (Bibliothèque des Cahiers de l'Institut de Linguistique de Louvain-19). Cabay, Louvain-la-Neuve.

Franks, S., and Progovac, L. (1994) "On the Placement of Serbo-Croatian Clitics," in G. Fowler, H. Cooper, Jr., and J. Ludwig (eds.), *Indiana Slavic Studies*, 7, 69–78.

Fraser, B. (1966) "Some Remarks on the Verb-particle Construction in English," in F. P. Dinneen (ed.), *17th Annual Round Table*, Institute of Languages and Linguistics, Georgetown University, 45–61.

Fraser, B. (1976) *The Verb-Particle Combination in English*. Academic Press, New York.

Freeze, R. (1992) "Existentials and Other Locatives," *Language*, 68, 553–595.

Fresina, C. (1980) *Aspects de la grammaire transformationnelle de l'italien*. Thèse de 3ème cycle, Université de Paris VIII.

Fresina, C. (1982) "Les verbes de mouvement et les aspectuels en italien." *Lingvisticae Investigationes*, 6, 283–331.

Fukui, N. (1989) "Strong Barriers and Weak Barriers," paper presented at Syntax Circle, Rutgers University.

Gaatone, D. (1992) "De quelques notions de base dans une grammaire de l'ordre des mots," in L. Tasmowski and A. Zribi-Hertz (eds.), *Hommages à Nicolas Ruwet*, Communication and Cognition, Ghent, 244–254.

Galet, Y. (1971) *L'évolution de l'ordre des mots dans la phrase française de 1600 à 1700*. PUF, Paris.

Ganzoni, G. P. (1983a) *Grammatica ladina. Grammatica sistematica dal rumantsch d'Engiadina Bassa per scolars e creschüts da lingua rumantscha e francesa*. Lia Rumantscha, Samedan.

Ganzoni, G. P. (1983b) *Grammatica ladina: Grammatica sistematica dal rumauntsch d'Engiadin' Ota*. Lia Rumantscha, Samedan.

Gatti, T. (1990) *Confronto tra fenomeni sintattici nell'italiano e nel dialetto trentino: participio passato, accordo e ausiliari*. Tesi di laurea, University of Trento.

Gesner, B. E. (1979) "Etude morphosyntaxique du parler acadien de la Baie Sainte-Marie, Nouvelle-Ecosse (Canada)," Publication B-85, Centre international de recherche sur le bilinguisme, Québec.

Giammarco, E. (1973) "Selezione del verbo ausiliare nei paradigmi dei tempi composti." *Abruzzo*, 11, 152–178.

Giorgi, A. (1984) "Toward a Theory of Long Distance Anaphors: A GB Approach." *Linguistic Review*, 3, 307–361.

Giorgi, A., and F. Pianesi (1997) *Tense and Aspect. From Semantics to Morphosyntax*. Oxford University Press, New York.

Giupponi, E. (1988) *Pro-Drop-Parameter und Restrukturierung im Trentino*. Diplomarbeit zur Erlangung des Magistergrades, University of Vienna.

Giusti, G. (1992) *La sintassi dei sintagmi nominali quantificati. Uno studio comparativo*. Tesi di dottorato, University of Padua/University of Venice.

Goodall, G. (1985) "Parallel Structures in Syntax." *Linguistic Review*, 5, 173–184.

Gougenheim, G. (1971) *Etude sur les périphrases verbales de la langue française*. Nizet, Paris.

Granier, S. (1978) *Petite grammaire de l'occitan*. Escola Occitana d'Estiu, Villeneuve/Lot.

Grevisse, M. (1964) *Le bon usage* (8th ed.). J. Duculot, Gembloux.

Grevisse, M. (1993) *Le bon usage* (13th ed., by André Goosse). Duculot, Paris.

Grimshaw, J. (1991) "Extended Projection." Ms., Brandeis University.

Groat, E., and J. O'Neil (1996) "Spell-out at the LF interface," in W. Abraham, S. D. Epstein,

H. Thráinsson, and C. J.-W. Zwart (eds.), *Minimal ideas. Syntactic studies in the minimalist framework*, John Benjamins, Amsterdam, 113–139.

Groos, A., and van Riemsdijk, H. (1981) "Matching Effects in Free Relatives: A Parameter of Core Grammar," in A. Belletti, L. Brandi, and L. Rizzi (eds.), *Theory of Markedness in Generative Grammar. Proceedings of the 1979 GLOW Conference*, Scuola Normale Superiore, Pisa, 171–216.

Gross, M. (1968) *Grammaire transformationnelle du français. Syntaxe du verbe*. Larousse, Paris.

Gross, M. (1975) *Méthodes en syntaxe. Régime des constructions complétives*. Hermann, Paris.

Guasti, M. T. (1990) "The *faire-par* Construction in Romance and Germanic," in L. Halpern (ed.), *Proceedings of the Ninth West Coast Conference on Formal Linguistics*, CSLI, 205–217.

Gulli, A. (1997) "Free Relatives and DP-reduplication." Ms., New York University.

Guéron, J. (1980) "On the Syntax and Semantics of PP Extraposition." *Linguistic Inquiry*, 11, 637–678.

Haegeman, L. (1993) "The Morphology and Distribution of Object Clitics in West Flemish." *Studia Linguistica*, 47, 57–94.

Haegeman, L. (1995) *The Syntax of Negation*. Cambridge University Press, Cambridge.

Haegeman, L. (1996) "Negative Inversion, the Neg-criterion and the Structure of CP." *Geneva Generative Papers*, 4, 93–119.

Haegeman, L., and H. van Riemsdijk (1986) "Verb Projection Raising, Scope, and the Typology of Rules Affecting Verbs." *Linguistic Inquiry*, 17, 417–466.

Haegeman, L., and R. Zanuttini (1996) "Negative Concord in West Flemish" in A. Belletti and L. Rizzi (eds.), *Parameters and Functional Heads. Essays in Comparative Syntax*, Oxford University Press, New York, 117–179.

Haider, H. (1985) "Von *sein* oder nicht *sein*: Zur Grammatik des Pronomens *sich*," in W. Abraham (ed.) *Erklärende Syntax des Deutschen*, Gunter Narr, Tübingen, 223–254.

Haider, H., and R. Rindler-Schjerve (1988) "The Parameter of Auxiliary Selection: Italian-German Contrasts." *Linguistics*, 25, 1029–1055.

Haiman, J. (1980) *HUA: A Papuan Language of the Eastern Highlands of New Guinea*. John Benjamins, Amsterdam.

Haiman, J. (1988) "Rhaeto-Romance," in M. Harris and N. Vincent (eds.), *The Romance Languages*, Oxford University Press, New York, 351–390.

Hale, K. (1973) "Person Marking in Walbiri," in S. R. Anderson and P. Kiparsky (eds.), *A Festschrift for Morris Halle*, Holt, Rinehart and Winston, New York, 308–344.

Harmer, L. C. (1979) *Uncertainties in French Grammar*. Cambridge University Press, Cambridge.

Harris, J. W. (1969) *Spanish Phonology*. MIT Press, Cambridge, Mass.

Harris, J. W. (1991) "The Exponence of Gender in Spanish." *Linguistic Inquiry*, 22, 27–62.

Harris, J. W. (1997) "Morphologie autonome et pronoms clitiques en catalan et en espagnol," in A. Zribi-Hertz (ed.), *Les pronoms. Morphologie, syntaxe et typologie*, Presses Universitaires de Vincennes, Saint-Denis, 35–55.

Harris, J. (1993) "The Grammar of Irish English," in J. Milroy and L. Milroy (eds.), *Real English. The Grammar of English Dialects in the British Isles*, Longman, London, pp. 139–186.

Harris, R. (1969) "Pronominal Postposition in Valdôtain." *Revue de linguistique romane*, 33, 133–143.

Harves, S. (1998) "The syntax of negated prepositional phrases in Slavic." In Z. Bošković, S. Franks and W. Snyder (eds.), *Formal Approaches to Slavic Linguistics #6*, Michigan Slavic Publications, Ann Arbor.

Hauchard, V. (1994) *Vie et Parler traditionnels dans le canton de Condé-sur-Noireau, Calvados*. Presses Universitaires de Caen, Charles Corlet, Caen/Condé-sur-Noireau.

Heim, I., H. Lasnik, and R. May (1991) "Reciprocity and Plurality." *Linguistic Inquiry*, 22, 63–101.

Helke, M. (1973) "On Reflexives in English." *Linguistics*, 106, 5–23.

Hellan, L., and K. C. Christensen, eds. (1986) *Topics in Scandinavian Syntax*. Reidel, Dordrecht.

Henry, A. (1995) *Belfast English and Standard English. Dialect Variation and Parameter Setting*. Oxford University Press, New York.

Henry, A. (1996) "Imperative Inversion in Belfast English," in J. R. Black and V. Motapanyane, eds., *Microparametric Syntax and Dialect Variation*, Benjamins, Amsterdam, 79–93.

Herburger, E. (1993) "Focus and Scrambling: The Need for Hierarchy Preservation" (abstract), University of Southern California.

Hernanz, M. L., and G. Rigau (1984) "Auxiliaritat i reestructuració." Els Marges 31, 29–51.

Hervé, B. (1973) *Le parler de Plouguenast*. Master's thesis, University of Haute Bretagne.

Hestvik, A. G. (1990) *LF-Movement of Pronouns and the Computation of Binding Domains*. Doctoral dissertation, Brandeis University, Waltham, Mass.

Hestvik, A. G. (1992) "LF Movement of Pronouns and Antisubject Orientation." *Linguistic Inquiry*, 23, 557–594.

Higginbotham, J. (1983) "Logical Form, Binding, and Nominals." *Linguistic Inquiry*, 14, 395–420.

Higginbotham, J. (1989) "Reference and Control." *Rivista di Linguistica*, 1, 301–326.

Higginbotham, J. (1995) "Semantic computation." Ms., Somerville College, Oxford.

Hill, A. A. (1958) *Introduction to Linguistic Structures*. Harcourt, Brace and Company, New York.

Hinterhölzl, R. (1997) "An XP-movement Account of Restructuring." Ms., University of Southern California.

Hirschbühler, P., and Rivero, M.-L. (1983) "Remarks on Free Relatives and Matching Phenomena," *Linguistic Inquiry*, 14, 505–520.

Hoekstra, T. (1984) *Transitivity. Grammatical Relations in Government-Binding Theory*. Foris, Dordrecht.

Hoekstra, T. (1995) "To Have to Be Dative," in H. Haider, S. Olsen, and S. Vikner (eds.), *Studies in Comparative Germanic Syntax*, Kluwer, Dordrecht, 119–137.

Hoekstra, T. (1999) "Parallels between Nominal and Verbal Projections," in D. Adger et al. (eds.) *Specifiers*, Oxford University Press, 163–187.

Hoekstra, T., and R. Mulder (1990) "Unergatives as Copular Verbs; Locational and Existential predication." *Linguistic Review*, 7, 1–79.

Holmberg, A. (1986) *Word Order and Syntactic Features in the Scandinavian Languages and English*. Doctoral dissertation, University of Stockholm.

Holmberg, A. (1987) "The IP/VP Parameter," talk presented at the Fourth Workshop on Comparative Germanic Syntax, McGill University, Montreal.

Holmberg, A. (1990) "On Bare Infinitivals in Swedish," in J. Mascaró and M. Nespor (eds.), *Grammar in Progress. Glow Essays for Henk van Riemsdijk*, Foris, Dordrecht, 237–245.

Holmberg, A. (1999) "Remarks on Holmberg's Generalization," *Studia Linguistica 53*, 1–39.

Holmberg, A., and C. Platzack (1995) *The Role of Inflection in Scandinavian Syntax*. Oxford University Press, New York.

Holmes, P., and I. Hinchliffe (1994) *Swedish. A Comprehensive Grammar*. Routledge, London.

Honda, K. (1997) "The "VP"-constituent in Japanese and Its Theoretical Implications." *Dokkyo Working Papers in Linguistics*, 14, 5–40.

Horn, L. R. (1978) "Remarks on Neg-raising," in P. Cole (ed.), *Syntax and Semantics 9. Pragmatics*, Academic Press, New York, 129–220.

Horn, L. R. (1989) *A Natural History of Negation*. University of Chicago Press, Chicago, Ill.

Hornstein, N. (1990) "Sequence of Tense and Infinitives," paper presented at the M.I.T. Conference on Time in Language.

Hornstein, N. (1994) "An Argument for Minimalism: The Case of Antecedent-contained Deletion." *Linguistic Inquiry*, 25, 455–480.

Hornstein, N. (1995) *Logical Form. From GB to Minimalism*. Blackwell, Oxford.

Horvath, J. (1995) "Structural Focus, Structural Case, and the Notion of Feature-assignment," in K. E. Kiss (ed.), *Discourse Configurational Languages*, Oxford University Press, New York, 28–64.

Horvath, J. (1997) "The Status of 'Wh-expletives' and the Partial Wh-movement Construction of Hungarian." *Natural Language and Linguistic Theory*, 15, 509–572.

Hovdhaugen, E., I. Hoëm, C. M. Iosefo, and A. M. Vonen (1989) *A Handbook of the Tokelau Language*. Norwegian University Press: The Institute for Comparative Research in Human Culture and Office for Tokelau Affairs, Oslo and Apia.

Huang, C.-T. J. (1982a) *Logical Relations in Chinese and the Theory of Grammar*, Ph.D. dissertation, Massachusetts Institute of Technology, Cambridge, Mass.

Huang, C.-T. J. (1982b) "Move WH in a Language without WH Movement." *Linguistic Review*, 1, 369–416.

Huang, C.-T. J. (1983) "A Note on the Binding Theory." *Linguistic Inquiry*, 14, 554–561.

Huang, C.-T. J. (1989) "Pro-Drop in Chinese: A Generalized Control Theory," in O. Jaeggli and K. J. Safir (eds.), *The Null Subject Parameter*, Kluwer, Dordrecht, 185–214.

Huang, C.-T. J. (1993) "Reconstruction and the Structure of VP: Some Theoretical Consequences." *Linguistic Inquiry*, 24, 103–138.

Hull, A. (1988) "The First Person Plural Form: *Je Parlons*," *French Review*, 62, 242–247.

Huot, H. (1974) "Les relatives parenthétiques," in C. Rohrer and N. Ruwet (eds.), *Actes du Colloque Franco-allemand de Grammaire Transformationnelle I*, Niemeyer, Tübingen, 31–62.

Huot, H. (1981) *Constructions infinitives du français. Le subordonnant* de. Droz, Geneva-Paris.

Iatridou, S. (1988) "Clitics, Anaphors, and a Problem of Coindexation." *Linguistic Inquiry*, 19, 698–703.

Jackendoff, R. S. (1972) *Semantic Interpretation in Generative Grammar*. MIT Press, Cambridge, Mass.

Jaeggli, O. (1986) "Passive." *Linguistic Inquiry*, 17, 587–622.

Jayaseelan, K. A. (1996) "Anaphors as Pronouns." *Studia Linguistica* 50, 207–255.

Jayaseelan, K. A. (1998) "Blocking Effects and the Syntax of Malayalam *Taan*," in R. Singh (ed.), *The Yearbook of South Asian Languages and Linguistics*, Sage, New Dehli, 11–27.

Jespersen, O. (1961) *A Modern English Grammar on Historical Principles, Part V*. George Allen and Unwin, London, and Ejnar Munksgaard, Copenhagen.

Johansson, S. (1979) "American and British English Grammar: An Elicitation Experiment." *English Studies*, 60, 195–215.

Johnson, K. (1988) "Verb Raising and 'Have'," *McGill Working Papers in Linguistics. Special Issue on Comparative Germanic Syntax*, Montreal, 156–167.

Johnson, K. (1991) "Object Positions." *Natural Language and Linguistic Theory*, 9, 577–636.

Johnson, K. (1994) "Bridging the Gap." Ms., University of Massachusetts, Amherst.

Johnson, K. (1996) "In Search of the English Middle Field," Ms., University of Massachusetts, Amherst.

Johnson, K. (1997) "A Way to Hide Scope," paper presented at the Graduate Center, CUNY.

Johnson, K. and S. Tomioka (1998) "Lowering and Mid-Size Clauses," In Proceedings of the

1997 Tübingen Workshop on Reconstruction, 185–206. Sprachteoretische Grundlagen für die Computer Linguistik, Tübingen, Germany.

Jones, M. (1988) "Sardinian," in M. Harris and N. Vincent (eds.), *The Romance Languages*, Oxford University Press, New York, 314–350.

Jones, M. (1990) "Some Distinctive Properties of Sardinian Syntax," paper presented at the conference on Central Romance, University of Geneva.

Jones, M. A. (1993) *Sardinian Syntax*. Routledge, London.

Jones, M. A. (1996) "The Pronoun ~ Determiner Debate: Evidence From Sardinian and Repercussions for French," paper presented at Linguistic Symposium for Romance Languages 26, Mexico City.

Jónsson, J. G. (1996) *Clausal Architecture and Case in Icelandic*. Doctoral dissertation, University of Massachusetts, Amherst.

Kany, C. E. (1976) *Sintaxis Hispanoamericana*. Editorial Gredos, Madrid.

Katz, J. J., and P. M. Postal (1964) *An Integrated Theory of Linguistic Descriptions*. MIT Press, Cambridge, Mass.

Kawashima, R. (1993) "Indefinite Wh Pronouns and the Morpheme *mo* in Japanese," in P. M. Clancy (ed.), *Japanese/Korean Linguistics*, Vol. 2, CSLI, Stanford University, 267–282.

Kayne, R. S. (1972) "Subject Inversion in French Interrogatives," in J. Casagrande and B. Saciuk (eds.), *Generative Studies in Romance Languages*, Newbury House, Rowley, Mass., 70–126.

Kayne, R. S. (1975) *French Syntax. The Transformational Cycle*. MIT Press, Cambridge, Mass.

Kayne, R. S. (1976) "French Relative 'que'," in F. Hensey and M. Luján (eds.), *Current Studies in Romance Linguistics*, Georgetown University Press, Washington, D.C., 255–299.

Kayne, R. S. (1980a) "Vers une solution d'un problème grammatical: *Je l'ai voulu lire, j'ai tout voulu lire*," *Langue Française*, 46, 32–40.

Kayne, R. S. (1980b) "Extensions of Binding and Case-marking." *Linguistic Inquiry*, 11, 75–96 (reprinted in Kayne (1984)).

Kayne, R. S. (1981a) "Two Notes on the NIC," in A. Belletti, L. Brandi, and L. Rizzi (eds.), *Theory of Markedness in Generative Grammar. Proceedings of the 1979 GLOW Conference*, Scuola Normale Superiore, Pisa, 317–346 (reprinted in Kayne (1984)).

Kayne, R. S. (1981b) "Binding, Quantifiers, Clitics, and Control," in F. Heny (ed.), *Binding and Filtering*, Croom Helm, London, 191–211 (reprinted in Kayne (1984)).

Kayne, R. S. (1981c) "Unambiguous Paths," in R. May and J. Koster (eds.), *Levels of Syntactic Representation*, Foris, Dordrecht, 143–183 (reprinted in Kayne (1984)).

Kayne, R. S. (1981d) "ECP extensions." *Linguistic Inquiry*, 12, 93–133 (reprinted in Kayne (1984)).

Kayne, R. S. (1981e) "On Certain Differences between French and English." *Linguistic Inquiry*, 12, 349–371 (reprinted in Kayne (1984)).

Kayne, R. S. (1982) "Predicates and Arguments, Verbs and Nouns," paper presented at the GLOW Conference, *GLOW Newsletter*, 8, 24.

Kayne, R. S. (1983a) "Connectedness." *Linguistic Inquiry*, 14, 223–249 (reprinted in Kayne (1984)).

Kayne, R. S. (1983b) "Chains, Categories External to S, and French Complex Inversion," *Natural Language and Linguistic Theory*, 1, 107–139 (reprinted in Kayne (1984)).

Kayne, R. S. (1983c) "Le datif en français et en anglais", in M. Herslund, O. Mordrup, and F. Sorensen (eds.), *Analyses grammaticales du français. Etudes publiées à l'occasion du 50e anniversaire de Carl Vikner*, *Revue Romane*, Numéro spécial 24, 86–98 (English version in Kayne (1984)).

Kayne, R. S. (1984) *Connectedness and Binary Branching*. Foris, Dordrecht.

Kayne, R. S. (1985) "Principles of Particle Constructions," in J. Guéron, H.-G. Obenauer, and J.-Y. Pollock (eds.), *Grammatical Representation*, Foris, Dordrecht, 101–140.

Kayne, R. S. (1986a) "Connexité et inversion du sujet," in M. Ronat and D. Couquaux (eds.), *La grammaire modulaire*, Editions de Minuit, Paris, 127–147.

Kayne, R. S. (1986b) "Thematic and Case-assigning Properties of Past Participles" (abstract of) paper presented at the Princeton Workshop on Comparative Grammar, Princeton.

Kayne, R. S. (1987) "Binary Branching as a Source of Adjacency Effects." *GLOW Newsletter* (Tilburg University), 18, 39.

Kayne, R. S. (1988) "Romance *Se/Si*," paper presented at the GLOW Colloquium, Budapest, *GLOW Newsletter*, 20.

Kayne, R. S. (1990) "Romance Clitics and PRO," *Proceedings of the 20th Annual Meeting of NELS*, GLSA, University of Massachusetts, Amherst.

Kayne, R. S. (1994) *The Antisymmetry of Syntax*. MIT Press, Cambridge, Mass.

Kayne, R. S. (1997a) "Antisymmetry and Typology," LSA Summer Institute course.

Kayne, R. S. (1997b) "Movement and Binding Theory," paper presented at M.I.T. and the University of Massachusetts, Amherst.

Kayne, R. S., and J.-Y. Pollock (1978) "Stylistic Inversion, Successive Cyclicity, and Move NP in French." *Linguistic Inquiry*, 9, 595–621.

Kelly, R. C. (1973) *A Descriptive Analysis of Gascon*. Mouton, The Hague.

Kennedy, C. (1997) "Antecedent-contained Deletion and the Syntax of Quantification." *Linguistic Inquiry*, 28, 662–688.

Keyser, S. J., and T. Roeper (1984) "On the Middle and Ergative Constructions in English." *Linguistic Inquiry*, 15, 381–416.

Kihm, A. (1997) "Wolof Noun Phrase Structure: Implications for the Position of Gender and the Merger vs. Fusion Contrast." Ms., Centre National de la Recherche Scientifique-Langues et Civilisations à Tradition Orale.

Kimball, J., and J. Aissen (1971) "I Think, You Think, He Think." *Linguistic Inquiry*, 2, 242–246.

Kitagawa, Y. (1986) *Subjects in Japanese and English*. Doctoral dissertation, University of Massachusetts, Amherst.

Kitahara, H. (1996) "Raising Quantifiers without Quantifier Raising," in W. Abraham, S. D. Epstein, H. Thráinsson, and C. J.-W. Zwart (eds.), *Minimal Ideas. Syntactic Studies in the Minimalist Framework*, John Benjamins, Amsterdam, 189–198.

Klima, E. S. (1964a) "Negation in English," in J. A. Fodor and J. J. Katz (eds.), *The Structure of Language. Readings in the Philosophy of Language*, Prentice Hall, Englewood Cliffs, N.J., 246–323.

Klima, E. S. (1964b) "Relatedness between Grammatical Systems." *Language*, 40, 1–20 (reprinted in D. A. Reibel and S. A. Schane (eds.), (1969) *Modern Studies in English*, Prentice-Hall, Englewood Cliffs, N.J., 227–246).

Koizumi, M. (1993) "Modal Phrase and Adjuncts," in P. M. Clancy (ed.), *Japanese/Korean Linguistics*, Vol. 2, CSLI, Stanford, 409–428.

Kok, A. C. de (1985) *La place du pronom personnel régime conjoint en français: une étude diachronique*. Doctoral dissertation, University of Amsterdam.

Koopman, H. (1993) "The Internal and External Distribution of Pronominal DPs." Ms., UCLA.

Koopman, H. (1994) "Licensing Heads," in D. Lightfoot and N. Hornstein (eds.), *Verb Movement*, Cambridge University Press, Cambridge, 261–296.

Koopman, H. (1995) "The position of incorporated heads in the verbal complex." Ms., UCLA (Dutch version in *TABU* 1995).

Koopman, H. (1996) "Antisymmetry and the Doubly-filled C Filter." Ms., UCLA.

Koopman, H. (1997) "Unifying Predicate Cleft Constructions," paper presented at BLS Special Session, Berkeley.

Koopman, H., and D. Sportiche (1991) "The Position of Subjects." *Lingua*, 85, 211–258.

Koopman, H., and A. Szabolcsi (1997) "The Hungarian Verbal Complex: Incorporation as XP-movement." Ms., UCLA.

Koster, Jan (1978) "Why Subject Sentences Don't Exist," in S. J. Keyser (ed.), *Recent Transformational Studies in European Languages*, MIT Press, Cambridge, Mass., 53–64.

Koster, J. (1987) *Domains and Dynasties. The Radical Autonomy of Syntax*. Foris, Dordrecht.

Koster, J. (1994) "Predicate Incorporation and the Word Order of Dutch," in G. Cinque, J. Koster, J.-Y. Pollock, L. Rizzi, and R. Zanuttini (eds.), *Paths toward Universal Grammar. Studies in Honor of Richard S. Kayne*, Georgetown University Press, Washington, D.C., 255–276.

Kroch, A. S. (1979) review of Fraser (1976), *Language*, 55, 219–224.

Kuno, S. (1973) "Constraints on Internal Clauses and Sentential Subjects." *Linguistic Inquiry*, 4, 363–385.

Kuno, S., and K. Takami (1997) "Remarks on Negative Islands." *Linguistic Inquiry*, 28, 553–576.

Kupferman, L. (1986) "Le pronom réfléchi non-clitique existe-t-il en français?" in D. Kremer (ed.), *Actes du 19e Congrès de Linguistique et de Philologie Romanes*, vol. 2, Max Niemeyer, Tübingen, 485–494.

Labov, W. (1972) *Language in the Inner City: Studies in the Black English Vernacular*. University of Pennsylvania Press, Philadelphia.

La Fauci, N., and M. Loporcaro (1989) "Passifs, avancements de l'objet indirect et formes verbales périphrastiques dans le dialecte d'Altamura (Pouilles)." *Rivista di Linguistica*, 1, 161–196.

La Fauci, N., and M. Loporcaro (1993) "Grammatical Relations and Syntactic Levels in Bonorvese Morphosyntax," in A. Belletti (ed.), *Syntactic Theory and the Dialects of Italy*, Rosenberg and Sellier, Turin.

Lafont, R. (1967) *La phrase occitane. Essai d'analyse systématique*. Presses Universitaires de France.

Laka, I. (1990) *Negation in syntax: On the nature of functional categories and projections*. Doctoral dissertation, Massachusetts Institute of Technology, Cambridge, Mass.

Lamouche, L. (1902) *Essai de grammaire languedocienne *Dialectes de Montpellier et de Lodève)*. H. Welter, Paris.

Lapointe, S. (1980) "A Lexical Analysis of the English Auxiliary Verb System," in T. Hoekstra, H. van der Hulst, and M. Moortgat (eds.), *Lexical Grammar*, Foris, Dordrecht, 215–254.

Larson, R. K. (1985) "On the Syntax of Disjunction Scope." *Natural Language and Linguistic Theory*, 3, 217–264.

Larson, R. K. (1988) "On the Double Object Construction." *Linguistic Inquiry*, 19, 335–391.

Larson, R. K. (1990) "Double Objects Revisited: Reply to Jackendoff." *Linguistic Inquiry* 21, 589–632.

Lasnik, H. (1989) "Control and Binding Theory," paper presented at the M.I.T. Workshop on Control, Cambridge, Mass.

Lasnik, H. (1995a) "Verbal Morphology: *Syntactic Structures* Meets the Minimalist Program," in H. Campos and P. Kempchinsky (eds.), *Evolution and Revolution in Linguistic Theory*, Georgetown University Press, Washington, D.C., 251–275.

Lasnik, H. (1995b) "A Note on Pseudogapping," *MIT Working Papers in Linguistics*, 27, 143–163.

Lasnik, H., and M. Saito (1984) "On the Nature of Proper Government." *Linguistic Inquiry* 15, 235–289.

Lebeaux, D. (1984) "Anaphoric Binding and the Definition of PRO," in *Proceedings of NELS 14*, University of Massachusetts, Amherst.

Lee, F. (1998) "VP Remnant Movement and VSO in Quiaviní Zapotec." Ms., UCLA.

Legendre, G. (1997) "Secondary Predication and Functional Projections in French." *Natural Language and Linguistic Theory* 15, 43–87.

Legendre, G., P. Smolensky, and C. Wilson (1998) "When Is Less More? Faithfulness and Minimal Links in *wh*-Chains," in Barbosa et al. (1998), 249–289.

Lencho, M. (1992) "Evidence That "To" Is a Complementizer" (abstract), University of Tromsø.

Lepelley, R. (1974) *Le parler normand du Val de Saire (Manche)* (Cahier des Annales de Normandie no. 7). Musée de Normandie, Caen.

Lepschy, A. L., and G. Lepschy (1977) *The Italian Language Today*. Hutchinson, London.

Lepschy, A. L., and G. Lepschy (1981) *La lingua italiana: storia, varietà dell'uso, grammatica*. Bompiani, Milan.

Li, Y-H. A. (1992) "Indefinite *wh* in Mandarin Chinese." *Journal of East Asian Linguistics*, 1, 125–155.

Lobeck, A. (1995) *Ellipsis. Functional Heads, Licensing, and Identification*. Oxford University Press, New York.

Lo Cascio, V. (1970) *Strutture pronominali e verbali italiane*. Zanichelli, Bologna.

Lockwood, W. B. (1977) *An Introduction to Modern Faroese*. Foroya Skúlabókagrunnar, Tórshavn.

Loi Corvetto, I. (1982) *L'italiano regionale di Sardegna*. Zanichelli, Bologna.

Lois, X. (1990) "Auxiliary Selection and Past Participle Agreement in Romance." *Probus*, 2, 233–255.

Long, M. E. (1976) "Semantic Verb Classes and Their role in French Predicate Complementation." *Indiana University Linguistics Club*.

Longobardi, G. (1980) "Remarks on Infinitives: A Case for a Filter." *Journal of Italian Linguistics* 5, 101–155.

Longobardi, G. (1985) "Connectedness, Scope, and C-command." *Linguistic Inquiry*, 16, 163–192.

Longobardi, G. (1992) "In Defense of the Correspondence Hypothesis: Island Effects and Parasitic Constructions in Logical Form," in C.-T. J. Huang and R. May (eds.), *Logical Structure and Linguistic Structure. Cross-Linguistic Perspectives*, Kluwer, Dordrecht, 149–196.

Longobardi, G. (1994) "Reference and Proper Names." *Linguistic Inquiry* 25, 609–665.

Loporcaro, M. (1988) *Grammatica Storica del Dialetto di Altamura*. Giardini, Pisa.

Luján, M. (1978) "Clitic Promotion and Mood in Spanish Verbal Complements." *Montreal Working Papers in Linguistics*, 10, 103–190; also in *Linguistics*, 18 (1980), 381–484.

Lurà, F. 1990. *Il dialetto del Mendrisiotto, terza edizione*. Edizioni Unione di Banche Svizzere, Mendrisio-Chiasso.

Lyons, J. (1968) *Introduction to Theoretical Linguistics*. Cambridge University Press, Cambridge.

Mahajan, A. (1994) "The Ergativity Parameter: *have-be* Alternation, Word Order and Split Ergativity," in M. Gonzalez (ed.), *Proceedings of NELS 24*, GLSA, University of Massachusetts, Amherst.

Mainoldi, P. (1950) *Manuale dell'odierno dialetto bolognese*. Società Tipografica Mareggiani, Bologna.

Manzini, M. R. (1979) "Una teoria del controllo." *Rivista di Grammatica Generativa*, 4, 139–163.

Manzini, M. R. (1982) "Italian Prepositions before Infinitives." *MIT Working Papers in Linguistics*, 4, 115–122.

Manzini, M. R. (1983a) *Restructuring and Reanalysis*. Doctoral dissertation, Massachusetts Institute of Technology, Cambridge, Mass.

Manzini, M. R. (1983b) "On Control and Control Theory." *Linguistic Inquiry*, 14, 421–446.

Manzini, M. R., and L. Savoia (1998) "Clitics and Auxiliary Choice in Italian Dialects: Their Relevance for the Person Ergativity Split," *Recherches Linguistiques de Vincennes*, 27, 115–138.

Marcellesi, J.-B. (1986) "Le 'complément d'objet direct' en corse: *à* + SN de GV, 0 + SN de GV," in *Morphosyntaxe des langues romanes* (Actes du XVIIᵉ congrès international de linguistique et philologie romanes, Vol. 4), Université de Provence, Aix-en-Provence, 127–138.

Marshall, M. M. (1984) *The Dialect of Notre-Dame-de-Sanilhac: A Natural Generative Phonology* (Stanford French and Italian Studies 31). Anma Libri, Saratoga, Calif.

Martin, R., and M. Wilmet (1980) *Manuel du français du moyen âge: 2. Syntaxe du moyen français*. SOBODI, Bordeaux.

Martineau, F., and V. Motapanyane (1996) "Hypothetical Infinitives and Crosslinguistic Variation in Continental and Québec French," in J. R. Black and V. Motapanyane, eds., *Microparametric Syntax and Dialect Variation*, John Benjamins, Amsterdam, 145–168.

Martinon, P. (1927) *Comment on parle en français*. Larousse, Paris.

Mastrangelo Latini, G. (1981) "Note di morfologia dialettale." *Quaderni di filologia e lingue romanze*, 3, 241–249.

Mattesini, E. 1976. Tre microsistemi morfologici del dialetto di Borgo Sansepolcro (Arezzo), in *Problemi di morfosintassi dialettale*, Pacini, Pisa, 177–202.

Matthews, S., and V. Yip (1994) *Cantonese. A Comprehensive Grammar*. Routledge, London.

Mattoso Camara, Jr., J. (1972) *The Portuguese Language*. University of Chicago Press, Chicago.

May, R. (1985) *Logical Form. Its Structure and Derivation*. MIT Press, Cambridge, Mass.

Maze, C. (1969) *Etude sur le langage de la banlieue du Havre*. Slatkine Reprints, Geneva (1903).

McCawley, J. D. (1988) *The Syntactic Phenomena of English*, Vol. 1, University of Chicago Press, Chicago.

McCloskey, J. (1986) "Inflection and Conjunction in Modern Irish." *Natural Language and Linguistic Theory*, 4, 245–281.

McCloskey, J., and K. Hale (1984) "On the Syntax of Person-Number Inflection in Modern Irish." *Natural Language and Linguistic Theory*, 1, 487–533.

McCloskey, J., and P. Sells (1988) "Control and A-Chains in Modern Irish." *Natural Language and Linguistic Theory*, 6, 143–189.

McGinnis, M. J. (1998) "Locality in A-Movement," Ph.D. dissertation. Massachusetts Institute of Technology, Cambridge, Mass.

Mencken, H. L. (1937) *The American Language. An Inquiry into the Development of English in the United States*, 4th ed., Alfred A. Knopf, New York.

Mencken, H. L. (1948) *The American Language. An Inquiry into the Development of English in the United States. Supplement II*. Alfred A. Knopf, New York.

Merat, F. (1974) *Une comparaison grammaticale et lexicale de l'anglais britannique et américain enseigné aux étrangers*. Thèse de Doctorat de 3e Cycle, Université de Paris VII.

Miller, J. (1993) "The Grammar of Scottish English," in J. Milroy and L. Milroy (eds.), *Real*

English. The Grammar of English Dialects in the British Isles, Longman, London, pp. 99–138.

Milner, J.-C. (1978) "Le système du réfléchi en latin." *Langages* 50, 73–86.

Milner, J.-C. (1982) *Ordres et raisons de langue*. Editions du Seuil, Paris.

Miremont, P. (1976) *La syntaxe occitane du Périgord*, Cuers.

Montaut, A. (1997) "Les pronoms personnels, emphatiques et réfléchis dans les langues indiennes," in A. Zribi-Hertz (ed.), *Les pronoms. Morphologie, syntaxe et typologie*, Presses Universitaires de Vincennes, Saint-Denis, 101–128.

Montgomery, M. 1988 "The Roots of Appalachian English" in A. R. Thomas (ed.), *Methods in Dialectology*, Multilingual Matters Ltd., Clevedon and Philadelphia, 480–491.

Moreira da Silva, S. (1983) *Etudes sur la symétrie et l'asymétrie SUJET/OBJET dans le portugais du Brésil*, Thèse de 3ème cycle, Université de Paris VIII.

Morin, Y.-C. (1979a) "La morphophonologie des pronoms clitiques en français populaire." *Cahier de linguistique no. 9*, Les Presses de l'Université du Québec, Montréal, 1–36.

Morin, Y.-C. (1979b) "More Remarks on French Clitic Order." *Linguistic Analysis* 5, 293–312.

Moro, A. (1997) *The Raising of Predicates. Predicative Noun Phrases and the Theory of Clause Structure*. Cambridge University Press, Cambridge.

Motapanyane, V. (1989) "La position du sujet dans une langue à L'ordre SVO/VSO." Ms., University of Geneva.

Mouchaweh, L. (1984) "En faveur des 'small clauses'," *Recherches Linguistiques*, 12, Université de Paris VIII, 92–124.

Mouchaweh, L. (1985) "De la quantification à distance et des nominalisations en français." *Modèles Linguistiques*, 7, 91–117.

Müller, G. (1998) *Incomplete Category Fronting. A Derivational Approach to Remnant Movement in German*. Kluwer, Dordrecht.

Murasugi, K. (1994) "Head-internal Relative Clauses as Adjunct Pure Complex NPs," in S. Chiba et al. (eds.), *Synchronic and Diachronic Approaches to Language*, Liber Press, Tokyo, 425–437.

Nadahalli, J. (1998) "Aspects of Kannada Grammar." Ph.D. dissertation, New York University.

Napoli, D. J. (1976) "Infinitival Relatives in Italian," in M. Luján and F. Hensey (eds.), *Current Studies in Romance Linguistics*, Georgetown University Press, Washington, D.C., 300–329.

Napoli, D. J. (1981a) "Subject Pronouns: The Pronominal System of Italian vs. French." *Chicago Linguistic Society*, 17, 249–276.

Napoli, D. J. (1981b) "Semantic Interpretation vs. Lexical Governance: Clitic Climbing in Italian." *Language*, 57, 841–887.

Nash, L. (1997) "La partition personnelle dans les langues ergatives," in A. Zribi-Hertz (ed.), *Les pronoms. Morphologie, syntaxe et typologie*, Presses Universitaires de Vincennes, Saint-Denis, 129–149.

Nelson, N. (1997) "The Structure of Exclamatives: An Extension of Kayne's (1997) Analysis of Sentential Negation." Ms., Rutgers University.

Nicoli, F. (1983) *Grammatica milanese*. Bramante Editrice, Busto Arsizio.

Nishigauchi, T. (1992) "Construing *WH*," in C.-T. J. Huang and R. May (eds.), *Logical Structure and Linguistic Structure. Cross-linguistic Perspectives*, Kluwer, Dordrecht, 197–231.

Nkemnji, M. A. (1995) "Heavy Pied-piping in Nweh. Ph.D. dissertation, University of California at Los Angeles.

Nunes, J. M. (1995) *The Copy Theory of Movement and Linearization of Chains in the Minimalist Program*. Doctoral dissertation, University of Maryland, College Park.

Obenauer, H.-G. (1984) "On the Identification of Empty Categories." *Linguistic Review*, 4, 153–202.

Obenauer, H.-G. (1994) *Aspects de la syntaxe A-barre. Effets d'intervention et mouvements des quantifieurs.* Thèse de doctorat d'Etat, Université de Paris VIII.

Olszyna-Marzys, Z. (1964) *Les pronoms dans les patois du Valais central* (Romanica Helvetica, 76). Francke, Bern.

O'Neil, J. (1997) *Means of Control: Deriving the Properties of PRO in the Minimalist Program.* Doctoral dissertation, Harvard University.

Ordóñez, F. (1997) *Word Order and Clause Structure in Spanish and Other Romance Languages.* Doctoral dissertation, Graduate Center, City University of New York.

Ordóñez, F., and E. Treviño (1999) "Left Dislocated Subjects and the Pro-drop Parameter: A Case Study of Spanish." *Lingua*, 107, 39–68.

Paddock, H. (1990) "On Explaining Macrovariation in the Sibiliant and Nasal Suffixes of English." *Folia Linguistica Historica*, 9, 235–269.

Page, L. (1985) *Le patois fribourgeois*, 2nd ed., La Sarine, Fribourg.

Parisi, D. (1976) "The Past Participle." *Italian Linguistics* 1, 77–106.

Parkinson, S. (1988) "Portuguese," in M. Harris and N. Vincent (eds.), *The Romance Languages*, Oxford University Press, New York, 131–169.

Parry, M. (1984) *The Dialect of Cairo Montenotte.* Doctoral dissertation, University of Wales.

Parry, M. (1989) "Some Observations on the Syntax of Clitic Pronouns in Piedmontese." Ms., University of Wales, Aberystwyth.

Payne, J. R. (1985) "Negation," in T. Shopen (ed.), *Language Typology and Syntactic Description. Vol. I. Clause Structure*, Cambridge University Press, Cambridge, 197–242.

Pearson, M. (1997a) "Feature Inheritance, Head Movement, and Pied Piping: Deriving Head-Final Structures." Ms., UCLA (paper presented at the Japanese Syntax in a Comparative Context Workshop, Cornell University, July 1997).

Pearson, M. (1997b) "Pied-Piping into the Left Periphery." *Proceedings of NELS*, 27.

Pelliciardi, F. (1977) *Grammatica del dialetto romagnolo.* Longo, Ravenna.

Perlmutter, D. M. (1970) "On the Article in English," in M. Bierwisch and K. E. Heidolph (eds.), *Progress in Linguistics*, Mouton, The Hague, 233–248.

Perlmutter, D. M. (1971) *Deep and Surface Structure Constraints in Syntax.* Holt, Rinehart and Winston, New York.

Perlmutter, D. M. (1978) "Impersonal Passives and the Unaccusative Hypothesis." *Proceedings of the Fourth Annual Meeting of the Berkeley Linguistics Society*, UCLA.

Perlmutter, D. M. (1983) "Personal vs. Impersonal Constructions." *Natural Language and Linguistic Theory*, 1, 141–200.

Perlmutter, D. M. (1989) "Multiattachment and the Unaccusative Hypothesis: The Perfect Auxiliary in Italian." *Probus*, 1, 63–119.

Pesetsky, D. (1982) *Paths and Categories.* Doctoral dissertation, Massachusetts Institute of Technology, Cambridge, Mass.

Pesetsky, D. (1984) "Extraction Domains and a Surprising Subject-Object Asymmetry," paper presented at the GLOW Colloquium, Copenhagen.

Pesetsky, D. (1989) "Language-Particular Processes and the Earliness Principle," paper presented at the GLOW Colloquium, Utrecht, *GLOW Newsletter*, 22, 48–49.

Pesetsky, D. (1995) *Zero Syntax. Experiencers and Cascades.* MIT Press, Cambridge, Mass.

Pesetsky, D. (1997) "Optimality Theory and Syntax: Movement and Pronunciation," in D. Archangeli and D. T. Langendoen (eds.), *Optimality theory: An overview*, Blackwell, Oxford, 134–170.

Petrovitz, W. (1990) *Argument Opacity.* Doctoral dissertation, Graduate Center, City of University of New York.

Pica, P. (1984) "Liage et contiguïté," in *Recherches sur l'anaphore*, D.R.L., Université de Paris VII, 119–164.

Pica, P. (1987) "On the Nature of the Reflexivization Cycle," in *Proceedings of NELS 17*, GLSA, University of Massachusetts, Amherst, 483–499.

Picabia, L. (1997) "Les traits du pronom-accord en grand-comorien," in A. Zribi-Hertz (ed.), *Les pronoms. Morphologie, syntaxe et typologie*, Presses Universitaires de Vincennes, Saint-Denis, 151–179.

Picallo, M. C. (1991) "Nominals and Nominalizations in Catalan." *Probus*, 3, 279–316.

Picallo, M. C. (1994) "Catalan Possessive Pronouns: The Avoid Pronoun Principle Revisited." *Natural Language and Linguistic Theory*, 12, 259–299.

Pizzini, Q. A. (1981) "The Placement of Clitic Pronouns in Portuguese." *Linguistic Analysis*, 8, 403–430.

Platzack, C. (1986a) "COMP, INFL, and Germanic Word Order," in L. Hellan and K. K. Christensen (eds.), *Topics in Scandinavian Syntax*, Reidel, Dordrecht, 185–234.

Platzack, C. (1986b) "The Structure of Infinitive Clauses in Danish and Swedish," in Ö. Dahl and A. Holmberg (eds.), *Scandinavian Syntax*, Institute of Linguistics, University of Stockholm, 123–137.

Platzack, C., and A. Holmberg (1989) "The Role of AGR and Finiteness in Germanic VO-languages," paper presented at the GLOW Colloquium, Utrecht, and in *Working Papers in Scandinavian Syntax*, 43, University of Lund, 51–76.

Poletto, C. (1990a) "L'inversione soggetto clitico/verbo nei dialetti veneti." Ms., Università degli Studi di Padova e Venezia/Université de Genève.

Poletto, C. (1990b) "The Subject Clitic System in Basso Polesano and the Theory of PRO" paper presented at the ESF Workshop on Clitics and Their Hosts, University of Geneva.

Poletto, C. (1993) *La sintassi del soggetto nei dialetti italiani settentrionali* (Quaderni Patavini di Linguistica. Monografie. 12). Unipress, University of Padua/CNR.

Poletto, C. (1995) "Split Agr and Subject Clitics in the Northern Italian Dialects," paper presented at the 18th GLOW Colloquium, *GLOW Newsletter*, 34, 46–47.

Poletto, C. (2000) *The Higher Functional Field in the Northern Italian Dialects*. Oxford University Press, New York.

Pollock, J.-Y. (1981) "On Case and Impersonal Constructions," in R. May and J. Koster (eds.), *Levels of Syntactic Representation*, Foris, Dordrecht, 219–252.

Pollock, J.-Y. (1983a) "Accord, chaînes impersonnelles et variables." *Lingvisticae Investigationes*, 7, 131–181.

Pollock, J.-Y. (1983b) "Sur quelques propriétés des phrases copulatives en français." *Langue Française*, 58, 89–125.

Pollock, J.-Y. (1985) "On Case and the Syntax of Infinitives in French," in J. Guéron, H.-G. Obenauer, and J.-Y. Pollock (eds.), *Grammatical Representation*, Foris, Dordrecht, 293–326.

Pollock, J.-Y. (1986) "Sur la syntaxe de *en* et le paramètre du sujet nul," in M. Ronat and D. Couquaux (eds.), *La grammaire modulaire*, Editions de Minuit, Paris, 211–246.

Pollock, J.-Y. (1989) "Verb Movement, Universal Grammar, and the Structure of IP." *Linguistic Inquiry*, 20, 365–424.

Pollock, J.-Y. (1992) "Opérateurs nuls, *dont*, questions indirectes, et théorie de la quantification," in L. Tasmowski and A. Zribi-Hertz (eds.), *Hommages à Nicolas Ruwet*, Communication and Cognition, Ghent, 440–463.

Pollock, J.-Y. (1994) "Checking Theory and Bare Verbs," in G. Cinque, J. Koster, J.-Y. Pollock, L. Rizzi, and R. Zanuttini (eds.), *Paths toward Universal Grammar. Studies in Honor of Richard S. Kayne*, Georgetown University Press, Washington, D.C., 293–310.

Pollock, J.-Y. (1996) "Case checking and particle constructions." Ms., Harvard University.

Pollock, J.-Y. (1998) "On the Syntax of Subnominal Clitics: Cliticization and Ellipsis." *Syntax*, 1, 300–330.

Postal, P. M. 1966. "On So-Called 'Pronouns' in English," in F. P. Dineen, ed., *Report of the Seventeenth Annual Roundtable Meeting on Linguistics and Language Studies*, Georgetown University Press, Washington, D.C., 177–206 (reprinted in D. A. Reibel and S. A. Schane (eds.), *Modern Studies in English* (1969), Prentice-Hall, Englewood Cliffs, N.J.).

Postal, P. M. (1970) "On Coreferential Complement Subject Deletion." *Linguistic Inquiry*, 1, 439–500.

Postal, P. M. (1974) *On Raising. One Rule of English Grammar and Its Theoretical Implications*. MIT Press, Cambridge, Mass.

Postal, P. M. (1988) Anaphoric Islands, in E. Schiller et al. (eds.), *The Best of CLS. A Selection of Out-of-print Papers from 1968 to 1975*, Chicago Linguistic Society, Chicago, 67–94.

Postal, P. M. (1990) "French Indirect Object Demotion," in P. M. Postal and B. D. Joseph (eds.), *Studies in Relational Grammar 3*, University of Chicago Press, Chicago, 104–200.

Postma, G. (1994) "The indefinite reading of WH," in R. Bok-Bennema and C. Cremers (eds.), *Linguistics in the Netherlands 1994*, John Benjamins, Amsterdam, 187–198.

Potsdam, E. (1997) "NegP and Subjunctive Complements in English." *Linguistic Inquiry*, 28, 533–541.

Price, G. (1967) "Influences espagnole, italienne et occitane sur la langue de Brantôme." *Revue de linguistique romane*, 31, 147–179.

Progovac, L. (1993) "Negation and Comp." *Rivista di Linguistica*, 5, 329–347.

Progovac, L. (1994) *Negative and Positive Polarity. A Binding Approach*. Cambridge University Press, Cambridge.

Pullum, G., and D. Wilson (1977) "Autonomous Syntax and the Analysis of Auxiliaries." *Language*, 53, 741–788.

Quicoli, A. C. (1976) "Conditions on Clitic-Movement in Portuguese." *Linguistic Analysis*, 2, 199–223.

Quirk, R., S. Greenbaum, G. Leech, and J. Svartvik (1972) *A Grammar of Contemporary English*. Longman, London.

Randolph, V. (1927) "The Grammar of the Ozark Dialect." *American Speech*, 3, 1–11.

Raposo, E. (1987a) "Romance Infinitival Clauses and Case Theory," in C. Neidle and R. Nuñez-Cedeño (eds.), *Studies in Romance Languages*, Foris, Dordrecht, 237–249.

Raposo, E. (1987b) "Case Theory and Infl-to-Comp: The Inflected Infinitive in European Portuguese." *Linguistic Inquiry*, 18, 85–109.

Ratel, V. (1958) *Morphologie du patois de Saint-Martin-la-Porte (Savoie)* (Publications de l'Institut de Linguistique Romane de Lyon, 13). Les Belles Lettres, Paris.

Reinhart, T. (1983) *Anaphora and semantic interpretation*. Croom Helm, London.

Reinholtz, C. (1989) "Verb-'Second' and Danish," paper presented at the Sixth Workshop in Comparative Germanic Syntax, Lund, Sweden.

Remacle, L. (1952) *Syntaxe du parler wallon de La Gleize, Tome I*, Bibliothèque de la Faculté de Philosophie et Lettres de l'Université de Liège, Fascicule CXXVI. Les Belles Lettres, Paris.

Remacle, L. (1956) *Syntaxe du parler wallon de La Gleize, Tome 2*, Bibliothèque de la Faculté de Philosophie et Lettres de l'Université de Liège, Fascicule CXXXIX. Les Belles Lettres, Paris.

Renzi, L. (1989) "Two Types of Clitics in Natural Languages." *Rivista di Linguistica*, 1, 355–372.

Renzi, L., and L. Vanelli (1983) "I pronomi soggetto in alcune varietà romanze," in *Scritti linguistici in onore di Giovan Battista Pellegrini*, Pacini, Pisa, 121–145.

Reuland, E. (1983a) "Governing -ing." *Linguistic Inquiry*, 14, 101–136.

Reuland, E. (1983b) "The Extended Projection Principle and the Definiteness Effect," in M. Barlow et al. (eds.), *Proceedings of the West Coast Conference on Formal Linguistics*, Stanford Linguistics Association, 217–236.

Reymond, J., and M. Bossard (1979) *Le patois vaudois*, 2d ed., Payot, Lausanne.

Richards, N. (1997) *What Moves Where When in Which Language?* Doctoral dissertation, Massachusetts Institute of Technology, Cambridge, Mass.

Rickard, P. (1970) "*(Il) Estuet, (Il) Convient, (Il) Faut* and Their Constructions in Old and Middle French," in T. G. S. Combe and P. Rickard (eds.), *The French Language. Studies Presented to Lewis Charles Harmer*, George G. Harrap, London, 65–92.

Rigau, G. (1984) "De com *si* no és conjunció i d'altres elements interrogatius." *Estudis Gramaticals 1*, Universitat Autònoma de Barcelona, Bellaterra, 249–278.

Rigau, G. (1988) "Strong Pronouns." *Linguistic Inquiry*, 19, 503–511.

Rigau, G. (1991) "On the Functional Properties of AGR" in A. Branchadell et al. (eds.), *Catalan Working Papers in Linguistics*, Universitat Autònoma de Barcelona, 235–260.

Rigau, G. (1994) "Locative Sentences in Catalan: *ésser/haver-hi* Alternation," paper presented at the Graduate Center, CUNY.

Ritter, E. (1991) "Two Functional Categories in Noun Phrases: Evidence from Modern Hebrew," in S. Rothstein (ed.), *Perspectives on Phrase Structure: Heads and Licensing*, Syntax and Semantics 25, Academic Press, San Diego, 37–62.

Ritter, E. (1995) "On the Syntactic Category of Pronouns and Agreement." *Natural Language and Linguistic Theory*, 13, 405–443.

Rivero, M.-L. (1988) "The Structure of IP and V-movement in the Languages of the Balkans." Ms., University of Ottawa.

Rizzi, L. (1976) "Ristrutturazione." *Rivista de Grammatica Generativa* 1, 1–54.

Rizzi, L. (1981) "Nominative Marking in Italian Infinitives and the Nominative Island Constraint," in F. Heny (ed.), *Binding and Filtering*, Croom Helm, London, 129–157.

Rizzi, L. (1982a) *Issues in Italian Syntax*. Foris, Dordrecht.

Rizzi, L. (1982b) "Comments on Chomsky's Chapter, 'On the Representation of Form and Function'," in J. Mehler, E. C. T. Walker, and M. Garrett (eds.), *Perspectives on Mental Representation*, Lawrence Erlbaum, Hillsdale, N.J., 441–451.

Rizzi, L. (1986a) "Null Objects in Italian and the Theory of *pro*." *Linguistic Inquiry*, 17, 501–557.

Rizzi, L. (1986b) "On the Status of Subject Clitics in Romance," in O. Jaeggli and C. Silva-Corvalán (eds.), *Studies in Romance Linguistics*, Foris, Dordrecht.

Rizzi, L. (1986c) "On Chain Formation," in H. Borer (ed.), *Syntax and Semantics. Vol. 19. The Syntax of Pronominal Clitics*, Academic Press, Orlando, Fla. 65–95.

Rizzi, L. (1988) "Il sintagma preposizionale," in L. Renzi (ed.), *Grande grammatica italiana di consultazione. Vol. I. La frase. I sintagmi nominale e preposizionale*, Il Mulino, Bologna, 507–531.

Rizzi, L. (1990) *Relativized Minimality*. MIT Press, Cambridge, Mass.

Rizzi, L. (1991) "Proper Head Government and the Definition of A Positions," paper presented at the GLOW Conference, *GLOW Newsletter*, 26, 46–47.

Rizzi, L. (1996) "Residual Verb Second and the *Wh*-criterion," in A. Belletti and L. Rizzi (eds.), *Parameters and Functional Heads. Essays in Comparative Syntax*, Oxford University Press, New York, 63–90.

Rizzi, L. (1997) "The Fine Structure of the Left Periphery," in L. Haegeman (ed.), *Elements of Grammar. Handbook of Generative Syntax*, Kluwer, Dordrecht, 281–337.

Rizzi, L., and I. Roberts (1989) "Complex Inversion in French." *Probus*, 1, 1–30.

Roberts, I. G. (1985) "Agreement Parameters and the Development of English Modal Auxiliaries." *Natural Language and Linguistic Theory*, 3, 21–58.

Roberts, I. G. (1991) "Excorporation and Minimality." *Linguistic Inquiry*, 22, 209–218.

Roberts, I. G. (1993) *Verbs and Diachronic Syntax. A Comparative History of English and French*. Kluwer, Dordrecht.

Roberts, I. G. (1997) "Restructuring, Head Movement, and Locality." *Linguistic Inquiry*, 28, 423–460.

Roca, F. (1992) *On the Licensing of Pronominal Clitics: The Properties of Object Clitics in Spanish and Catalan*. Treball de recerca, Universitat Autònoma de Barcelona.

Rochemont, M. S., and P. W. Culicover (1990) *English Focus Constructions and the Theory of Grammar*. Cambridge University Press, Cambridge.

Rögnvaldsson, E. (1987) "OV Word Order in Icelandic." *Proceedings of the Seventh Biennial Conference of Teachers of Scandinavian Studies in Great Britain and Northern Ireland*, University College, London, 33–49.

Rögnvaldsson, E., and H. Thráinsson (1990) "On Icelandic Word Order Once More," in J. Maling and A. Zaenen (eds.), *Syntax and Semantic. Vol. 24. Modern Icelandic Syntax*, Academic Press, San Diego, 3–40.

Rohlfs, G. (1969) *Grammatica storica della lingua italiana e dei suoi dialetti. Sintassi e formazione delle parole*. Einaudi, Turin.

Rohlfs, G. (1977) *Le gascon. Etudes de philologie pyrénéenne*. Max Niemeyer Verlag, Tübingen, and Marrimpouey Jeune, Pau.

Roldán, M. (1974) "Constraints on Clitic Insertion in Spanish," in R. J. Campbell, M. G. Goldin, and M. C. Wang (eds.), *Linguistic Studies in Romance Languages*, Georgetown University Press, Washington, D.C., 124–138.

Rooryck, J. (1987) *Les verbes de Contrôle*. Doctoral dissertation, Catholic University of Louvain.

Rooryck, J. (1992) "Romance Enclitic Ordering and Universal Grammar." *Linguistic Review* 9, 219–250.

Rosenbaum, P. S. (1967) *The Grammar of English Predicate Complement Constructions*. MIT Press, Cambridge, Mass.

Ross, J. R. (1967) "Auxiliaries as Main Verbs," in W. Todd (ed.), *Studies in Philosophical Linguistics. Series 1*, Great Expectations Press, Evanston, Ill.

Rossini, G. (1975) *Capitoli di morfologia e sintassi del dialetto cremonese* (Pubblicazioni della Facoltà di Lettere e Filosofia dell'Università di Milano, LXXVI—Sezione a cura dell'istituto di glottologia, 2). La Nuova Italia, Florence.

Rothstein, S. (1985) "The Syntax Forms of Predication." *Linguistic Review*, 5, 163–172.

Rouffiange, R. (1983) *Le patois et le français rural de Magny-Lès-Aubigny (Côte-d'Or)*. Association Bourguignonne de Dialectologie et d'Onomastique, Fontaine lès Dijon.

Rouveret, A. (1980) "Sur la notion de proposition finie, gouvernement et inversion." *Langages*, 60, 75–107.

Rouveret, A. (1991) "Functional Categories and Agreement." *Linguistic Review*, 8, 353–387.

Rouveret, A. (1997) "Les pronoms personnels du gallois: structure interne et syntaxe," in A. Zribi-Hertz (ed.), *Les pronoms. Morphologie, syntaxe et typologie*, Presses Universitaires de Vincennes, Saint-Denis, 181–212.

Rouveret, A., and J. R. Vergnaud (1980) "Specifying Reference to the Subject: French Causatives and Conditions on Representations." *Linguistic Inquiry*, 11, 97–202.

Ruwet, N. (1967) "Some Problems about Gender in French." Ms., M.I.T.

Ruwet, N. (1978) "Une construction absolue en français." *Lingvisticae Investigationes*, 2, 165–210 (reprinted in N. Ruwet, *Grammaire des insultes et autres études*. Editions du Seuil, Paris, 1982).

Ruwet, N. (1982) *Grammaire des insultes et autres études*. Editions du Seuil, Paris.

Ruwet, N. (1983) "Du bon usage des expressions idiomatiques." *Recherches Linguistiques*, 11, Université de Paris VIII, 5–84.

Ruwet, N. (1989) "Weather Verbs and the Unaccusative Hypothesis," in C. Kirschner and J. DeCesaris (eds.), *Studies in Romance Linguistics*, John Benjamins, Amsterdam, 313–345.

Safir, K. (1996) "Semantic Atoms of Anaphora." *Natural Language and Linguistic Theory*, 14, 545–589.

Salvi, G. (1991) "L'accordo," in L. Renzi and G. Salvi (eds.), *Grande grammatica italiana di consultazione. Vol. II. I sintagmi verbale, aggettivale, avverbiale. La subordinazione*, Il Mulino, Bologna, 227–244.

Salvioni, C. (1975) "Fonetica e morfologia del dialetto milanese, a cura di Dante Isella," *L'italia Dialettale*, 38, 1–46.

Sandfeld, K., and H. Olsen (1936) *Syntaxe roumaine I*. Droz, Paris.

Sankoff, G., and P. Thibault (1977) "L'alternance entre les auxiliaires *avoir* et *être* en français parlé à Montréal." *Langue Française*, 34, 81–108.

Sauzet, P. (1986) "Les clitiques occitans: Analyse métrique de leur variation dialectale," in *Morphosyntaxe des langues romanes* (Actes du XVIIᵉ congrès international de linguistique et philologie romanes), Vol. 4, Université de Provence, Aix-en-Provence, 153–180.

Sauzet, P. (1989) "Topicalisation et prolepse en occitan." *Revue des Langues Romanes*, 93, 235–273.

Schmitt, C. (1998) "Lack of Iteration: Accusative Clitic Doubling, Participial Absolutes and *Have* + Agreeing Participles." *Probus*, 10, 243–300.

Schwartz, A. (1972) "The VP Constituent of SVO Languages," in J. P. Kimball (ed.), *Syntax and Semantics,* Vol. I, Academic Press, New York, 213–235.

Séguy, J. (1950) *Le français parlé à Toulouse*. Edouard Privat, Toulouse.

Sells, P., J. Rickford, and T. Wasow (1996) "An Optimality Theoretic Approach to Variation in Negative Inversion in AAVE." *Natural Language and Linguistic Theory*, 14, 591–627.

Seuren, P. A. M. (1976) "Clitic Pronoun Clusters." *Italian Linguistics*, 2, 7–35.

Shlonsky, U. (1989) "The Hierarchical Representation of Subject-Verb Agreement." Ms., Univ. of Haifa.

Shlonsky, U. (1991) "Quantifiers as Functional Heads: A Study of Quantifier Float in Hebrew." *Lingua*, 84, 159–180.

Shlonsky, U. (1997) *Clause Structure and Word Order in Hebrew and Arabic. An Essay in Comparative Semitic Syntax*. Oxford University Press, New York.

Siegel, M. E. A. (1987) "Compositionality, Case, and the Scope of Auxiliaries." *Linguistics and Philosophy*, 10, 53–76.

Signorell, F., et al. (1987) *Normas surmiranas: Grammatica rumantscha digl idiom da Sur-e Sotses*. Tgesa editoura cantunala, Coira.

Sigurdsson, H. A. (1986) "Verb Post-second in a V2 Language," in Ö. Dahl and A. Holmberg (eds.), *Scandinavian Syntax*, University of Stockholm, 138–149.

Sigurdsson, H. A. (1989) *Verbal Syntax and Case in Icelandic*. Doctoral dissertation, University of Lund.

Simpson, A. (1995) *Wh-movement, Licensing and the Locality of Feature-checking*. Doctoral dissertation, School of Oriental and African Studies (SOAS), London.

Skytte, G., and G. Salvi (1991) "Frasi subordinate all'infinito," in L. Renzi and G. Salvi (eds.), *Grande grammatica italiana di consultazione. Vol. II. I sintagmi verbale, aggettivale, avverbiale. La subordinazione*, Il Mulino, Bologna, 497–569.

Slack, L. L., and D. Lebeaux (1996) "Kayne's Right-branching Structures and Incremental Movement." Ms., University of Maryland, College Park, and NEC Research Institute.

Spiess, F. 1976. "Di un'innovazione morfologica nel sistema dei pronomi personali oggetto del dialetto della Collina d'Oro." In *Problemi di morfosintassi dialettale*, Pacini, Pisa, 203–212.

Sportiche, D. (1983) *Structural Invariance and Symmetry in Syntax*. Doctoral dissertation, Massachusetts Institute of Technology, Cambridge, Mass.

Sportiche, D. (1988) "A Theory of Floating Quantifiers and Its Corollaries for Constituent Structure." *Linguistic Inquiry*, 19, 425–449.

Sportiche, D. (1990) "Movement, Agreement and Case." Ms., UCLA.

Sportiche, D. (1995a) "Clitic Constructions," in L. Zaring and J. Rooryck (eds.), *Phrase Structure and the Lexicon*, Kluwer, Dordrecht, 213–276.

Sportiche, Dominique (1995b) "Sketch of a Reductionist Approach to Syntactic Variation and Dependencies," in H. Campos and P. Kempchinsky (eds.), *Evolution and Revolution in Linguistic Theory*, Georgetown University Press, Washington, D.C., 356–398.

Starke, M. (1993) "Notes on Prepositions and Clause-Structure." Mini-Mémoire, University of Geneva.

Stowell, T. (1981) *Origins of Phrase Structure*. Doctoral dissertation, Massachusetts Institute of Technology, Cambridge, Mass.

Stowell, T. (1982) "The Tense of Infinitives." *Linguistic Inquiry*, 13, 561–570.

Stowell, T. (1983) "Subjects across Categories," *Linguistic Review*, 2, 285–312.

Stowell, T. (1989) "Subjects, Specifiers and X-Bar Theory," in M. R. Baltin and A. S. Kroch (eds.), *Alternative Conceptions of Phrase Structure*, University of Chicago Press, Chicago, 232–262.

Stowell, T. (1991) "Small Clause Restructuring," in R. Freidin (ed.), *Principles and Parameters in Comparative Grammar*, MIT Press, Cambridge, Mass., 182–218.

Strandskogen, A.-B. and Strandskogen, R. (1989) *Norwegian. An Essential Grammar*. Routledge, London.

Strozer, J. R. (1976) *Clitics in Spanish*. Doctoral dissertation, University of Califorina at Los Angeles.

Svenonius, P. (1994) "C-selection as Feature-checking." *Studia Linguistica*, 48, 133–155.

Svenonius, P. (1996) "The Verb-particle Alternation in the Scandinavian Languages." Ms., University of Tromsø.

Szabolcsi, A. (1981) "The Possessive Construction in Hungarian: A Configurational Category in a Non-Configurational Language.," *Acta Linguistica Academiae Scientiarum Hungaricae*, 31, 261–289.

Szabolcsi, A. (1983) "The Possessor That Ran Away from Home." *The Linguistic Review*, 3, 89–102.

Szabolcsi, A. (1994) "The Noun Phrase," in F. Kiefer and K. E. Kiss (eds.), *Syntax and Semantics 27. The Syntactic Structure of Hungarian*, Academic Press, San Diego, 179–274.

Takano, Y. (1996) *Movement and Parametric Variation in Syntax*, Doctoral dissertation, University of California at Irvine.

Taljaard, P. C., J. N. Khumalo, and S. E. Bosch (1991) *Handbook of Siswati*. J. L. van Schaik, Pretoria.

Taraldsen, K. T. (1981) "The Head of S in Germanic and Romance," in T. Fretheim and L. Hellan (eds.), *Papers from the Sixth Scandinavian Conference of Linguistics*, Tapir, 151–161.

Taraldsen, K. T. (1983) *Parametric Variation in Phrase Structure: A Case Study*. Doctoral dissertation, University of Tromsø.

Taraldsen, K. T. (1984) "Some Phrase Structure Dependent Differences between Swedish and Norwegian," *Working Papers in Scandinavian Syntax*, 9, 1–45.

Taraldsen, K. T. (1991) "A Directionality Parameter for Subject-Object Linking," in R. Freidin (ed.), *Principles and Parameters in Comparative Grammar*, MIT Press, Cambridge, Mass., 219–268.

Taraldsen, K. T. (1992) "Agreement as Pronoun Incorporation," paper presented at the fifteenth GLOW Colloquium, *GLOW Newsletter*, 28, 50–51.

Taraldsen, K. T. (1994) "Agreement, Case and the Notion of Specifier," paper presented at the Graduate Center, CUNY.

Taverdet, G. (1971) "Traits mériodionaux et franco-provençaux dans les parlers bourguignons. *Revue de linguistique romane*, 35, 59–73.

Terzi, A. (1996) "Clitic Climbing from Finite Clauses and Tense Raising." *Probus*, 8, 273–295.

Thráinsson, H. (1984) "Different Types of Infinitival Complements in Icelandic," in W. de Geest and Y. Putseys (eds.), *Sentential Complementation*, Foris, Dordrecht, 247–255.

Thráinsson, H. (1986) "On Auxiliaries, AUX and VPs in Icelandic," in L. Hellan and K. K. Christensen (eds.), *Topics in Scandinavian Syntax*, Reidel, Dordrecht, 235–265.

Thráinsson, H. (1994) "Icelandic," in E. König and J. van der Auwera (eds.), *The Germanic Languages*, Routledge, London, 142–189.

Tintou, M. (1969) *Abrégé pratique de grammaire limousine*. Lemouzi, Tulle.

Togeby, K. (1983) *Grammaire française. Vol. III: Les Formes Impersonnelles du Verbe et la construction des verbes* (*Revue Romane Numéro Spécial Hors série*), M. Berg, Gh. Merad, and E. Spang-Hanssen (eds.), Akademisk Forlag, Copenhagen.

Torrego, E. (1983) "More Effects of Successive Cyclic Movement." *Linguistic Inquiry*, 14, 561–565.

Torrego, E. (1984a) "On Inversion in Spanish and Some of Its Effects," *Linguistic Inquiry*, 15, 103–129.

Torrego, E. (1984b) "Algunas observaciones sobre las oraciones existenciales con 'haber' en español." *Estudis Gramaticals-1* (Working Papers in Linguistics), Universitat Autònoma de Barcelona, 329–339.

Torrego, E. (1998) *The Dependencies of Objects*. MIT Press, Cambridge, Mass.

Tranel, B. (1981) *Concreteness in Generative Phonology. Evidence from French*. University of California Press, Berkeley.

Travis, L. (n.d.) "Derived Objects, Inner Aspect, and the Structure of VP." Ms., McGill University.

Trudgill, P., and J. K. Chambers, eds. (1991) *Dialects of English. Studies in Grammatical Variation*. Longman, London.

Trudgill, P., and J. Hannah (1994) *International English. A Guide to Varieties of Standard English*, 3rd ed., Edward Arnold, London.

Tuaillon, G. (1988) "Le français régional. Formes de rencontre," in G. Vermes (ed.) *Vingt-cinq communautés linguistiques de la France*, L'Harmattan, 291–300. Paris.

Turri, C. (1973) *Grammatica del Dialetto Novarese*. La Famiglia Nuaresa, Novara.

Tuttle, E. F. (1986) "The Spread of *ESSE* as Universal Auxiliary in Central Italo-Romance," *Medioevo Romanzo*, 11, 229–287.

Uriagereka, J. (1995) "Aspects of the Syntax of Clitic Placement in Western Romance," *Linguistic Inquiry*, 26, 79–123.

Uriagereka, J. (1988) *On Government*. Doctoral dissertation, University of Connecticut, Storrs.

Vanden Wyngaerd, G. (1996) "Particles and Bare Argument Structure," in W. Abraham, S. D. Epstein, H. Thráinsson, and C. J.-W. Zwart (eds.), *Minimal Ideas. Syntactic Studies in the Minimalist Framework*, John Benjamins, Amsterdam, 283–304.

Vanelli, L. (1998) *I dialetti italiani settentrionali nel panorama romanzo. Studi di sintassi e morfologia*. Bulzoni, Rome.

Van Riemsdijk, H. (1978) *A Case Study in Syntactic Markedness*. Peter de Ridder Press, Lisse.

Van Riemsdijk, H., and E. Williams (1981) "NP-structure," *Linguistic Review*, 1, 171–217.

Van Tiel-Di Maio, M. F. (1978) "Sur le phénomène dit du déplacement 'long' des clitiques et, en particulier, sur les constructions causatives," *Journal of Italian Linguistics*, 3, 73–136.

Vassere, S. (1993) *Sintassi formale e dialettologia. I pronomi clitici nel luganese*. FrancoAngeli, Milan.

Vergnaud, J.-R. (1974) *French Relative Clauses*. Doctoral dissertation, Massachusetts Institute of Technology, Cambridge, Mass.

Vey, E. (1978 (1911)) *Le dialecte de Saint-Etienne au XVIIᵉ siècle*. Laffitte Reprints, Marseille (Paris).

Vikner, S. (1995) *Verb Movement and Expletive Constructions in the Germanic Languages*. Oxford University Press, New York.

Vikner S., and R. A. Sprouse (1988) "*Have/Be* Selection as an A-Chain Membership Requirement." *Working Papers in Scandinavian Syntax*, 38,

Villalba, X. (1999) "Right Dislocation Is Not Right Dislocation," in O. Fullana and F. Roca (eds.), *Studies on the Syntax of Central Romance Languages. Proceedings of the III Symposium on the Syntax of Central Romance Languages*, Universitat de Girona, 227–241.

Villefranche, J.-M. (1978) *Essai de grammaire du patois lyonnais*. Slatkine Reprints, Geneva (Bourg, 1891).

Vizmuller-Zocco, J. (1984) "L'oscillazione tra enclisi e proclisi nell'italiano contemporaneo," in N. Villa and M. Danesi (eds.), *Studies in Italian Applied Linguistics* (Biblioteca di Quaderni d'italianistica, 1, Canadian Society for Italian Studies, Toronto.

Watanabe, A. (1992) "Subjacency and S-structure Movement of *Wh*-in-situ." *Journal of East Asian Linguistics*, 1, 255–291.

Watters, J. R., and J. Leroy (1989) "Southern Bantoid," in J. Bendor-Samuel (ed.), *The Niger-Congo Languages*, University Press of Americac, Lanham, Maryland, 431–449.

Whitman, J. (1999) "Kayne 1994: P. 143, fn. 3," in G. Alexandrova (ed.), *The Minimalist Parameter*, John Benjamins, Amsterdam.

Wilder, C. (1996) "English Finite Auxiliaries in Syntax and Phonology." In A. Alexiadou, N. Fuhrhop, P. Law, and S. Löhken (eds.), *ZAS Papers in Linguistics* 6, Zentrum für Allgemeine Sprachwissenschaft, Sprachtypologie und Universalienforschung, Berlin, 166–191.

Williams, E. S. (1977) "Discourse and Logical Form." *Linguistic Inquiry*, 8, 101–139.

Williams, E. (1981) "On the Notions 'Lexically Related' and 'Head of a Word'," *Linguistic Inquiry*, 12, 245–274.

Williams, E. (1982) "The NP Cycle." *Linguistic Inquiry*, 13, 277–295.

Williams, E. (1986) "A Reassignment of the Functions of LF." *Linguistic Inquiry*, 17, 265–299.

Williams, E. (1987) "Implicit Arguments, the Binding Theory, and Control." *Natural Language and Linguistic Theory*, 5, 151–180.

Williams, E. (1994) *Thematic Structure in Syntax*, MIT Press, Cambridge, Mass.

Wood, W. J. (1979) "Auxiliary Reduction in English: A Unified Account," in P. R. Clyne, W. F. Hanks, and C. L. Hofbauer (eds.), *Papers from the Fifteenth Regional Meeting. Chicago Linguistic Society*, University of Chicago, Chicago, Ill., 366–377.

Yvia Croce, H. (1979) *Grammaire corse*, 2d ed., Cyrnos et Méditerranée, Ajaccio.

Zandwoort, R. W. (1965) *A Handbook of English Grammar*, 3d ed. Longmans, London.

Zanuttini, R. (1987) "Negazione e concordanza negativa in italiano e in piemontese." *Rivista di Grammatica Generativa*, 12, 153–172.

Zanuttini, R. (1990) "Two Types of Negative Markers," in *Proceedings of the 20th Annual Meeting of NELS*, GLSA, University of Massachusetts, Amherst.

Zanuttini, R. (1996) "On the Relevance of Tense for Sentential Negation," in A. Belletti and L. Rizzi (eds.), *Parameters and Functional Heads. Essays in Comparative Syntax*, Oxford University Press, New York, 181–207.

Zanuttini, R. (1997) *Negation and Clausal Structure. A Comparative Study of Romance Languages*. Oxford University Press, New York.

Zaring, L. (1993) "On a type of Argument-island in French." *Natural Language and Linguistic Theory*, 11, 121–174.

Zepeda, O. (1983) *A Papago Grammar*. University of Arizona Press, Tucson.

Zribi-Hertz, A. (1980) "Coréférences et pronoms réfléchis: notes sur le contraste *lui/lui-même* en français." *Lingvisticae Investigationes* 4, 131–179.

Zribi-Hertz, A. (1998) "Les pronoms forts du français sont-ils [+animés]? Spécification morphologique et spécification sémantique." Ms., University of Paris VIII.

Zribi-Hertz, A., and L. Mbolatianavalona (1997) "De la structure à la référence: les pronoms du malgache," in A. Zribi-Hertz (ed.), *Les pronoms. Morphologie, syntaxe et typologie*, Presses Universitaires de Vincennes, Saint-Denis, 231–266.

Zubizarreta, M. L. (1980) "Pour une restructuration thématique." *Recherches Linguistiques*, 9 (Université de Paris VIII), 141–187.

Zubizarreta, M. L. (1986) "Le statut morpho-syntaxique des verbes causatifs dans les langues romanes," in M. Ronat and D. Couquaux (eds.), *La grammaire modulaire*, Editions de Minuit, Paris, 279–311.

Zwart, C. J.-W. (1994) "Dutch Is Head-initial," *Linguistic Review*, 11, 377–406.

Zwart, J.-W. (1996) "Verb Clusters in Continental West Germanic Dialects," in J. Black and V. Motapanyane (eds.), *Microparametric Syntax: Dialect Variation in Syntax*, John Benjamins, Amsterdam, 229–258.

Zwart, C. J.-W. (1997) *Morphosyntax of Verb Movement. A Minimalist Approach to the Syntax of Dutch*. Kluwer, Dordrecht.

Zwicky, A. M. (1970) "Auxiliary Reduction in English." *Linguistic Inquiry*, 1, 323–336.

Zwicky, A. M., and G. K. Pullum (1983) "Cliticization vs. Inflection: English *n't*." *Language*, 59, 502–513.

INDEX